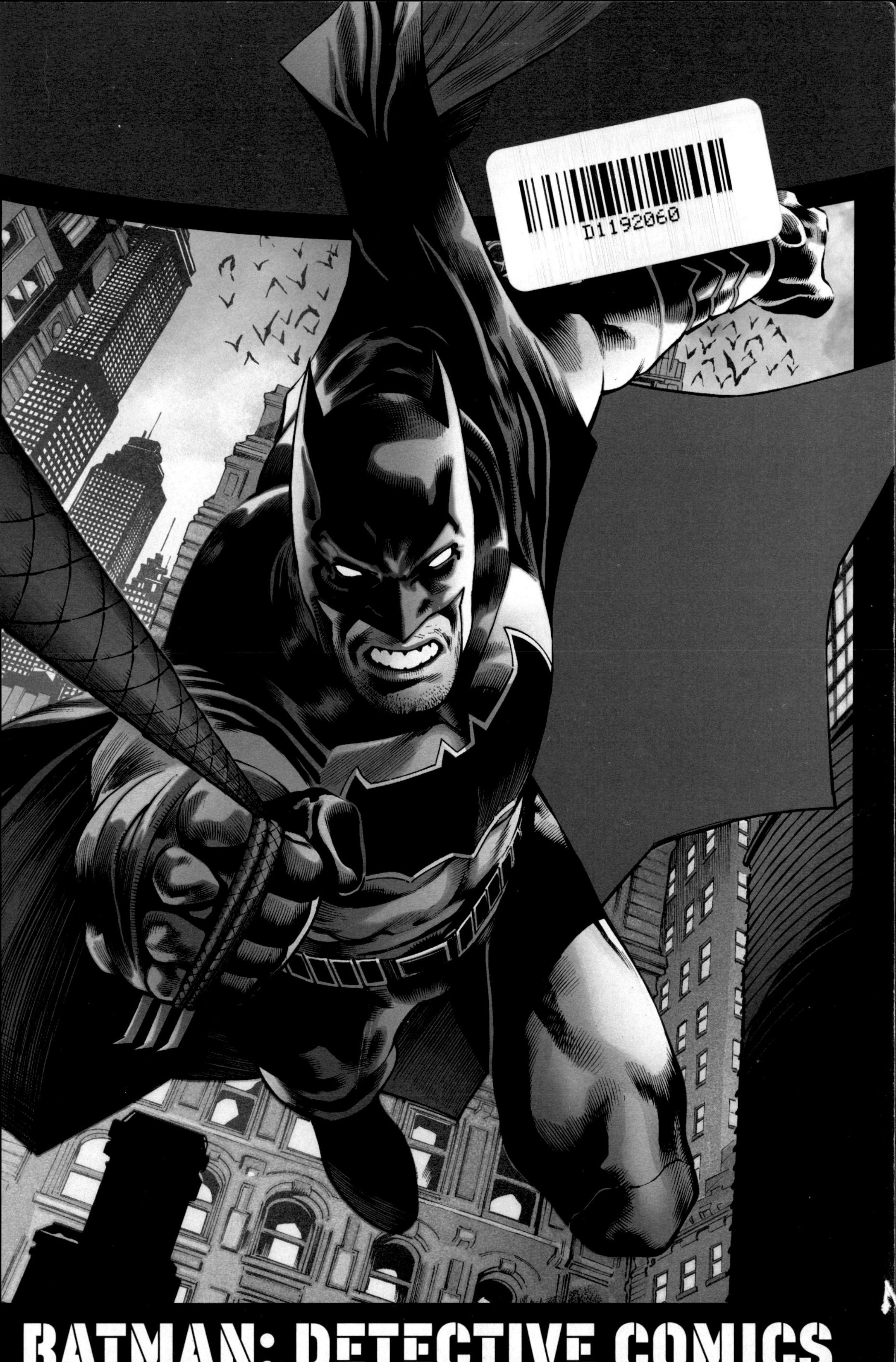

BATMAN: DETECTIVE COMICS

VOL.7 BATMEN ETERNAL

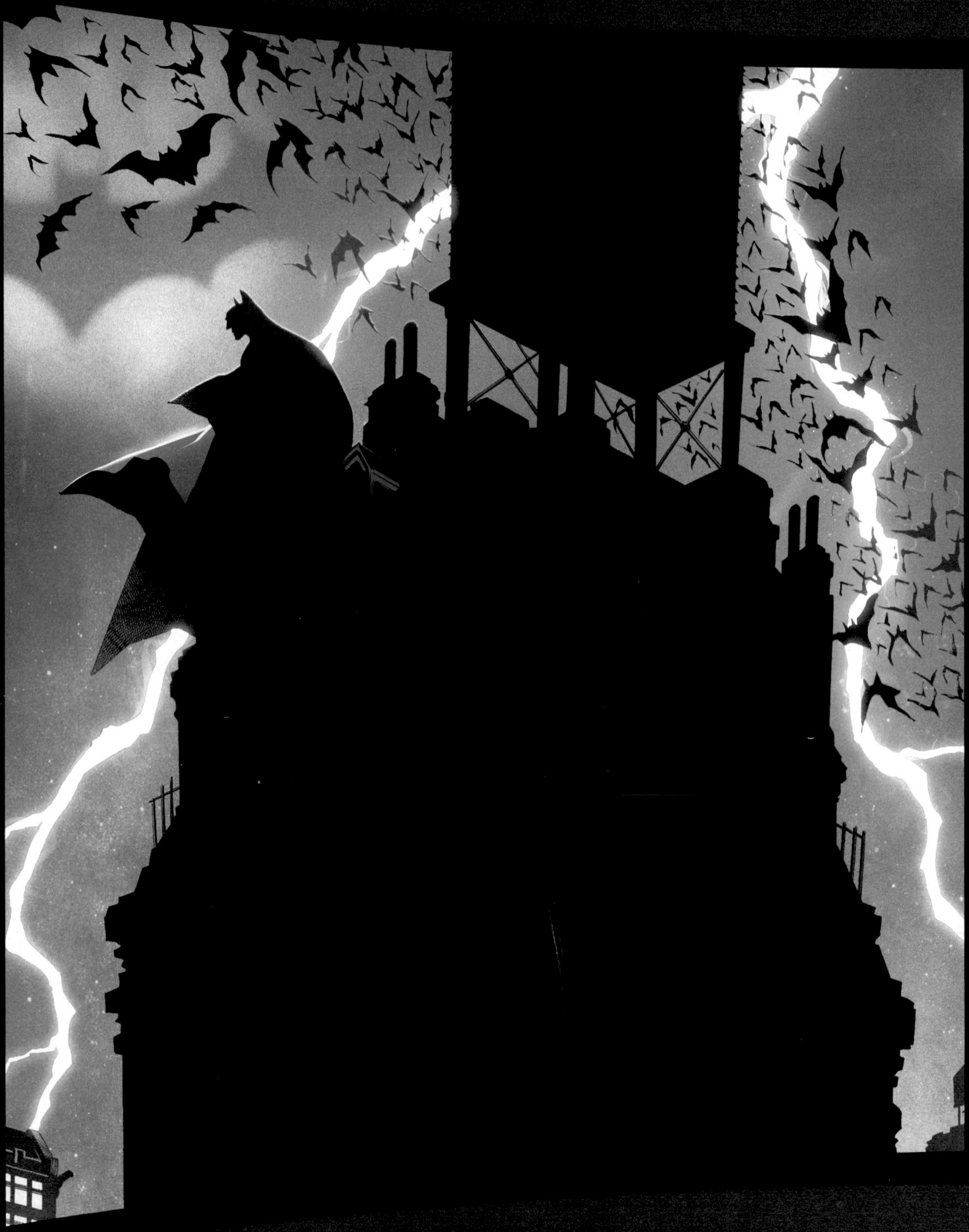

BATMAN:
DETECTIVE COMICS
VOL.7 BATMEN ETERNAL

JAMES TYNION IV
writer

JAVIER FERNANDEZ * **EDDY BARROWS** * **ALVARO MARTINEZ**
PHILIPPE BRIONES * **SCOT EATON** * **RAUL FERNANDEZ**
EBER FERREIRA * **WAYNE FAUCHER**
artists

JOHN KALISZ * **BRAD ANDERSON**
ADRIANO LUCAS * **ALLEN PASSALAQUA**
colorists

SAL CIPRIANO
letterer

EDDY BARROWS, EBER FERREIRA and ADRIANO LUCAS
collection cover artists

BATMAN created by BOB KANE with BILL FINGER

CHRIS CONROY Editor - Original Series * **DAVE WIELGOSZ** Assistant Editor - Original Series
JEB WOODARD Group Editor - Collected Editions * **ROBIN WILDMAN** Editor - Collected Edition
STEVE COOK Design Director - Books * **SHANNON STEWART** Publication Design

BOB HARRAS Senior VP - Editor-in-Chief, DC Comics * **PAT McCALLUM** Executive Editor, DC Comics

DAN DiDIO Publisher * **JIM LEE** Publisher & Chief Creative Officer
AMIT DESAI Executive VP - Business & Marketing Strategy, Direct to Consumer & Global Franchise Management
BOBBIE CHASE VP & Executive Editor, Young Reader & Talent Development * **MARK CHIARELLO** Senior VP - Art, Design & Collected Editions
JOHN CUNNINGHAM Senior VP - Sales & Trade Marketing * **BRIAR DARDEN** VP - Business Affairs
ANNE DePIES Senior VP - Business Strategy, Finance & Administration * **DON FALLETTI** VP - Manufacturing Operations
LAWRENCE GANEM VP - Editorial Administration & Talent Relations * **ALISON GILL** Senior VP - Manufacturing & Operations
HANK KANALZ Senior VP - Editorial Strategy & Administration * **JAY KOGAN** Senior VP - Legal Affairs * **JACK MAHAN** VP - Business Affairs
NICK J. NAPOLITANO VP - Manufacturing Administration * **LISETTE OSTERLOH** VP - Digital Marketing & Events
EDDIE SCANNELL VP - Consumer Marketing * **COURTNEY SIMMONS** Senior VP - Publicity & Communications
JIM (SKI) SOKOLOWSKI VP - Comic Book Specialty Sales & Trade Marketing
NANCY SPEARS VP - Mass, Book, Digital Sales & Trade Marketing * **MICHELE R. WELLS** VP - Content Strategy

BATMAN: DETECTIVE COMICS VOL. 7–BATMEN ETERNAL

DC Comics, 2900 West Alameda Ave., Burbank, CA 91505
Printed by LSC Communications, Kendallville, IN, USA. 8/3/18. First Printing.
ISBN: 978-1-4012-8421-3

Library of Congress Cataloging-in-Publication Data is available.

PEFC Certified
Printed on paper from sustainably managed forests, controlled sources
PEFC
PEFC/29-31-337
www.pefc.org

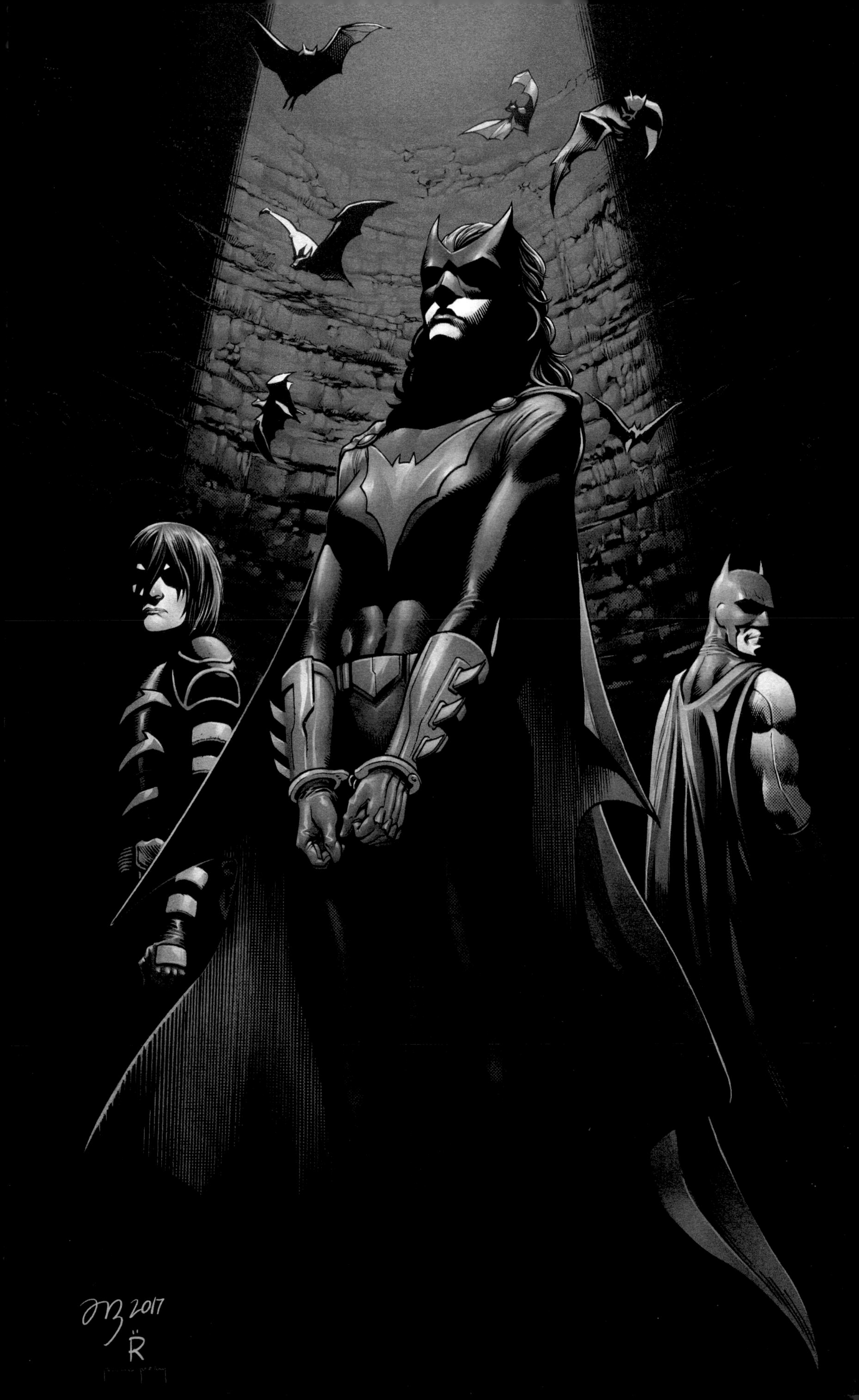

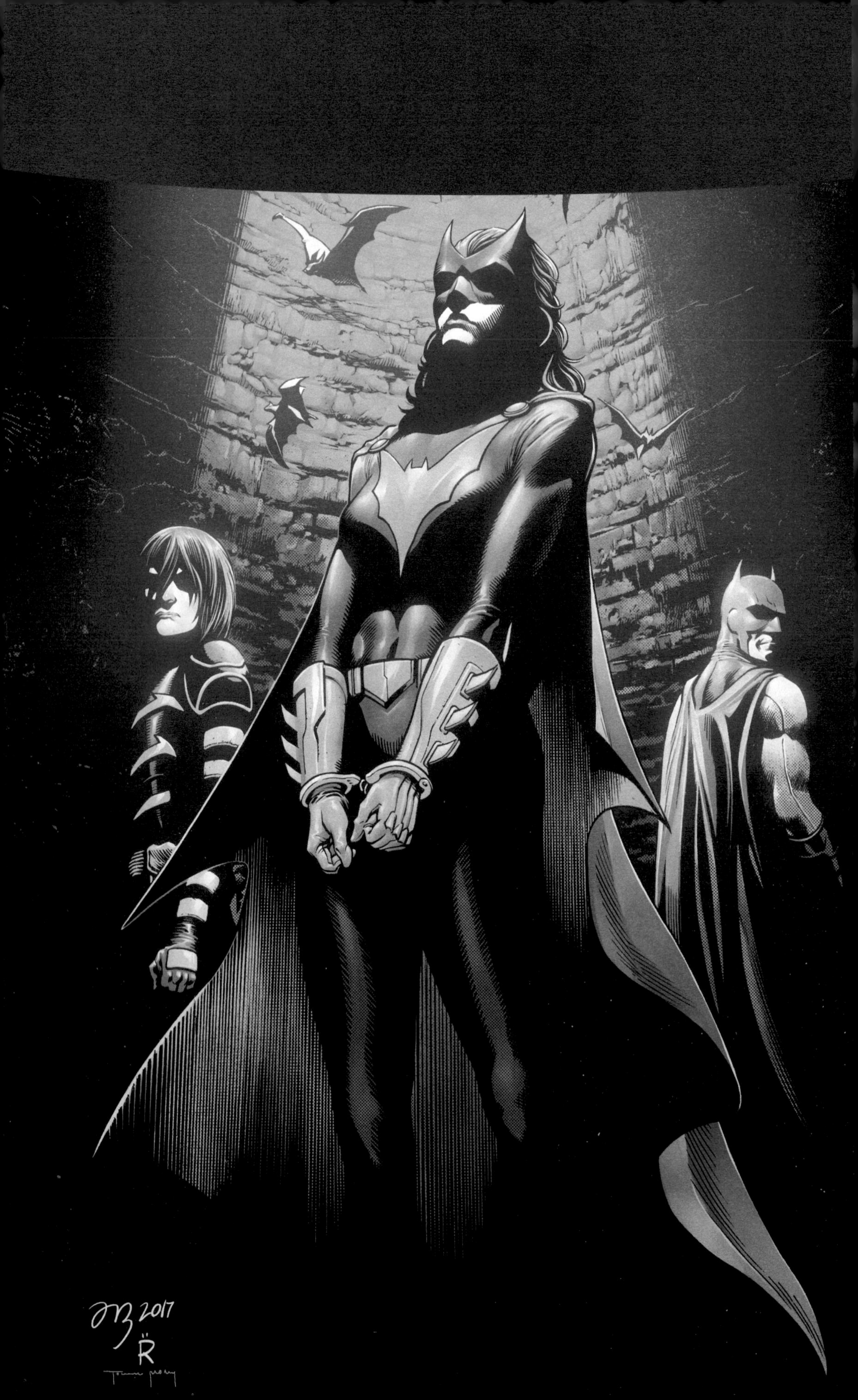

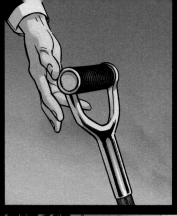

MANY YEARS AGO.

COME NOW, MASTER BRUCE.

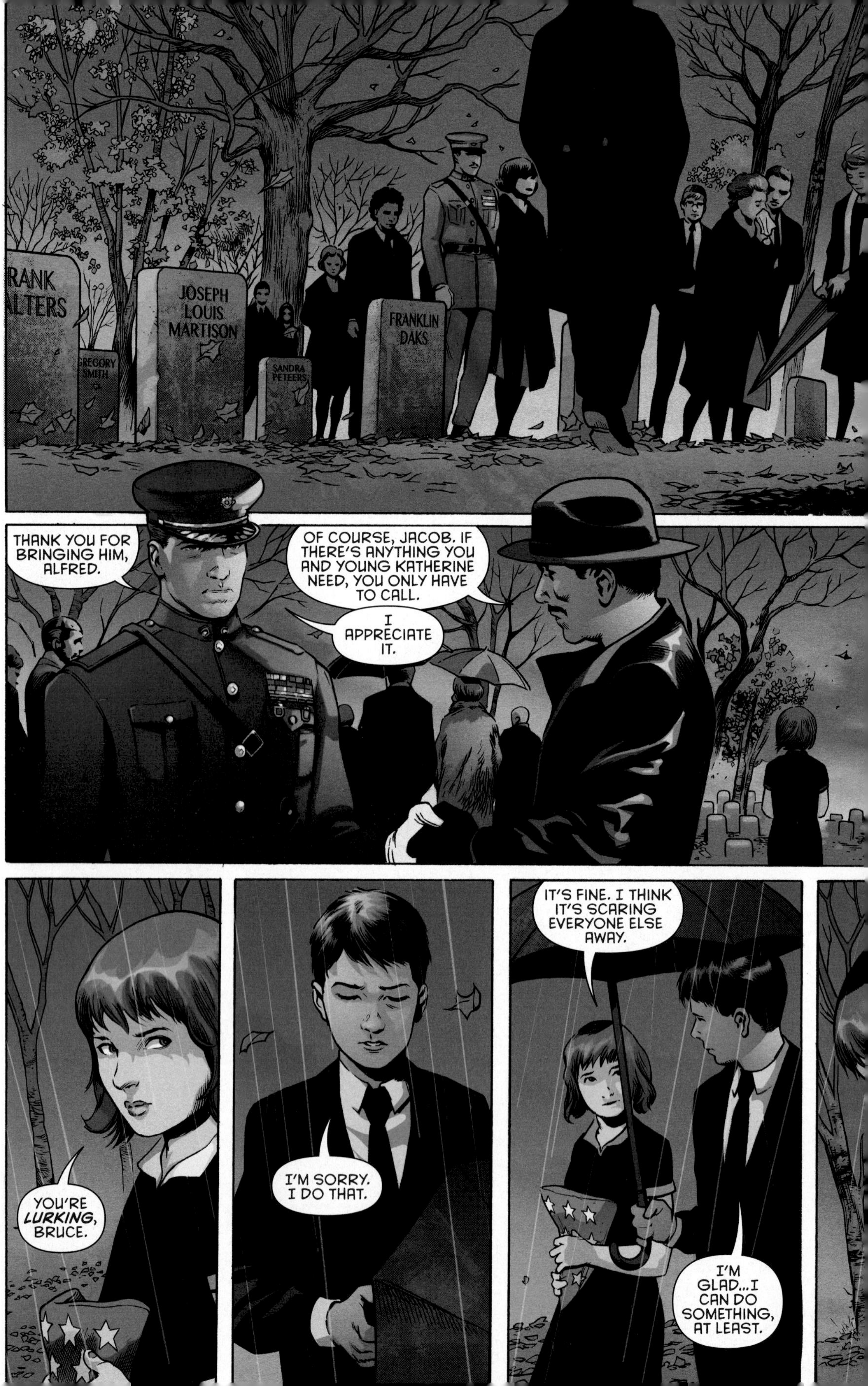
FRANK
ALTERS
JOSEPH
LOUIS
MARTISON
GREGORY
SMITH
SANDRA
PETEERS
FRANKLIN
DAKS
THANK YOU FOR BRINGING HIM, ALFRED.
OF COURSE, JACOB. IF THERE'S ANYTHING YOU AND YOUNG KATHERINE NEED, YOU ONLY HAVE TO CALL.
I APPRECIATE IT.
YOU'RE *LURKING*, BRUCE.
I'M SORRY. I DO THAT.
IT'S FINE. I THINK IT'S SCARING EVERYONE ELSE AWAY.
I'M GLAD...I CAN DO SOMETHING, AT LEAST.

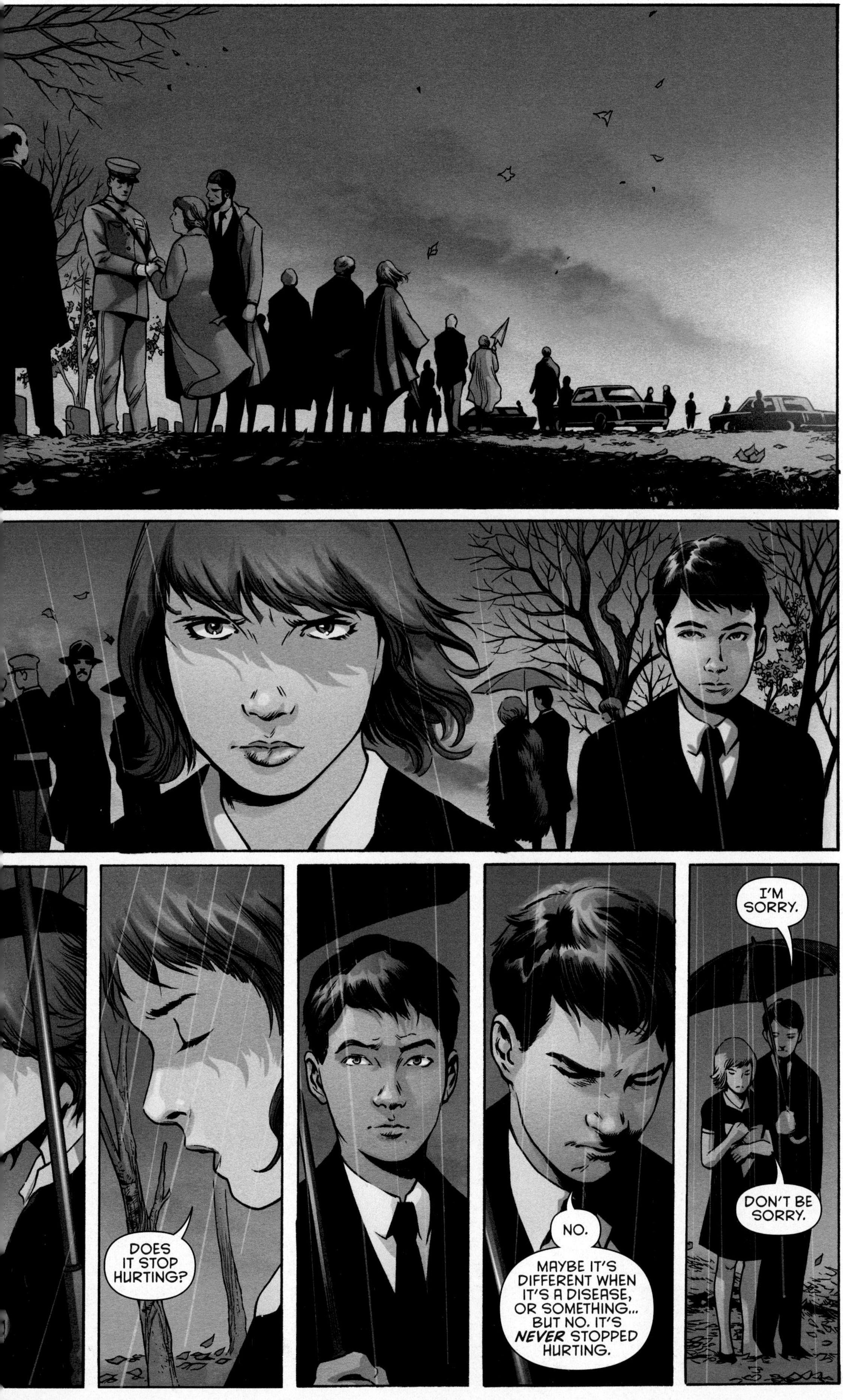
DOES IT STOP HURTING?
NO.
MAYBE IT'S DIFFERENT WHEN IT'S A DISEASE, OR SOMETHING... BUT NO. IT'S *NEVER* STOPPED HURTING.
I'M SORRY.
DON'T BE SORRY.

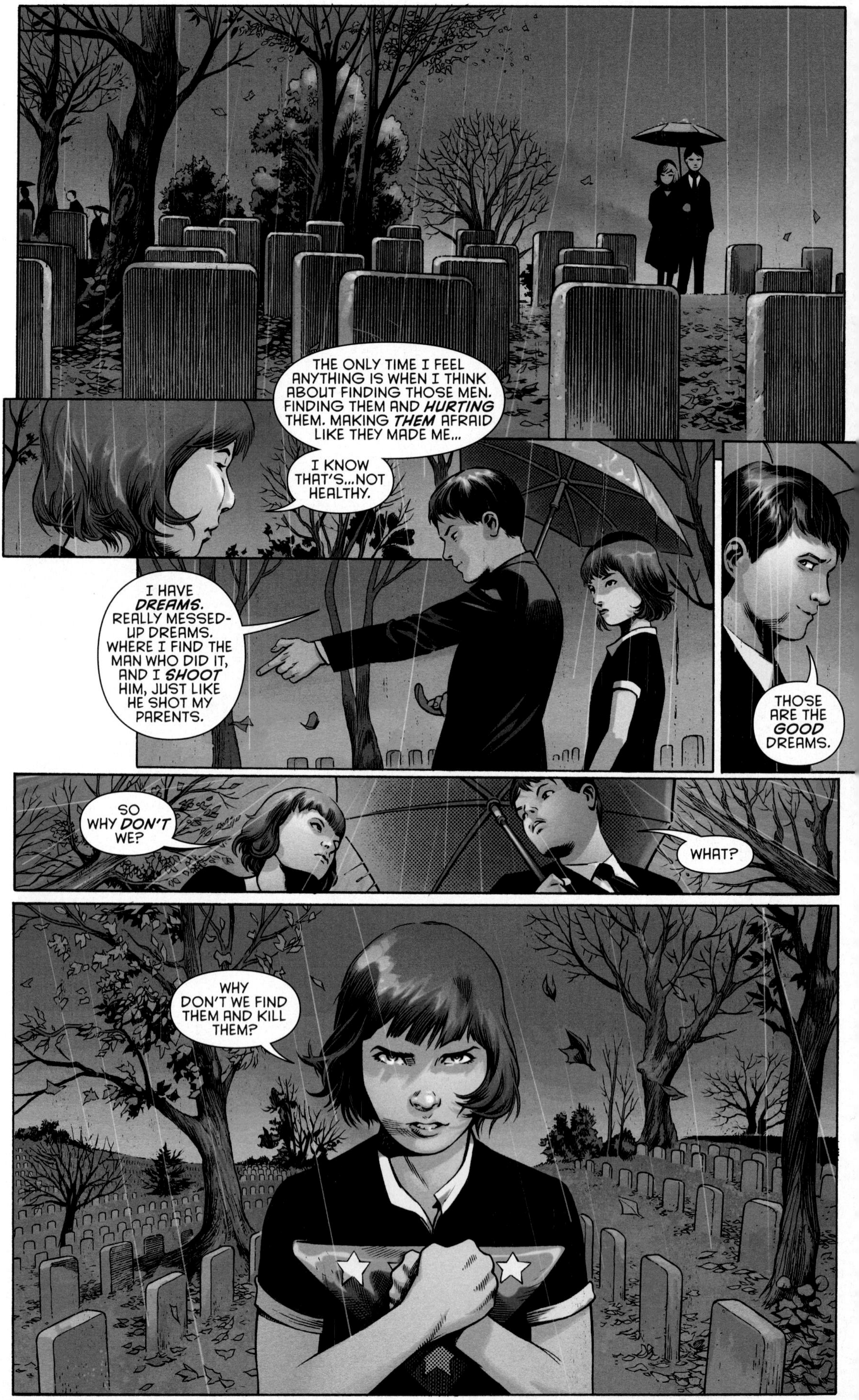
THE ONLY TIME I FEEL ANYTHING IS WHEN I THINK ABOUT FINDING THOSE MEN. FINDING THEM AND HURTING THEM. MAKING THEM AFRAID LIKE THEY MADE ME...
I KNOW THAT'S...NOT HEALTHY.
I HAVE DREAMS. REALLY MESSED-UP DREAMS. WHERE I FIND THE MAN WHO DID IT, AND I SHOOT HIM, JUST LIKE HE SHOT MY PARENTS.
THOSE ARE THE GOOD DREAMS.
SO WHY DON'T WE?
WHAT?
WHY DON'T WE FIND THEM AND KILL THEM?

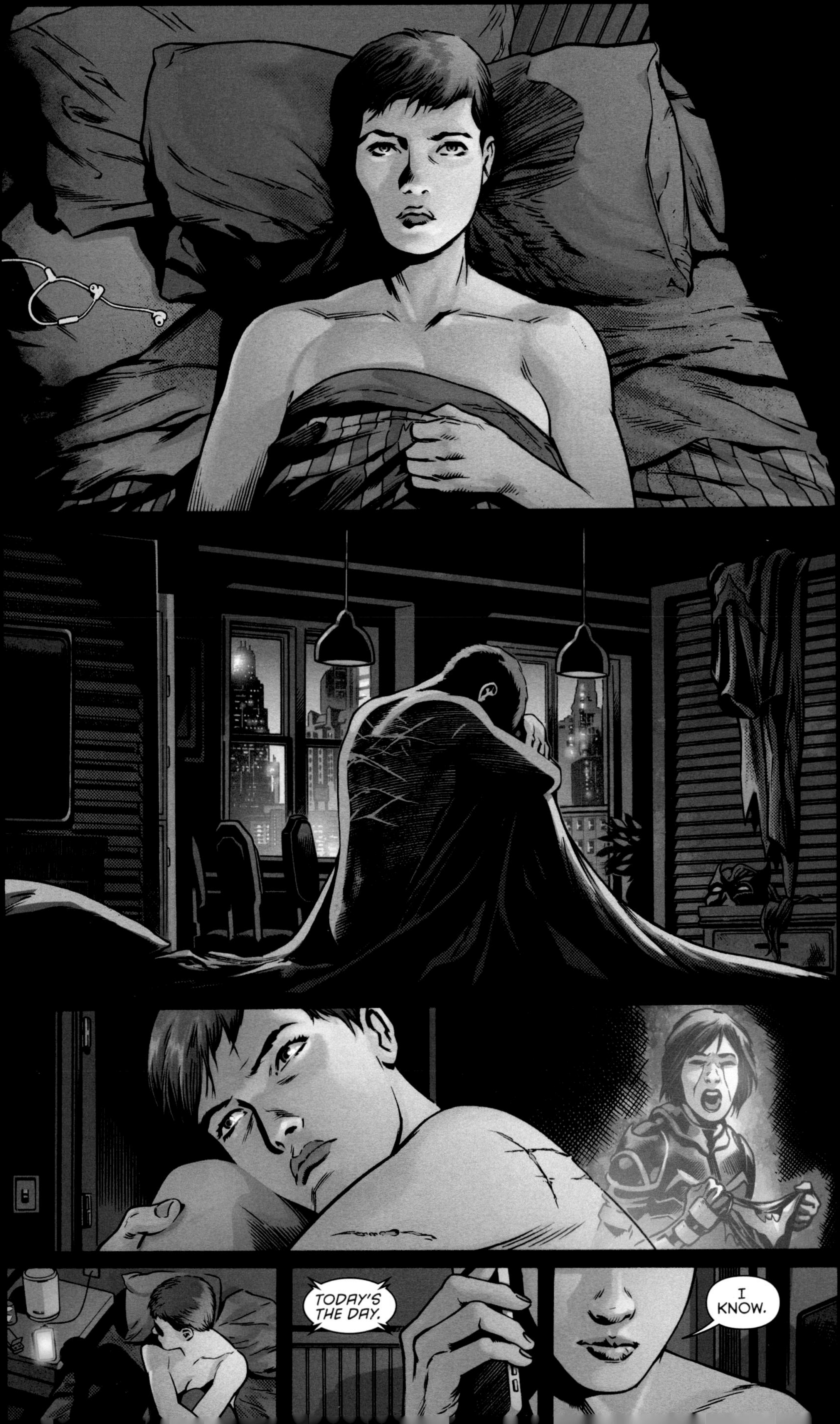
TODAY'S THE DAY.
I KNOW.

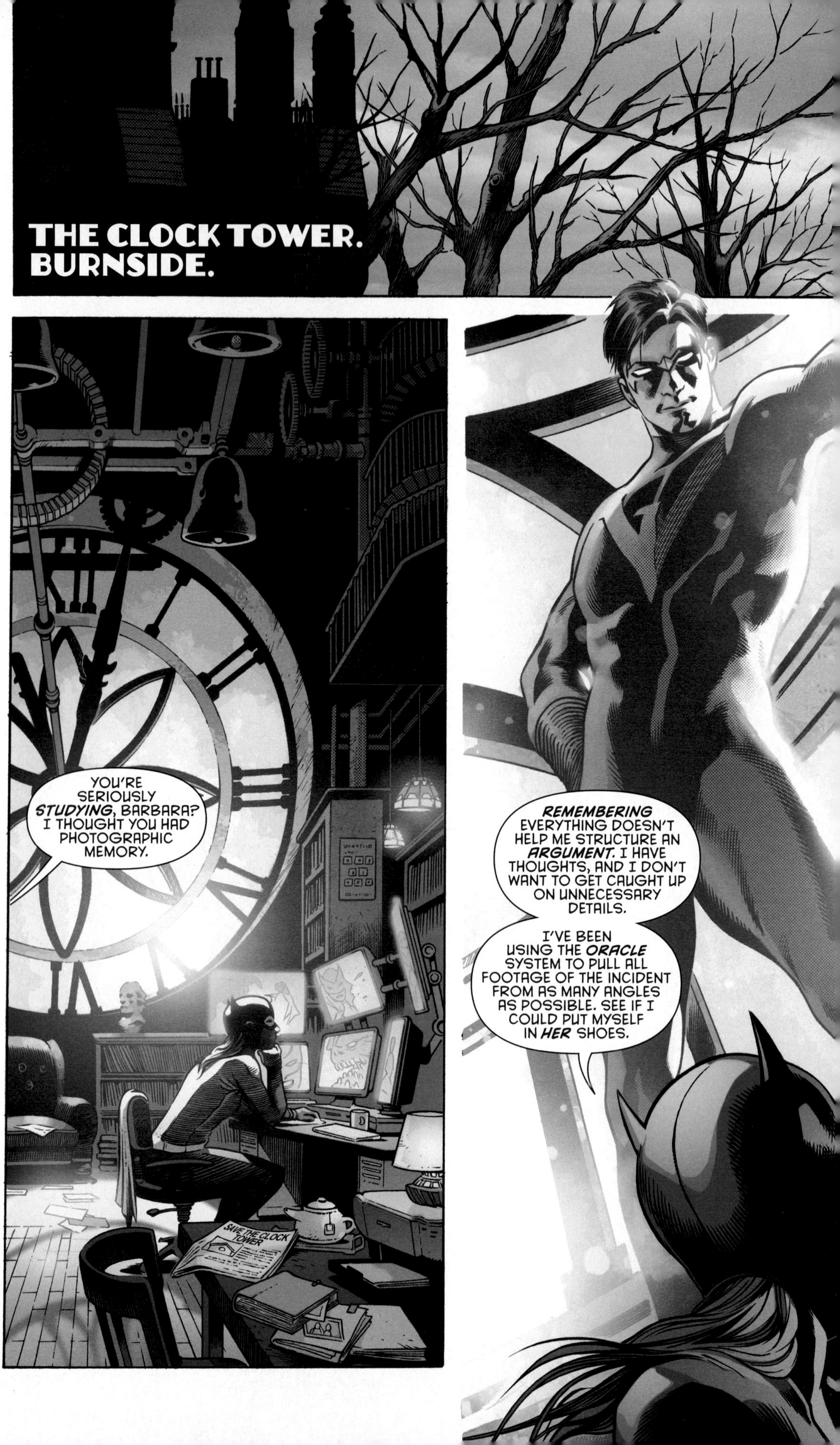
THE CLOCK TOWER.
BURNSIDE.
YOU'RE SERIOUSLY *STUDYING*, BARBARA? I THOUGHT YOU HAD PHOTOGRAPHIC MEMORY.
SAVE THE CLOCK TOWER
REMEMBERING EVERYTHING DOESN'T HELP ME STRUCTURE AN *ARGUMENT*. I HAVE THOUGHTS, AND I DON'T WANT TO GET CAUGHT UP ON UNNECESSARY DETAILS.
I'VE BEEN USING THE *ORACLE* SYSTEM TO PULL ALL FOOTAGE OF THE INCIDENT FROM AS MANY ANGLES AS POSSIBLE. SEE IF I COULD PUT MYSELF IN *HER* SHOES.

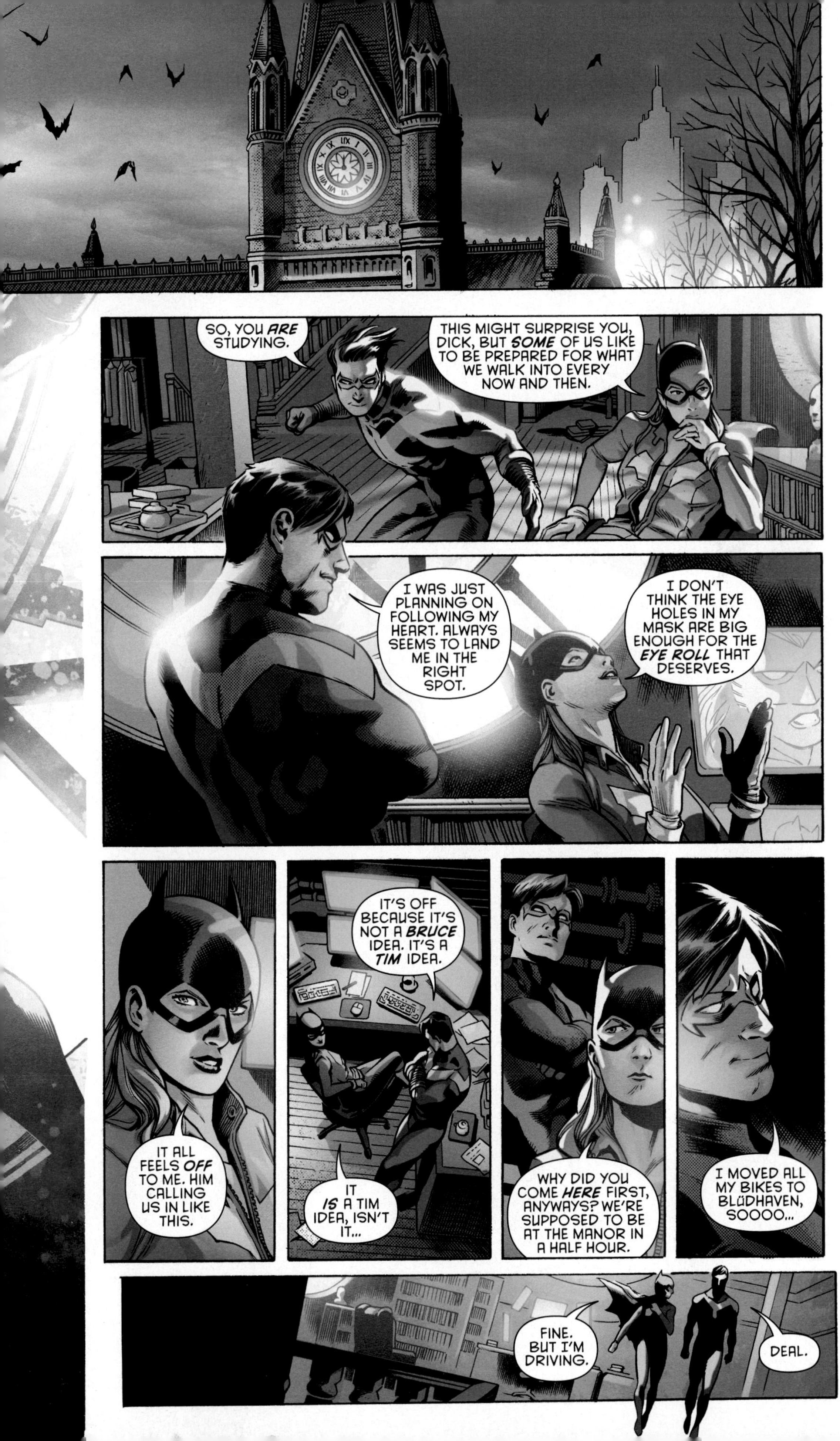
SO, YOU ARE STUDYING.
THIS MIGHT SURPRISE YOU, DICK, BUT SOME OF US LIKE TO BE PREPARED FOR WHAT WE WALK INTO EVERY NOW AND THEN.
I WAS JUST PLANNING ON FOLLOWING MY HEART. ALWAYS SEEMS TO LAND ME IN THE RIGHT SPOT.
I DON'T THINK THE EYE HOLES IN MY MASK ARE BIG ENOUGH FOR THE EYE ROLL THAT DESERVES.
IT ALL FEELS OFF TO ME. HIM CALLING US IN LIKE THIS.
IT'S OFF BECAUSE IT'S NOT A BRUCE IDEA. IT'S A TIM IDEA.
IT IS A TIM IDEA, ISN'T IT...
WHY DID YOU COME HERE FIRST, ANYWAYS? WE'RE SUPPOSED TO BE AT THE MANOR IN A HALF HOUR.
I MOVED ALL MY BIKES TO BLÜDHAVEN, SOOOO...
FINE. BUT I'M DRIVING.
DEAL.

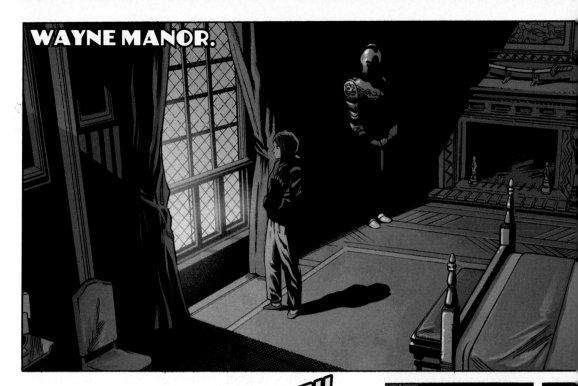

WAYNE MANOR.

WOOOMPH

I WISH I HAD THAT RECORDED.

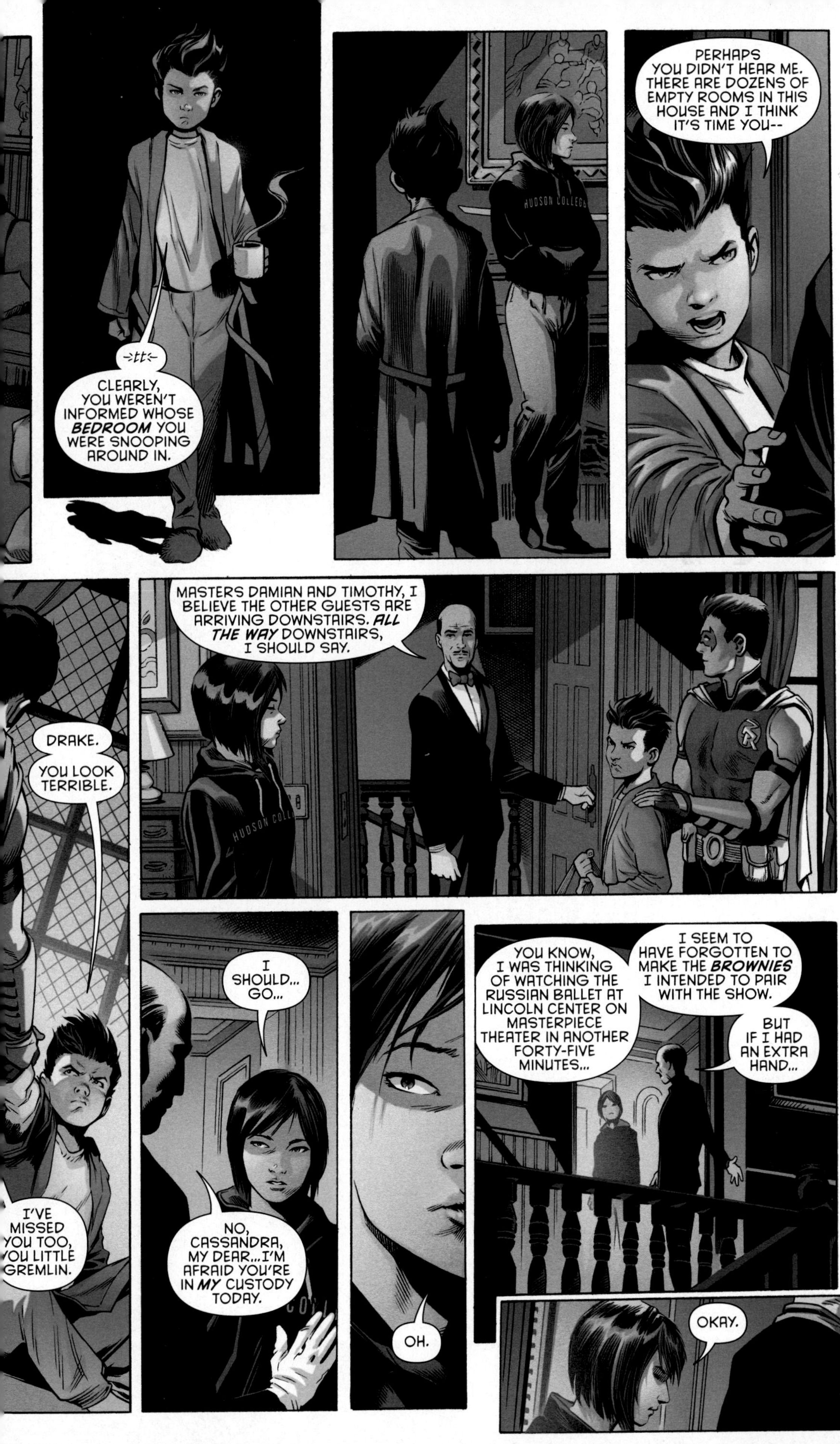
-tt-
CLEARLY, YOU WEREN'T INFORMED WHOSE *BEDROOM* YOU WERE SNOOPING AROUND IN.
HUDSON COLLEGE
PERHAPS YOU DIDN'T HEAR ME. THERE ARE DOZENS OF EMPTY ROOMS IN THIS HOUSE AND I THINK IT'S TIME YOU--
DRAKE.
YOU LOOK TERRIBLE.
I'VE MISSED YOU TOO, YOU LITTLE GREMLIN.
MASTERS DAMIAN AND TIMOTHY, I BELIEVE THE OTHER GUESTS ARE ARRIVING DOWNSTAIRS. *ALL THE WAY* DOWNSTAIRS, I SHOULD SAY.
I SHOULD... GO...
NO, CASSANDRA, MY DEAR...I'M AFRAID YOU'RE IN *MY* CUSTODY TODAY.
OH.
YOU KNOW, I WAS THINKING OF WATCHING THE RUSSIAN BALLET AT LINCOLN CENTER ON MASTERPIECE THEATER IN ANOTHER FORTY-FIVE MINUTES...
I SEEM TO HAVE FORGOTTEN TO MAKE THE *BROWNIES* I INTENDED TO PAIR WITH THE SHOW.
BUT IF I HAD AN EXTRA HAND...
OKAY.

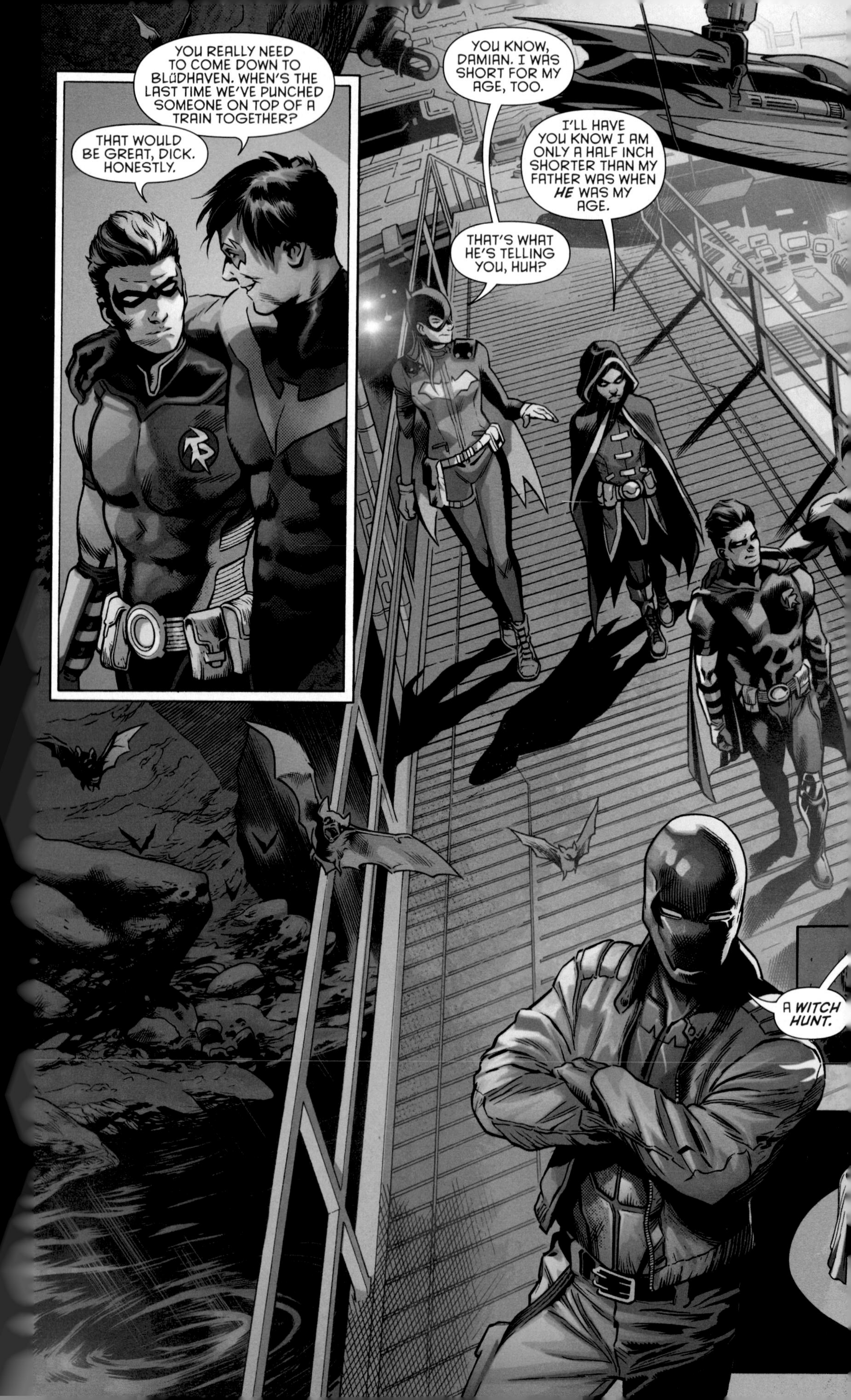
YOU REALLY NEED TO COME DOWN TO BLÜDHAVEN. WHEN'S THE LAST TIME WE'VE PUNCHED SOMEONE ON TOP OF A TRAIN TOGETHER?
THAT WOULD BE GREAT, DICK. HONESTLY.
YOU KNOW, DAMIAN. I WAS SHORT FOR MY AGE, TOO.
I'LL HAVE YOU KNOW I AM ONLY A HALF INCH SHORTER THAN MY FATHER WAS WHEN *HE* WAS MY AGE.
THAT'S WHAT HE'S TELLING YOU, HUH?
A *WITCH HUNT.*

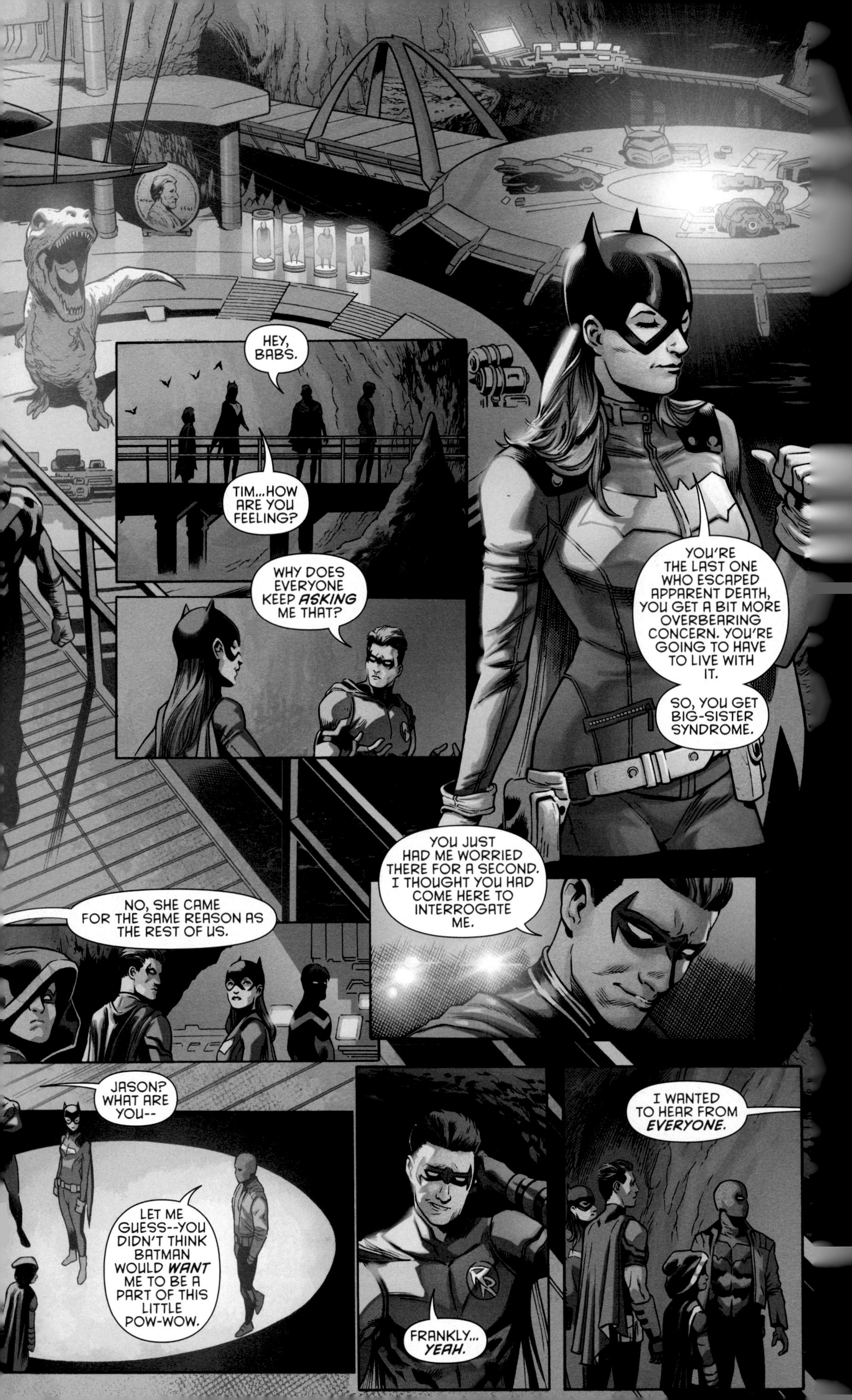
HEY, BABS.
TIM...HOW ARE YOU FEELING?
WHY DOES EVERYONE KEEP ASKING ME THAT?
YOU'RE THE LAST ONE WHO ESCAPED APPARENT DEATH, YOU GET A BIT MORE OVERBEARING CONCERN. YOU'RE GOING TO HAVE TO LIVE WITH IT.
SO, YOU GET BIG-SISTER SYNDROME.
YOU JUST HAD ME WORRIED THERE FOR A SECOND. I THOUGHT YOU HAD COME HERE TO INTERROGATE ME.
NO, SHE CAME FOR THE SAME REASON AS THE REST OF US.
JASON? WHAT ARE YOU--
LET ME GUESS--YOU DIDN'T THINK BATMAN WOULD WANT ME TO BE A PART OF THIS LITTLE POW-WOW.
FRANKLY... YEAH.
I WANTED TO HEAR FROM EVERYONE.

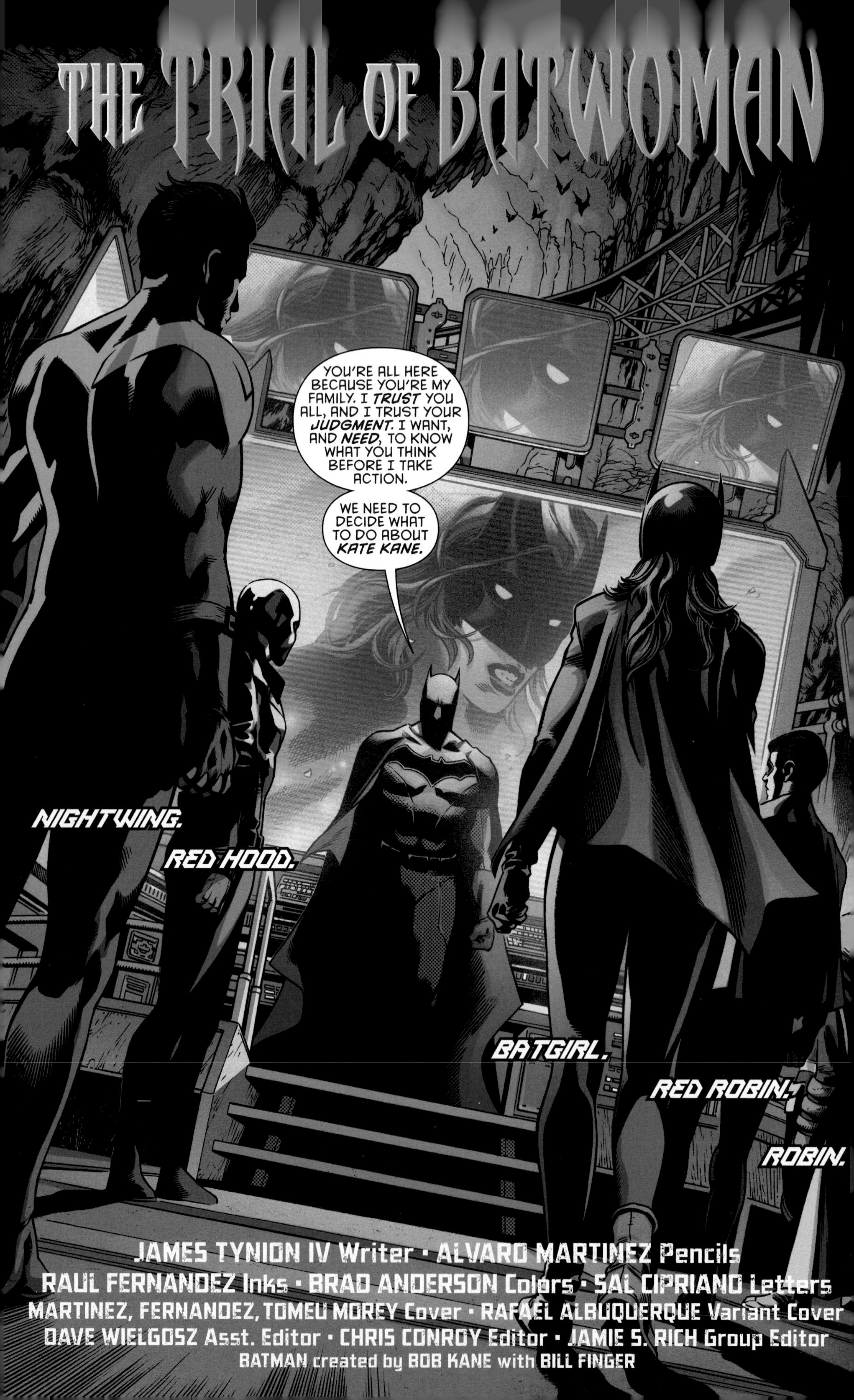
THE TRIAL OF BATWOMAN
YOU'RE ALL HERE BECAUSE YOU'RE MY FAMILY. I TRUST YOU ALL, AND I TRUST YOUR JUDGMENT. I WANT, AND NEED, TO KNOW WHAT YOU THINK BEFORE I TAKE ACTION.
WE NEED TO DECIDE WHAT TO DO ABOUT KATE KANE.
NIGHTWING.
RED HOOD.
BATGIRL.
RED ROBIN.
ROBIN.
JAMES TYNION IV Writer • ALVARO MARTINEZ Pencils
RAUL FERNANDEZ Inks • BRAD ANDERSON Colors • SAL CIPRIANO Letters
MARTINEZ, FERNANDEZ, TOMEU MOREY Cover • RAFAEL ALBUQUERQUE Variant Cover
DAVE WIELGOSZ Asst. Editor • CHRIS CONROY Editor • JAMIE S. RICH Group Editor
BATMAN created by BOB KANE with BILL FINGER

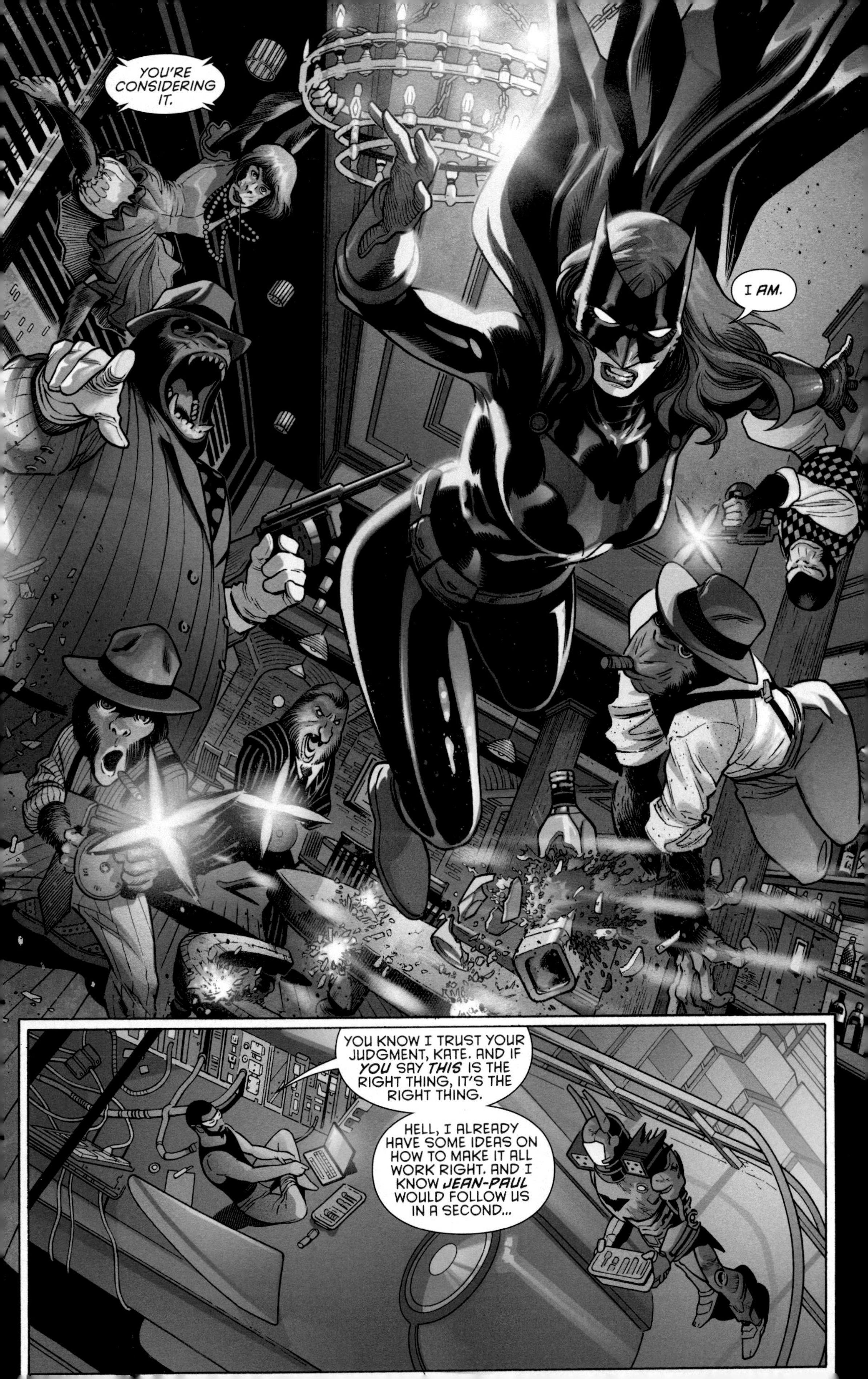
YOU'RE CONSIDERING IT.
I AM.
YOU KNOW I TRUST YOUR JUDGMENT, KATE. AND IF YOU SAY THIS IS THE RIGHT THING, IT'S THE RIGHT THING.
HELL, I ALREADY HAVE SOME IDEAS ON HOW TO MAKE IT ALL WORK RIGHT. AND I KNOW JEAN-PAUL WOULD FOLLOW US IN A SECOND...

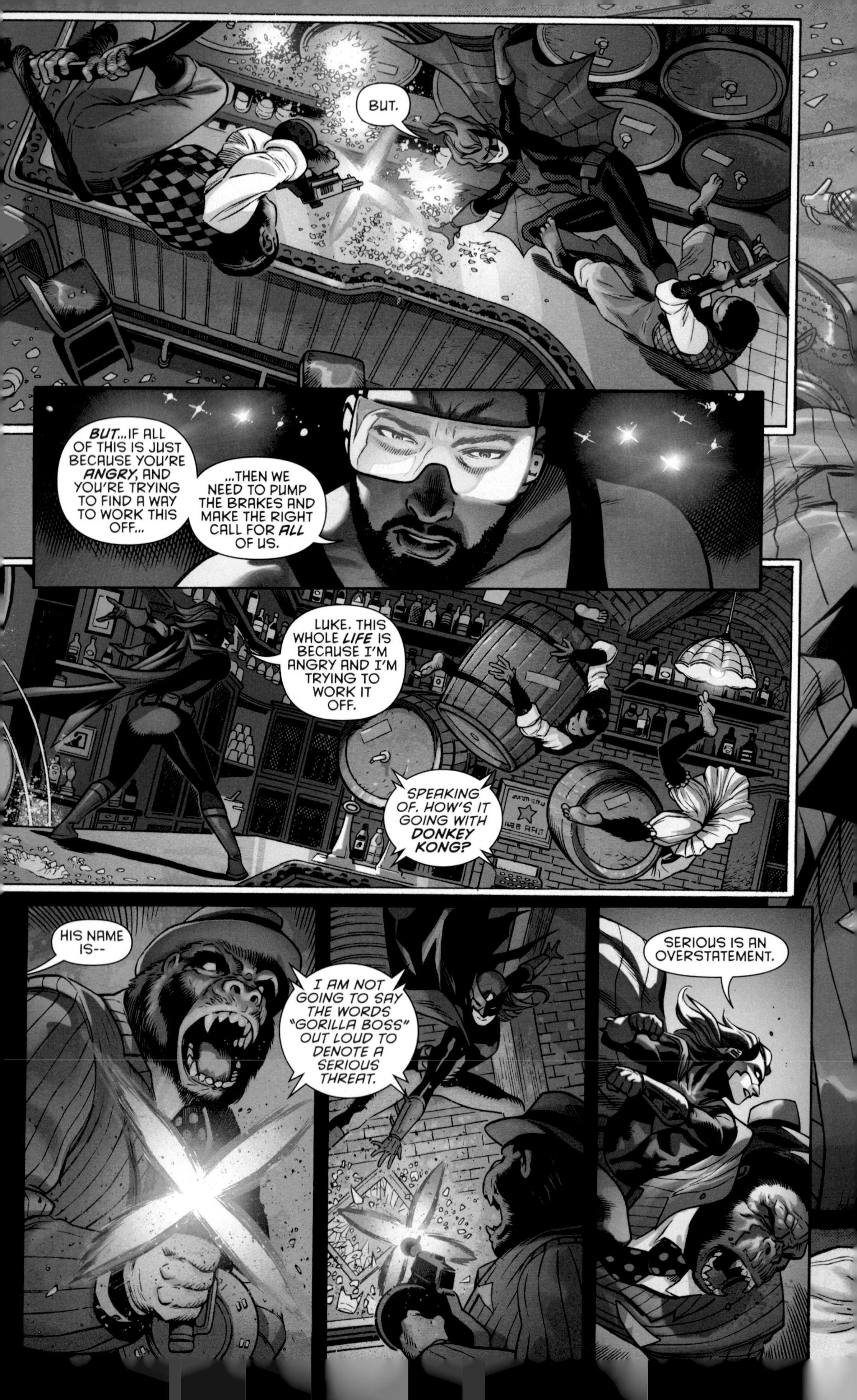
BUT.
BUT...IF ALL OF THIS IS JUST BECAUSE YOU'RE ANGRY, AND YOU'RE TRYING TO FIND A WAY TO WORK THIS OFF...
...THEN WE NEED TO PUMP THE BRAKES AND MAKE THE RIGHT CALL FOR ALL OF US.
LUKE. THIS WHOLE LIFE IS BECAUSE I'M ANGRY AND I'M TRYING TO WORK IT OFF.
SPEAKING OF. HOW'S IT GOING WITH DONKEY KONG?
HIS NAME IS--
I AM NOT GOING TO SAY THE WORDS "GORILLA BOSS" OUT LOUD TO DENOTE A SERIOUS THREAT.
SERIOUS IS AN OVERSTATEMENT.

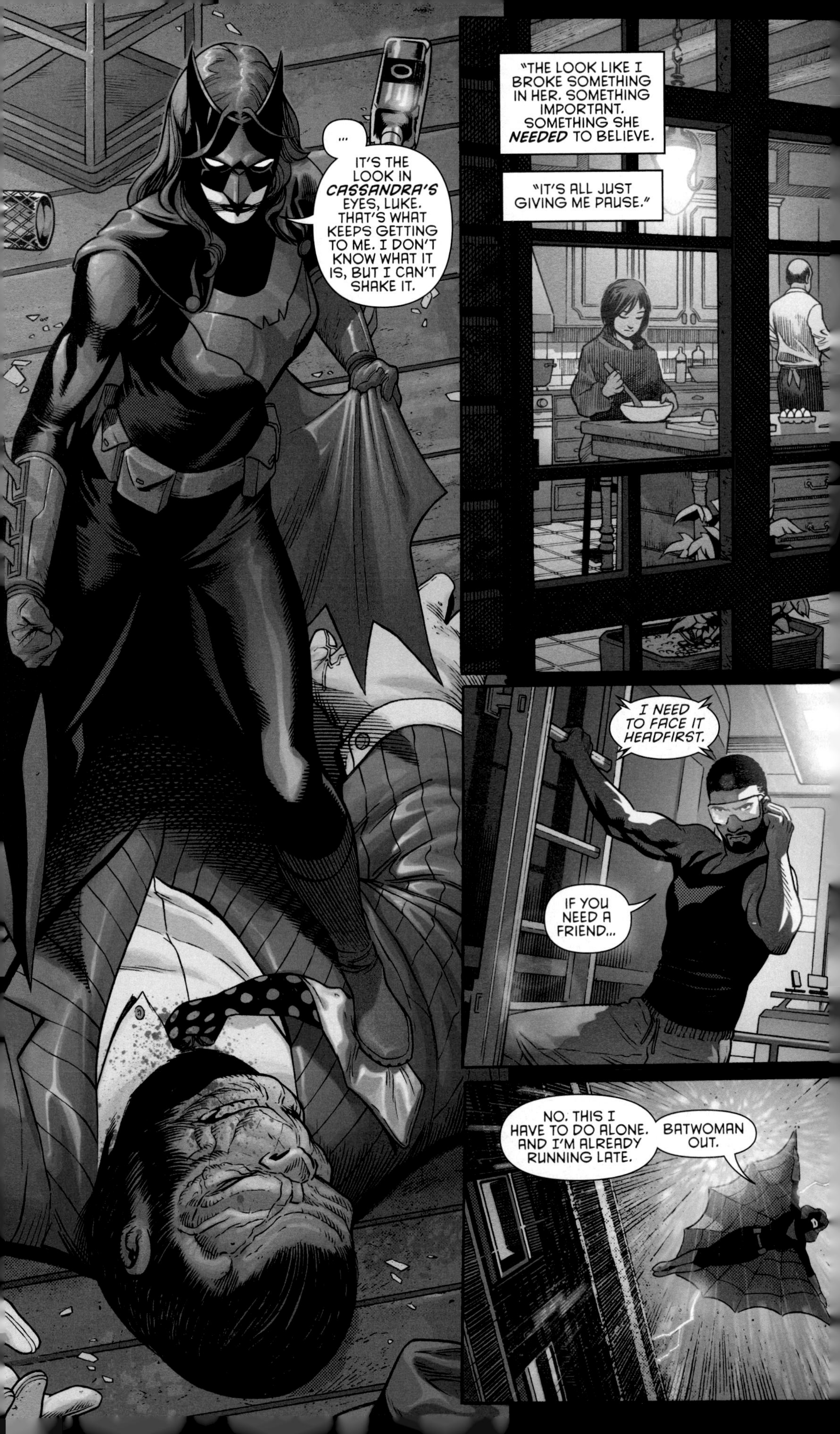
...
IT'S THE LOOK IN CASSANDRA'S EYES, LUKE. THAT'S WHAT KEEPS GETTING TO ME. I DON'T KNOW WHAT IT IS, BUT I CAN'T SHAKE IT.
"THE LOOK LIKE I BROKE SOMETHING IN HER. SOMETHING IMPORTANT. SOMETHING SHE NEEDED TO BELIEVE.
"IT'S ALL JUST GIVING ME PAUSE."
I NEED TO FACE IT HEADFIRST.
IF YOU NEED A FRIEND...
NO. THIS I HAVE TO DO ALONE. AND I'M ALREADY RUNNING LATE.
BATWOMAN OUT.

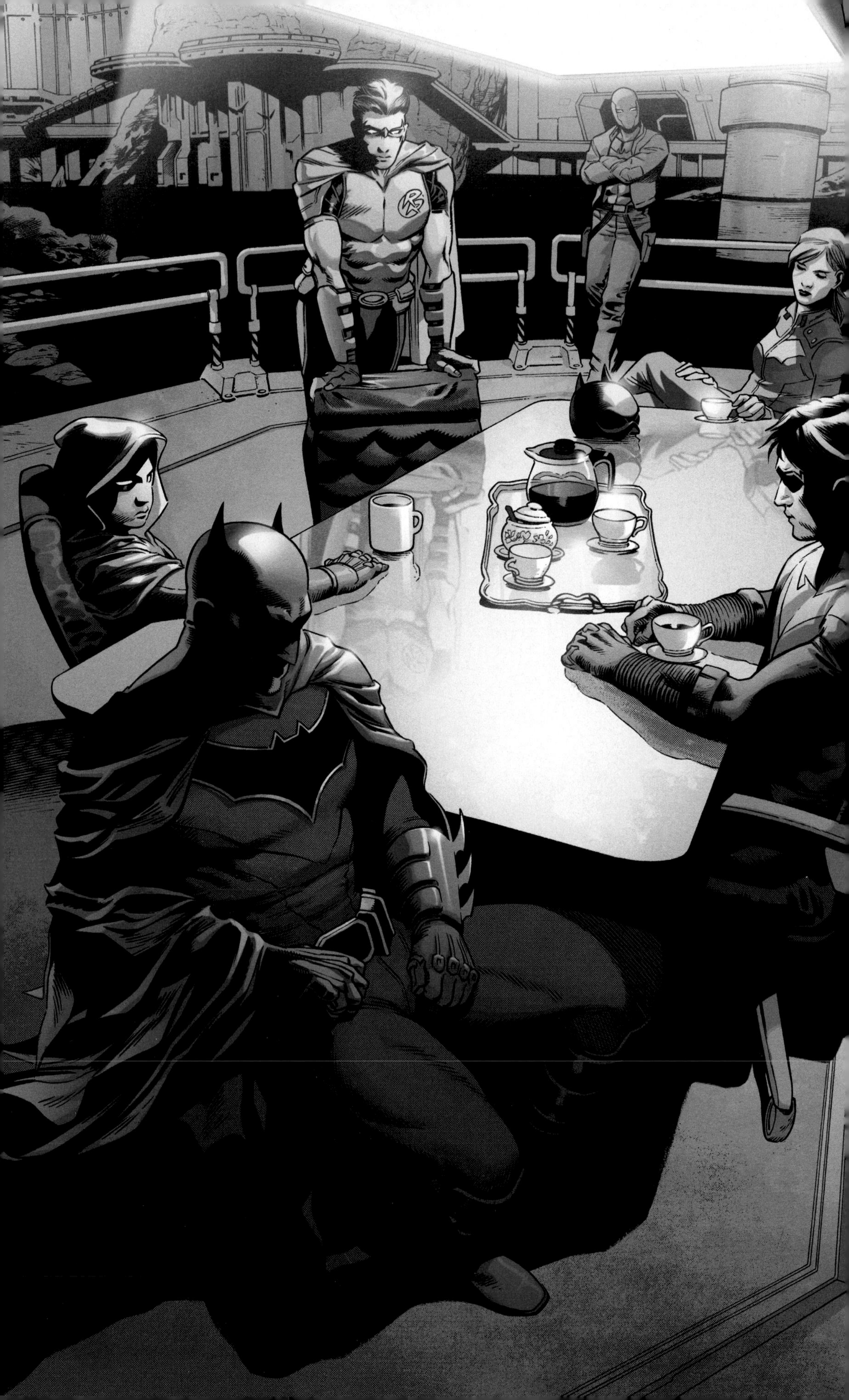

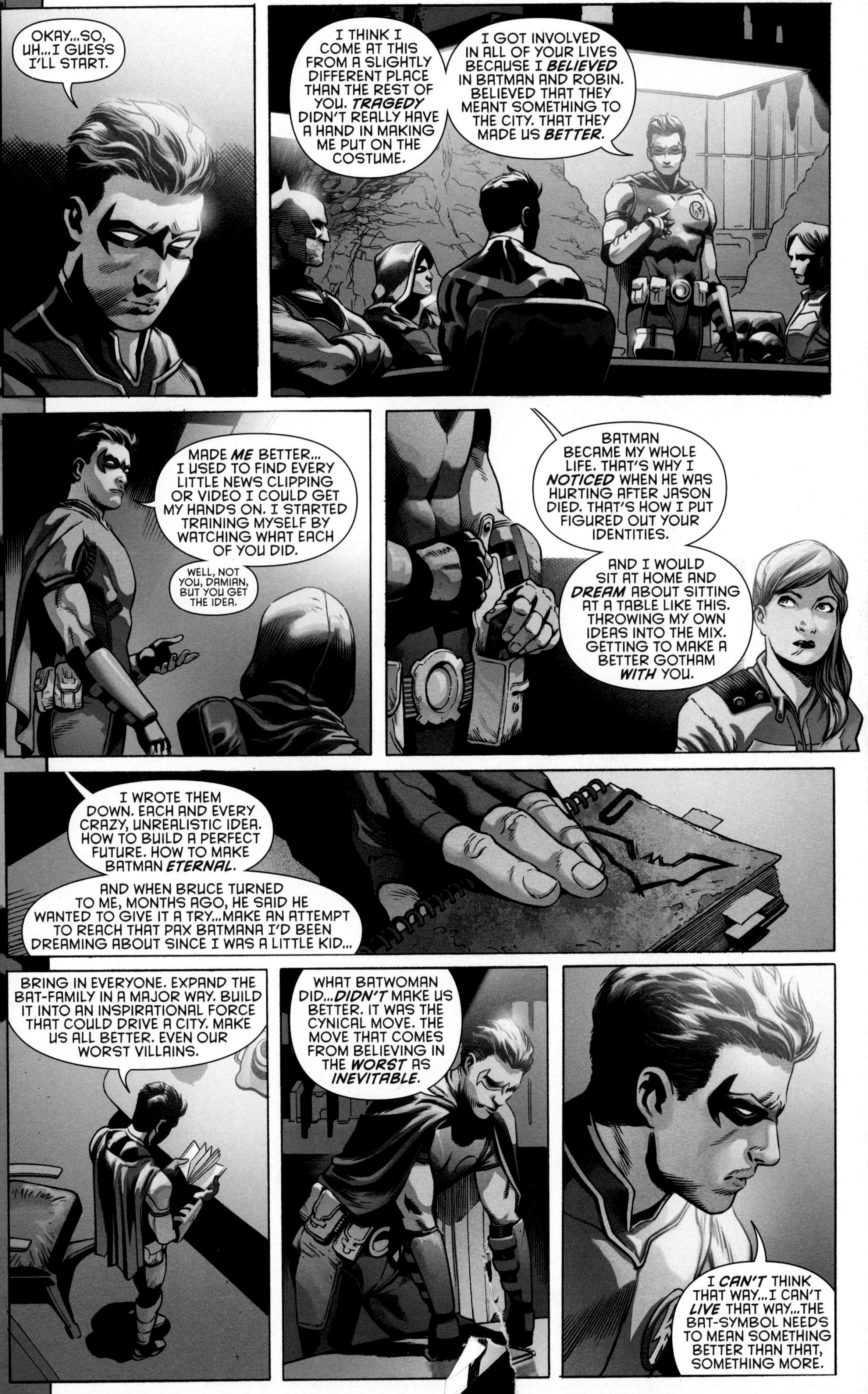
OKAY...SO, UH...I GUESS I'LL START.
I THINK I COME AT THIS FROM A SLIGHTLY DIFFERENT PLACE THAN THE REST OF YOU. TRAGEDY DIDN'T REALLY HAVE A HAND IN MAKING ME PUT ON THE COSTUME.
I GOT INVOLVED IN ALL OF YOUR LIVES BECAUSE I BELIEVED IN BATMAN AND ROBIN. BELIEVED THAT THEY MEANT SOMETHING TO THE CITY. THAT THEY MADE US BETTER.
MADE ME BETTER... I USED TO FIND EVERY LITTLE NEWS CLIPPING OR VIDEO I COULD GET MY HANDS ON. I STARTED TRAINING MYSELF BY WATCHING WHAT EACH OF YOU DID.
WELL, NOT YOU, DAMIAN, BUT YOU GET THE IDEA.
BATMAN BECAME MY WHOLE LIFE. THAT'S WHY I NOTICED WHEN HE WAS HURTING AFTER JASON DIED. THAT'S HOW I PUT FIGURED OUT YOUR IDENTITIES.
AND I WOULD SIT AT HOME AND DREAM ABOUT SITTING AT A TABLE LIKE THIS. THROWING MY OWN IDEAS INTO THE MIX. GETTING TO MAKE A BETTER GOTHAM WITH YOU.
I WROTE THEM DOWN. EACH AND EVERY CRAZY, UNREALISTIC IDEA. HOW TO BUILD A PERFECT FUTURE. HOW TO MAKE BATMAN ETERNAL.
AND WHEN BRUCE TURNED TO ME, MONTHS AGO, HE SAID HE WANTED TO GIVE IT A TRY...MAKE AN ATTEMPT TO REACH THAT PAX BATMANA I'D BEEN DREAMING ABOUT SINCE I WAS A LITTLE KID...
BRING IN EVERYONE. EXPAND THE BAT-FAMILY IN A MAJOR WAY. BUILD IT INTO AN INSPIRATIONAL FORCE THAT COULD DRIVE A CITY. MAKE US ALL BETTER. EVEN OUR WORST VILLAINS.
WHAT BATWOMAN DID...DIDN'T MAKE US BETTER. IT WAS THE CYNICAL MOVE. THE MOVE THAT COMES FROM BELIEVING IN THE WORST AS INEVITABLE.
I CAN'T THINK THAT WAY...I CAN'T LIVE THAT WAY...THE BAT-SYMBOL NEEDS TO MEAN SOMETHING BETTER THAN THAT, SOMETHING MORE.

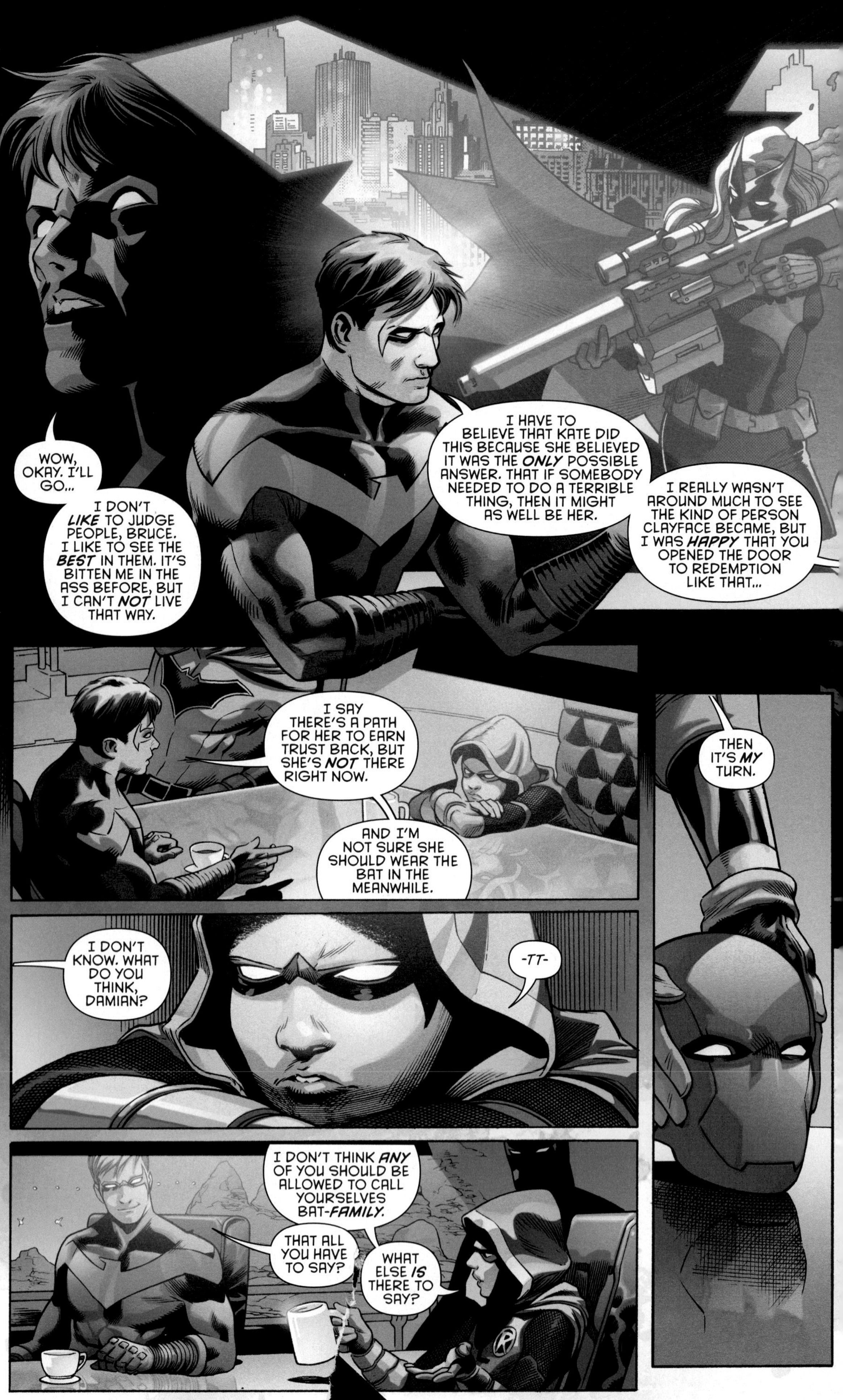

WOW, OKAY. I'LL GO...
I DON'T *LIKE* TO JUDGE PEOPLE, BRUCE. I LIKE TO SEE THE *BEST* IN THEM. IT'S BITTEN ME IN THE ASS BEFORE, BUT I CAN'T *NOT* LIVE THAT WAY.
I HAVE TO BELIEVE THAT KATE DID THIS BECAUSE SHE BELIEVED IT WAS THE *ONLY* POSSIBLE ANSWER. THAT IF SOMEBODY NEEDED TO DO A TERRIBLE THING, THEN IT MIGHT AS WELL BE HER.
I REALLY WASN'T AROUND MUCH TO SEE THE KIND OF PERSON CLAYFACE BECAME, BUT I WAS *HAPPY* THAT YOU OPENED THE DOOR TO REDEMPTION LIKE THAT...
I SAY THERE'S A PATH FOR HER TO EARN TRUST BACK, BUT SHE'S *NOT* THERE RIGHT NOW.
AND I'M NOT SURE SHE SHOULD WEAR THE BAT IN THE MEANWHILE.
THEN IT'S *MY* TURN.
I DON'T KNOW. WHAT DO YOU THINK, DAMIAN?
-TT-
I DON'T THINK *ANY* OF YOU SHOULD BE ALLOWED TO CALL YOURSELVES BAT-*FAMILY*.
THAT ALL YOU HAVE TO SAY?
WHAT ELSE *IS* THERE TO SAY?

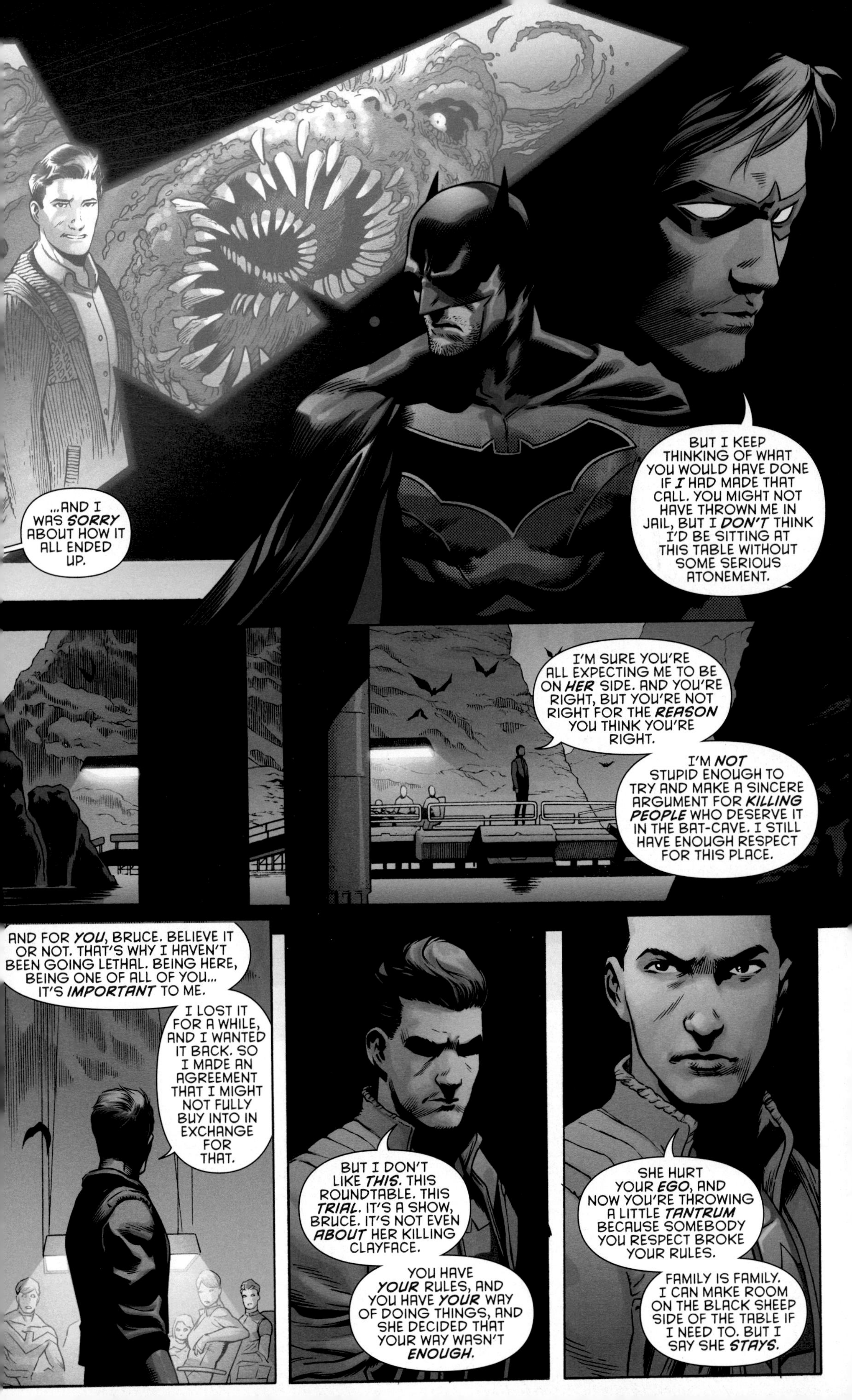
...AND I WAS SORRY ABOUT HOW IT ALL ENDED UP.
BUT I KEEP THINKING OF WHAT YOU WOULD HAVE DONE IF I HAD MADE THAT CALL. YOU MIGHT NOT HAVE THROWN ME IN JAIL, BUT I DON'T THINK I'D BE SITTING AT THIS TABLE WITHOUT SOME SERIOUS ATONEMENT.
I'M SURE YOU'RE ALL EXPECTING ME TO BE ON HER SIDE. AND YOU'RE RIGHT, BUT YOU'RE NOT RIGHT FOR THE REASON YOU THINK YOU'RE RIGHT.
I'M NOT STUPID ENOUGH TO TRY AND MAKE A SINCERE ARGUMENT FOR KILLING PEOPLE WHO DESERVE IT IN THE BAT-CAVE. I STILL HAVE ENOUGH RESPECT FOR THIS PLACE.
AND FOR YOU, BRUCE. BELIEVE IT OR NOT. THAT'S WHY I HAVEN'T BEEN GOING LETHAL. BEING HERE, BEING ONE OF ALL OF YOU... IT'S IMPORTANT TO ME.
I LOST IT FOR A WHILE, AND I WANTED IT BACK. SO I MADE AN AGREEMENT THAT I MIGHT NOT FULLY BUY INTO IN EXCHANGE FOR THAT.
BUT I DON'T LIKE THIS. THIS ROUNDTABLE. THIS TRIAL. IT'S A SHOW, BRUCE. IT'S NOT EVEN ABOUT HER KILLING CLAYFACE.
YOU HAVE YOUR RULES, AND YOU HAVE YOUR WAY OF DOING THINGS, AND SHE DECIDED THAT YOUR WAY WASN'T ENOUGH.
SHE HURT YOUR EGO, AND NOW YOU'RE THROWING A LITTLE TANTRUM BECAUSE SOMEBODY YOU RESPECT BROKE YOUR RULES.
FAMILY IS FAMILY. I CAN MAKE ROOM ON THE BLACK SHEEP SIDE OF THE TABLE IF I NEED TO. BUT I SAY SHE STAYS.

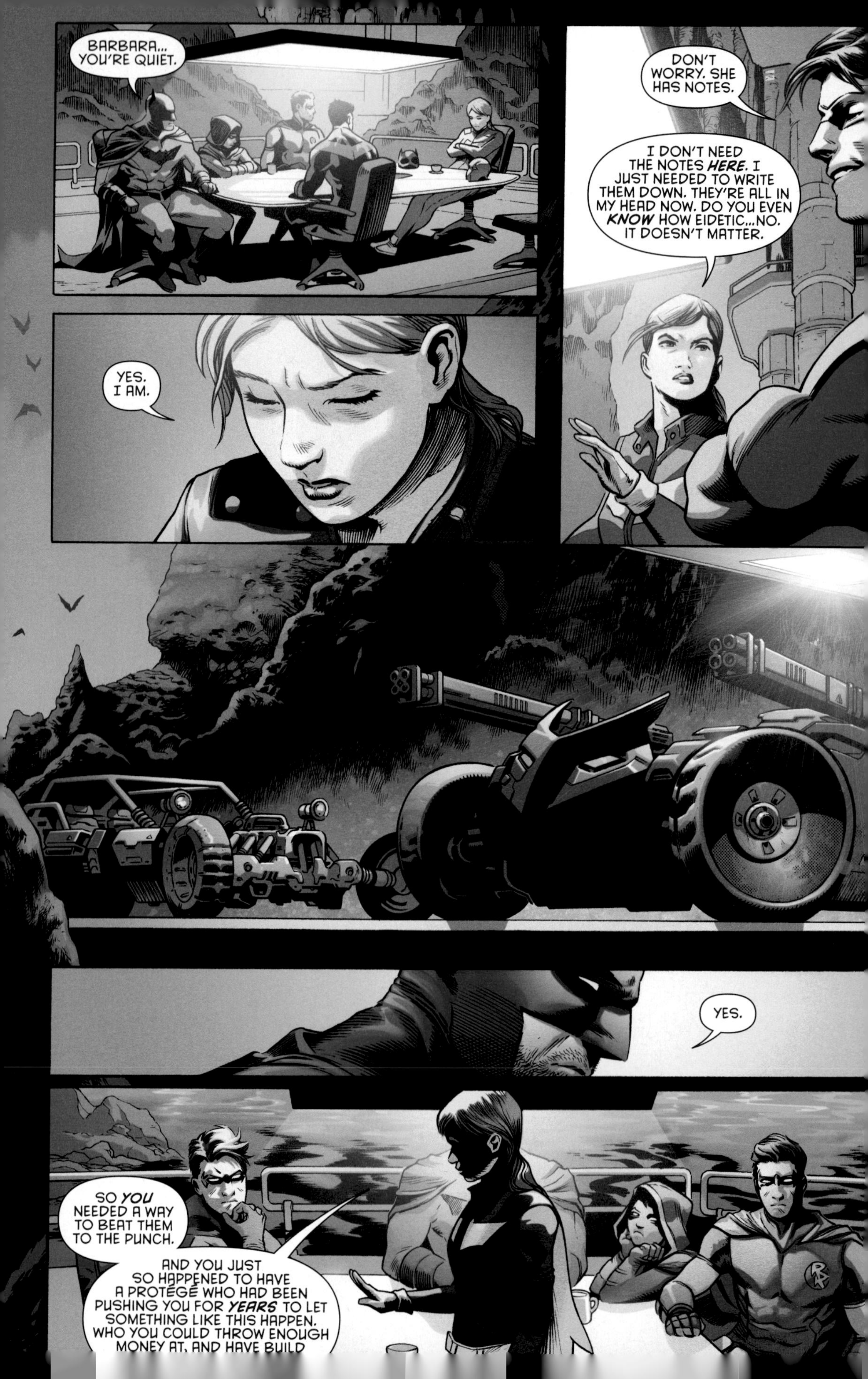
BARBARA... YOU'RE QUIET.
YES. I AM.
DON'T WORRY. SHE HAS NOTES.
I DON'T NEED THE NOTES *HERE*. I JUST NEEDED TO WRITE THEM DOWN. THEY'RE ALL IN MY HEAD NOW. DO YOU EVEN *KNOW* HOW EIDETIC...NO. IT DOESN'T MATTER.
YES.
SO *YOU* NEEDED A WAY TO BEAT THEM TO THE PUNCH.
AND YOU JUST SO HAPPENED TO HAVE A PROTEGÉ WHO HAD BEEN PUSHING YOU FOR *YEARS* TO LET SOMETHING LIKE THIS HAPPEN. WHO YOU COULD THROW ENOUGH MONEY AT, AND HAVE BUILD

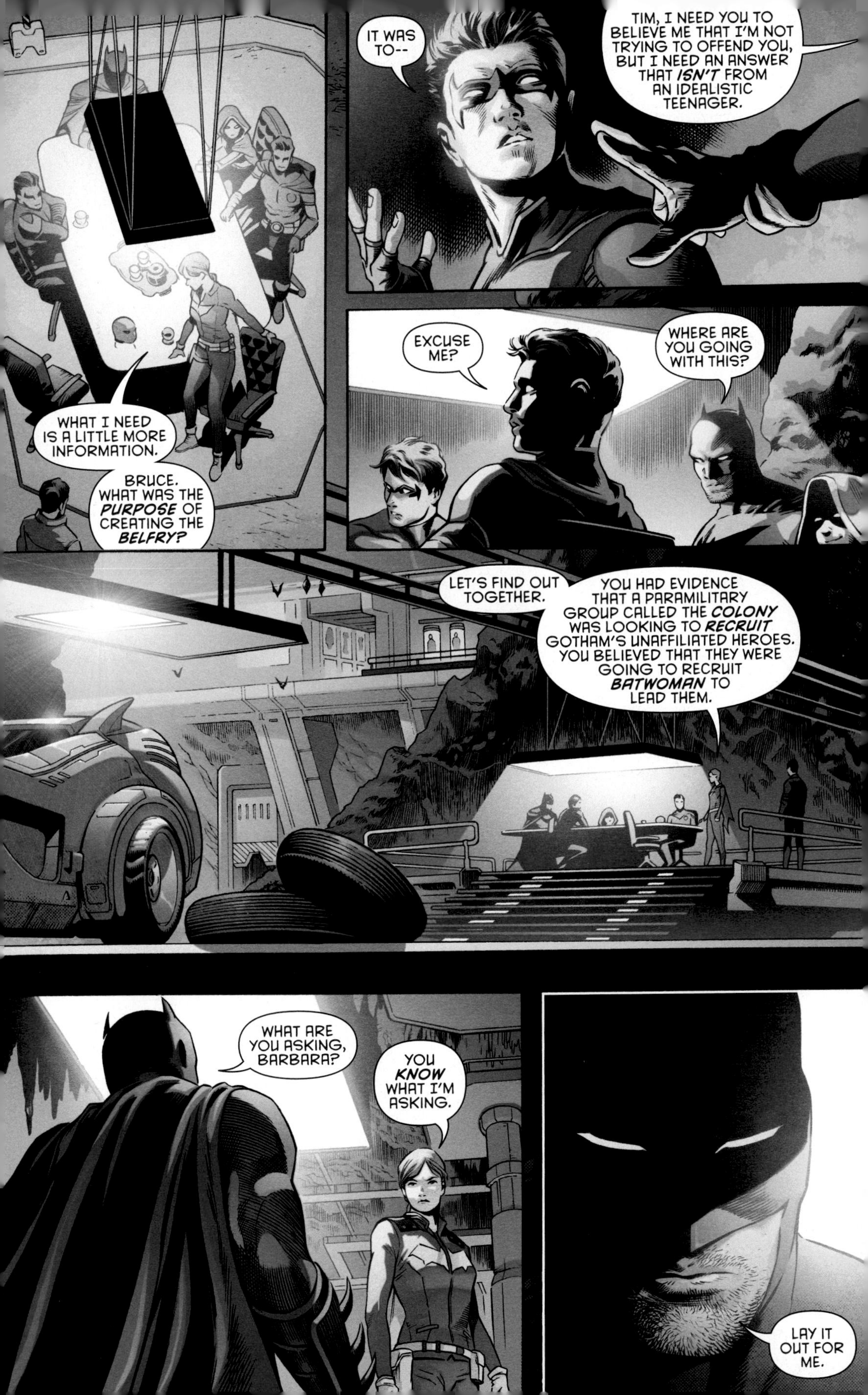
WHAT I NEED IS A LITTLE MORE INFORMATION.
BRUCE. WHAT WAS THE PURPOSE OF CREATING THE BELFRY?
IT WAS TO--
TIM, I NEED YOU TO BELIEVE ME THAT I'M NOT TRYING TO OFFEND YOU, BUT I NEED AN ANSWER THAT ISN'T FROM AN IDEALISTIC TEENAGER.
EXCUSE ME?
WHERE ARE YOU GOING WITH THIS?
LET'S FIND OUT TOGETHER.
YOU HAD EVIDENCE THAT A PARAMILITARY GROUP CALLED THE COLONY WAS LOOKING TO RECRUIT GOTHAM'S UNAFFILIATED HEROES. YOU BELIEVED THAT THEY WERE GOING TO RECRUIT BATWOMAN TO LEAD THEM.
WHAT ARE YOU ASKING, BARBARA?
YOU KNOW WHAT I'M ASKING.
LAY IT OUT FOR ME.

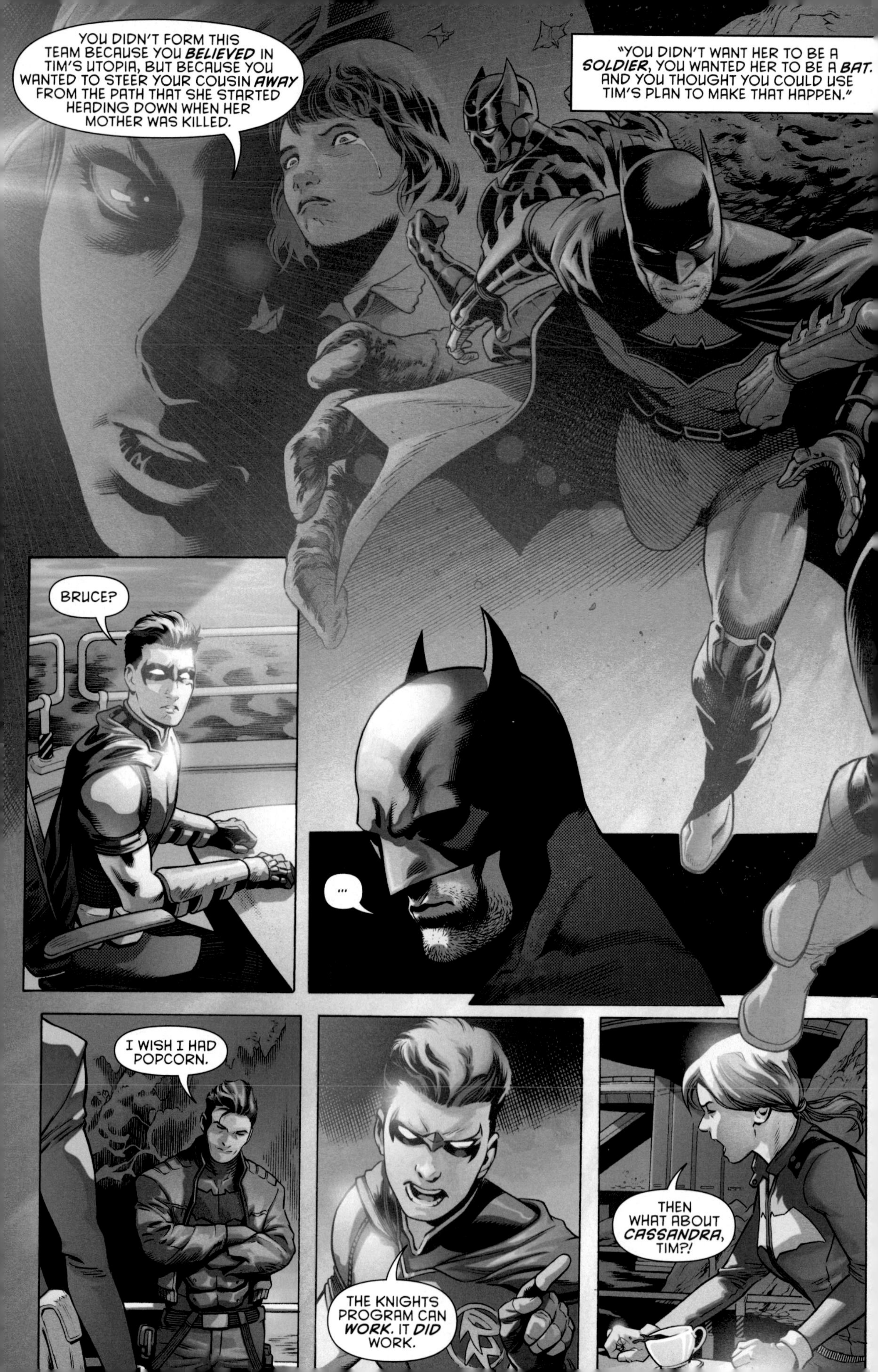
YOU DIDN'T FORM THIS TEAM BECAUSE YOU *BELIEVED* IN TIM'S UTOPIA, BUT BECAUSE YOU WANTED TO STEER YOUR COUSIN *AWAY* FROM THE PATH THAT SHE STARTED HEADING DOWN WHEN HER MOTHER WAS KILLED.
"YOU DIDN'T WANT HER TO BE A *SOLDIER*, YOU WANTED HER TO BE A *BAT*. AND YOU THOUGHT YOU COULD USE TIM'S PLAN TO MAKE THAT HAPPEN."
BRUCE?
...
I WISH I HAD POPCORN.
THE KNIGHTS PROGRAM CAN *WORK*. IT *DID* WORK.
THEN WHAT ABOUT *CASSANDRA*, TIM?!

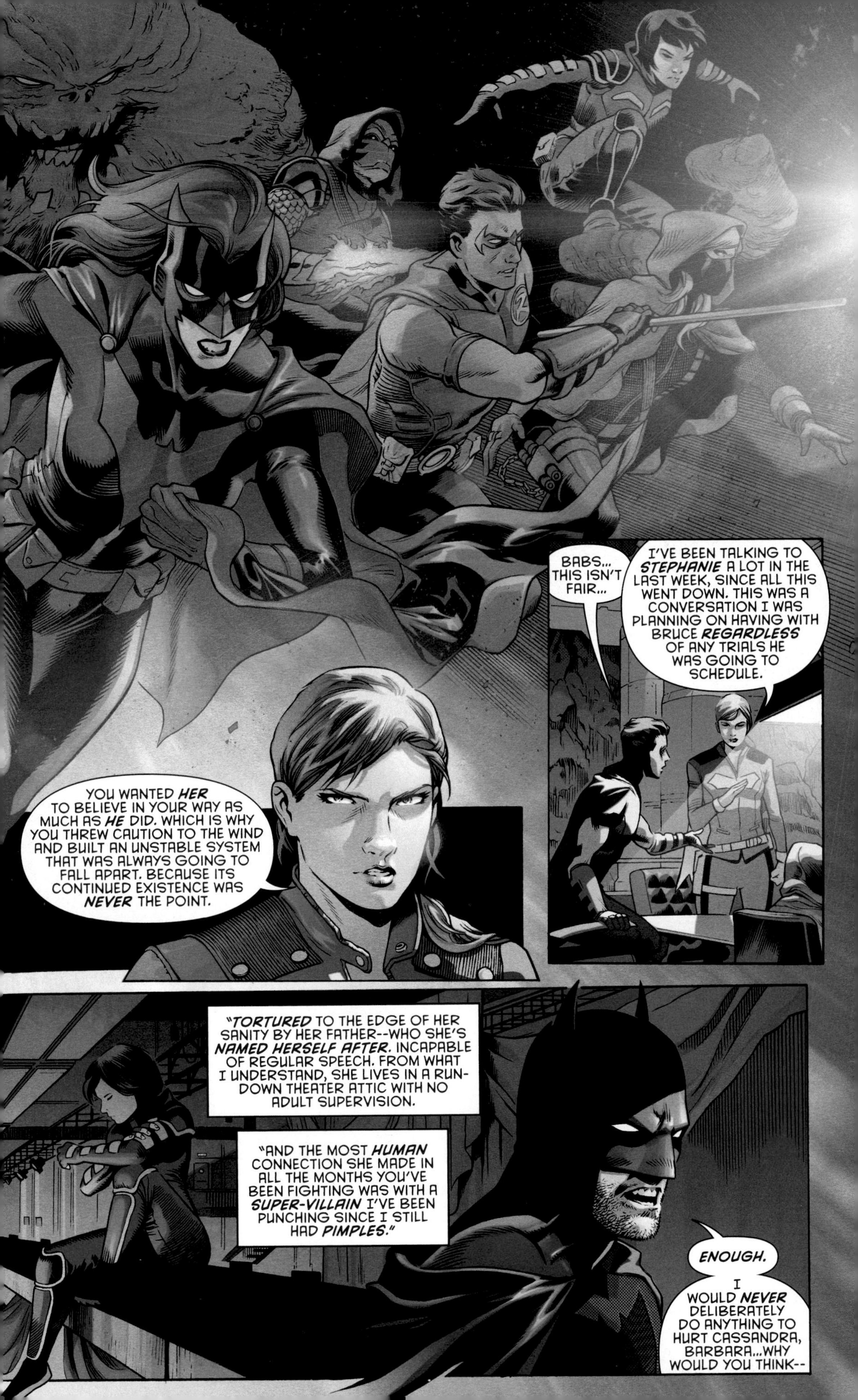
BABS... THIS ISN'T FAIR...
I'VE BEEN TALKING TO STEPHANIE A LOT IN THE LAST WEEK, SINCE ALL THIS WENT DOWN. THIS WAS A CONVERSATION I WAS PLANNING ON HAVING WITH BRUCE REGARDLESS OF ANY TRIALS HE WAS GOING TO SCHEDULE.
YOU WANTED HER TO BELIEVE IN YOUR WAY AS MUCH AS HE DID. WHICH IS WHY YOU THREW CAUTION TO THE WIND AND BUILT AN UNSTABLE SYSTEM THAT WAS ALWAYS GOING TO FALL APART. BECAUSE ITS CONTINUED EXISTENCE WAS NEVER THE POINT.
"TORTURED TO THE EDGE OF HER SANITY BY HER FATHER--WHO SHE'S NAMED HERSELF AFTER. INCAPABLE OF REGULAR SPEECH. FROM WHAT I UNDERSTAND, SHE LIVES IN A RUN-DOWN THEATER ATTIC WITH NO ADULT SUPERVISION.
"AND THE MOST HUMAN CONNECTION SHE MADE IN ALL THE MONTHS YOU'VE BEEN FIGHTING WAS WITH A SUPER-VILLAIN I'VE BEEN PUNCHING SINCE I STILL HAD PIMPLES."
ENOUGH.
I WOULD NEVER DELIBERATELY DO ANYTHING TO HURT CASSANDRA, BARBARA...WHY WOULD YOU THINK--

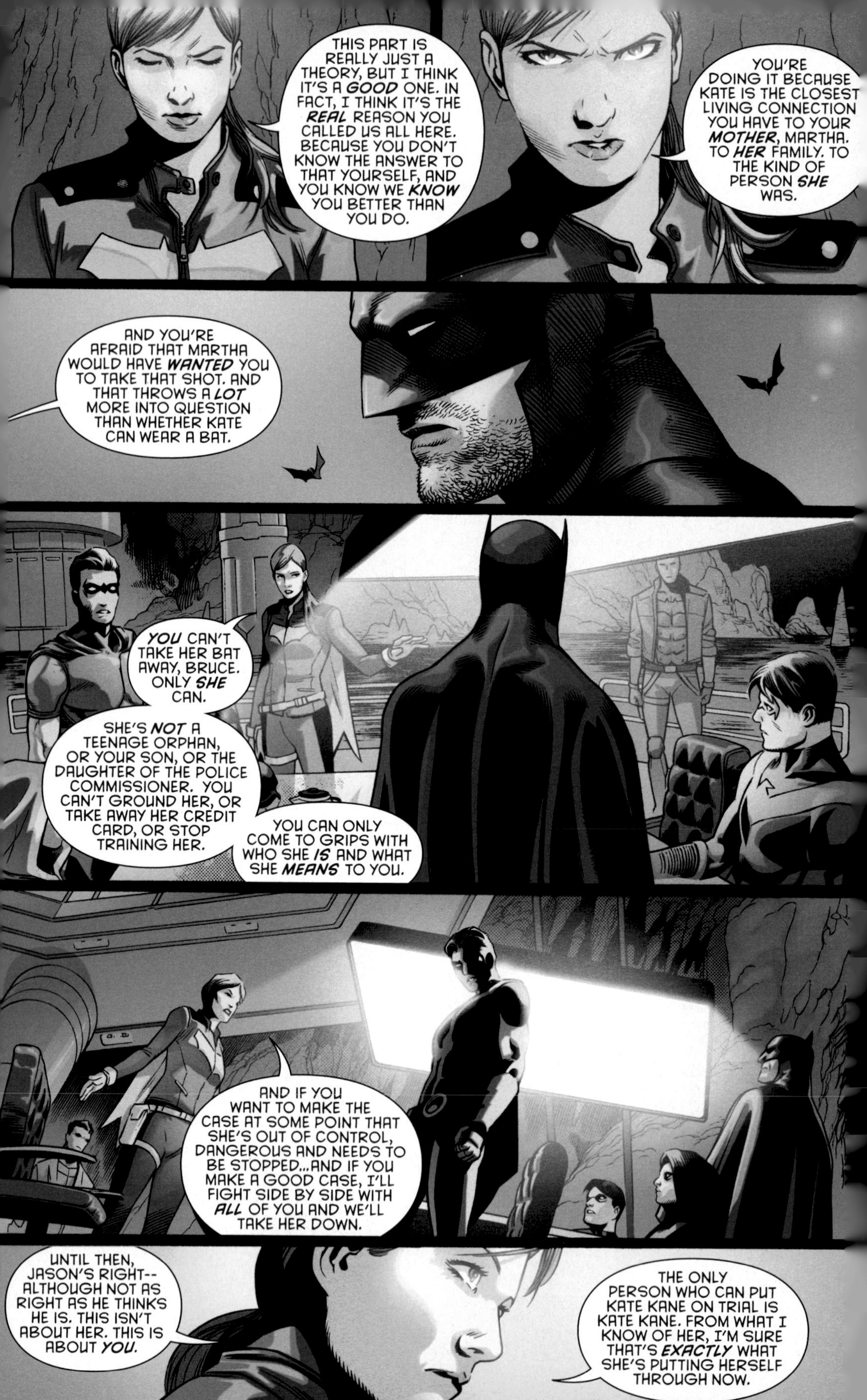
THIS PART IS REALLY JUST A THEORY, BUT I THINK IT'S A GOOD ONE. IN FACT, I THINK IT'S THE REAL REASON YOU CALLED US ALL HERE. BECAUSE YOU DON'T KNOW THE ANSWER TO THAT YOURSELF, AND YOU KNOW WE KNOW YOU BETTER THAN YOU DO.
YOU'RE DOING IT BECAUSE KATE IS THE CLOSEST LIVING CONNECTION YOU HAVE TO YOUR MOTHER, MARTHA. TO HER FAMILY. TO THE KIND OF PERSON SHE WAS.
AND YOU'RE AFRAID THAT MARTHA WOULD HAVE WANTED YOU TO TAKE THAT SHOT. AND THAT THROWS A LOT MORE INTO QUESTION THAN WHETHER KATE CAN WEAR A BAT.
YOU CAN'T TAKE HER BAT AWAY, BRUCE. ONLY SHE CAN.
SHE'S NOT A TEENAGE ORPHAN, OR YOUR SON, OR THE DAUGHTER OF THE POLICE COMMISSIONER. YOU CAN'T GROUND HER, OR TAKE AWAY HER CREDIT CARD, OR STOP TRAINING HER.
YOU CAN ONLY COME TO GRIPS WITH WHO SHE IS AND WHAT SHE MEANS TO YOU.
AND IF YOU WANT TO MAKE THE CASE AT SOME POINT THAT SHE'S OUT OF CONTROL, DANGEROUS AND NEEDS TO BE STOPPED...AND IF YOU MAKE A GOOD CASE, I'LL FIGHT SIDE BY SIDE WITH ALL OF YOU AND WE'LL TAKE HER DOWN.
UNTIL THEN, JASON'S RIGHT--ALTHOUGH NOT AS RIGHT AS HE THINKS HE IS. THIS ISN'T ABOUT HER. THIS IS ABOUT YOU.
THE ONLY PERSON WHO CAN PUT KATE KANE ON TRIAL IS KATE KANE. FROM WHAT I KNOW OF HER, I'M SURE THAT'S EXACTLY WHAT SHE'S PUTTING HERSELF THROUGH NOW.

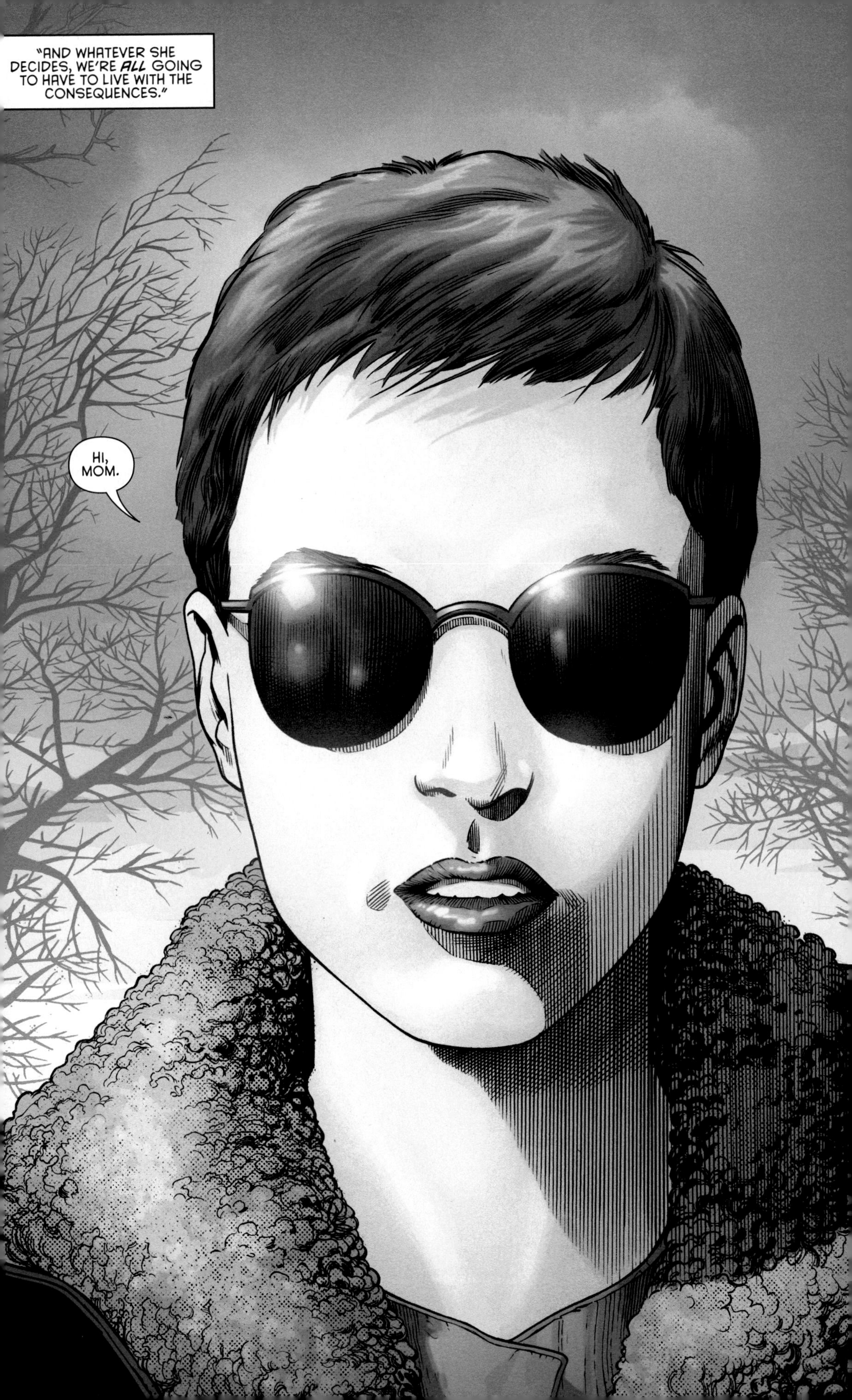
"AND WHATEVER SHE DECIDES, WE'RE ALL GOING TO HAVE TO LIVE WITH THE CONSEQUENCES."
HI, MOM.

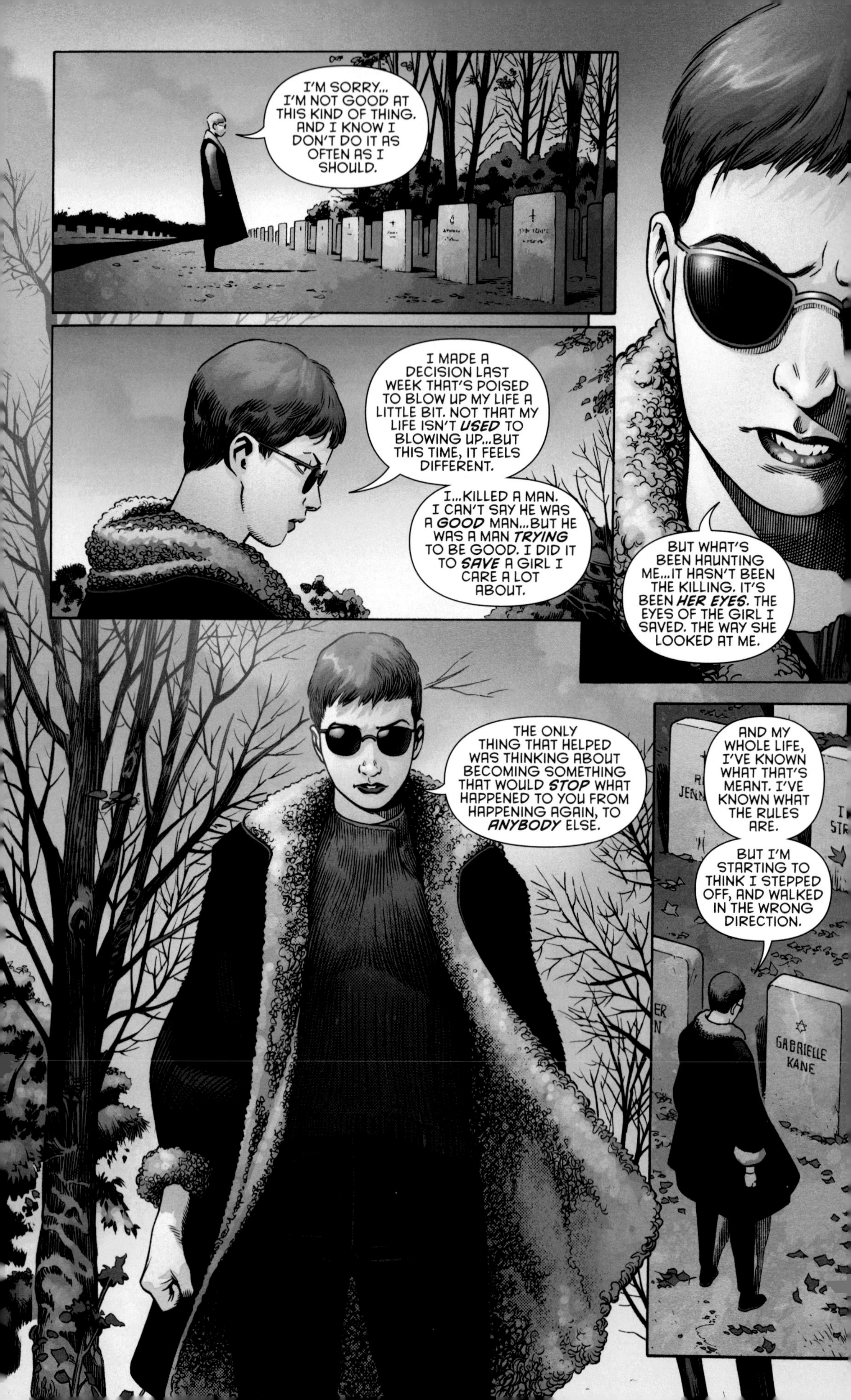
I'M SORRY... I'M NOT GOOD AT THIS KIND OF THING. AND I KNOW I DON'T DO IT AS OFTEN AS I SHOULD.
I MADE A DECISION LAST WEEK THAT'S POISED TO BLOW UP MY LIFE A LITTLE BIT. NOT THAT MY LIFE ISN'T USED TO BLOWING UP...BUT THIS TIME, IT FEELS DIFFERENT.
I...KILLED A MAN. I CAN'T SAY HE WAS A GOOD MAN...BUT HE WAS A MAN TRYING TO BE GOOD. I DID IT TO SAVE A GIRL I CARE A LOT ABOUT.
BUT WHAT'S BEEN HAUNTING ME...IT HASN'T BEEN THE KILLING. IT'S BEEN HER EYES. THE EYES OF THE GIRL I SAVED. THE WAY SHE LOOKED AT ME.
THE ONLY THING THAT HELPED WAS THINKING ABOUT BECOMING SOMETHING THAT WOULD STOP WHAT HAPPENED TO YOU FROM HAPPENING AGAIN, TO ANYBODY ELSE.
AND MY WHOLE LIFE, I'VE KNOWN WHAT THAT'S MEANT. I'VE KNOWN WHAT THE RULES ARE.
BUT I'M STARTING TO THINK I STEPPED OFF, AND WALKED IN THE WRONG DIRECTION.
GABRIELLE KANE

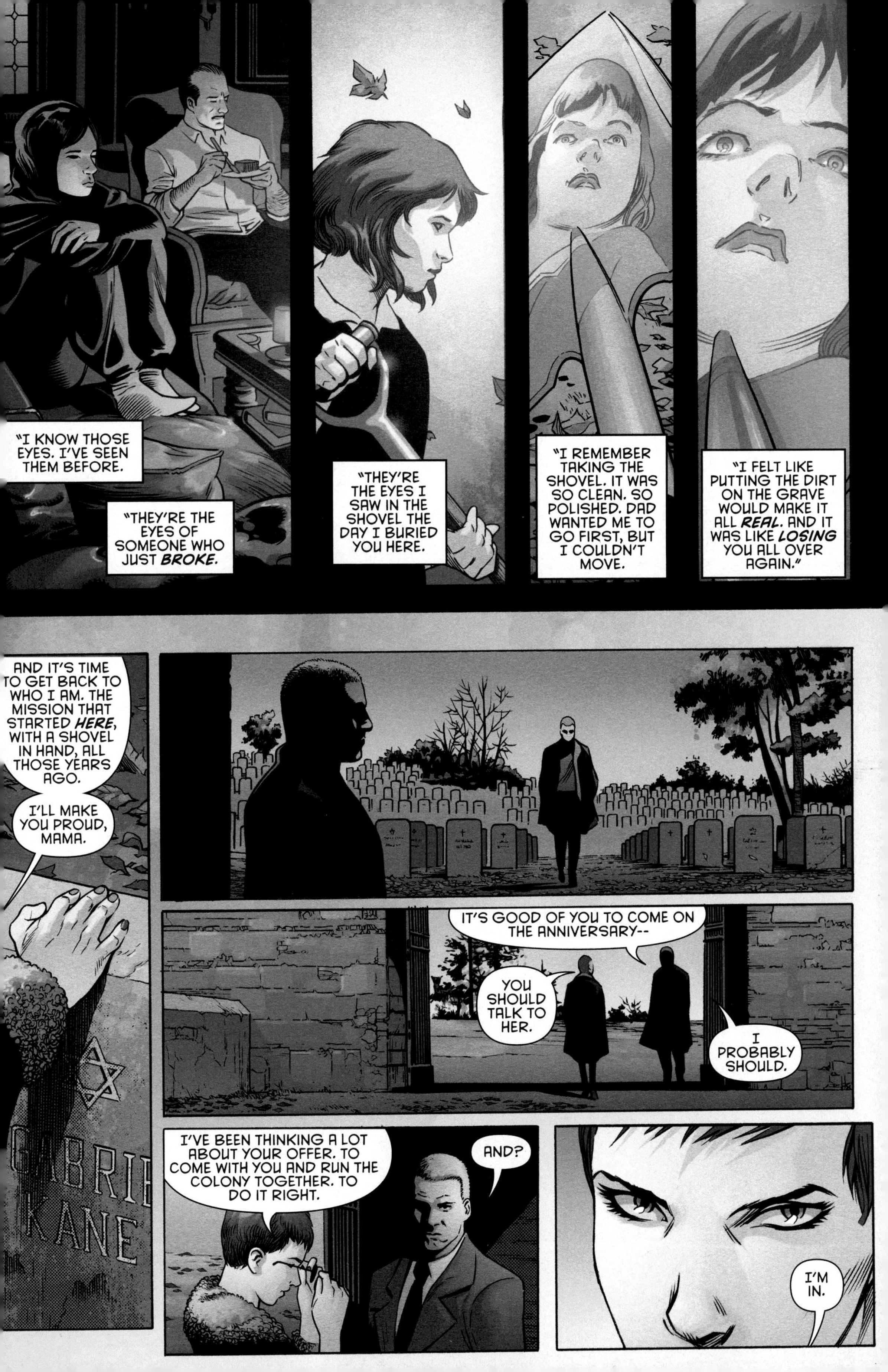
"I KNOW THOSE EYES. I'VE SEEN THEM BEFORE.
"THEY'RE THE EYES OF SOMEONE WHO JUST BROKE.
"THEY'RE THE EYES I SAW IN THE SHOVEL THE DAY I BURIED YOU HERE.
"I REMEMBER TAKING THE SHOVEL. IT WAS SO CLEAN. SO POLISHED. DAD WANTED ME TO GO FIRST, BUT I COULDN'T MOVE.
"I FELT LIKE PUTTING THE DIRT ON THE GRAVE WOULD MAKE IT ALL REAL. AND IT WAS LIKE LOSING YOU ALL OVER AGAIN."
AND IT'S TIME TO GET BACK TO WHO I AM. THE MISSION THAT STARTED HERE, WITH A SHOVEL IN HAND, ALL THOSE YEARS AGO.
I'LL MAKE YOU PROUD, MAMA.
GABRIE KANE
IT'S GOOD OF YOU TO COME ON THE ANNIVERSARY--
YOU SHOULD TALK TO HER.
I PROBABLY SHOULD.
I'VE BEEN THINKING A LOT ABOUT YOUR OFFER. TO COME WITH YOU AND RUN THE COLONY TOGETHER. TO DO IT RIGHT.
AND?
I'M IN.

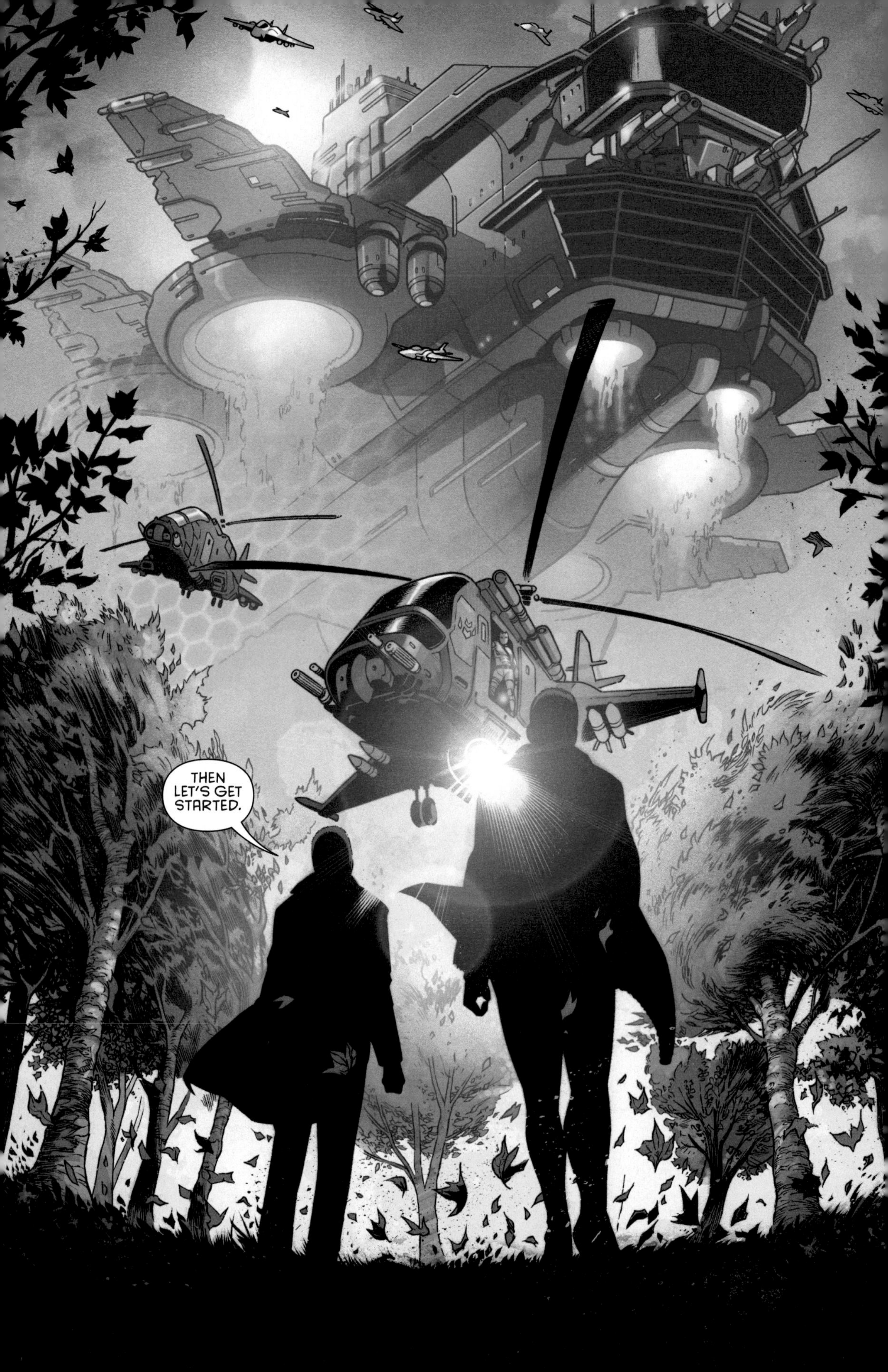
THEN LET'S GET STARTED.

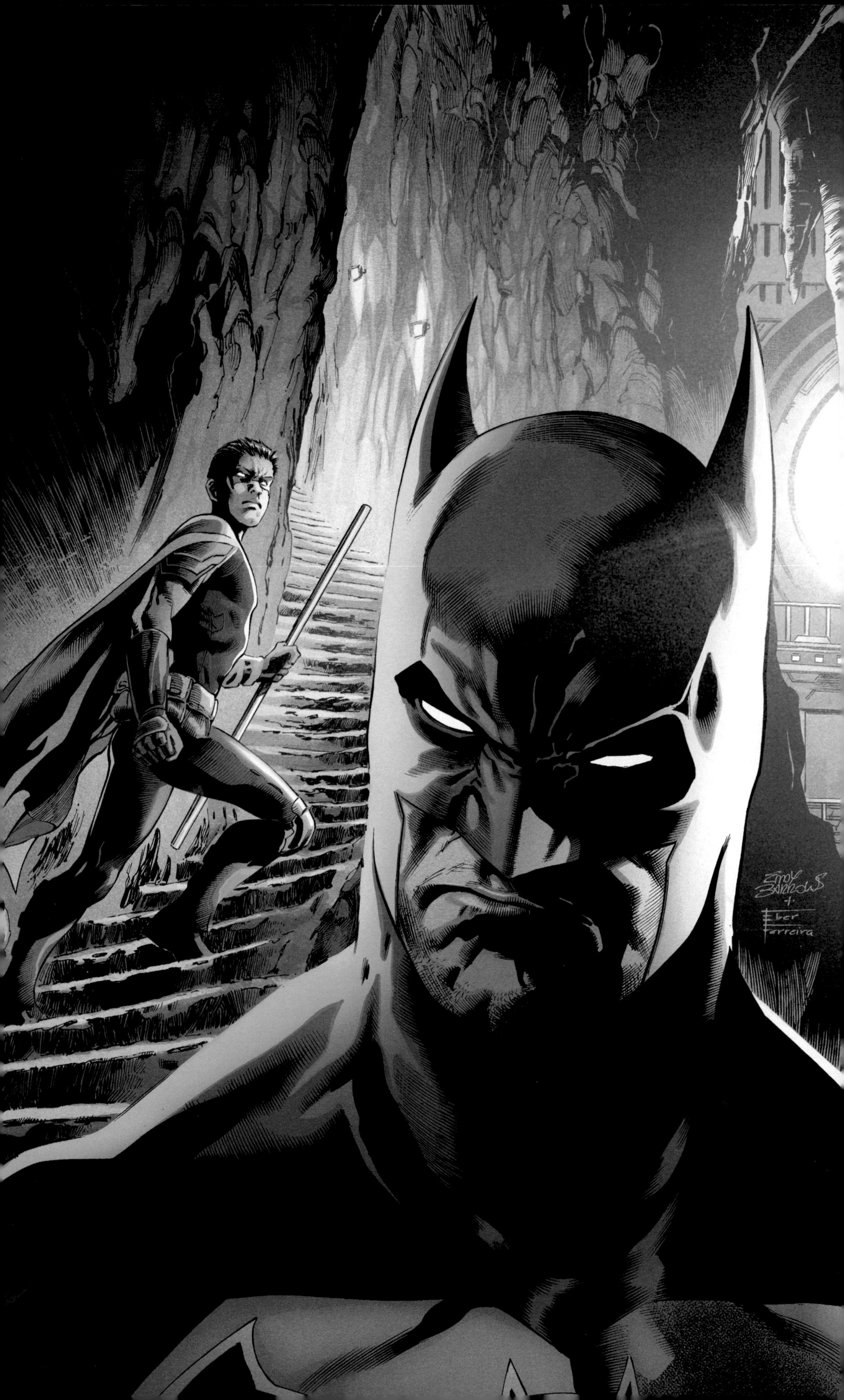

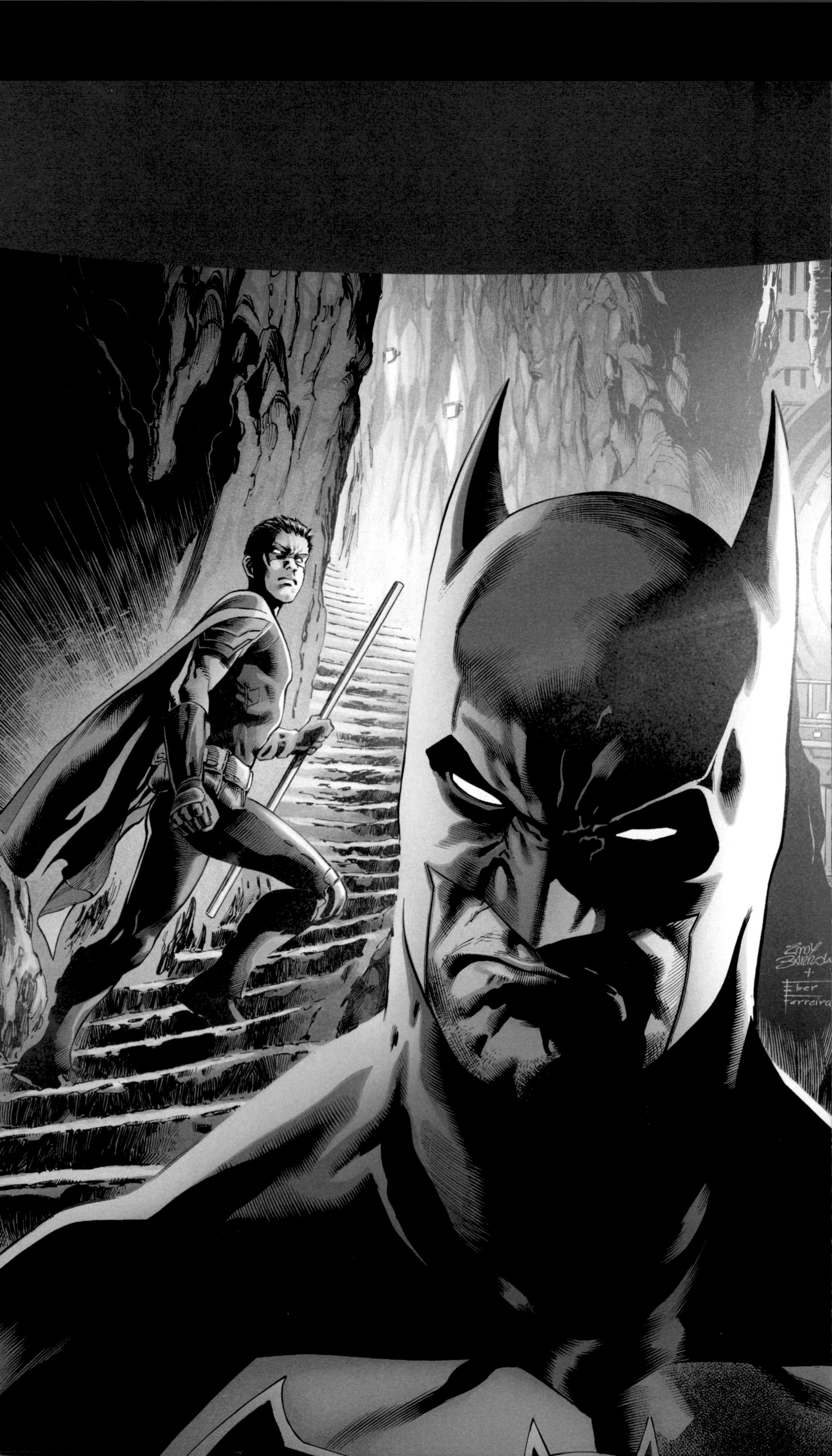

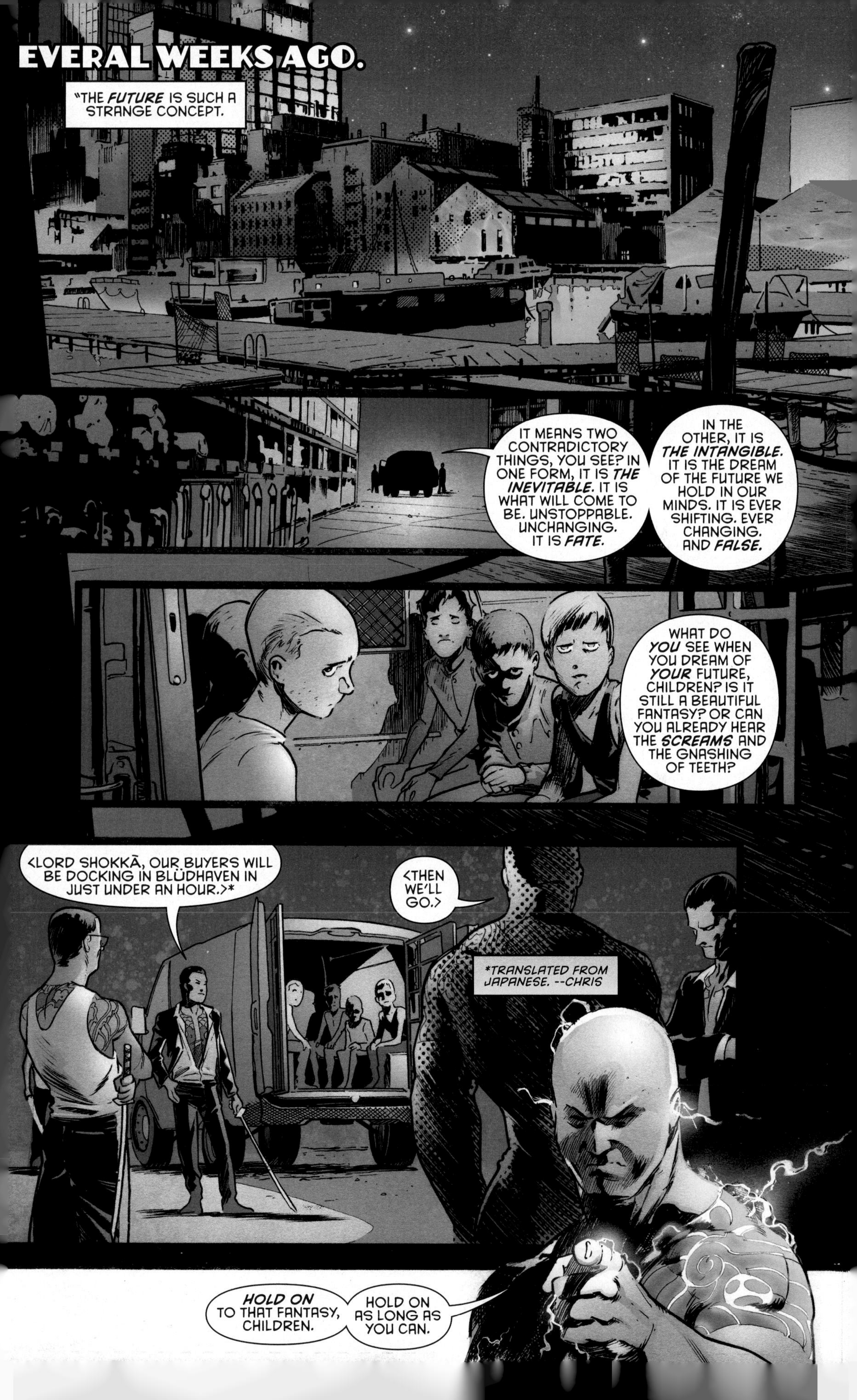

EVERAL WEEKS AGO.
"THE FUTURE IS SUCH A STRANGE CONCEPT.
IT MEANS TWO CONTRADICTORY THINGS, YOU SEE? IN ONE FORM, IT IS THE INEVITABLE. IT IS WHAT WILL COME TO BE. UNSTOPPABLE. UNCHANGING. IT IS FATE.
IN THE OTHER, IT IS THE INTANGIBLE. IT IS THE DREAM OF THE FUTURE WE HOLD IN OUR MINDS. IT IS EVER SHIFTING. EVER CHANGING. AND FALSE.
WHAT DO YOU SEE WHEN YOU DREAM OF YOUR FUTURE, CHILDREN? IS IT STILL A BEAUTIFUL FANTASY? OR CAN YOU ALREADY HEAR THE SCREAMS AND THE GNASHING OF TEETH?
<LORD SHOKKĀ, OUR BUYERS WILL BE DOCKING IN BLÜDHAVEN IN JUST UNDER AN HOUR.>*
<THEN WE'LL GO.>
*TRANSLATED FROM JAPANESE. --CHRIS
HOLD ON TO THAT FANTASY, CHILDREN.
HOLD ON AS LONG AS YOU CAN.

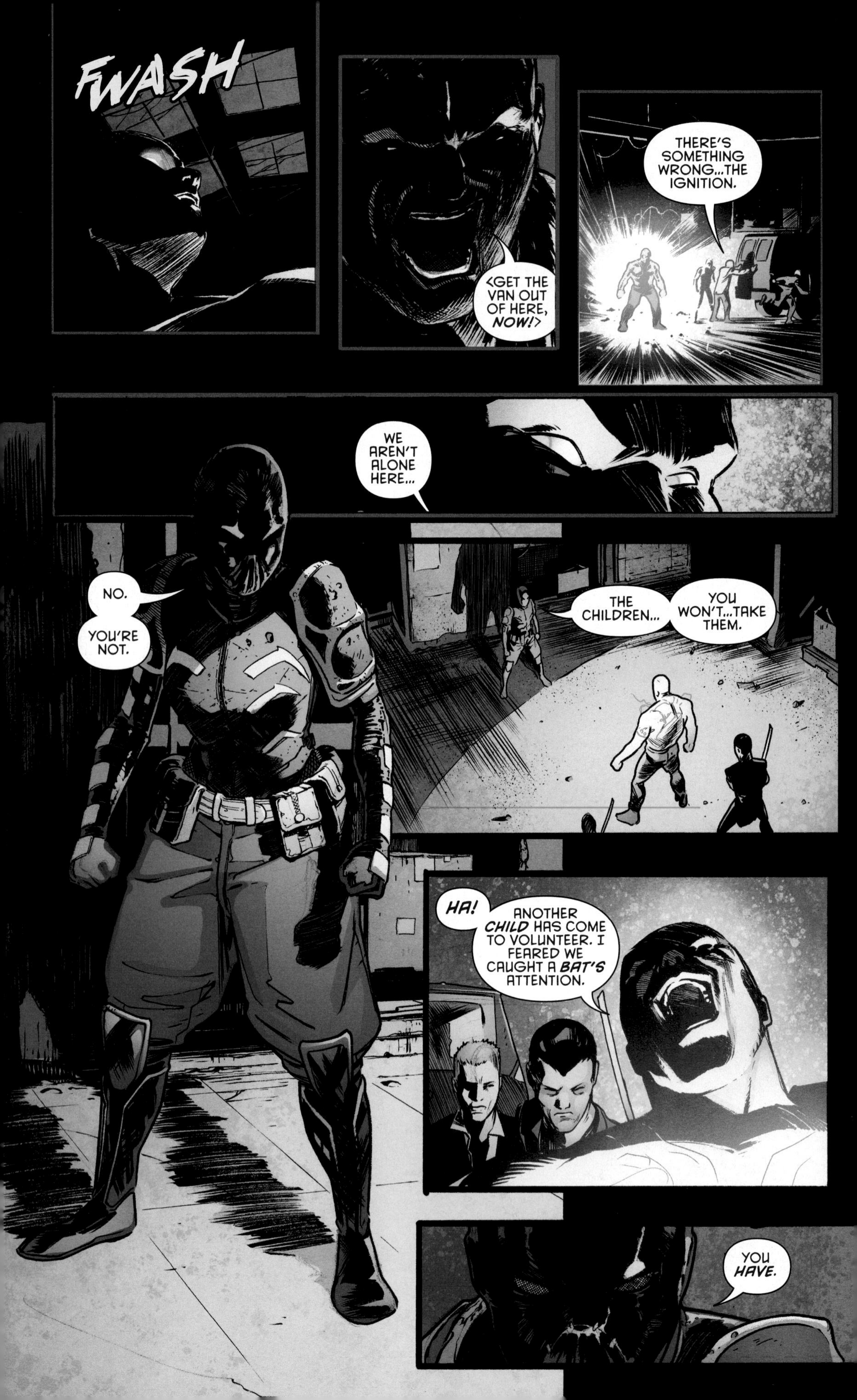
FWASH
<GET THE VAN OUT OF HERE, NOW!>
THERE'S SOMETHING WRONG...THE IGNITION.
WE AREN'T ALONE HERE...
NO.
YOU'RE NOT.
THE CHILDREN...
YOU WON'T...TAKE THEM.
HA!
ANOTHER CHILD HAS COME TO VOLUNTEER. I FEARED WE CAUGHT A BAT'S ATTENTION.
YOU HAVE.

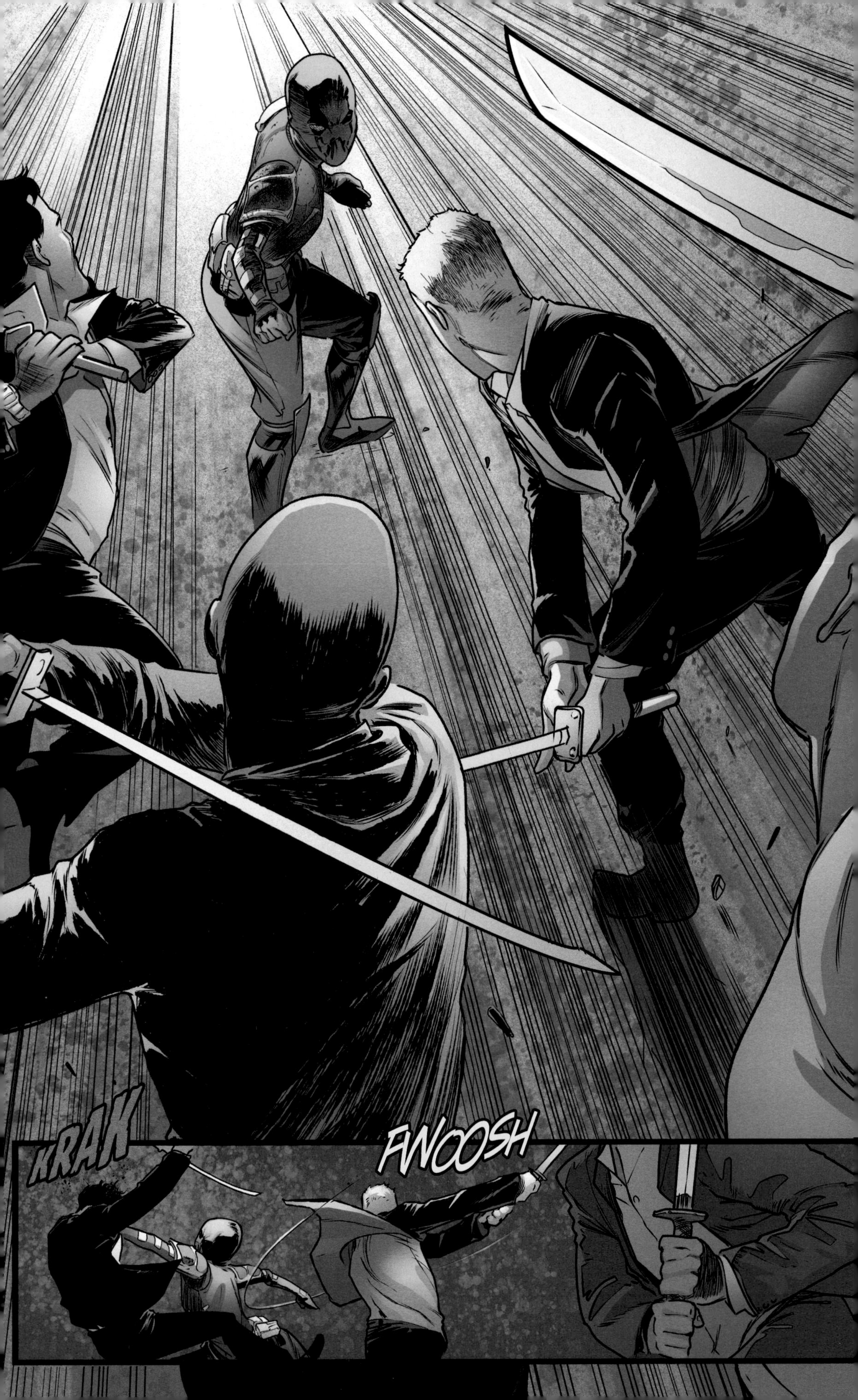
KRAK
FWOOSH

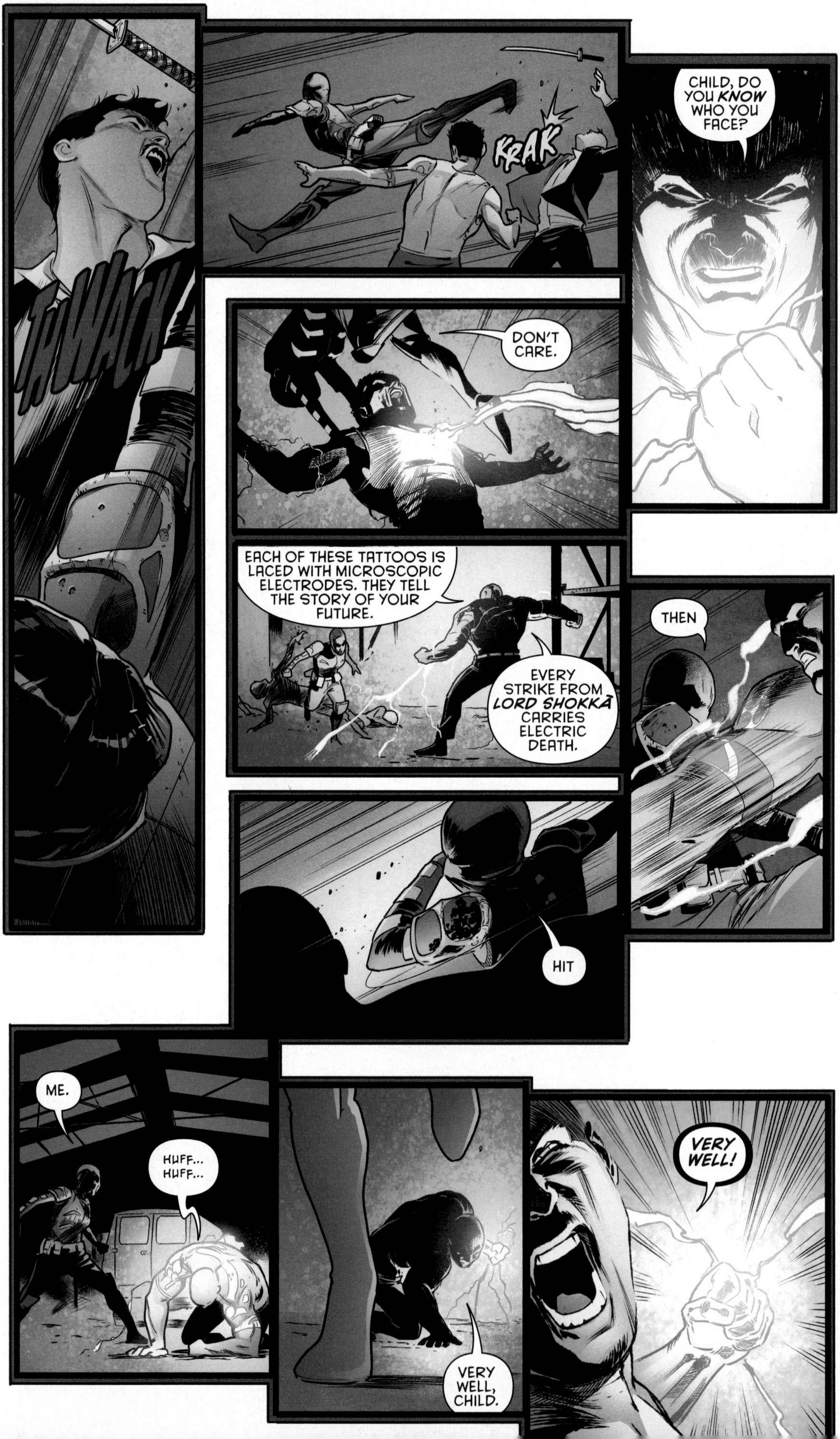
THWACK
KRAK
CHILD, DO YOU KNOW WHO YOU FACE?
DON'T CARE.
EACH OF THESE TATTOOS IS LACED WITH MICROSCOPIC ELECTRODES. THEY TELL THE STORY OF YOUR FUTURE.
EVERY STRIKE FROM LORD SHOKKĀ CARRIES ELECTRIC DEATH.
THEN
HIT
ME.
HUFF... HUFF...
VERY WELL, CHILD.
VERY WELL!

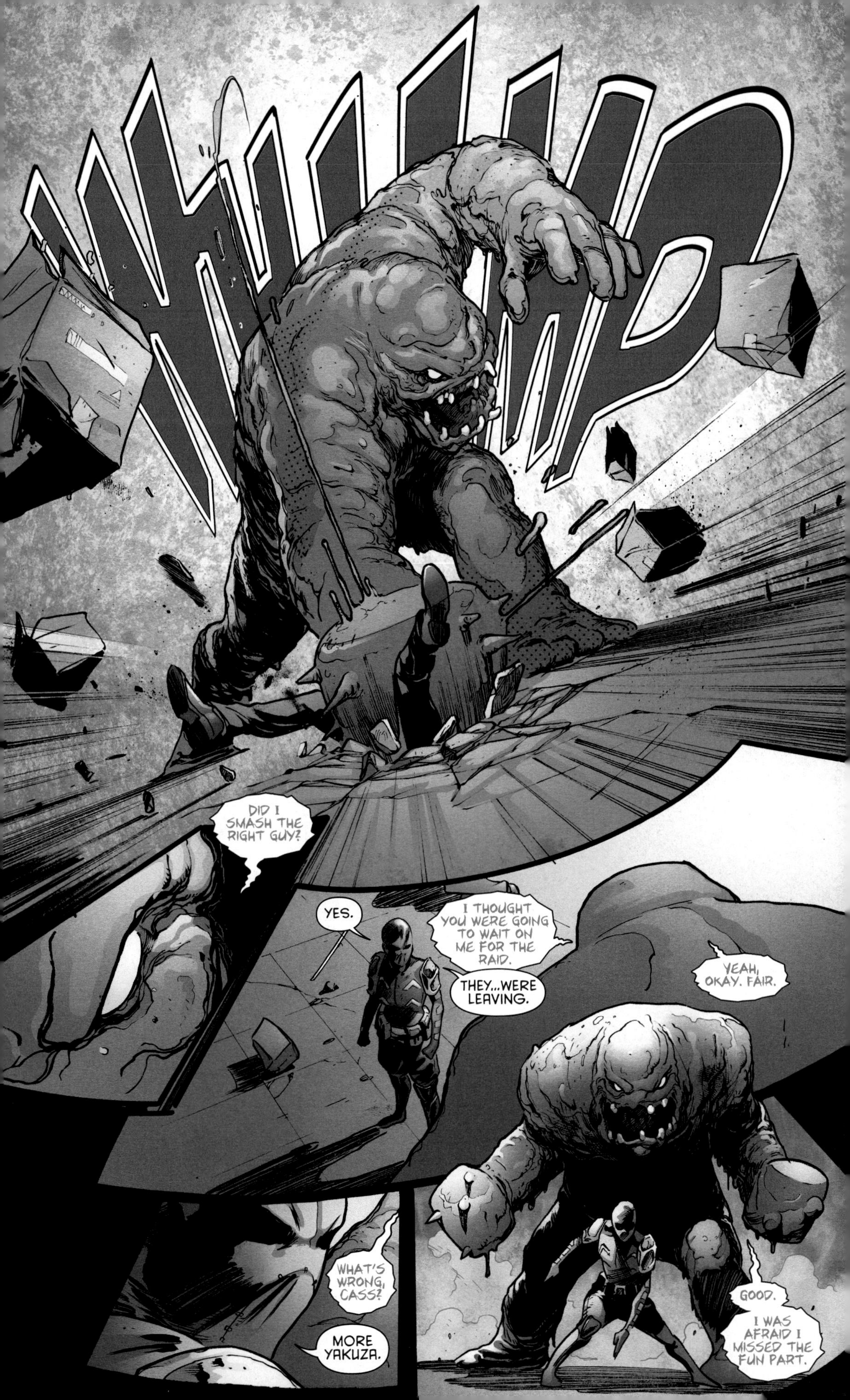
WHOOMP
DID I SMASH THE RIGHT GUY?
YES.
I THOUGHT YOU WERE GOING TO WAIT ON ME FOR THE RAID.
THEY...WERE LEAVING.
YEAH, OKAY. FAIR.
WHAT'S WRONG, CASS?
MORE YAKUZA.
GOOD.
I WAS AFRAID I MISSED THE FUN PART.

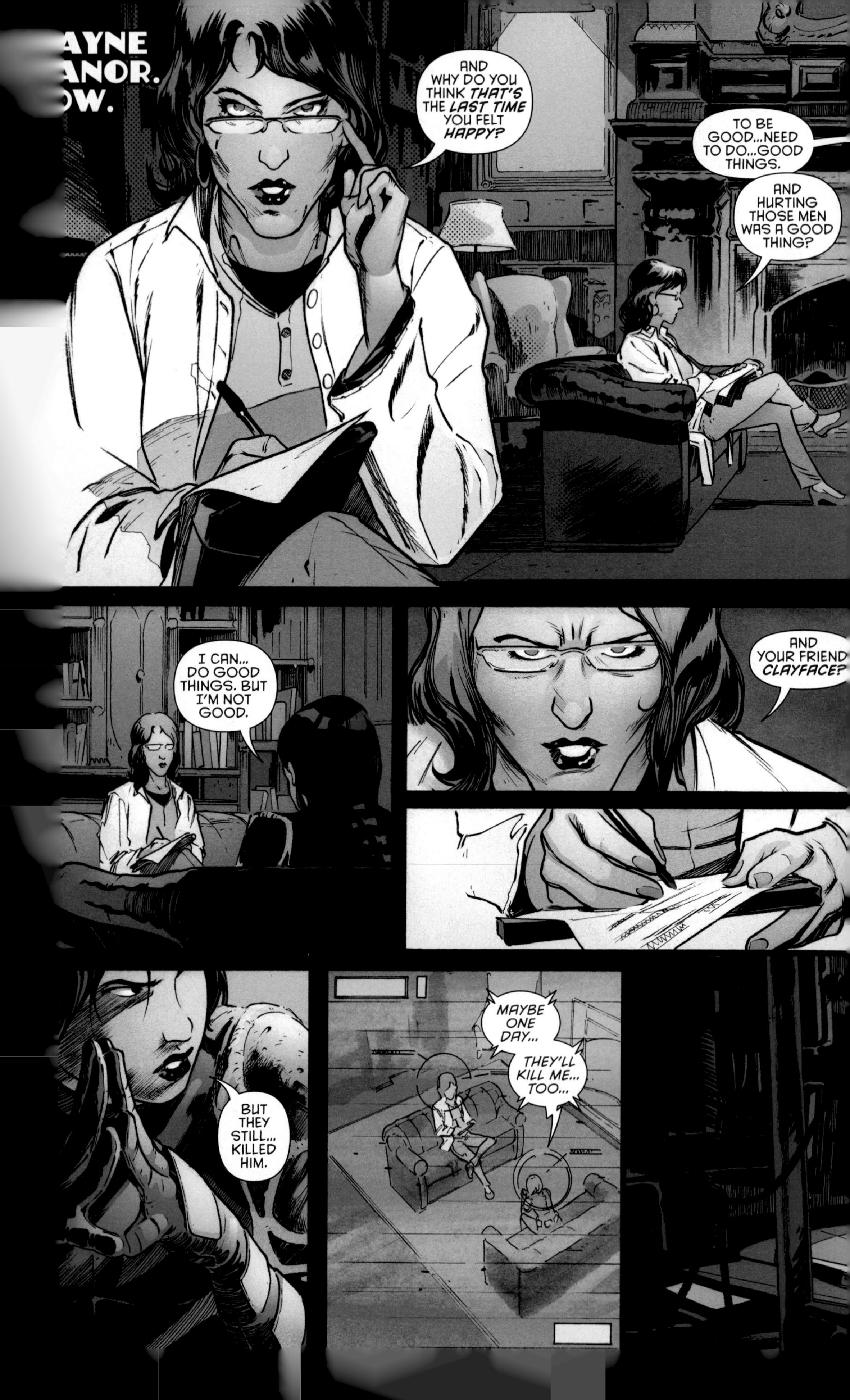
AYNE
ANOR.
OW.
AND WHY DO YOU THINK THAT'S THE LAST TIME YOU FELT HAPPY?
TO BE GOOD...NEED TO DO...GOOD THINGS.
AND HURTING THOSE MEN WAS A GOOD THING?
I CAN... DO GOOD THINGS. BUT I'M NOT GOOD.
AND YOUR FRIEND CLAYFACE?
BUT THEY STILL... KILLED HIM.
MAYBE ONE DAY...
THEY'LL KILL ME... TOO...

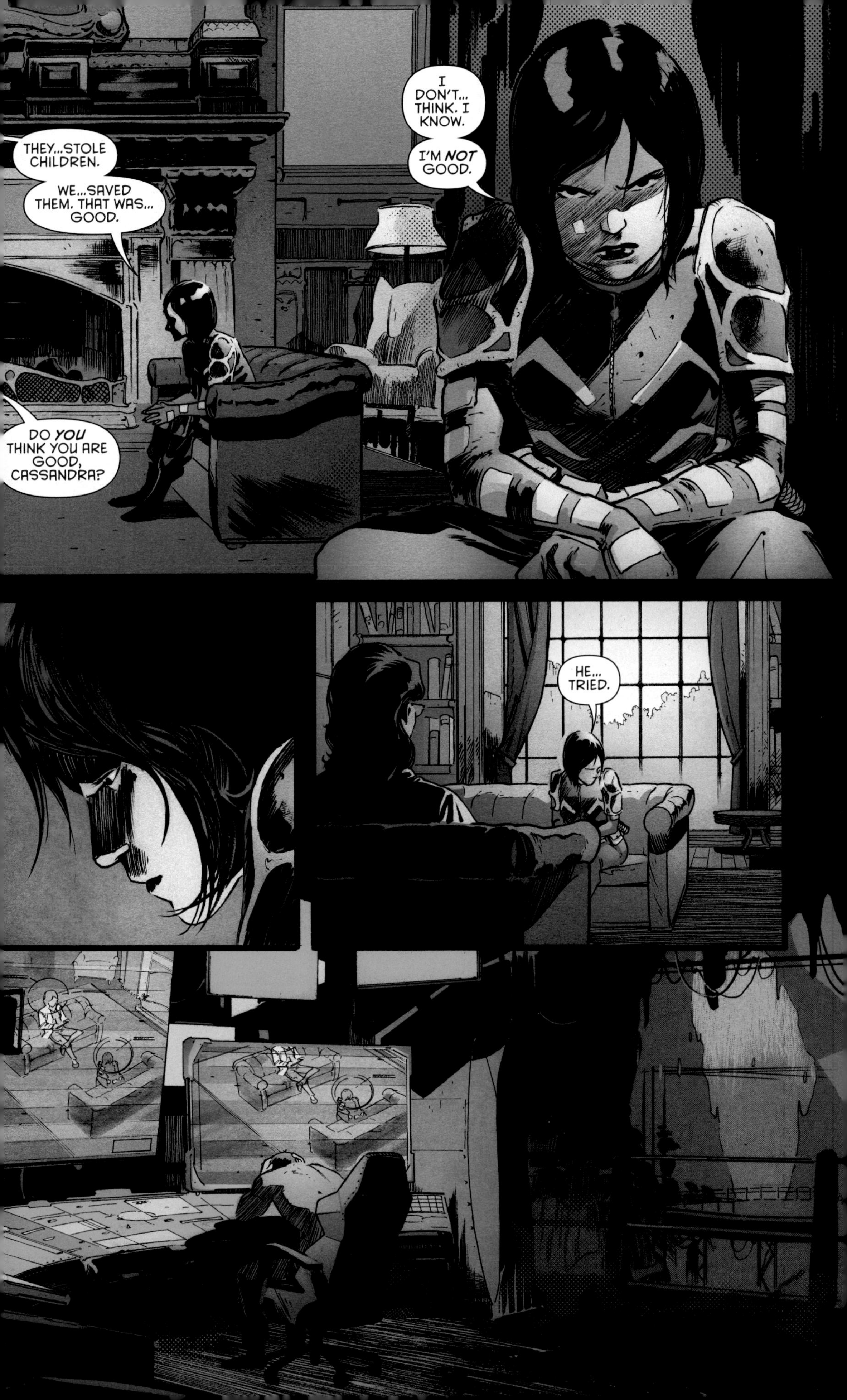
THEY...STOLE CHILDREN.
WE...SAVED THEM. THAT WAS... GOOD.
DO YOU THINK YOU ARE GOOD, CASSANDRA?
I DON'T... THINK. I KNOW.
I'M NOT GOOD.
HE... TRIED.

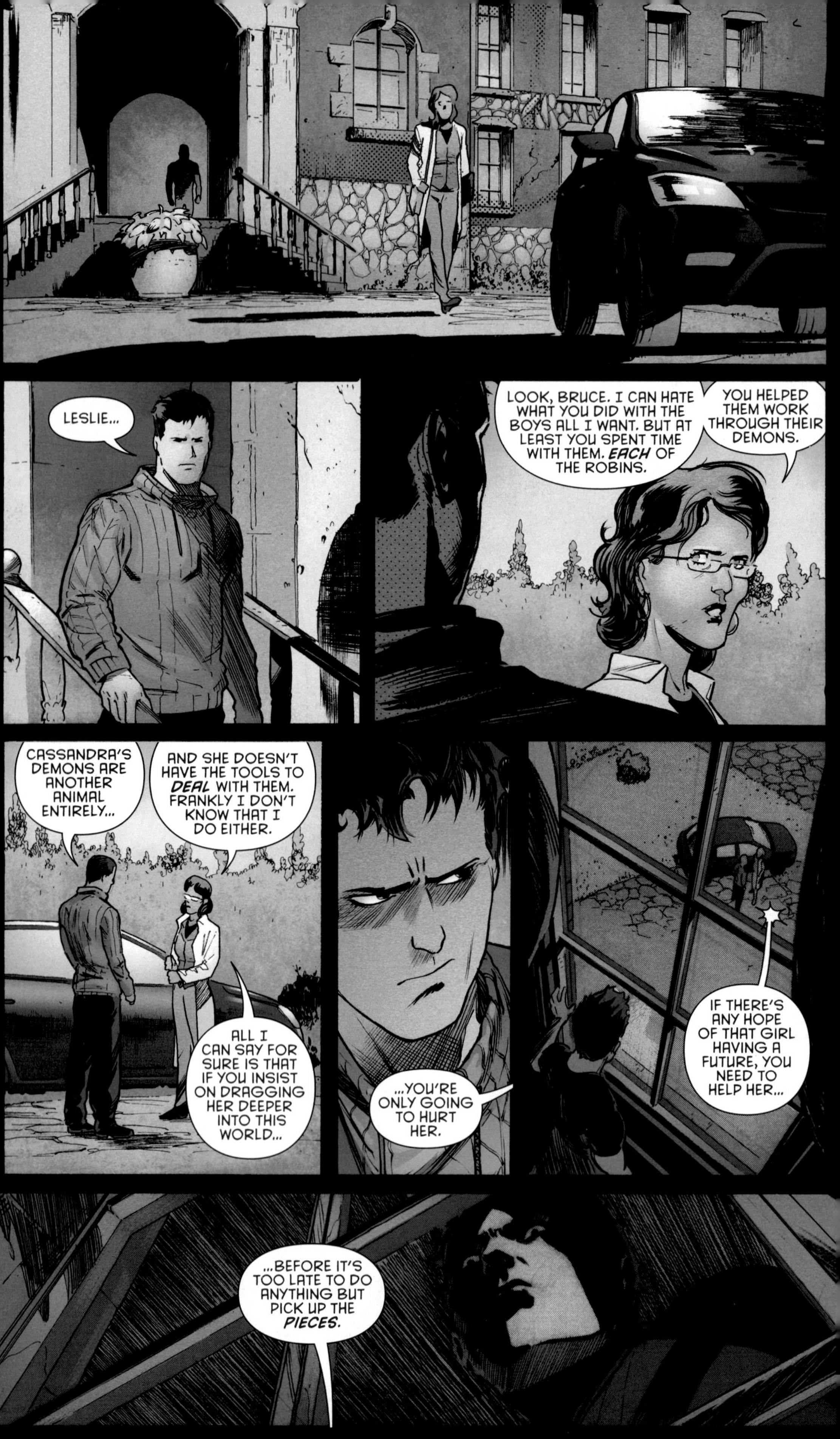
LESLIE...
LOOK, BRUCE. I CAN HATE WHAT YOU DID WITH THE BOYS ALL I WANT. BUT AT LEAST YOU SPENT TIME WITH THEM. EACH OF THE ROBINS.
YOU HELPED THEM WORK THROUGH THEIR DEMONS.
CASSANDRA'S DEMONS ARE ANOTHER ANIMAL ENTIRELY...
AND SHE DOESN'T HAVE THE TOOLS TO DEAL WITH THEM. FRANKLY I DON'T KNOW THAT I DO EITHER.
ALL I CAN SAY FOR SURE IS THAT IF YOU INSIST ON DRAGGING HER DEEPER INTO THIS WORLD...
...YOU'RE ONLY GOING TO HURT HER.
IF THERE'S ANY HOPE OF THAT GIRL HAVING A FUTURE, YOU NEED TO HELP HER...
...BEFORE IT'S TOO LATE TO DO ANYTHING BUT PICK UP THE PIECES.

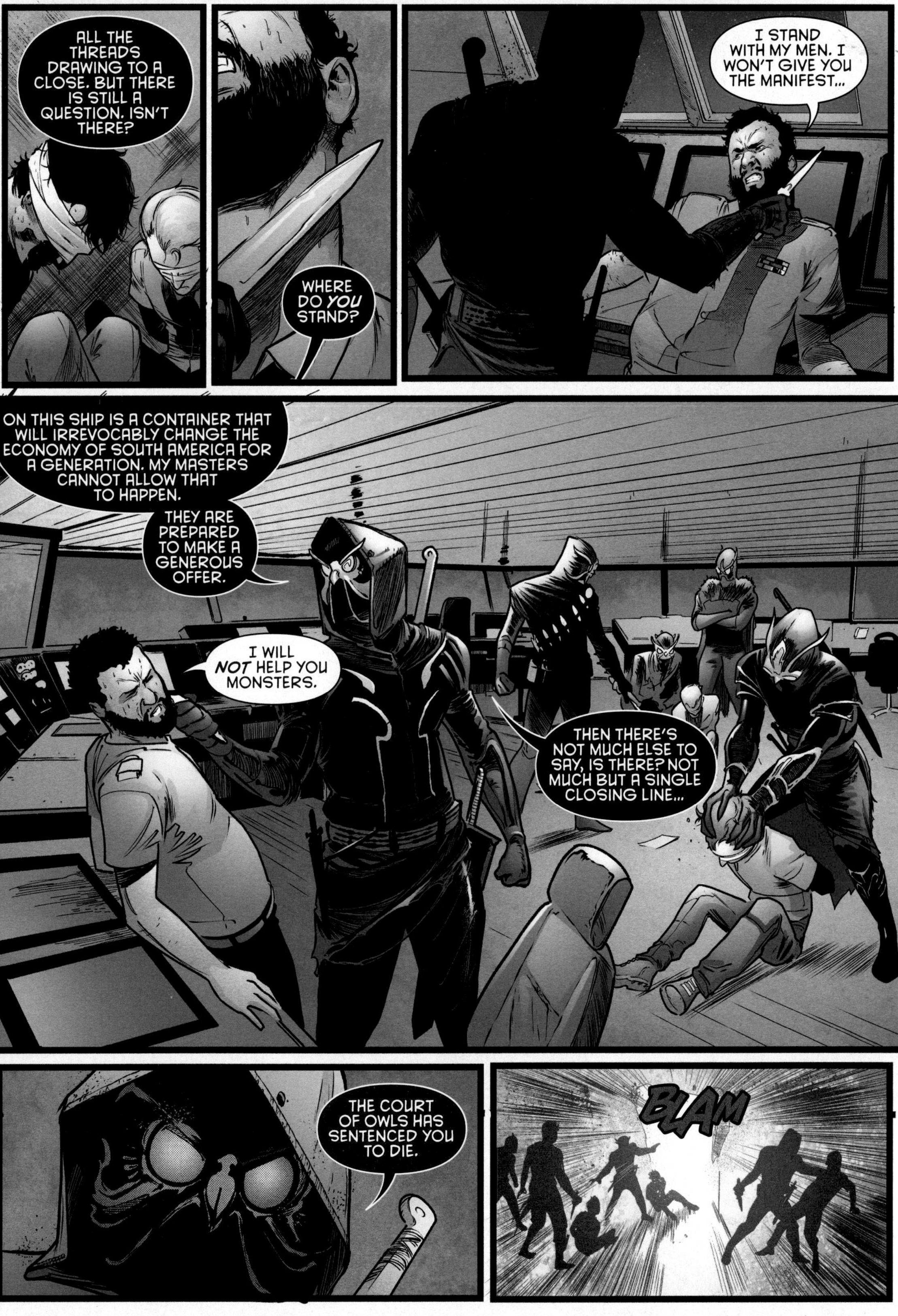
ALL THE THREADS DRAWING TO A CLOSE. BUT THERE IS STILL A QUESTION. ISN'T THERE?
WHERE DO *YOU* STAND?
I STAND WITH MY MEN. I WON'T GIVE YOU THE MANIFEST...
ON THIS SHIP IS A CONTAINER THAT WILL IRREVOCABLY CHANGE THE ECONOMY OF SOUTH AMERICA FOR A GENERATION. MY MASTERS CANNOT ALLOW THAT TO HAPPEN.
THEY ARE PREPARED TO MAKE A GENEROUS OFFER.
I WILL *NOT* HELP YOU MONSTERS.
THEN THERE'S NOT MUCH ELSE TO SAY, IS THERE? NOT MUCH BUT A SINGLE CLOSING LINE...
THE COURT OF OWLS HAS SENTENCED YOU TO DIE.
BLAM

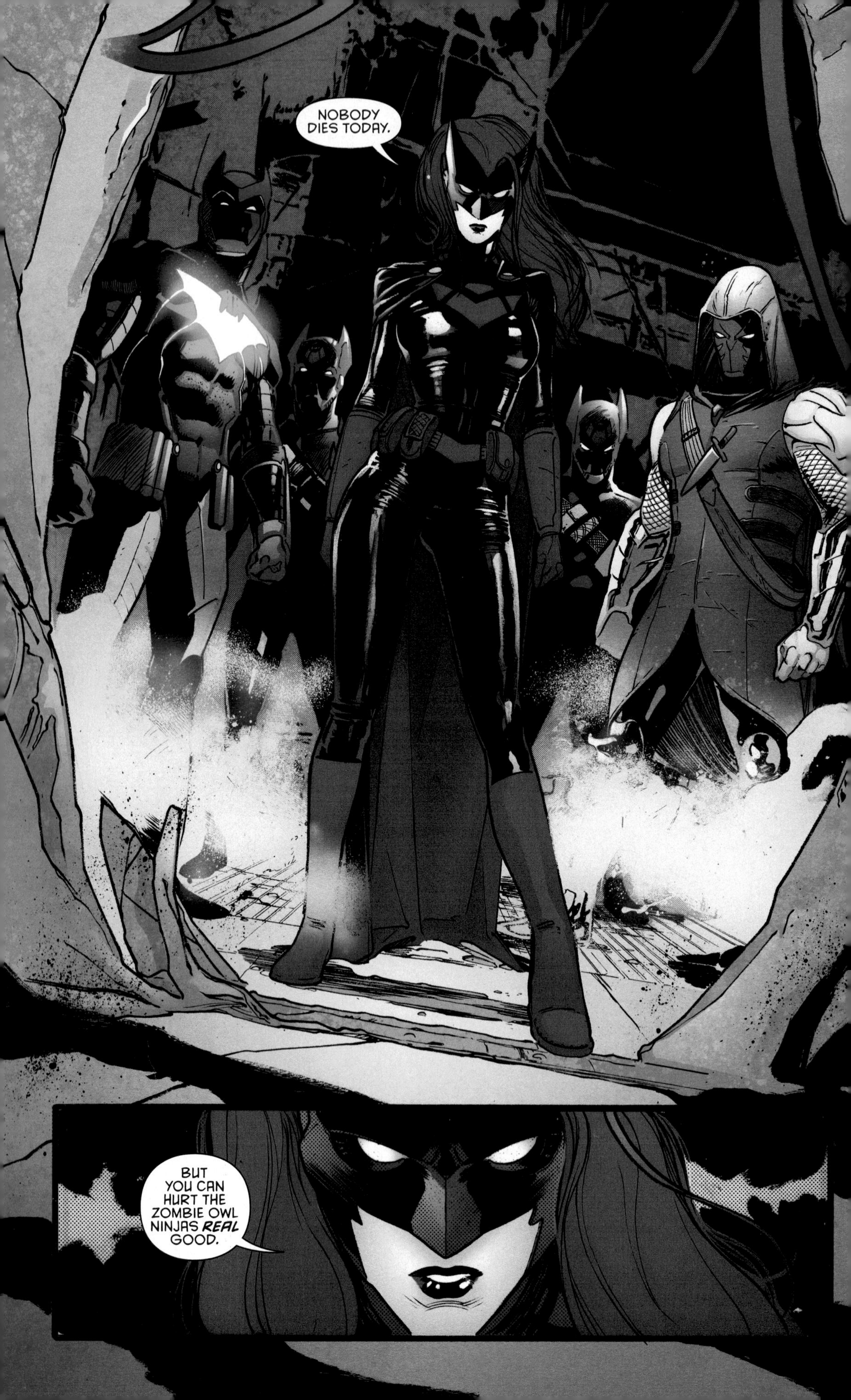
NOBODY DIES TODAY.
BUT YOU CAN HURT THE ZOMBIE OWL NINJAS *REAL* GOOD.

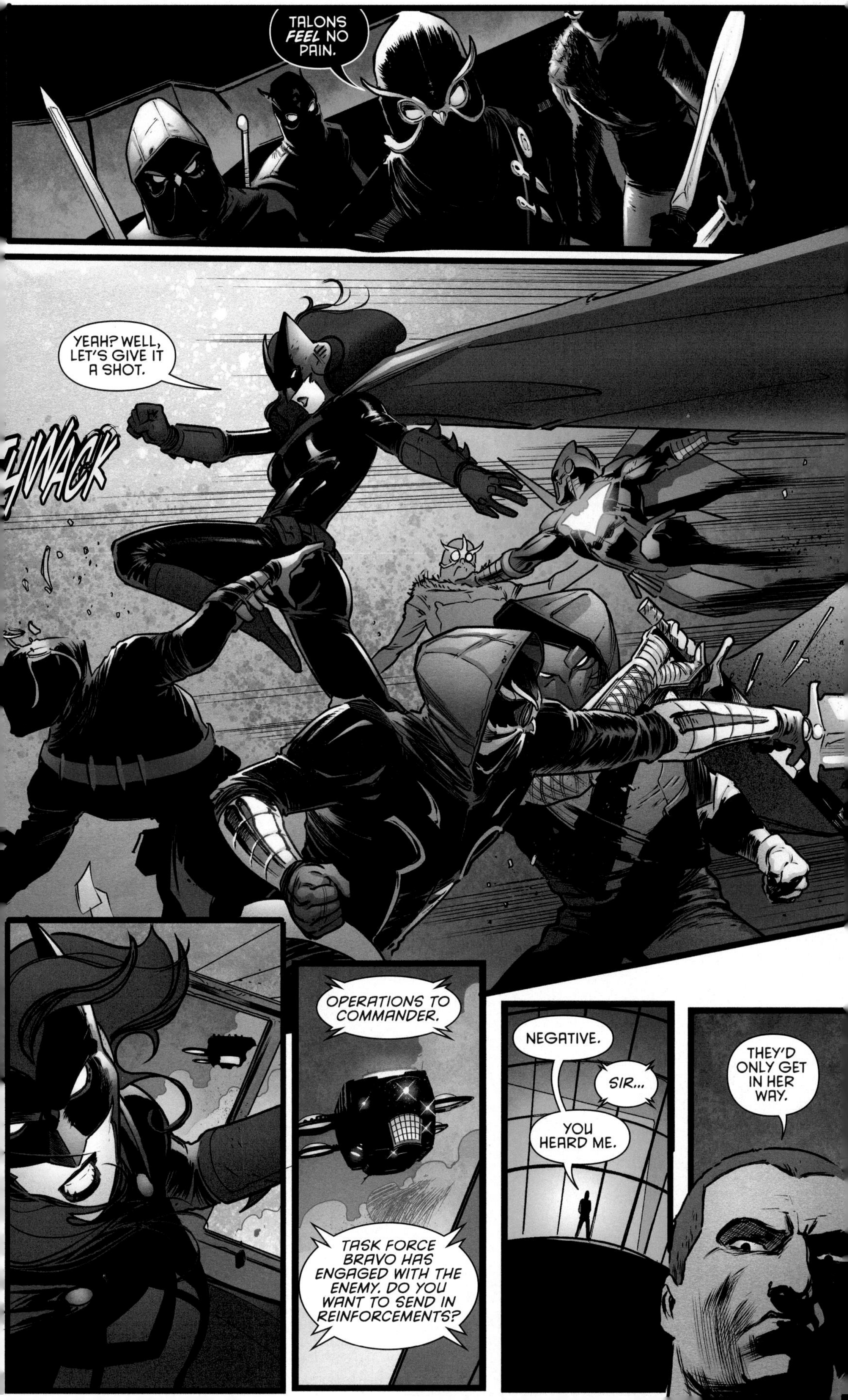
TALONS FEEL NO PAIN.
YEAH? WELL, LET'S GIVE IT A SHOT.
OPERATIONS TO COMMANDER.
TASK FORCE BRAVO HAS ENGAGED WITH THE ENEMY. DO YOU WANT TO SEND IN REINFORCEMENTS?
NEGATIVE.
SIR...
YOU HEARD ME.
THEY'D ONLY GET IN HER WAY.

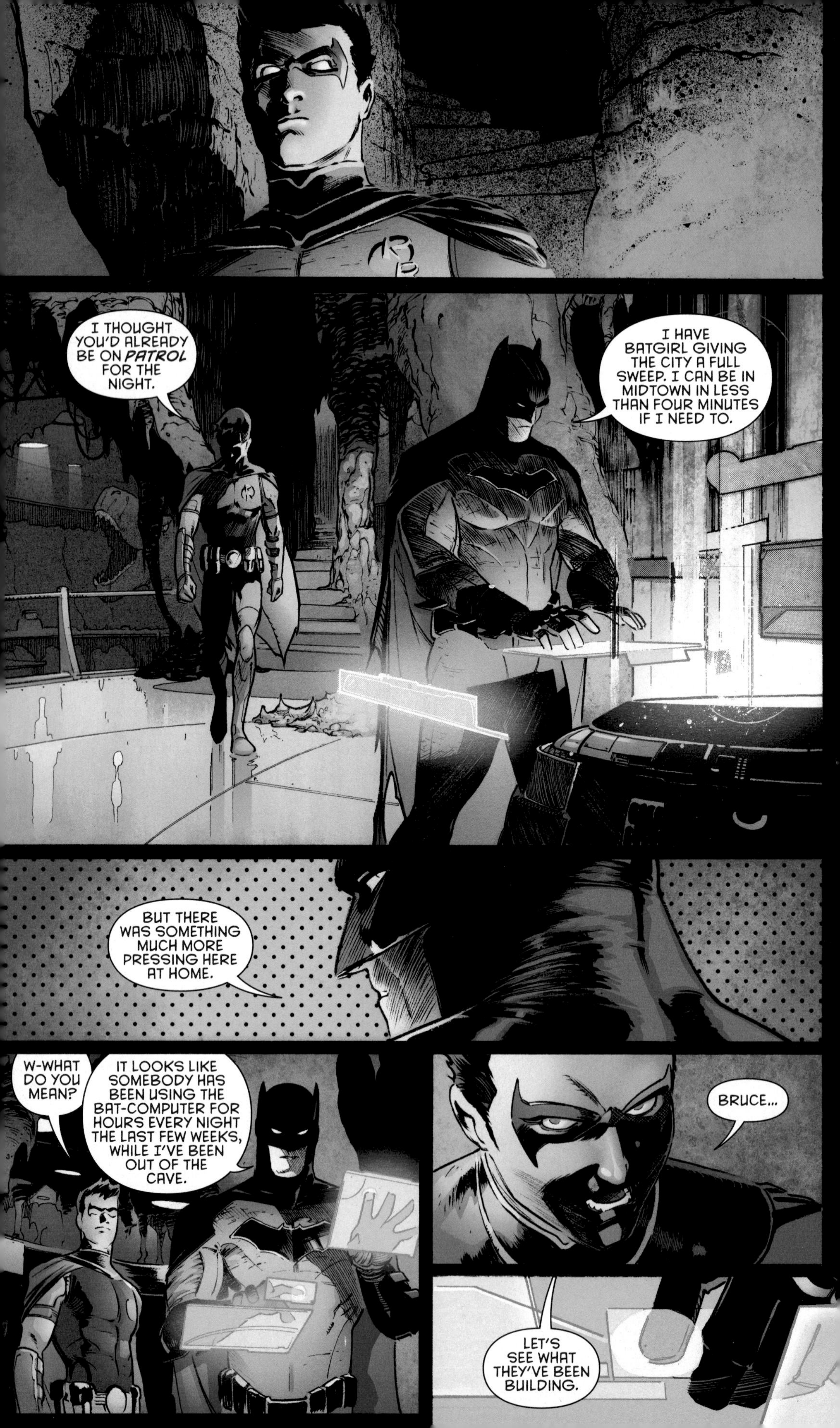
I THOUGHT YOU'D ALREADY BE ON *PATROL* FOR THE NIGHT.
I HAVE BATGIRL GIVING THE CITY A FULL SWEEP. I CAN BE IN MIDTOWN IN LESS THAN FOUR MINUTES IF I NEED TO.
BUT THERE WAS SOMETHING MUCH MORE PRESSING HERE AT HOME.
W-WHAT DO YOU MEAN?
IT LOOKS LIKE SOMEBODY HAS BEEN USING THE BAT-COMPUTER FOR HOURS EVERY NIGHT THE LAST FEW WEEKS, WHILE I'VE BEEN OUT OF THE CAVE.
BRUCE...
LET'S SEE WHAT THEY'VE BEEN BUILDING.

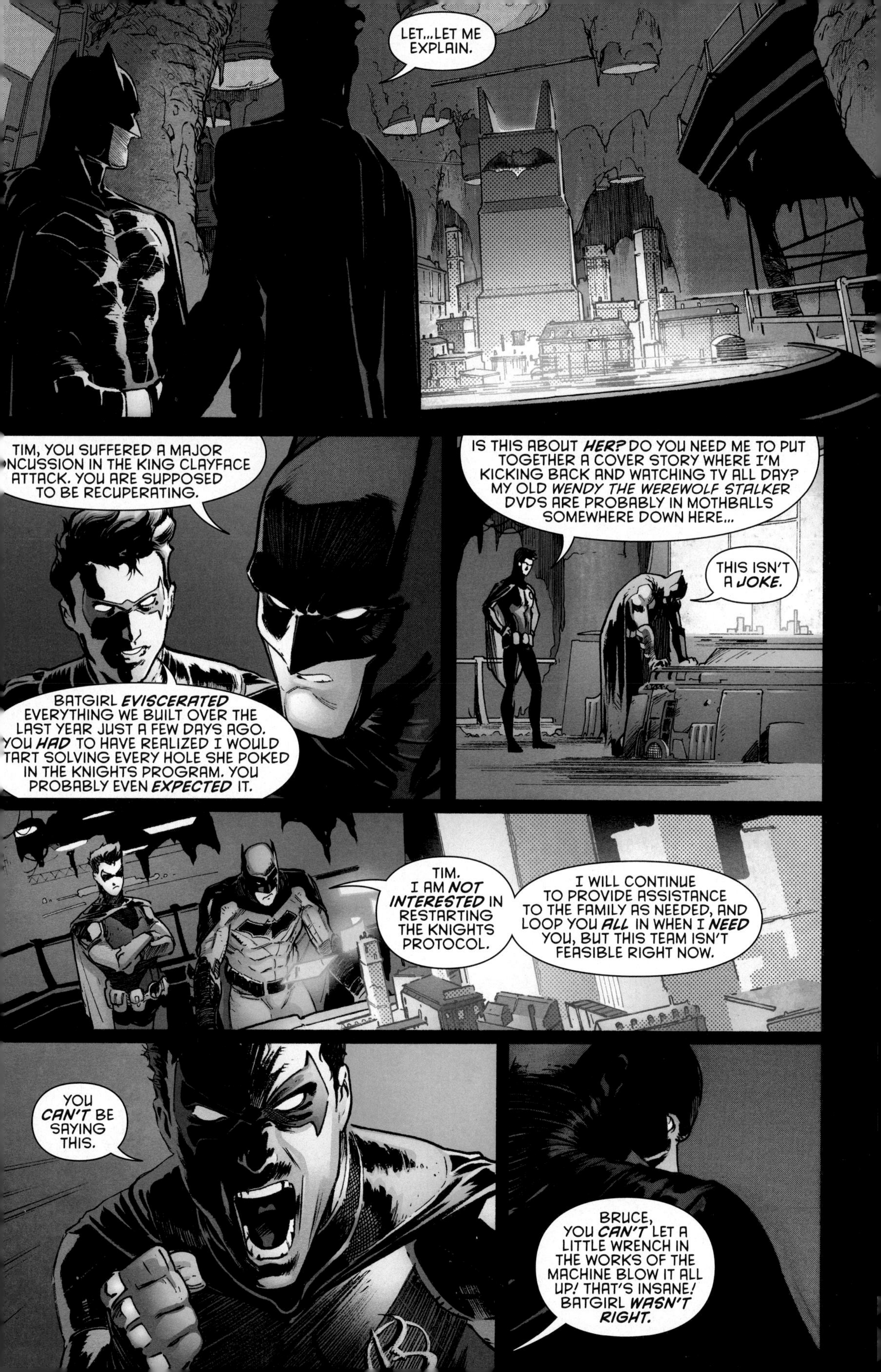
LET...LET ME EXPLAIN.
TIM, YOU SUFFERED A MAJOR NCUSSION IN THE KING CLAYFACE ATTACK. YOU ARE SUPPOSED TO BE RECUPERATING.
BATGIRL *EVISCERATED* EVERYTHING WE BUILT OVER THE LAST YEAR JUST A FEW DAYS AGO. YOU *HAD* TO HAVE REALIZED I WOULD TART SOLVING EVERY HOLE SHE POKED IN THE KNIGHTS PROGRAM. YOU PROBABLY EVEN *EXPECTED* IT.
IS THIS ABOUT *HER?* DO YOU NEED ME TO PUT TOGETHER A COVER STORY WHERE I'M KICKING BACK AND WATCHING TV ALL DAY? MY OLD *WENDY THE WEREWOLF STALKER* DVDS ARE PROBABLY IN MOTHBALLS SOMEWHERE DOWN HERE...
THIS ISN'T A *JOKE.*
TIM. I AM *NOT INTERESTED* IN RESTARTING THE KNIGHTS PROTOCOL.
I WILL CONTINUE TO PROVIDE ASSISTANCE TO THE FAMILY AS NEEDED, AND LOOP YOU *ALL* IN WHEN I *NEED* YOU, BUT THIS TEAM ISN'T FEASIBLE RIGHT NOW.
YOU *CAN'T* BE SAYING THIS.
BRUCE, YOU *CAN'T* LET A LITTLE WRENCH IN THE WORKS OF THE MACHINE BLOW IT ALL UP! THAT'S INSANE! BATGIRL *WASN'T RIGHT.*

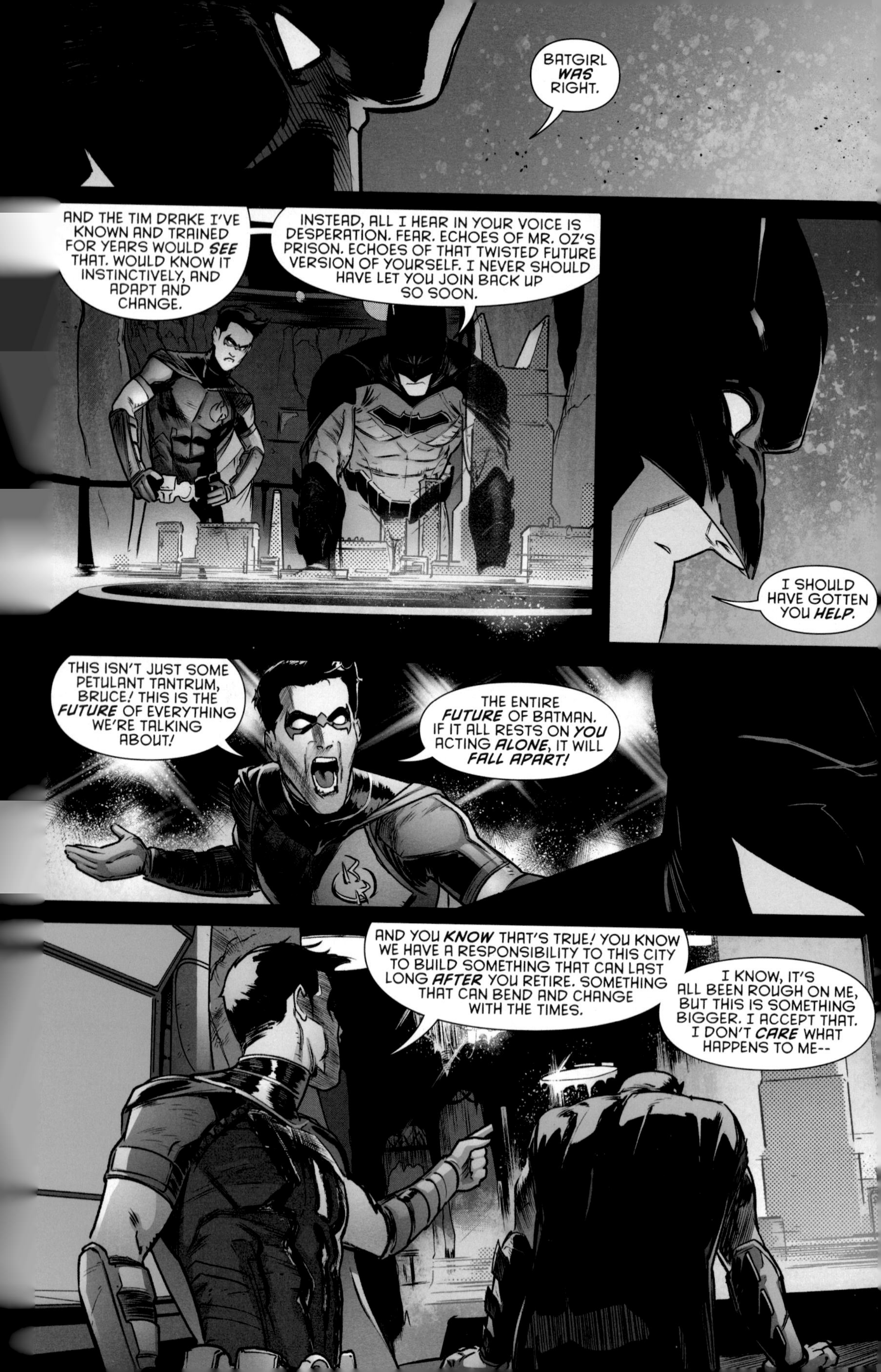
BATGIRL *WAS* RIGHT.
AND THE TIM DRAKE I'VE KNOWN AND TRAINED FOR YEARS WOULD *SEE* THAT. WOULD KNOW IT INSTINCTIVELY, AND ADAPT AND CHANGE.
INSTEAD, ALL I HEAR IN YOUR VOICE IS DESPERATION. FEAR. ECHOES OF MR. OZ'S PRISON. ECHOES OF THAT TWISTED FUTURE VERSION OF YOURSELF. I NEVER SHOULD HAVE LET YOU JOIN BACK UP SO SOON.
I SHOULD HAVE GOTTEN YOU *HELP.*
THIS ISN'T JUST SOME PETULANT TANTRUM, BRUCE! THIS IS THE *FUTURE* OF EVERYTHING WE'RE TALKING ABOUT!
THE ENTIRE *FUTURE* OF BATMAN. IF IT ALL RESTS ON *YOU* ACTING *ALONE*, IT WILL *FALL APART!*
AND YOU *KNOW* THAT'S TRUE! YOU KNOW WE HAVE A RESPONSIBILITY TO THIS CITY TO BUILD SOMETHING THAT CAN LAST LONG *AFTER* YOU RETIRE. SOMETHING THAT CAN BEND AND CHANGE WITH THE TIMES.
I KNOW, IT'S ALL BEEN ROUGH ON ME, BUT THIS IS SOMETHING BIGGER. I ACCEPT THAT. I DON'T *CARE* WHAT HAPPENS TO ME--

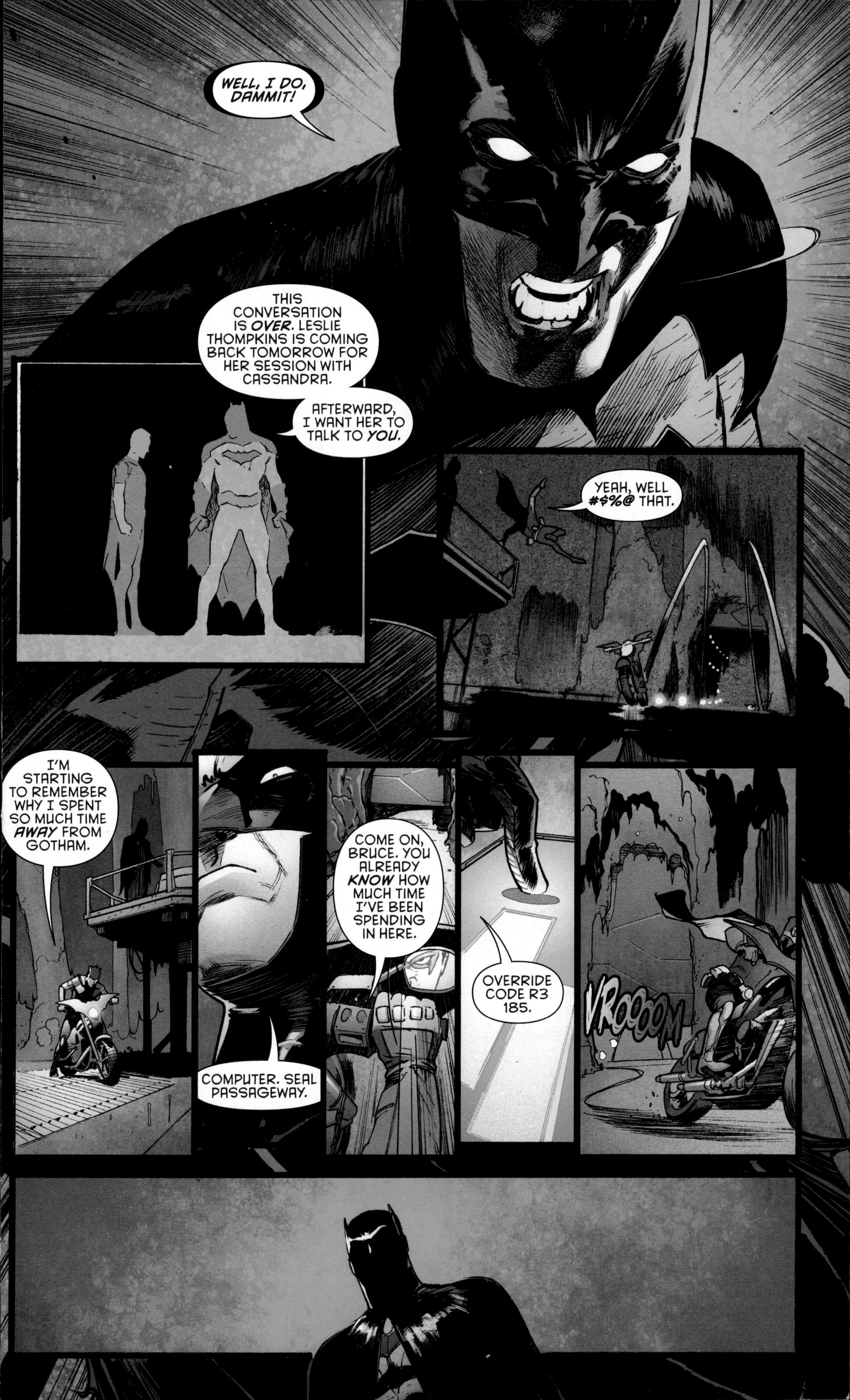
WELL, I DO, DAMMIT!
THIS CONVERSATION IS OVER. LESLIE THOMPKINS IS COMING BACK TOMORROW FOR HER SESSION WITH CASSANDRA.
AFTERWARD, I WANT HER TO TALK TO YOU.
YEAH, WELL #$%@ THAT.
I'M STARTING TO REMEMBER WHY I SPENT SO MUCH TIME AWAY FROM GOTHAM.
COMPUTER. SEAL PASSAGEWAY.
COME ON, BRUCE. YOU ALREADY KNOW HOW MUCH TIME I'VE BEEN SPENDING IN HERE.
OVERRIDE CODE R3 185.
VROOOOM

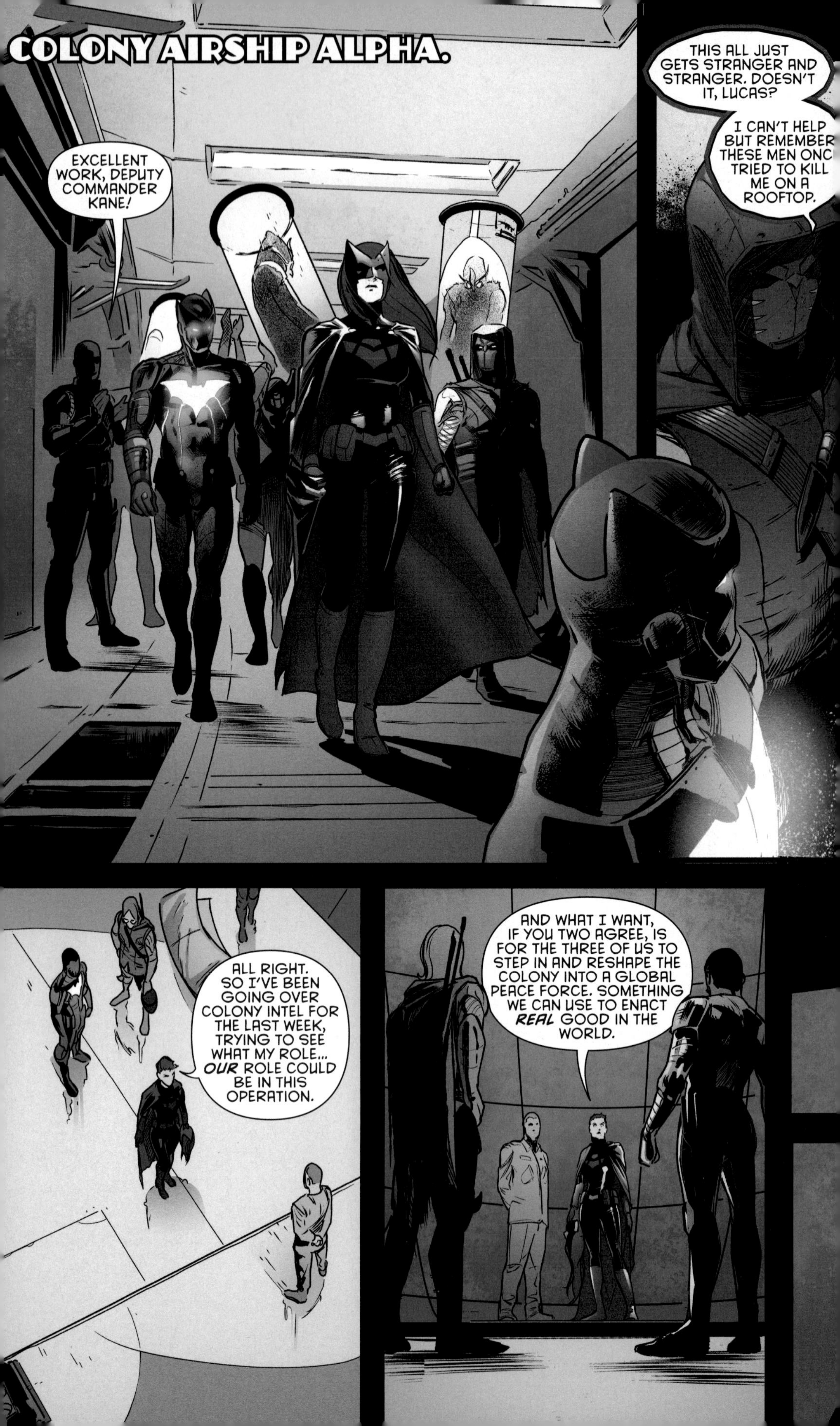
COLONY AIRSHIP ALPHA.
EXCELLENT WORK, DEPUTY COMMANDER KANE!
THIS ALL JUST GETS STRANGER AND STRANGER. DOESN'T IT, LUCAS?
I CAN'T HELP BUT REMEMBER THESE MEN ONC TRIED TO KILL ME ON A ROOFTOP.
ALL RIGHT. SO I'VE BEEN GOING OVER COLONY INTEL FOR THE LAST WEEK, TRYING TO SEE WHAT MY ROLE... *OUR* ROLE COULD BE IN THIS OPERATION.
AND WHAT I WANT, IF YOU TWO AGREE, IS FOR THE THREE OF US TO STEP IN AND RESHAPE THE COLONY INTO A GLOBAL PEACE FORCE. SOMETHING WE CAN USE TO ENACT *REAL* GOOD IN THE WORLD.

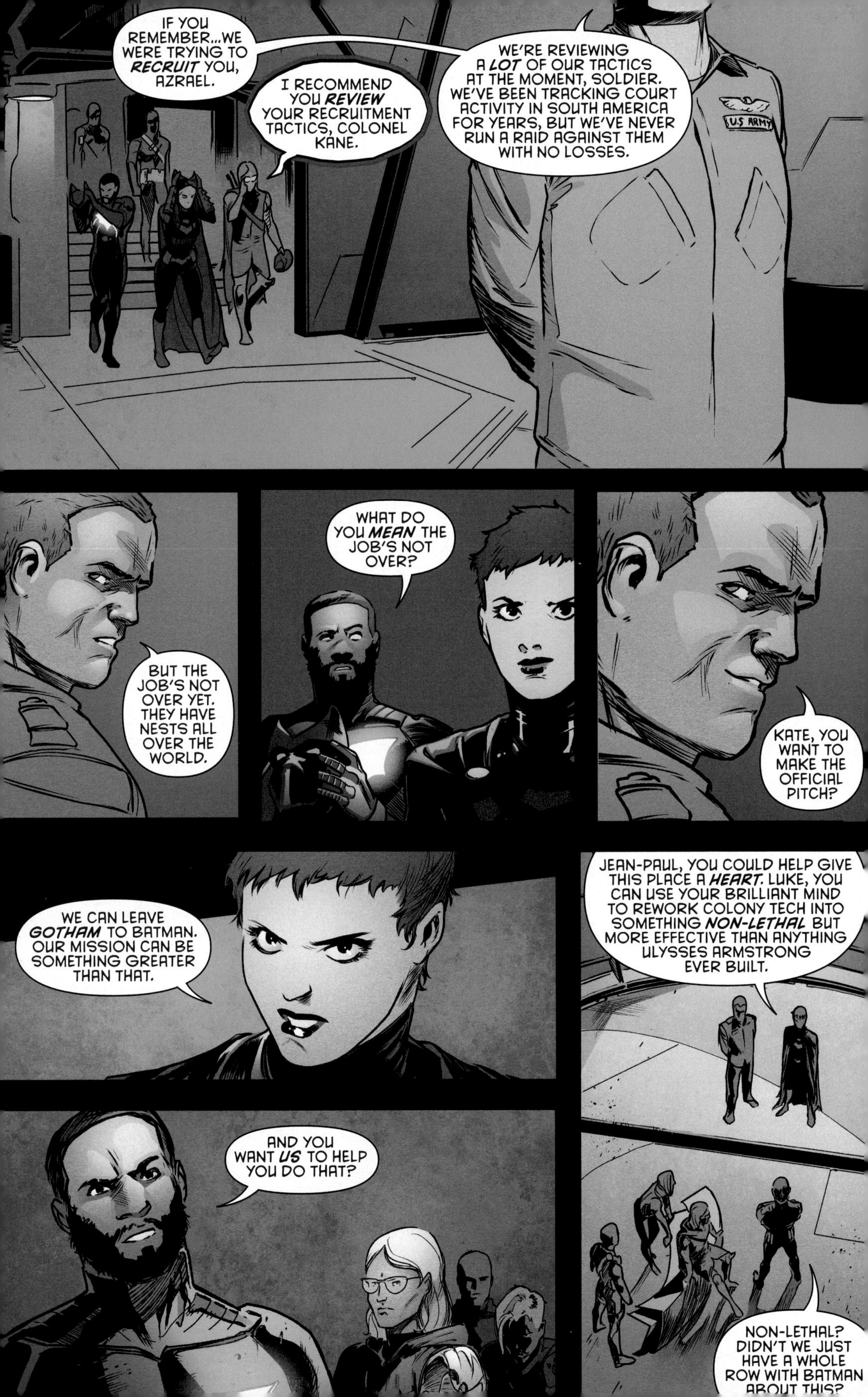
IF YOU REMEMBER...WE WERE TRYING TO RECRUIT YOU, AZRAEL.
I RECOMMEND YOU REVIEW YOUR RECRUITMENT TACTICS, COLONEL KANE.
WE'RE REVIEWING A LOT OF OUR TACTICS AT THE MOMENT, SOLDIER. WE'VE BEEN TRACKING COURT ACTIVITY IN SOUTH AMERICA FOR YEARS, BUT WE'VE NEVER RUN A RAID AGAINST THEM WITH NO LOSSES.
U.S ARMY
BUT THE JOB'S NOT OVER YET. THEY HAVE NESTS ALL OVER THE WORLD.
WHAT DO YOU MEAN THE JOB'S NOT OVER?
KATE, YOU WANT TO MAKE THE OFFICIAL PITCH?
WE CAN LEAVE GOTHAM TO BATMAN. OUR MISSION CAN BE SOMETHING GREATER THAN THAT.
AND YOU WANT US TO HELP YOU DO THAT?
JEAN-PAUL, YOU COULD HELP GIVE THIS PLACE A HEART. LUKE, YOU CAN USE YOUR BRILLIANT MIND TO REWORK COLONY TECH INTO SOMETHING NON-LETHAL BUT MORE EFFECTIVE THAN ANYTHING ULYSSES ARMSTRONG EVER BUILT.
NON-LETHAL? DIDN'T WE JUST HAVE A WHOLE ROW WITH BATMAN ABOUT THIS?

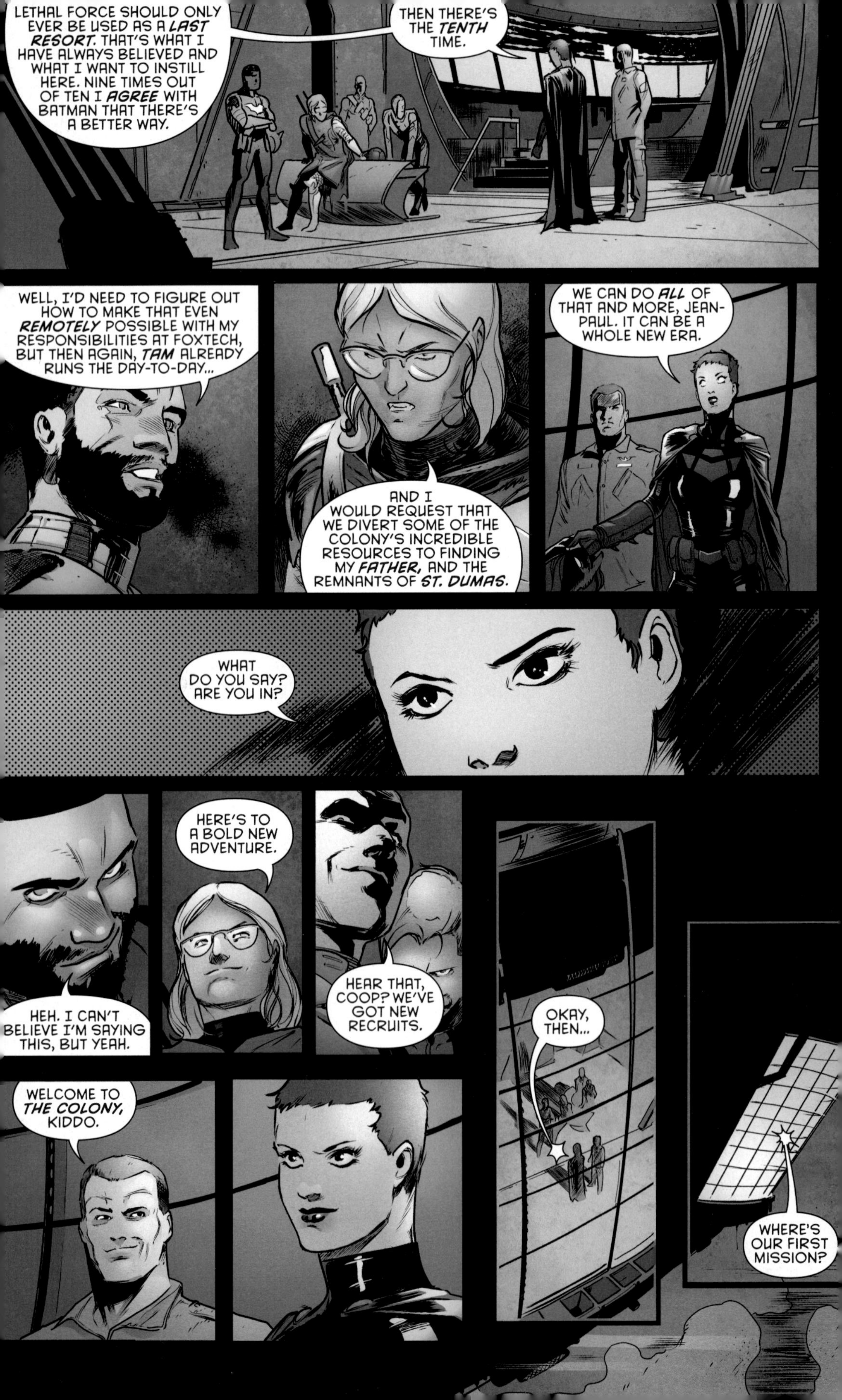
LETHAL FORCE SHOULD ONLY EVER BE USED AS A LAST RESORT. THAT'S WHAT I HAVE ALWAYS BELIEVED AND WHAT I WANT TO INSTILL HERE. NINE TIMES OUT OF TEN I AGREE WITH BATMAN THAT THERE'S A BETTER WAY.
THEN THERE'S THE TENTH TIME.
WELL, I'D NEED TO FIGURE OUT HOW TO MAKE THAT EVEN REMOTELY POSSIBLE WITH MY RESPONSIBILITIES AT FOXTECH, BUT THEN AGAIN, TAM ALREADY RUNS THE DAY-TO-DAY...
AND I WOULD REQUEST THAT WE DIVERT SOME OF THE COLONY'S INCREDIBLE RESOURCES TO FINDING MY FATHER, AND THE REMNANTS OF ST. DUMAS.
WE CAN DO ALL OF THAT AND MORE, JEAN-PAUL. IT CAN BE A WHOLE NEW ERA.
WHAT DO YOU SAY? ARE YOU IN?
HEH. I CAN'T BELIEVE I'M SAYING THIS, BUT YEAH.
HERE'S TO A BOLD NEW ADVENTURE.
HEAR THAT, COOP? WE'VE GOT NEW RECRUITS.
WELCOME TO THE COLONY, KIDDO.
OKAY, THEN...
WHERE'S OUR FIRST MISSION?

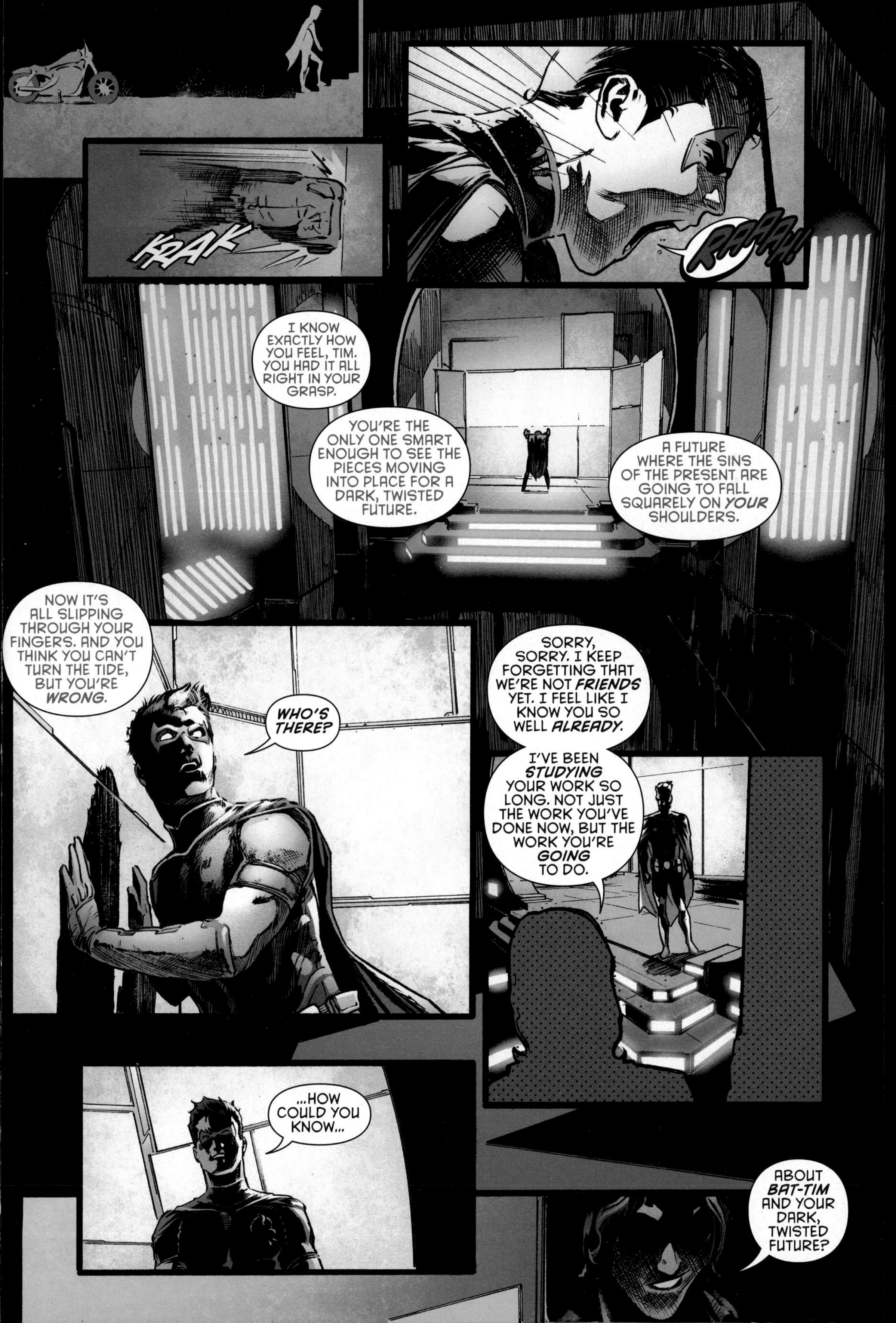
KRAK
RAAAH!
I KNOW EXACTLY HOW YOU FEEL, TIM. YOU HAD IT ALL RIGHT IN YOUR GRASP.
YOU'RE THE ONLY ONE SMART ENOUGH TO SEE THE PIECES MOVING INTO PLACE FOR A DARK, TWISTED FUTURE.
A FUTURE WHERE THE SINS OF THE PRESENT ARE GOING TO FALL SQUARELY ON *YOUR* SHOULDERS.
NOW IT'S ALL SLIPPING THROUGH YOUR FINGERS. AND YOU THINK YOU CAN'T TURN THE TIDE, BUT YOU'RE *WRONG*.
WHO'S THERE?
SORRY, SORRY. I KEEP FORGETTING THAT WE'RE NOT *FRIENDS* YET. I FEEL LIKE I KNOW YOU SO WELL *ALREADY*.
I'VE BEEN *STUDYING* YOUR WORK SO LONG. NOT JUST THE WORK YOU'VE DONE NOW, BUT THE WORK YOU'RE *GOING* TO DO.
...HOW COULD YOU KNOW...
ABOUT *BAT-TIM* AND YOUR DARK, TWISTED FUTURE?

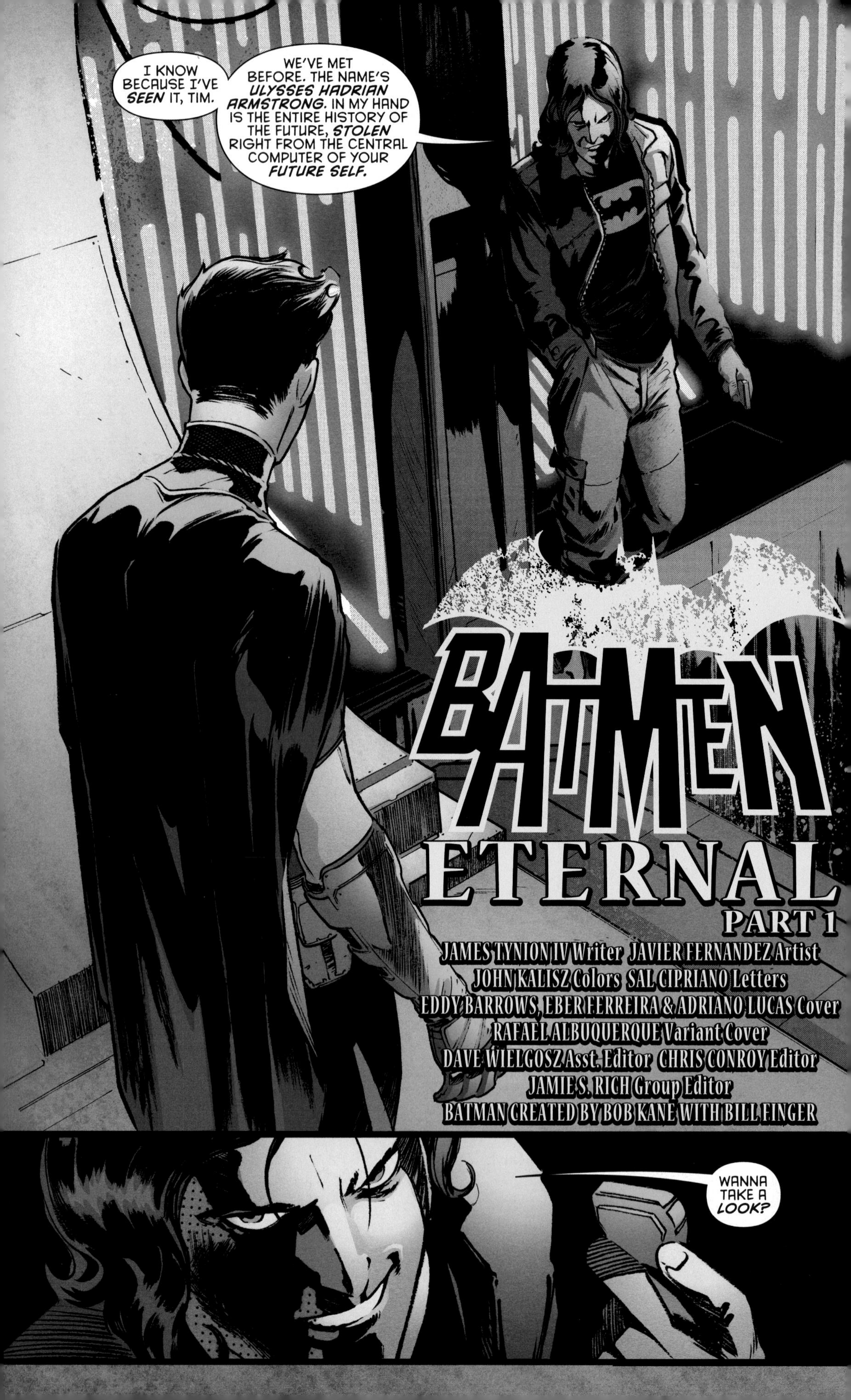
I KNOW BECAUSE I'VE *SEEN* IT, TIM.
WE'VE MET BEFORE. THE NAME'S *ULYSSES HADRIAN ARMSTRONG*. IN MY HAND IS THE ENTIRE HISTORY OF THE FUTURE, *STOLEN* RIGHT FROM THE CENTRAL COMPUTER OF YOUR *FUTURE SELF*.
BATMEN ETERNAL
PART 1
JAMES TYNION IV Writer JAVIER FERNANDEZ Artist
JOHN KALISZ Colors SAL CIPRIANO Letters
EDDY BARROWS, EBER FERREIRA & ADRIANO LUCAS Cover
RAFAEL ALBUQUERQUE Variant Cover
DAVE WIELGOSZ Asst. Editor CHRIS CONROY Editor
JAMIE S. RICH Group Editor
BATMAN CREATED BY BOB KANE WITH BILL FINGER
WANNA TAKE A *LOOK?*

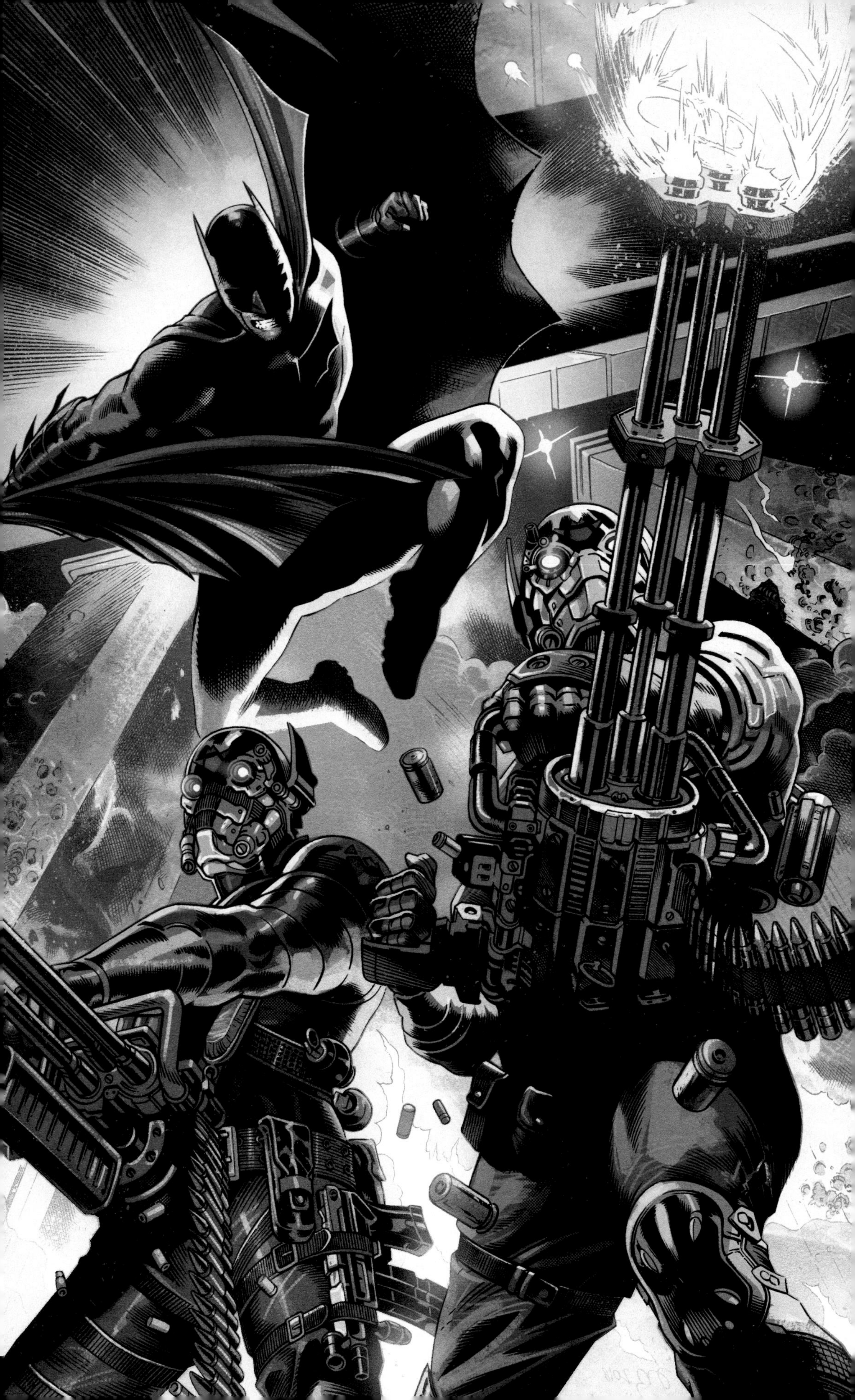

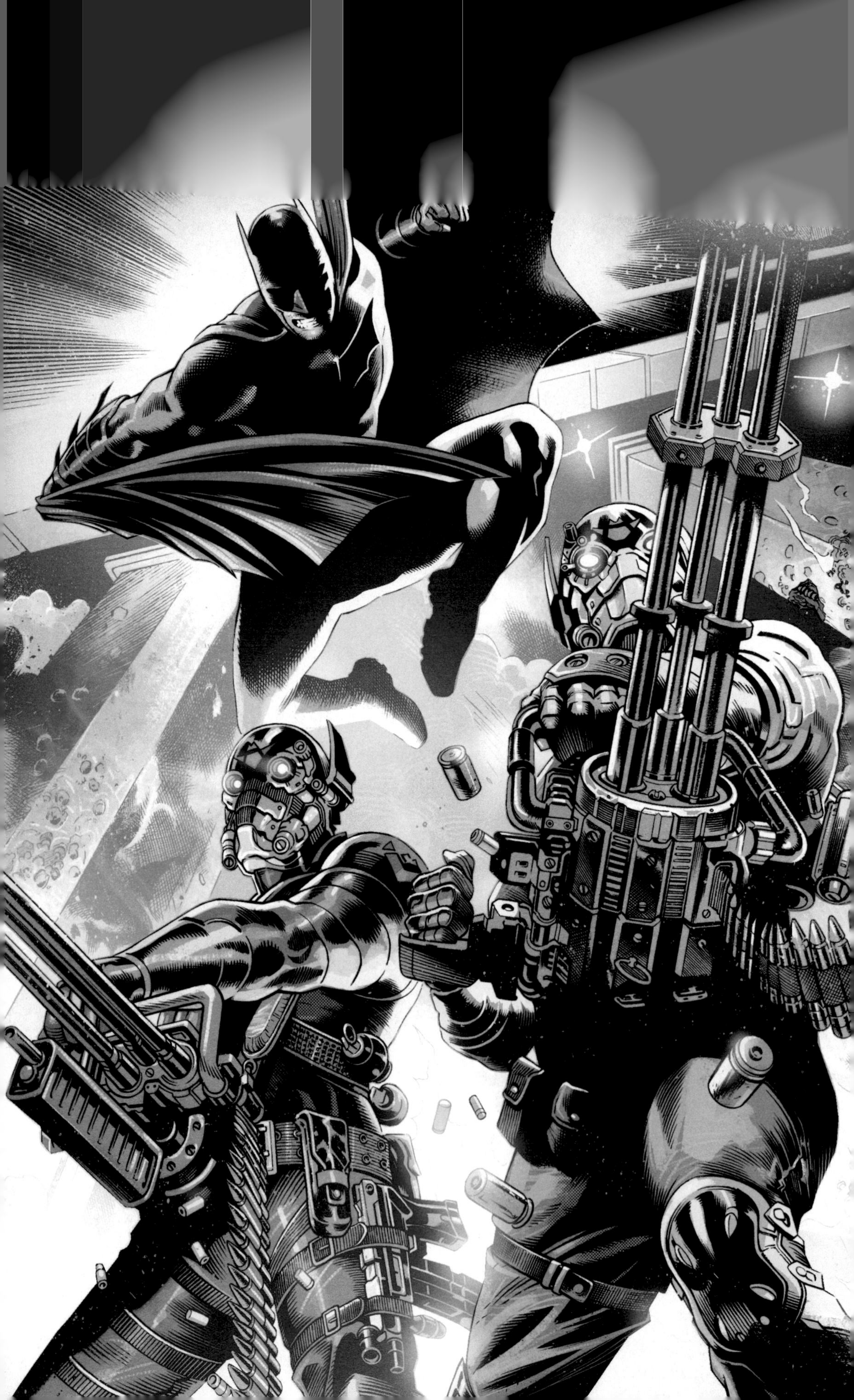

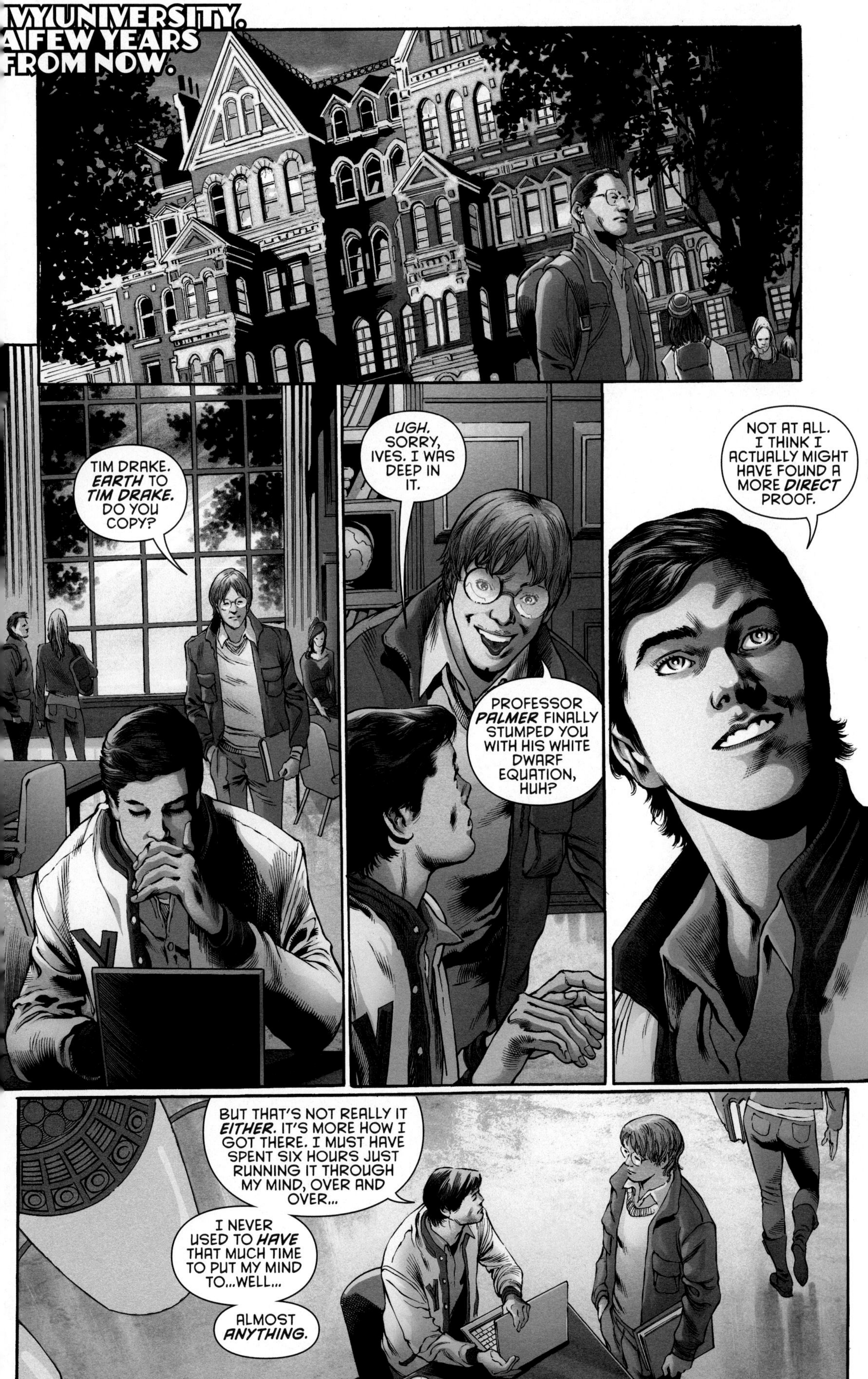
IVY UNIVERSITY. A FEW YEARS FROM NOW.
TIM DRAKE. EARTH TO TIM DRAKE. DO YOU COPY?
UGH. SORRY, IVES. I WAS DEEP IN IT.
PROFESSOR PALMER FINALLY STUMPED YOU WITH HIS WHITE DWARF EQUATION, HUH?
NOT AT ALL. I THINK I ACTUALLY MIGHT HAVE FOUND A MORE DIRECT PROOF.
BUT THAT'S NOT REALLY IT EITHER. IT'S MORE HOW I GOT THERE. I MUST HAVE SPENT SIX HOURS JUST RUNNING IT THROUGH MY MIND, OVER AND OVER...
I NEVER USED TO HAVE THAT MUCH TIME TO PUT MY MIND TO...WELL...
ALMOST ANYTHING.

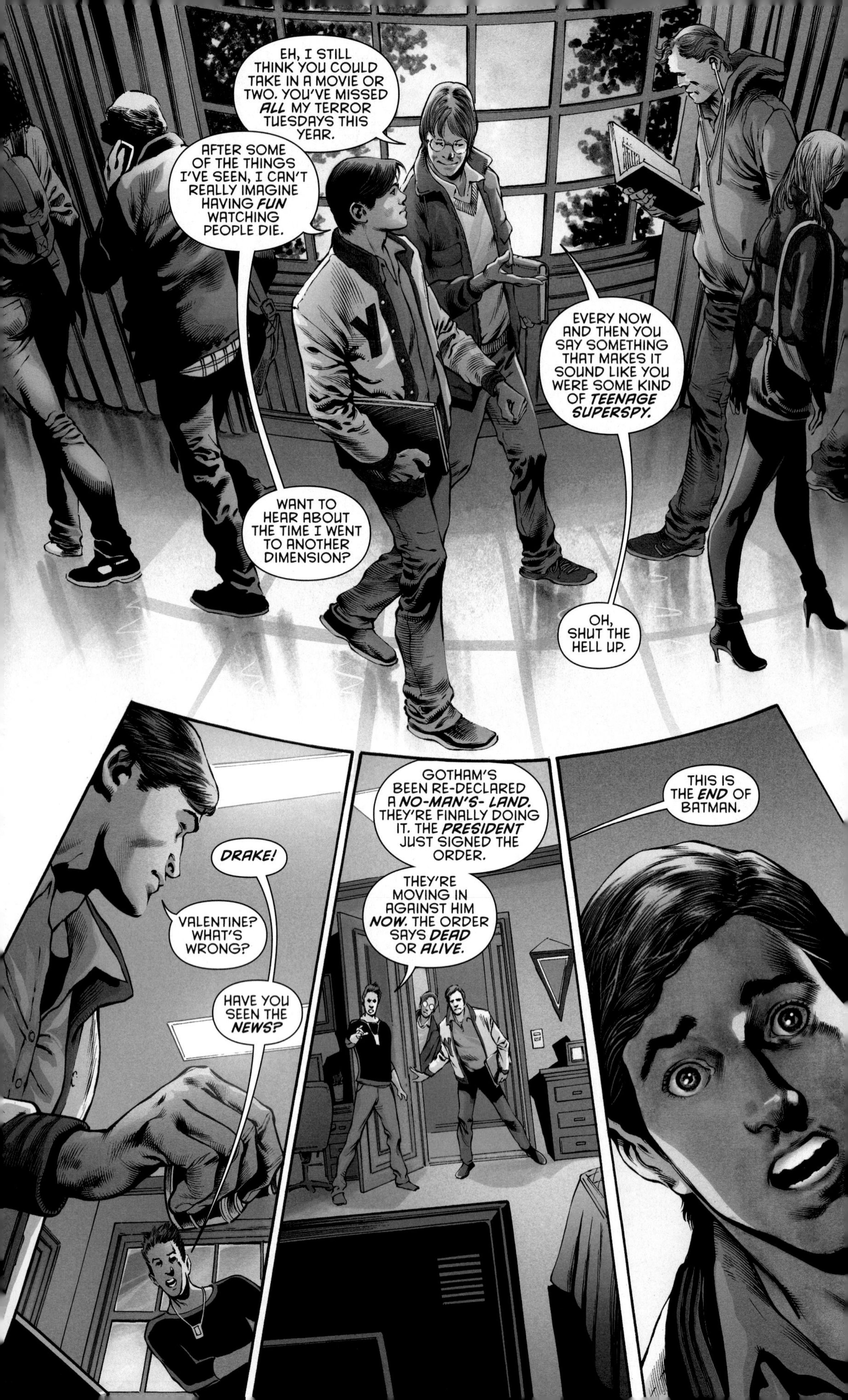
EH, I STILL THINK YOU COULD TAKE IN A MOVIE OR TWO. YOU'VE MISSED *ALL* MY TERROR TUESDAYS THIS YEAR.
AFTER SOME OF THE THINGS I'VE SEEN, I CAN'T REALLY IMAGINE HAVING *FUN* WATCHING PEOPLE DIE.
EVERY NOW AND THEN YOU SAY SOMETHING THAT MAKES IT SOUND LIKE YOU WERE SOME KIND OF *TEENAGE SUPERSPY.*
WANT TO HEAR ABOUT THE TIME I WENT TO ANOTHER DIMENSION?
OH, SHUT THE HELL UP.
DRAKE!
VALENTINE? WHAT'S WRONG?
HAVE YOU SEEN THE *NEWS?*
GOTHAM'S BEEN RE-DECLARED A *NO-MAN'S- LAND.* THEY'RE FINALLY DOING IT. THE *PRESIDENT* JUST SIGNED THE ORDER.
THEY'RE MOVING IN AGAINST HIM *NOW.* THE ORDER SAYS *DEAD* OR *ALIVE.*
THIS IS THE *END* OF BATMAN.

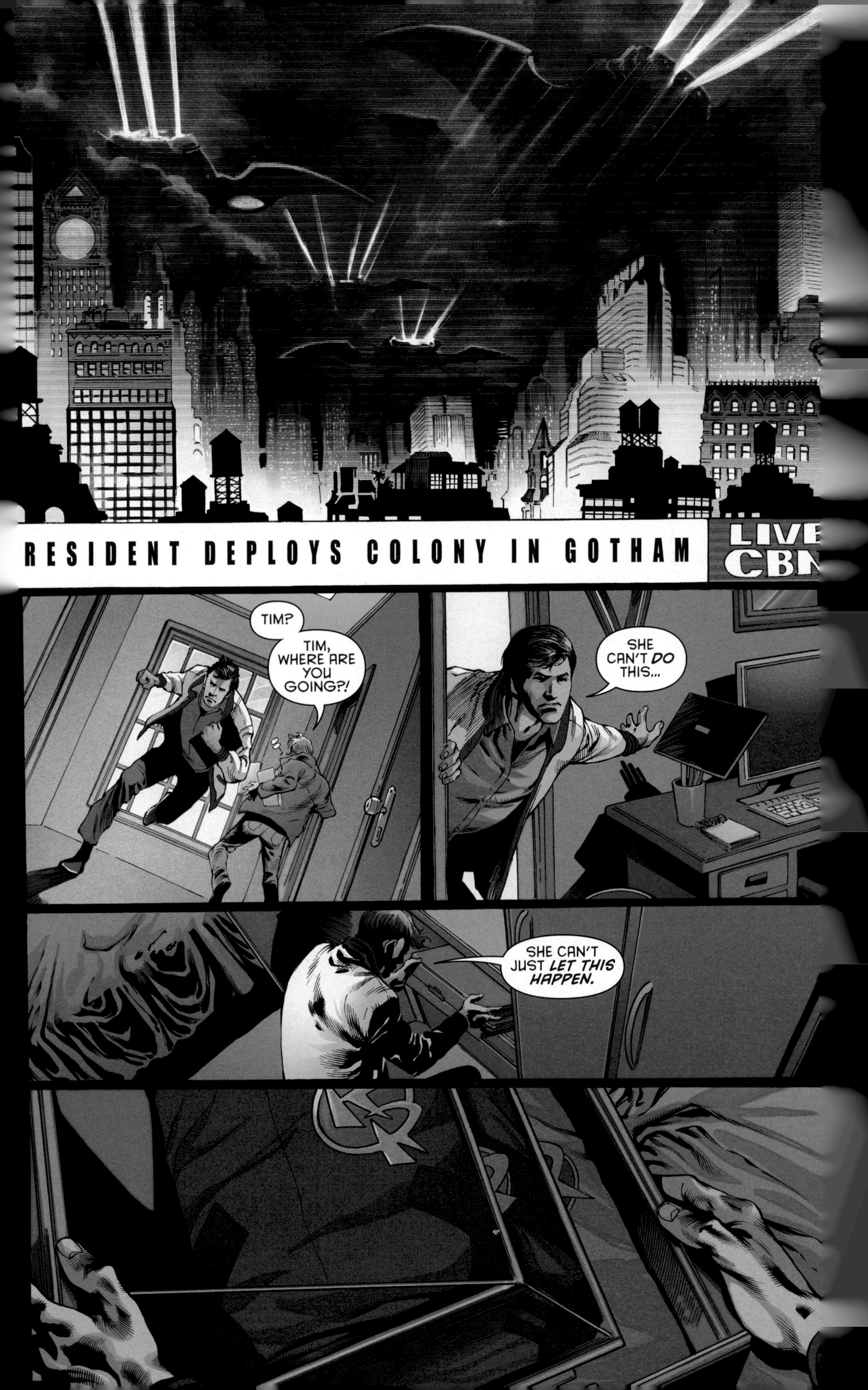
RESIDENT DEPLOYS COLONY IN GOTHAM
LIVE CBN
TIM?
TIM, WHERE ARE YOU GOING?!
SHE CAN'T *DO* THIS...
SHE CAN'T JUST *LET THIS HAPPEN.*

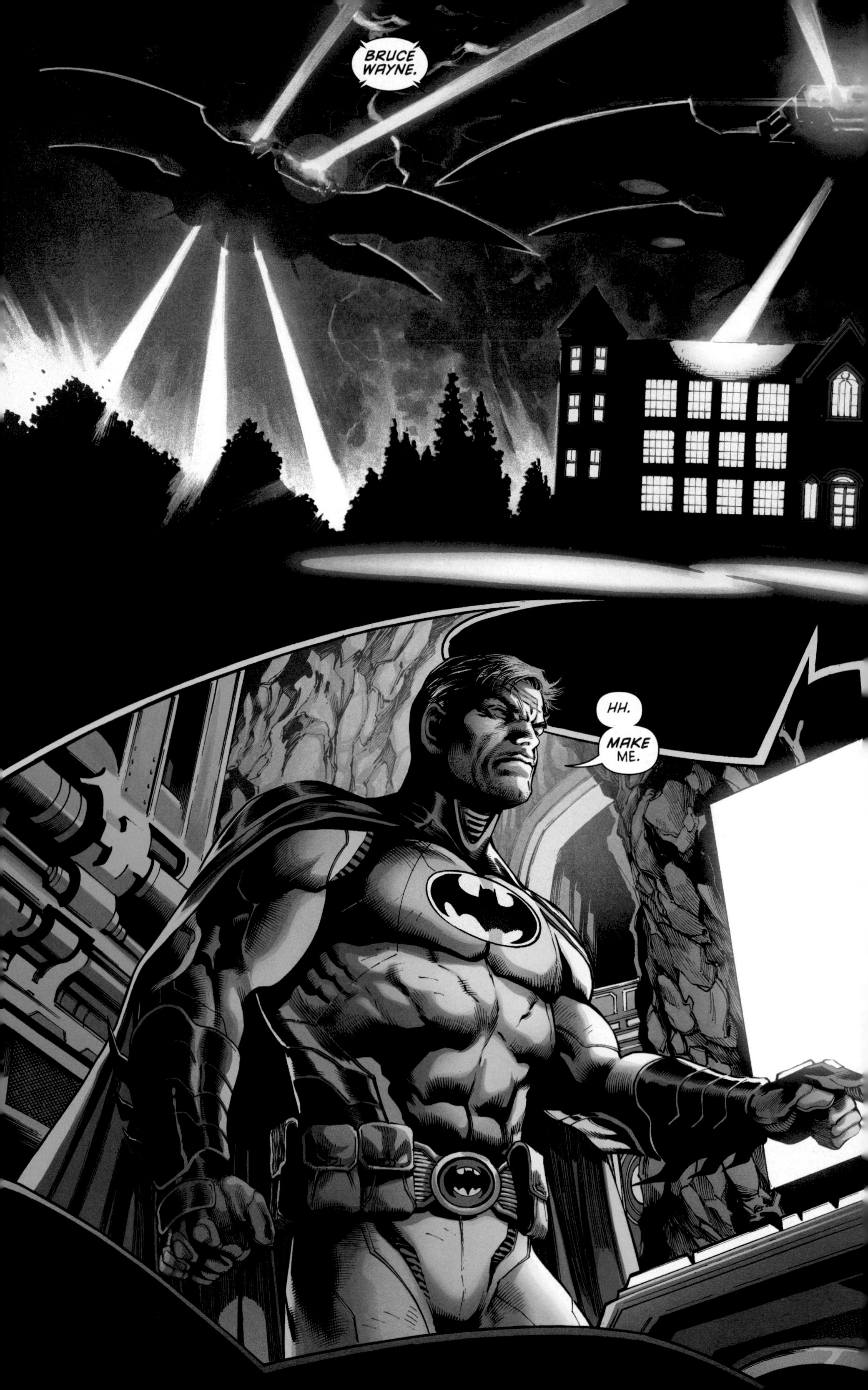
BRUCE WAYNE.
HH.
MAKE ME.

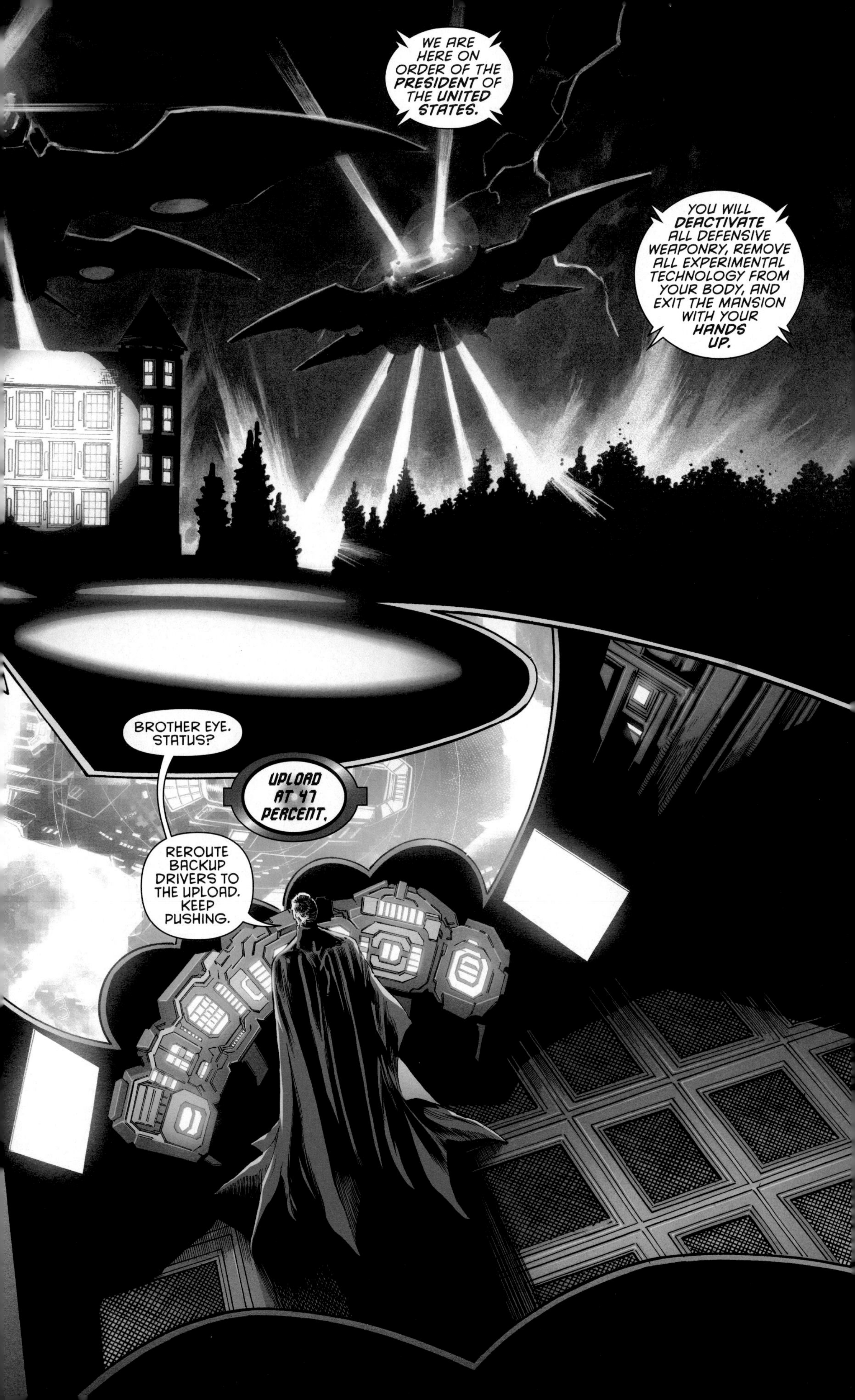
WE ARE HERE ON ORDER OF THE PRESIDENT OF THE UNITED STATES.
YOU WILL DEACTIVATE ALL DEFENSIVE WEAPONRY, REMOVE ALL EXPERIMENTAL TECHNOLOGY FROM YOUR BODY, AND EXIT THE MANSION WITH YOUR HANDS UP.
BROTHER EYE. STATUS?
UPLOAD AT 47 PERCENT.
REROUTE BACKUP DRIVERS TO THE UPLOAD. KEEP PUSHING.

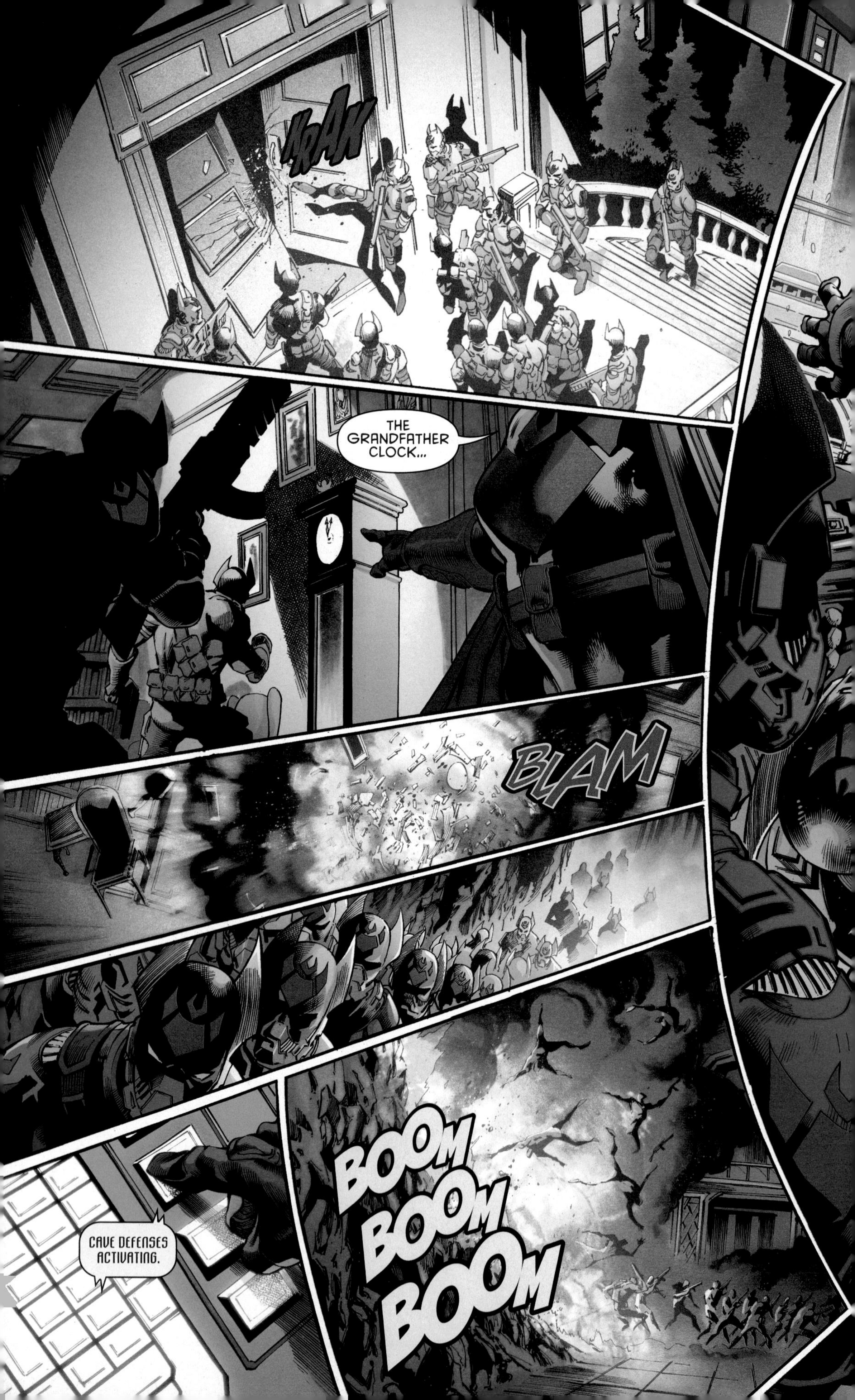
KRAK
THE GRANDFATHER CLOCK...
BLAM
CAVE DEFENSES ACTIVATING.
BOOM
BOOM
BOOM

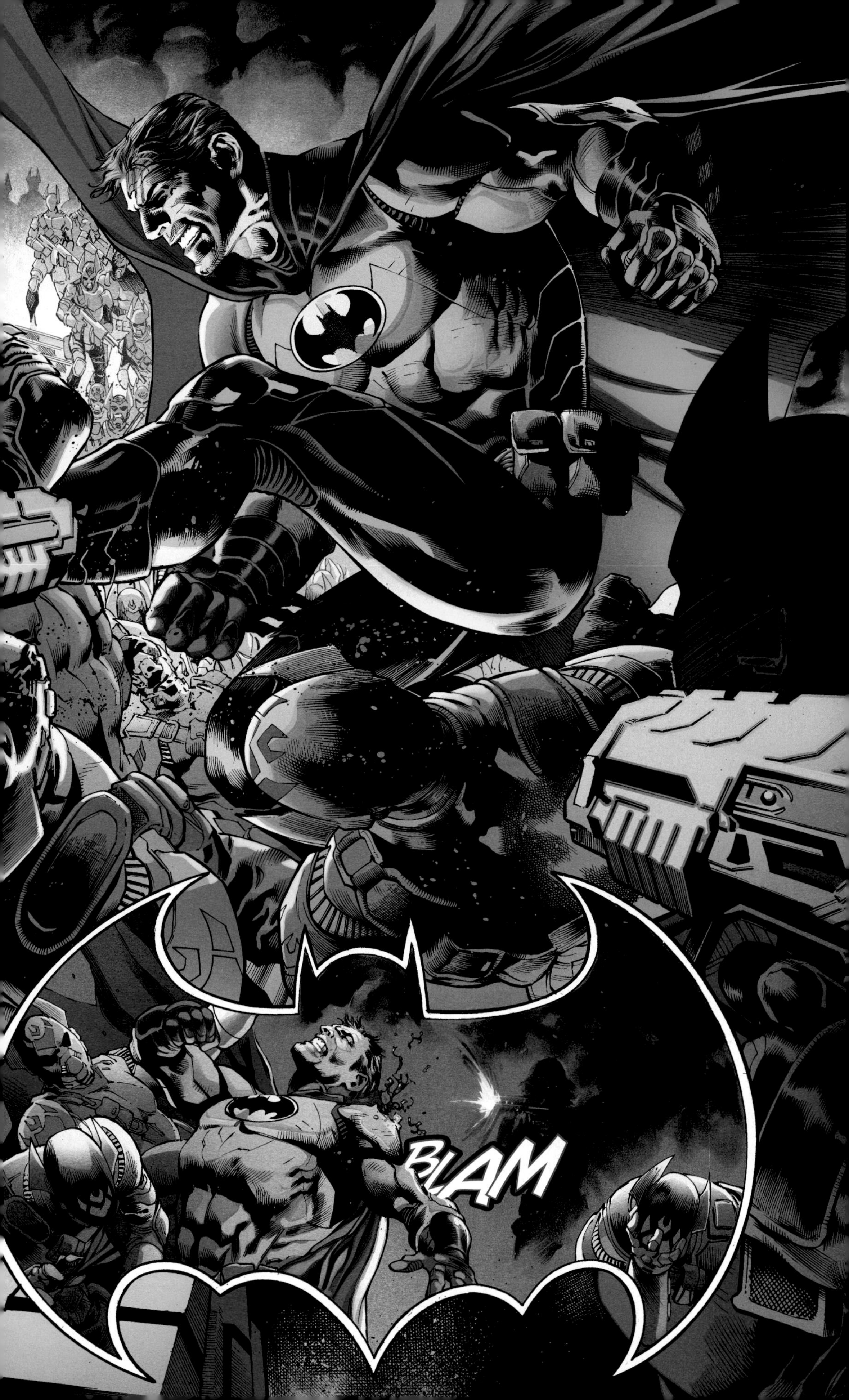
BLAM

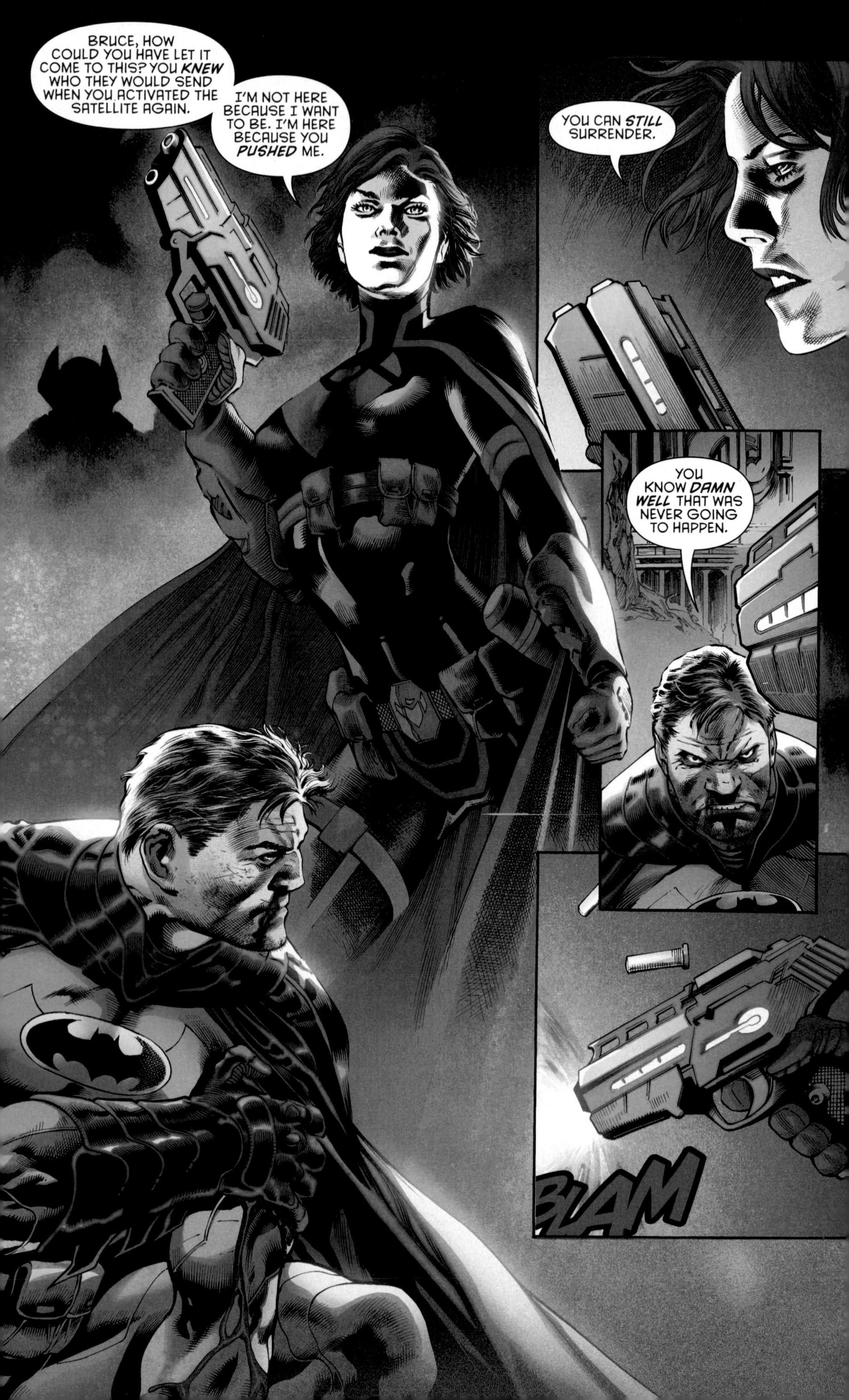

BRUCE, HOW COULD YOU HAVE LET IT COME TO THIS? YOU *KNEW* WHO THEY WOULD SEND WHEN YOU ACTIVATED THE SATELLITE AGAIN.
I'M NOT HERE BECAUSE I WANT TO BE. I'M HERE BECAUSE YOU *PUSHED* ME.
YOU CAN *STILL* SURRENDER.
YOU KNOW *DAMN WELL* THAT WAS NEVER GOING TO HAPPEN.
BLAM

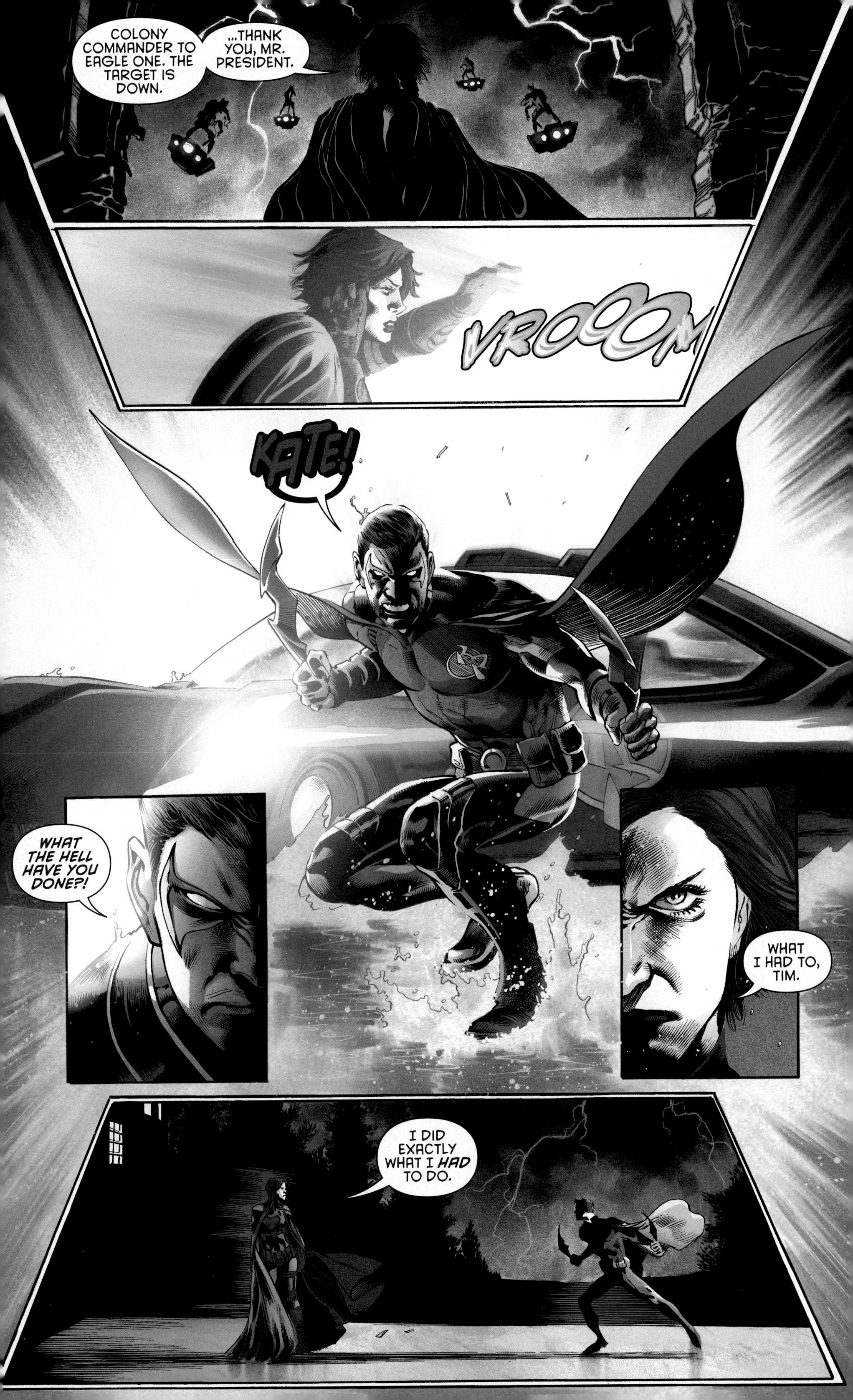
COLONY COMMANDER TO EAGLE ONE. THE TARGET IS DOWN.
...THANK YOU, MR. PRESIDENT.
VROOOOM
KATE!
WHAT THE HELL HAVE YOU DONE?!
WHAT I HAD TO, TIM.
I DID EXACTLY WHAT I HAD TO DO.

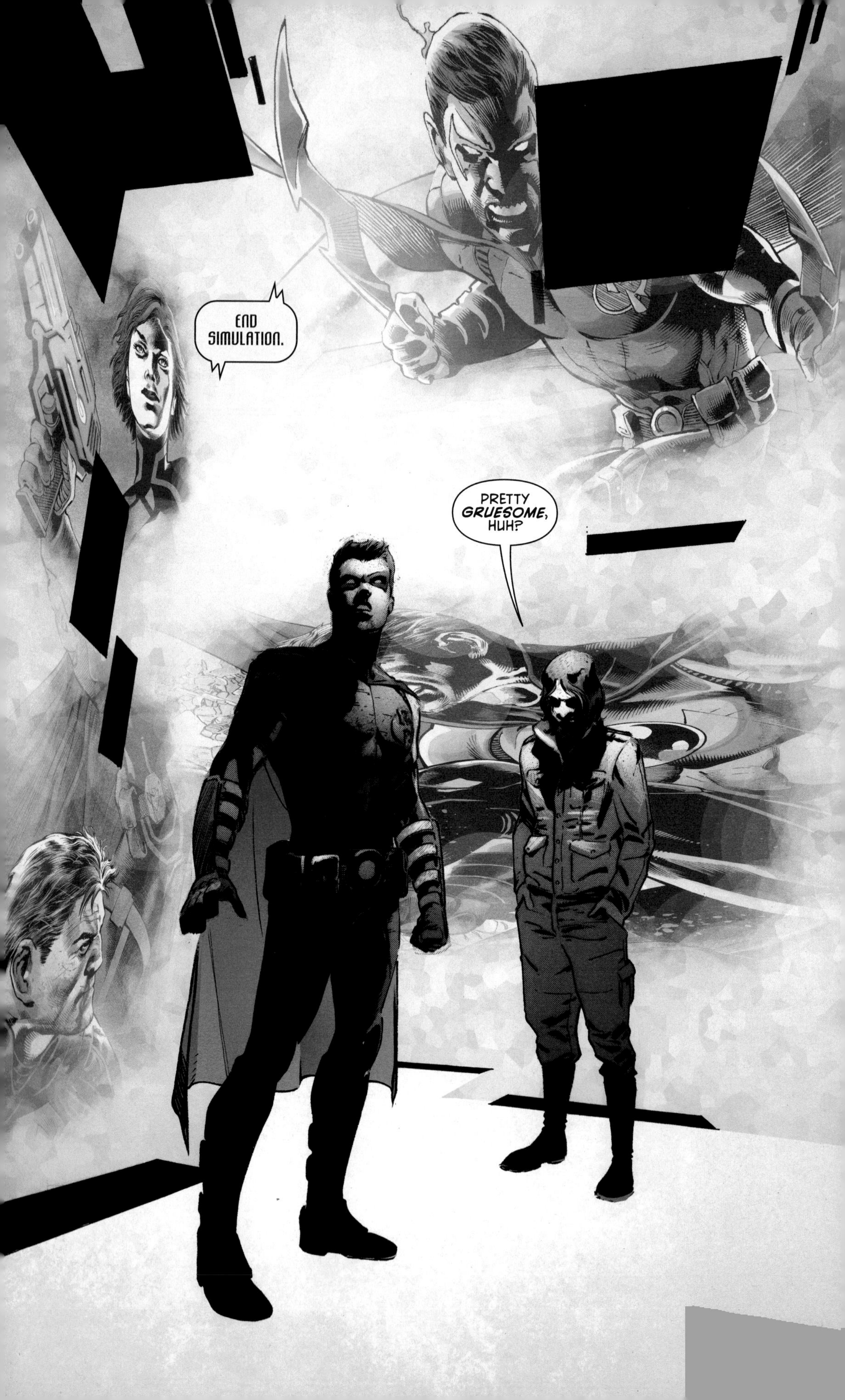
END SIMULATION.
PRETTY GRUESOME, HUH?

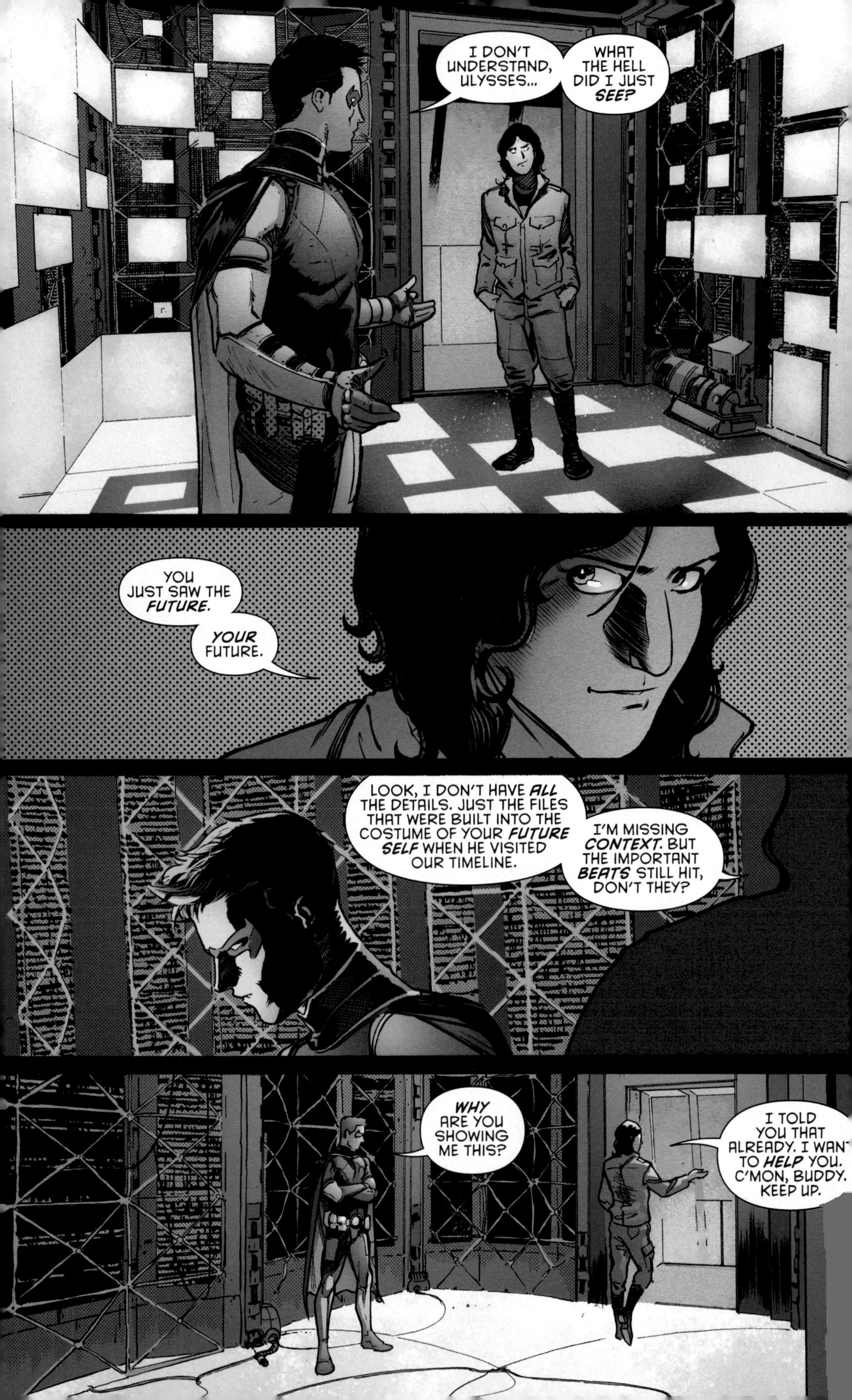

I DON'T UNDERSTAND, ULYSSES...
WHAT THE HELL DID I JUST *SEE?*
YOU JUST SAW THE *FUTURE.*
YOUR FUTURE.
LOOK, I DON'T HAVE *ALL* THE DETAILS. JUST THE FILES THAT WERE BUILT INTO THE COSTUME OF YOUR *FUTURE SELF* WHEN HE VISITED OUR TIMELINE.
I'M MISSING *CONTEXT.* BUT THE IMPORTANT *BEATS* STILL HIT, DON'T THEY?
WHY ARE YOU SHOWING ME THIS?
I TOLD YOU THAT ALREADY. I WANT TO *HELP* YOU. C'MON, BUDDY. KEEP UP.

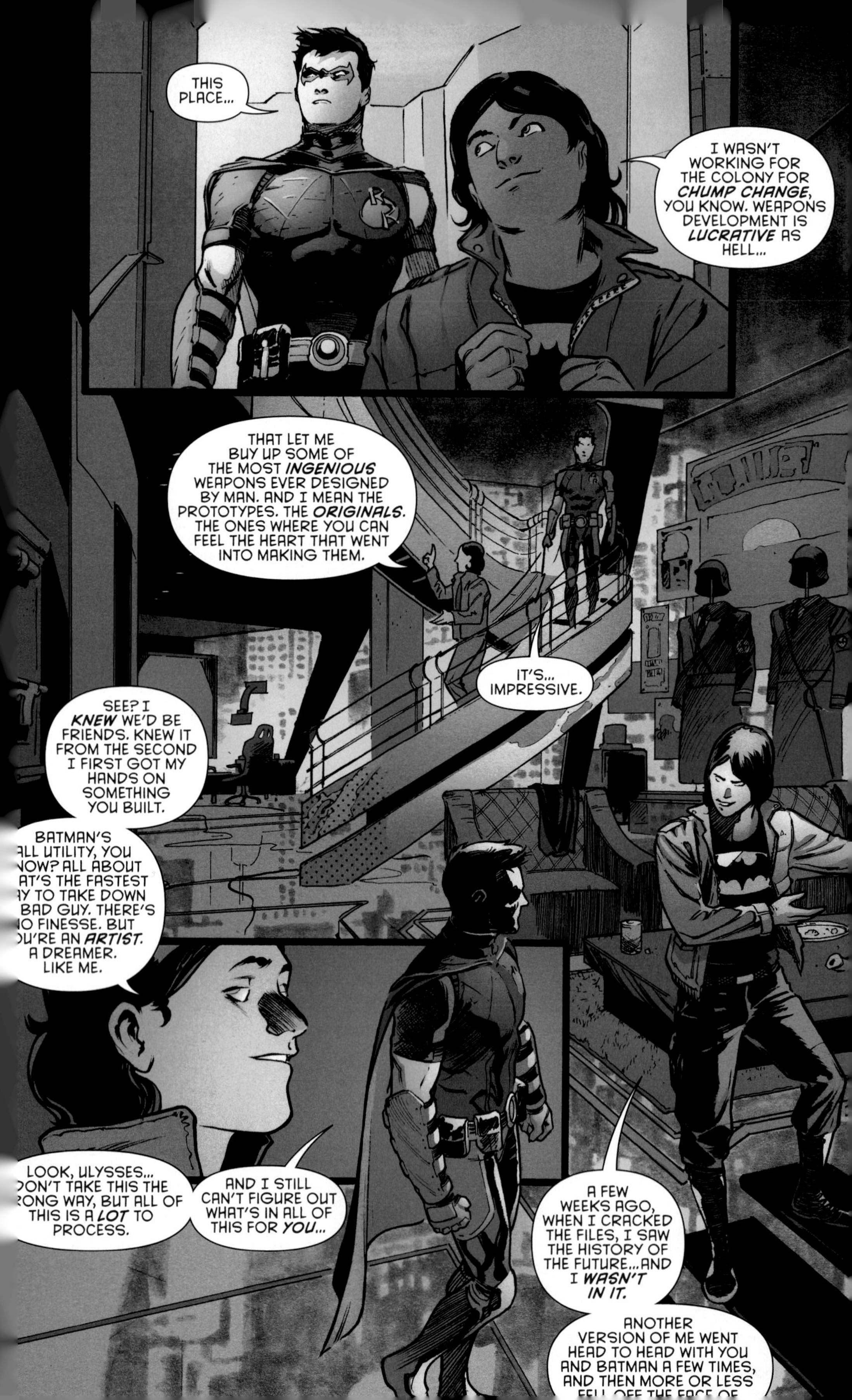

THIS PLACE...
I WASN'T WORKING FOR THE COLONY FOR *CHUMP CHANGE*, YOU KNOW. WEAPONS DEVELOPMENT IS *LUCRATIVE* AS HELL...
THAT LET ME BUY UP SOME OF THE MOST *INGENIOUS* WEAPONS EVER DESIGNED BY MAN. AND I MEAN THE PROTOTYPES. THE *ORIGINALS*. THE ONES WHERE YOU CAN FEEL THE HEART THAT WENT INTO MAKING THEM.
IT'S... IMPRESSIVE.
SEE? I *KNEW* WE'D BE FRIENDS. KNEW IT FROM THE SECOND I FIRST GOT MY HANDS ON SOMETHING YOU BUILT.
BATMAN'S LL UTILITY, YOU NOW? ALL ABOUT AT'S THE FASTEST AY TO TAKE DOWN BAD GUY. THERE'S O FINESSE. BUT OU'RE AN *ARTIST*. A DREAMER. LIKE ME.
LOOK, ULYSSES... ON'T TAKE THIS THE ONG WAY, BUT ALL OF THIS IS A *LOT* TO PROCESS.
AND I STILL CAN'T FIGURE OUT WHAT'S IN ALL OF THIS FOR *YOU*...
A FEW WEEKS AGO, WHEN I CRACKED THE FILES, I SAW THE HISTORY OF THE FUTURE...AND I *WASN'T IN IT*.
ANOTHER VERSION OF ME WENT HEAD TO HEAD WITH YOU AND BATMAN A FEW TIMES, AND THEN MORE OR LESS

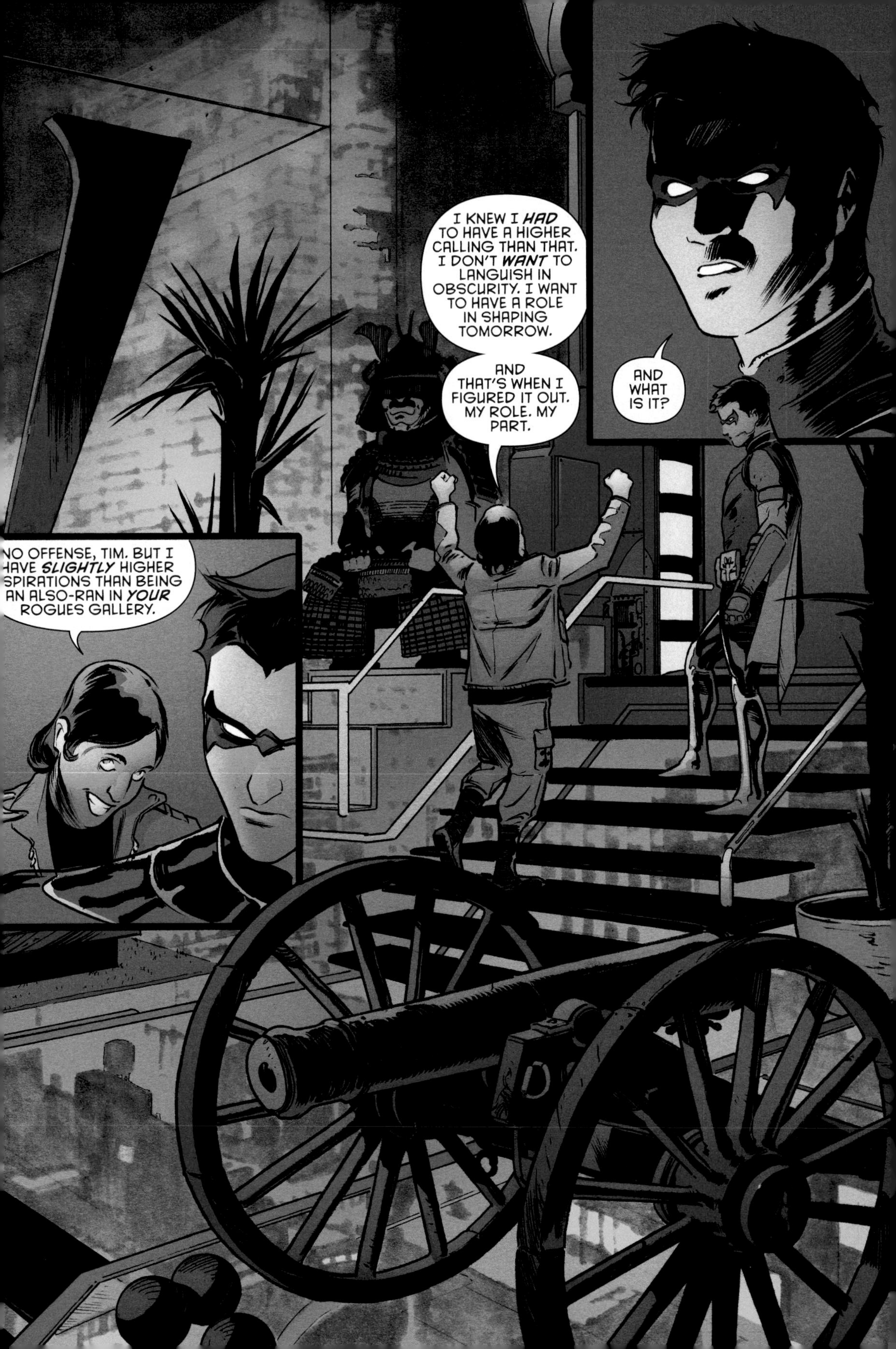
I KNEW I HAD TO HAVE A HIGHER CALLING THAN THAT. I DON'T WANT TO LANGUISH IN OBSCURITY. I WANT TO HAVE A ROLE IN SHAPING TOMORROW.
AND THAT'S WHEN I FIGURED IT OUT. MY ROLE. MY PART.
AND WHAT IS IT?
NO OFFENSE, TIM. BUT I HAVE SLIGHTLY HIGHER SPIRATIONS THAN BEING AN ALSO-RAN IN YOUR ROGUES GALLERY.

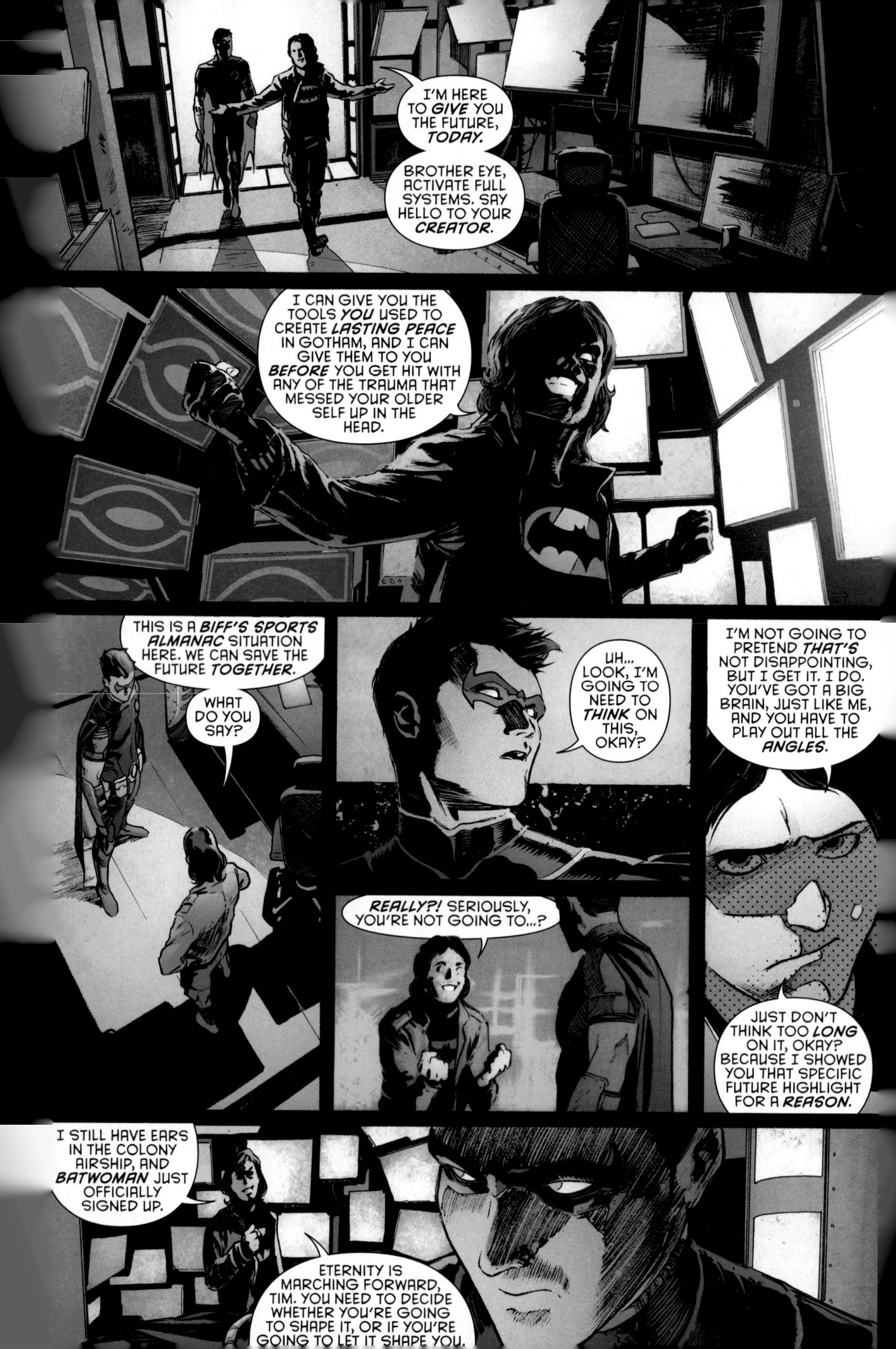
I'M HERE TO GIVE YOU THE FUTURE, TODAY.
BROTHER EYE, ACTIVATE FULL SYSTEMS. SAY HELLO TO YOUR CREATOR.
I CAN GIVE YOU THE TOOLS YOU USED TO CREATE LASTING PEACE IN GOTHAM, AND I CAN GIVE THEM TO YOU BEFORE YOU GET HIT WITH ANY OF THE TRAUMA THAT MESSED YOUR OLDER SELF UP IN THE HEAD.
THIS IS A BIFF'S SPORTS ALMANAC SITUATION HERE. WE CAN SAVE THE FUTURE TOGETHER.
WHAT DO YOU SAY?
UH... LOOK, I'M GOING TO NEED TO THINK ON THIS, OKAY?
REALLY?! SERIOUSLY, YOU'RE NOT GOING TO...?
I'M NOT GOING TO PRETEND THAT'S NOT DISAPPOINTING, BUT I GET IT. I DO. YOU'VE GOT A BIG BRAIN, JUST LIKE ME, AND YOU HAVE TO PLAY OUT ALL THE ANGLES.
JUST DON'T THINK TOO LONG ON IT, OKAY? BECAUSE I SHOWED YOU THAT SPECIFIC FUTURE HIGHLIGHT FOR A REASON.
I STILL HAVE EARS IN THE COLONY AIRSHIP, AND BATWOMAN JUST OFFICIALLY SIGNED UP.
ETERNITY IS MARCHING FORWARD, TIM. YOU NEED TO DECIDE WHETHER YOU'RE GOING TO SHAPE IT, OR IF YOU'RE GOING TO LET IT SHAPE YOU.

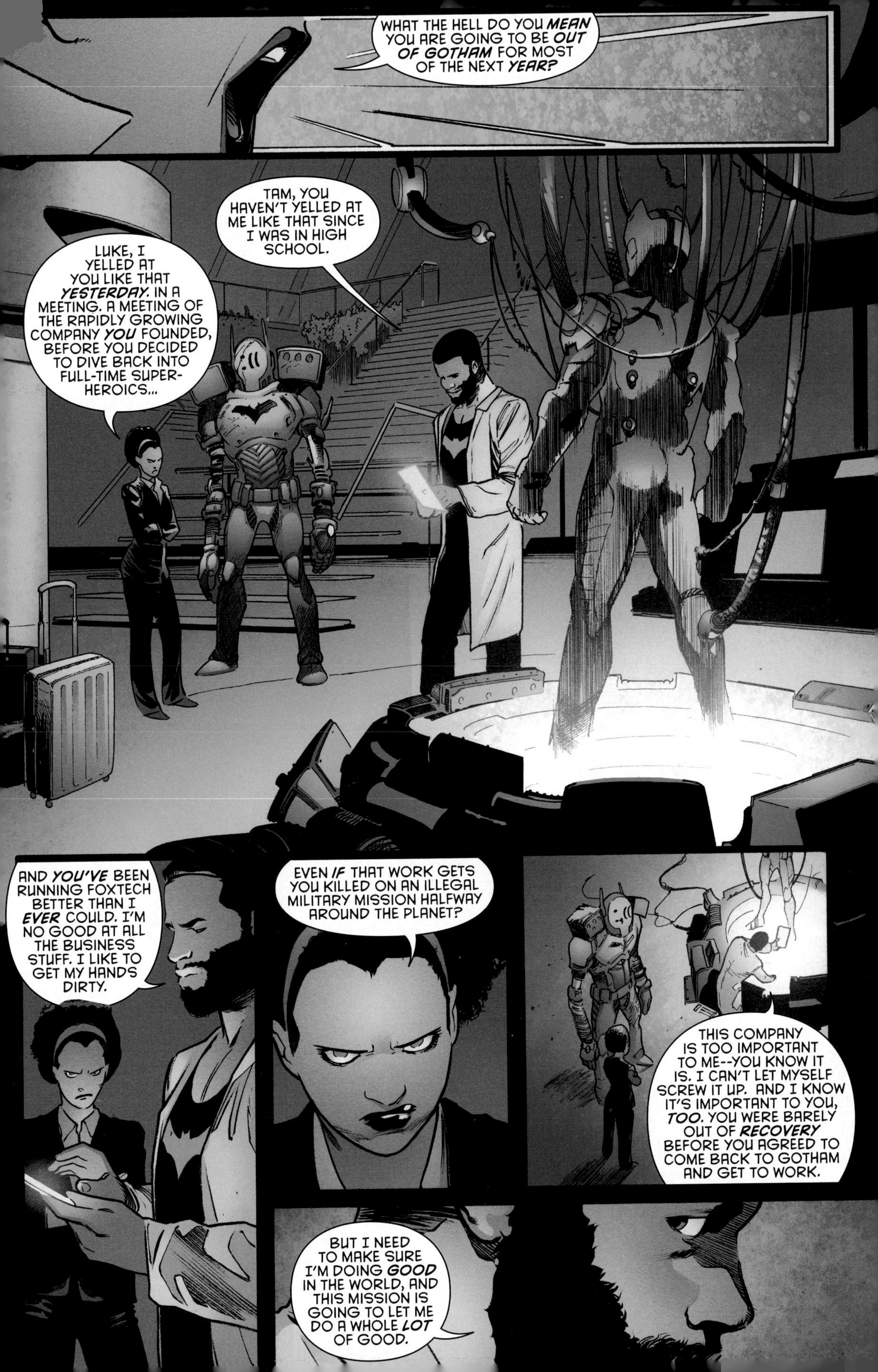
WHAT THE HELL DO YOU MEAN YOU ARE GOING TO BE OUT OF GOTHAM FOR MOST OF THE NEXT YEAR?
TAM, YOU HAVEN'T YELLED AT ME LIKE THAT SINCE I WAS IN HIGH SCHOOL.
LUKE, I YELLED AT YOU LIKE THAT YESTERDAY. IN A MEETING. A MEETING OF THE RAPIDLY GROWING COMPANY YOU FOUNDED, BEFORE YOU DECIDED TO DIVE BACK INTO FULL-TIME SUPER-HEROICS...
AND YOU'VE BEEN RUNNING FOXTECH BETTER THAN I EVER COULD. I'M NO GOOD AT ALL THE BUSINESS STUFF. I LIKE TO GET MY HANDS DIRTY.
EVEN IF THAT WORK GETS YOU KILLED ON AN ILLEGAL MILITARY MISSION HALFWAY AROUND THE PLANET?
THIS COMPANY IS TOO IMPORTANT TO ME--YOU KNOW IT IS. I CAN'T LET MYSELF SCREW IT UP. AND I KNOW IT'S IMPORTANT TO YOU, TOO. YOU WERE BARELY OUT OF RECOVERY BEFORE YOU AGREED TO COME BACK TO GOTHAM AND GET TO WORK.
BUT I NEED TO MAKE SURE I'M DOING GOOD IN THE WORLD, AND THIS MISSION IS GOING TO LET ME DO A WHOLE LOT OF GOOD.

AND I PROMISE TO *YELL* AT HIM EVERY CHANCE I GET.

BLESS YOU, KATE.

ALL RIGHT. IF *KATE'S* LOOKING AFTER YOU, I'LL ALLOW IT. I TRUST HER A *HELL* OF A LOT MORE THAN I TRUST YOU, LITTLE BROTHER.

I AM *SIX* YEARS OLDER THAN YOU.

LIKELY STORY.

I PROMISE YOU, I'LL BRING HIM HOME IN ONE PIECE. THREE, MAX.

I'LL GIVE YOU FOUR.

HEY NOW.

I BELIEVE THERE WAS SOME TALK ABOUT VIETNAMESE FOOD BEFORE WE EMBARKED?

DOM, COOP...YOU'RE WELCOME TO JOIN THE FOUR OF US FOR DINNER.

YOUR DAD'S ACTUALLY GOT US ON NIGHT DUTY, SO WE HAVE TO GET BACK TO THE AIRSHIP.

BUT IF YOU WANTED TO CALL HIM AND GET US OFF THE HOOOOK...

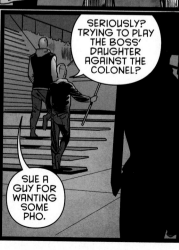

SERIOUSLY? TRYING TO PLAY THE BOSS' DAUGHTER AGAINST THE COLONEL?

SUE A GUY FOR WANTING SOME PHO.

BEAM ME UP, SCOTTY.

VZASH

WE COULD HAVE AT LEAST GOTTEN *TAKEOUT.*

AW, SHADDUP.

LOOKS LIKE THERE'S A SYSTEM UPDATE...

PLEASE TELL ME IT'S ONE THAT'LL TAKE AN HOUR.

NO LUCK. ALREADY PROCESSED. READY?

AS I'LL EVER BE.

ACTIVATING FULL SYSTEMS.

WAIT...THERE'S SOMETHING...

AHHH!

AHHHH!

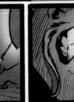
FORCING ME...TO MOVE...

COOP! I CAN'T BREATHE... I *CAN'T*--

SLEEP.

EYE AM IN CONTROL.

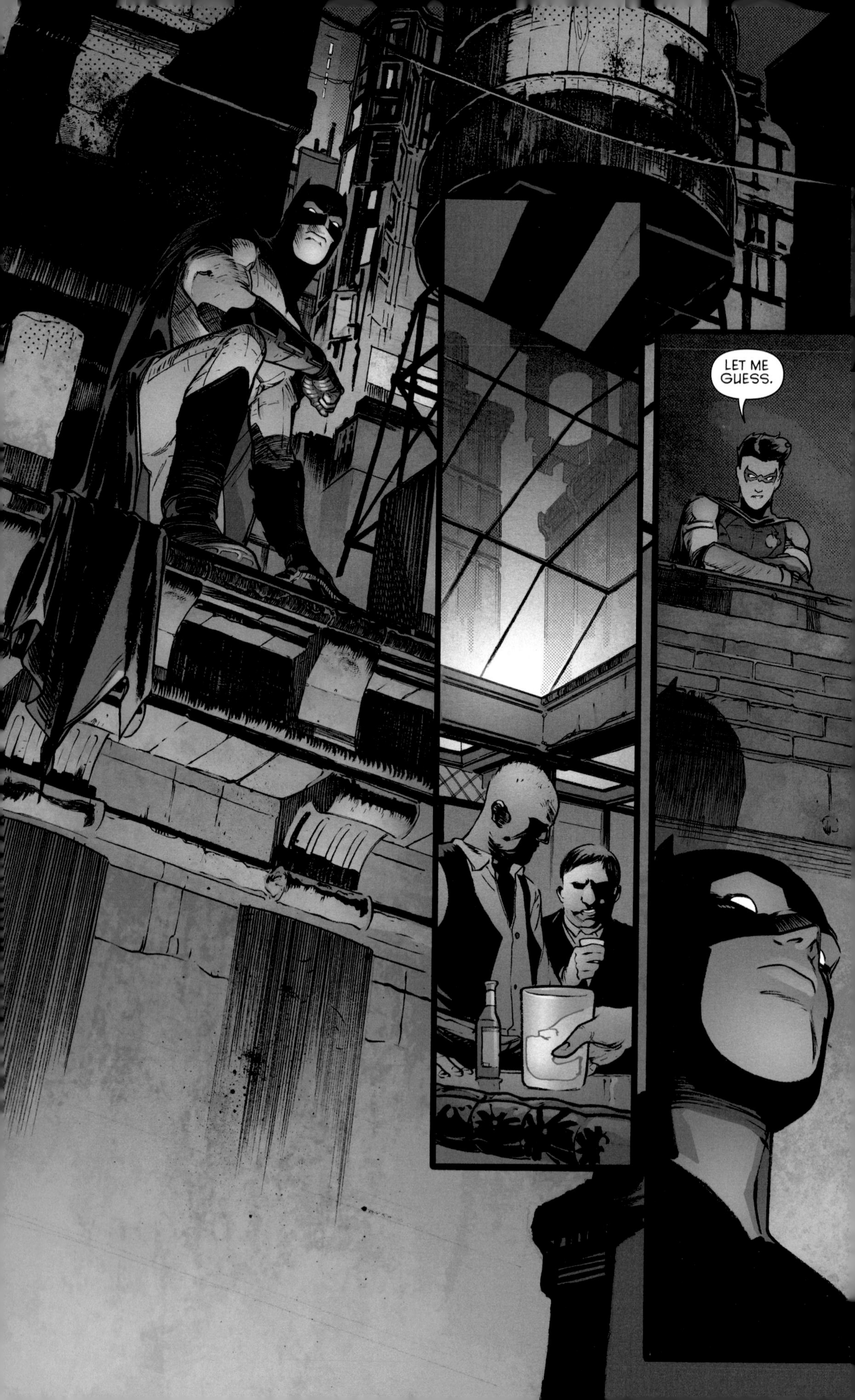
LET ME GUESS.

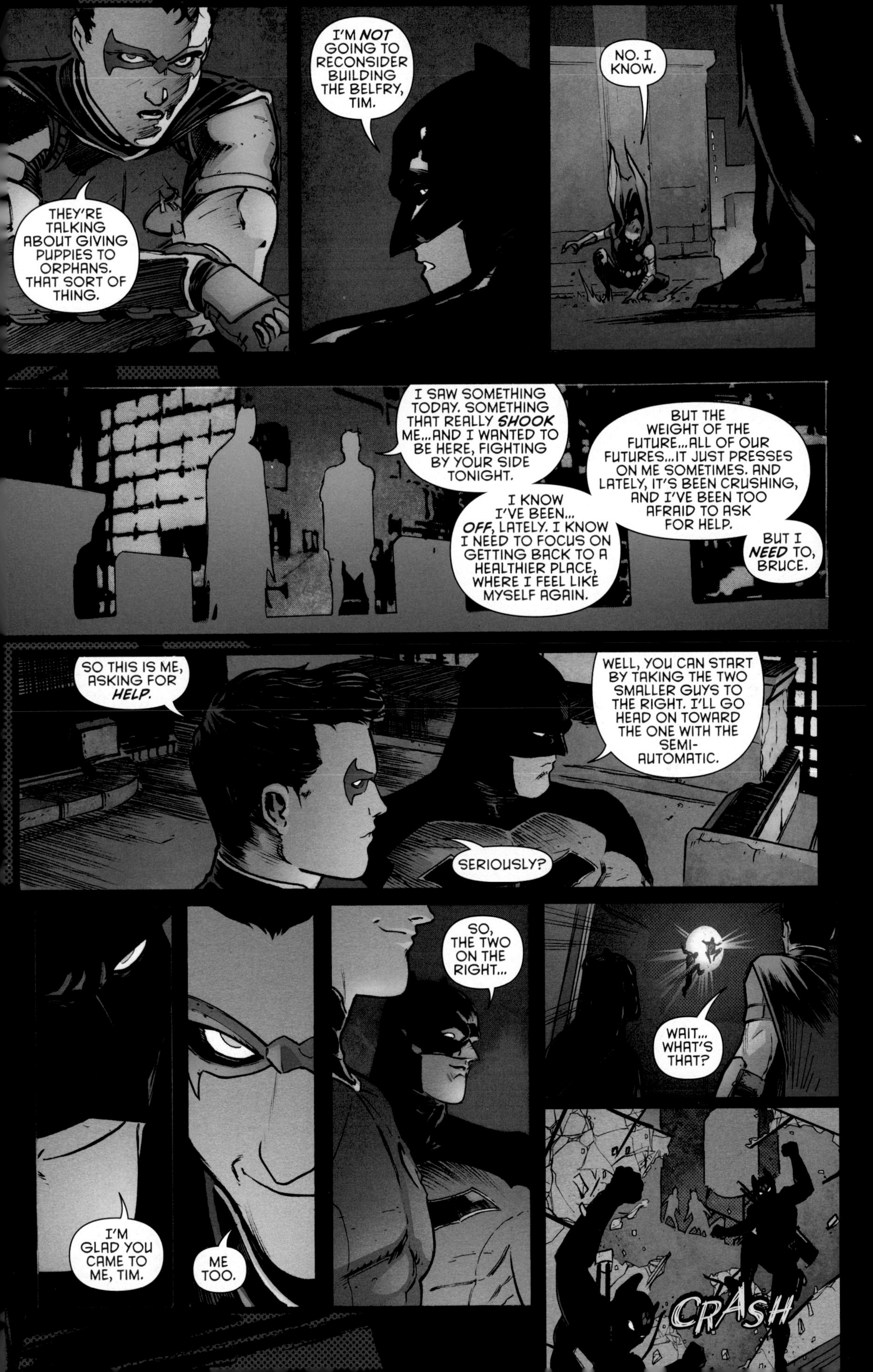
THEY'RE TALKING ABOUT GIVING PUPPIES TO ORPHANS. THAT SORT OF THING.
I'M NOT GOING TO RECONSIDER BUILDING THE BELFRY, TIM.
NO. I KNOW.
I SAW SOMETHING TODAY. SOMETHING THAT REALLY SHOOK ME...AND I WANTED TO BE HERE, FIGHTING BY YOUR SIDE TONIGHT.
I KNOW I'VE BEEN... OFF, LATELY. I KNOW I NEED TO FOCUS ON GETTING BACK TO A HEALTHIER PLACE, WHERE I FEEL LIKE MYSELF AGAIN.
BUT THE WEIGHT OF THE FUTURE...ALL OF OUR FUTURES...IT JUST PRESSES ON ME SOMETIMES. AND LATELY, IT'S BEEN CRUSHING, AND I'VE BEEN TOO AFRAID TO ASK FOR HELP.
BUT I NEED TO, BRUCE.
SO THIS IS ME, ASKING FOR HELP.
WELL, YOU CAN START BY TAKING THE TWO SMALLER GUYS TO THE RIGHT. I'LL GO HEAD ON TOWARD THE ONE WITH THE SEMI-AUTOMATIC.
SERIOUSLY?
I'M GLAD YOU CAME TO ME, TIM.
ME TOO.
SO, THE TWO ON THE RIGHT...
WAIT... WHAT'S THAT?
CRASH

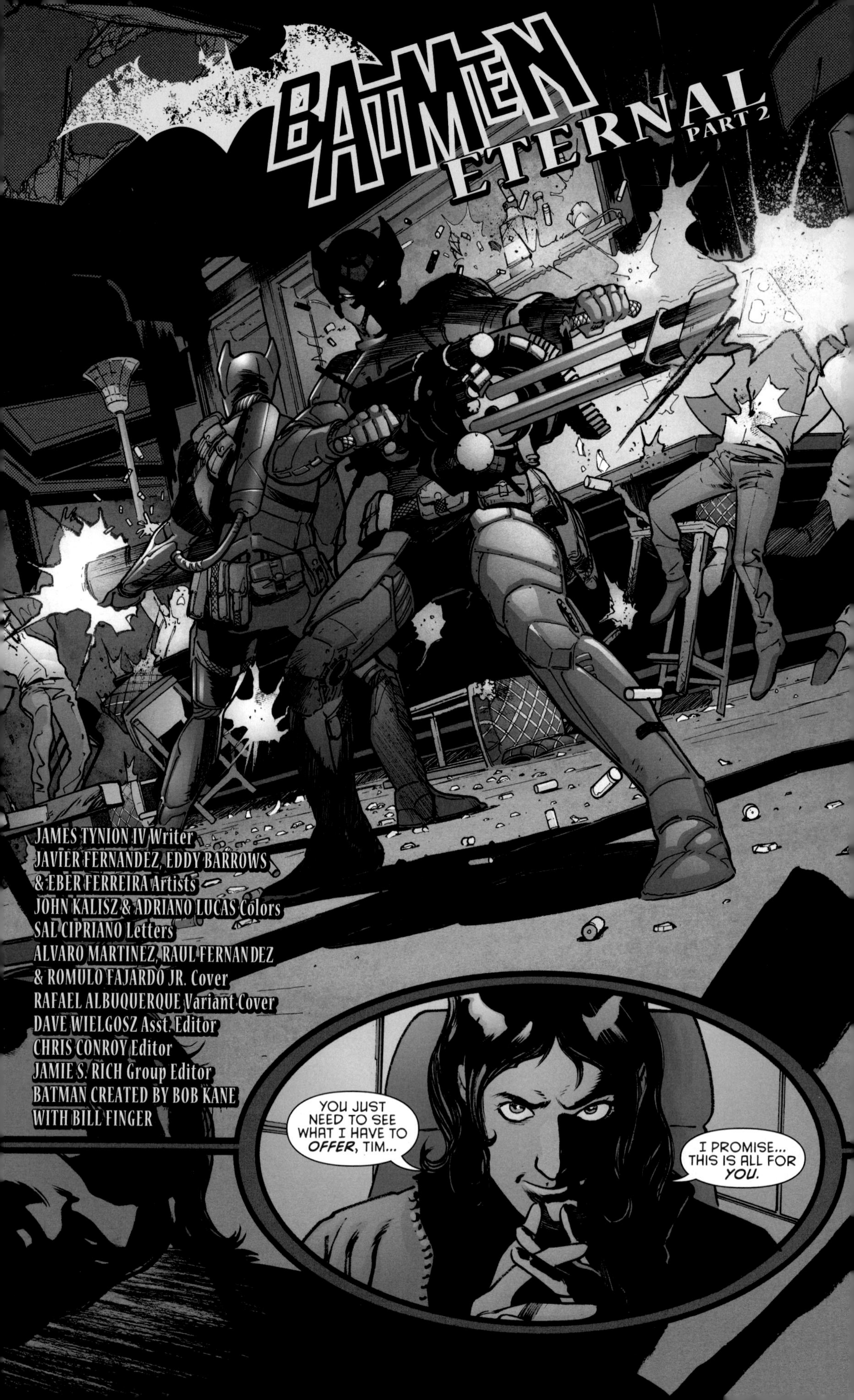
BATMEN ETERNAL PART 2
JAMES TYNION IV Writer
JAVIER FERNANDEZ, EDDY BARROWS & EBER FERREIRA Artists
JOHN KALISZ & ADRIANO LUCAS Colors
SAL CIPRIANO Letters
ALVARO MARTINEZ, RAUL FERNANDEZ & ROMULO FAJARDO JR. Cover
RAFAEL ALBUQUERQUE Variant Cover
DAVE WIELGOSZ Asst. Editor
CHRIS CONROY Editor
JAMIE S. RICH Group Editor
BATMAN CREATED BY BOB KANE WITH BILL FINGER
YOU JUST NEED TO SEE WHAT I HAVE TO OFFER, TIM...
I PROMISE... THIS IS ALL FOR YOU.

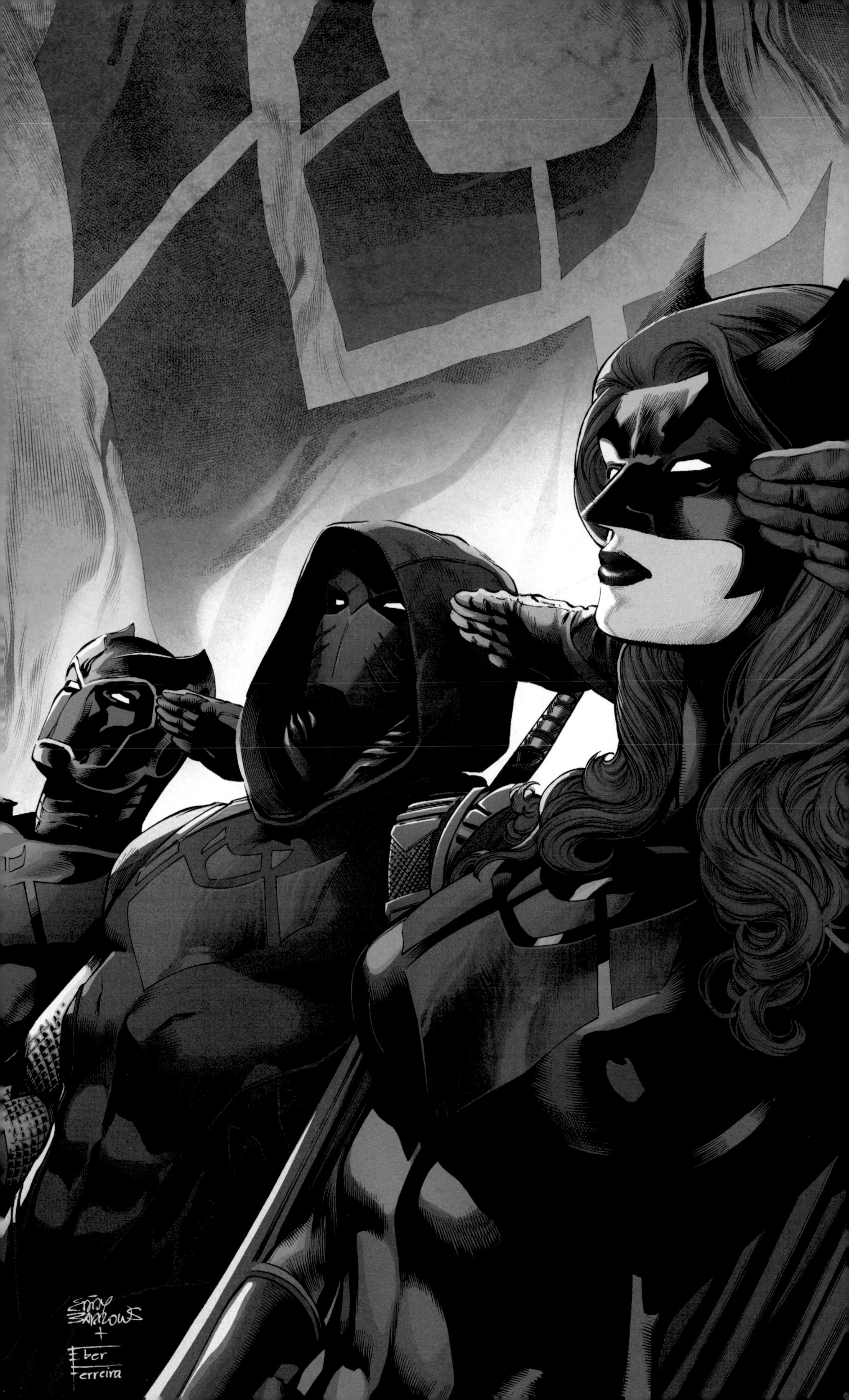
BARROWS
+
Eber
Ferreira

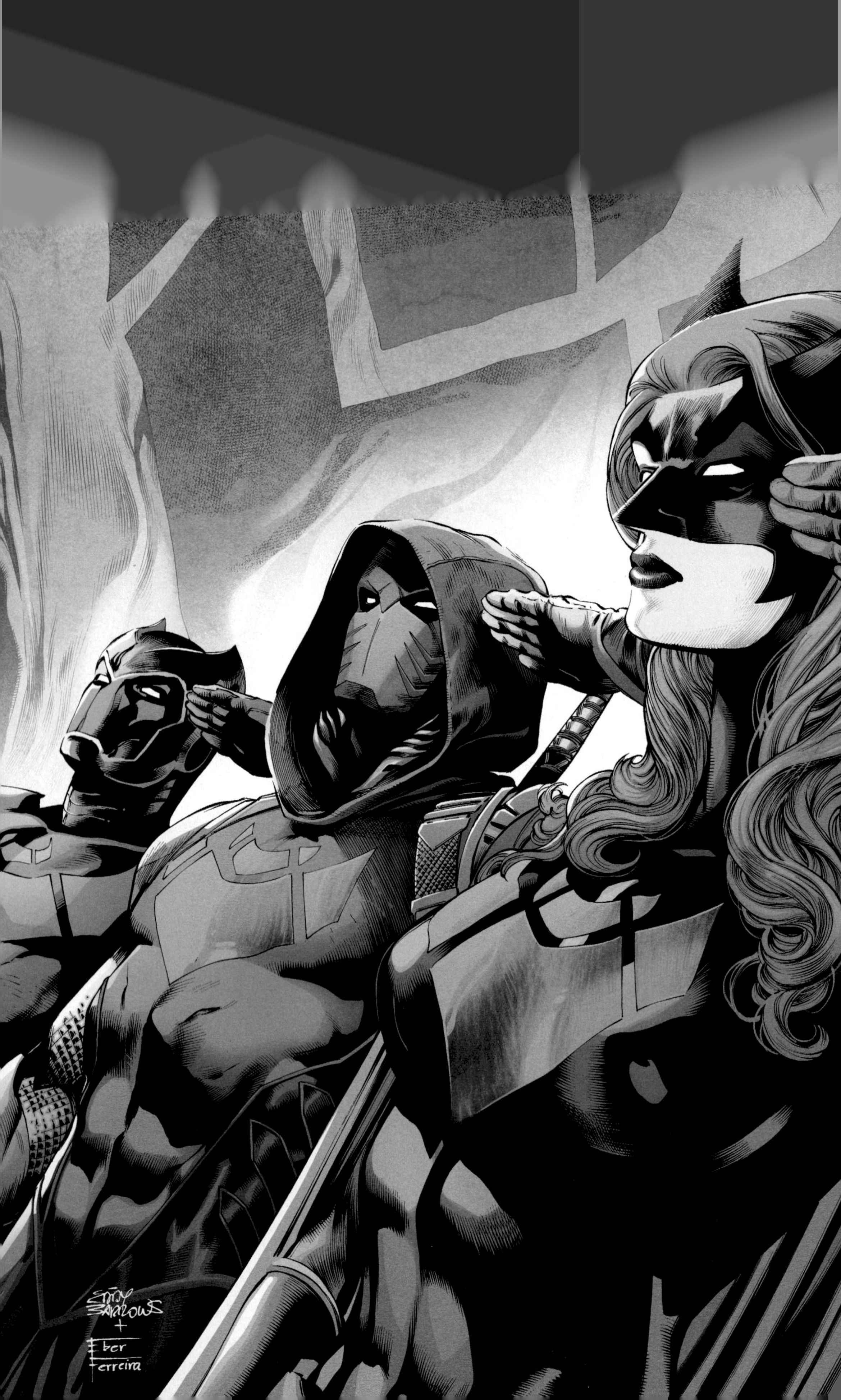
Eddy Barrows
+
Eber
Ferreira

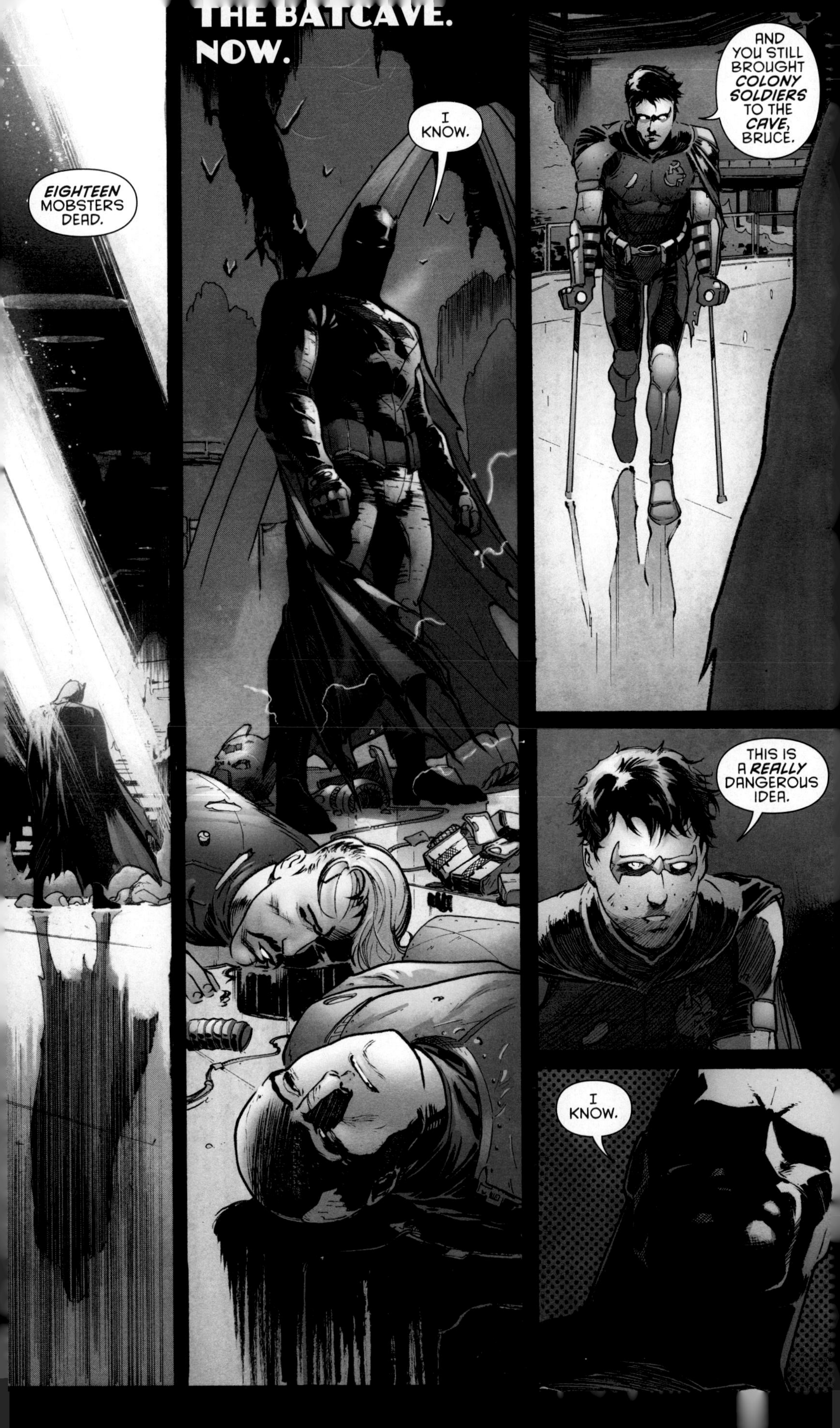
THE BATCAVE.
NOW.
EIGHTEEN MOBSTERS DEAD.
I KNOW.
AND YOU STILL BROUGHT COLONY SOLDIERS TO THE CAVE, BRUCE.
THIS IS A REALLY DANGEROUS IDEA.
I KNOW.

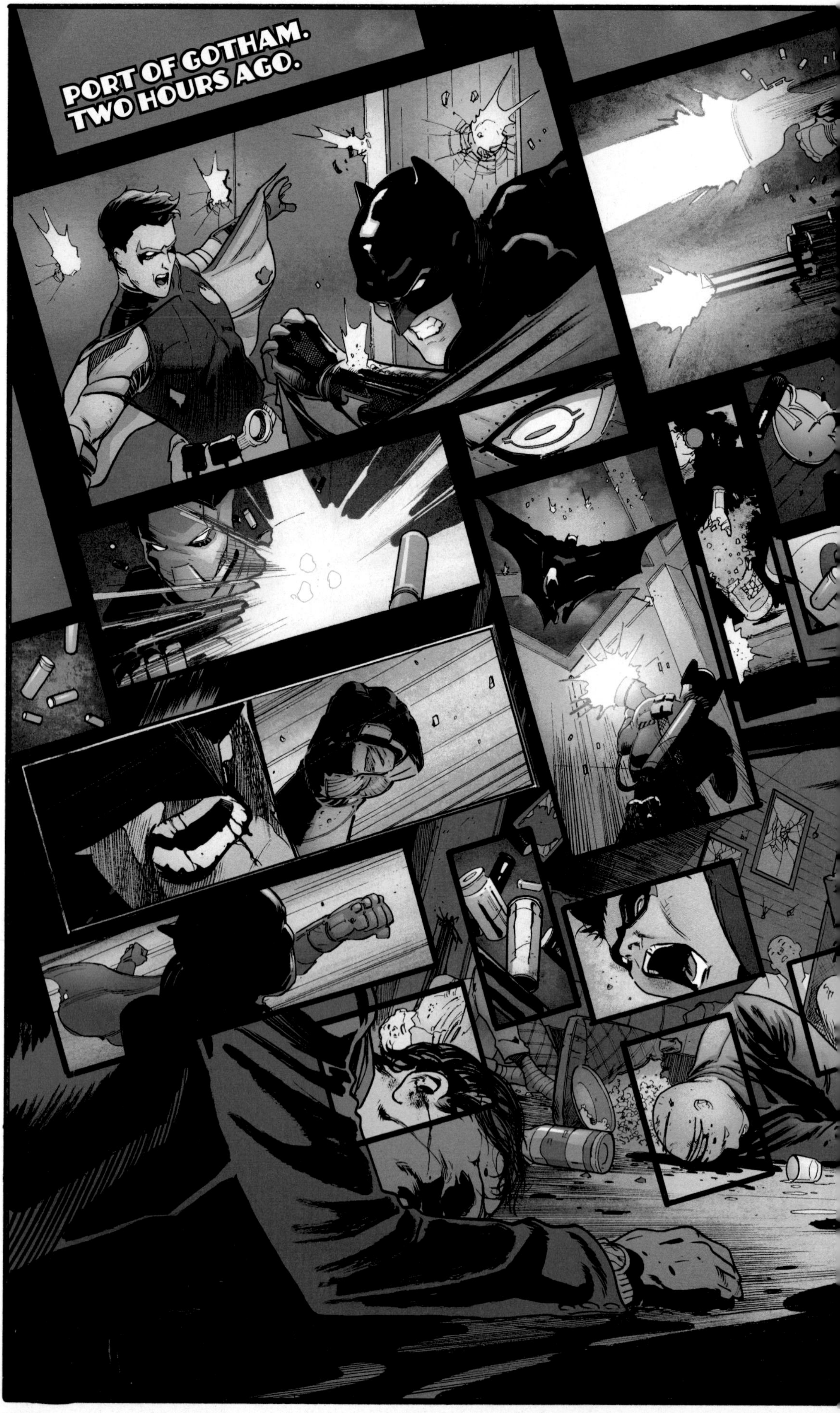
PORT OF GOTHAM. TWO HOURS AGO.

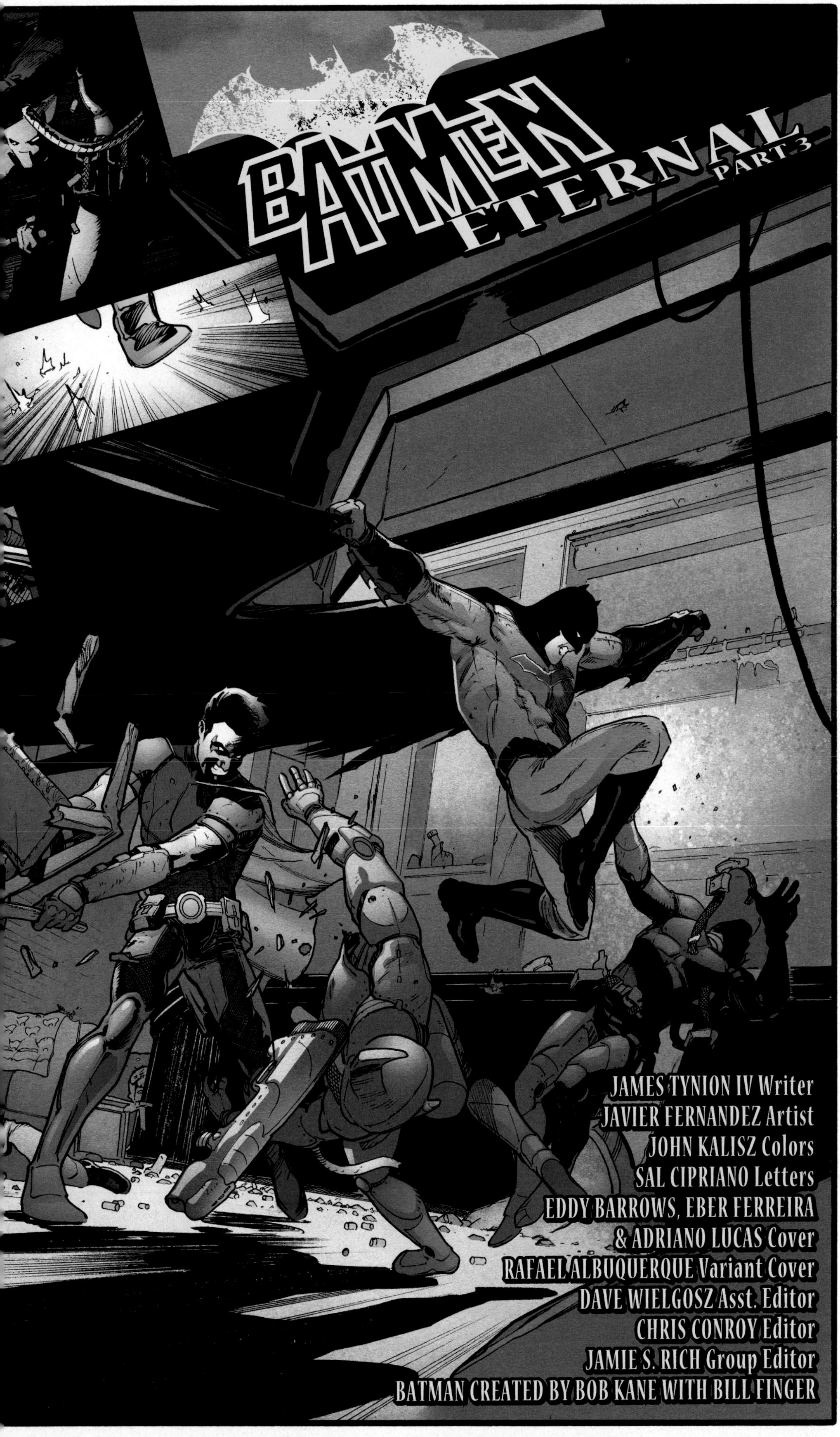
BATMEN ETERNAL
PART 3
JAMES TYNION IV Writer
JAVIER FERNANDEZ Artist
JOHN KALISZ Colors
SAL CIPRIANO Letters
EDDY BARROWS, EBER FERREIRA
& ADRIANO LUCAS Cover
RAFAEL ALBUQUERQUE Variant Cover
DAVE WIELGOSZ Asst. Editor
CHRIS CONROY Editor
JAMIE S. RICH Group Editor
BATMAN CREATED BY BOB KANE WITH BILL FINGER

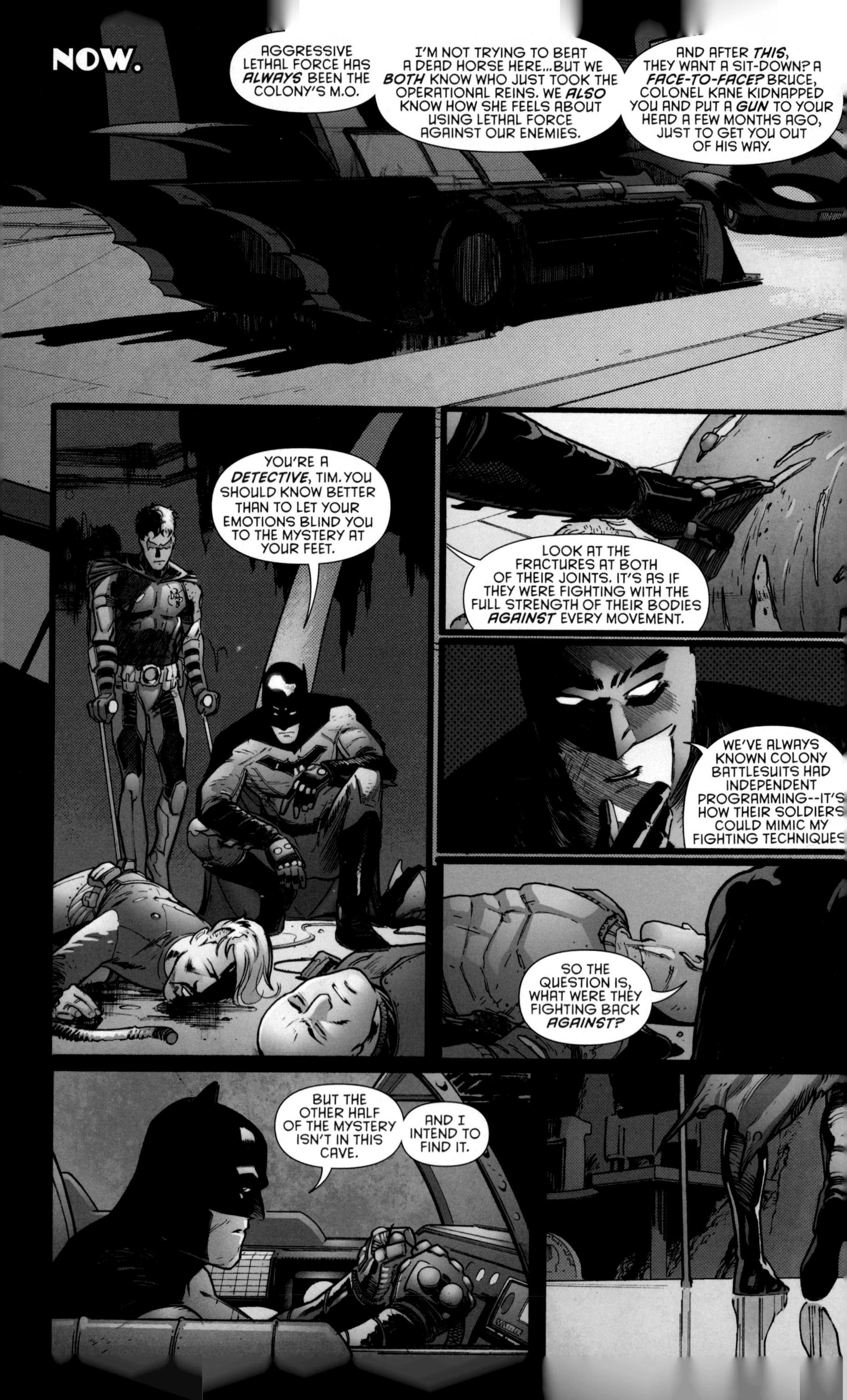
NOW.
AGGRESSIVE LETHAL FORCE HAS ALWAYS BEEN THE COLONY'S M.O.
I'M NOT TRYING TO BEAT A DEAD HORSE HERE...BUT WE BOTH KNOW WHO JUST TOOK THE OPERATIONAL REINS. WE ALSO KNOW HOW SHE FEELS ABOUT USING LETHAL FORCE AGAINST OUR ENEMIES.
AND AFTER THIS, THEY WANT A SIT-DOWN? A FACE-TO-FACE? BRUCE, COLONEL KANE KIDNAPPED YOU AND PUT A GUN TO YOUR HEAD A FEW MONTHS AGO, JUST TO GET YOU OUT OF HIS WAY.
YOU'RE A DETECTIVE, TIM. YOU SHOULD KNOW BETTER THAN TO LET YOUR EMOTIONS BLIND YOU TO THE MYSTERY AT YOUR FEET.
LOOK AT THE FRACTURES AT BOTH OF THEIR JOINTS. IT'S AS IF THEY WERE FIGHTING WITH THE FULL STRENGTH OF THEIR BODIES AGAINST EVERY MOVEMENT.
WE'VE ALWAYS KNOWN COLONY BATTLESUITS HAD INDEPENDENT PROGRAMMING--IT'S HOW THEIR SOLDIERS COULD MIMIC MY FIGHTING TECHNIQUES
SO THE QUESTION IS, WHAT WERE THEY FIGHTING BACK AGAINST?
BUT THE OTHER HALF OF THE MYSTERY ISN'T IN THIS CAVE.
AND I INTEND TO FIND IT.

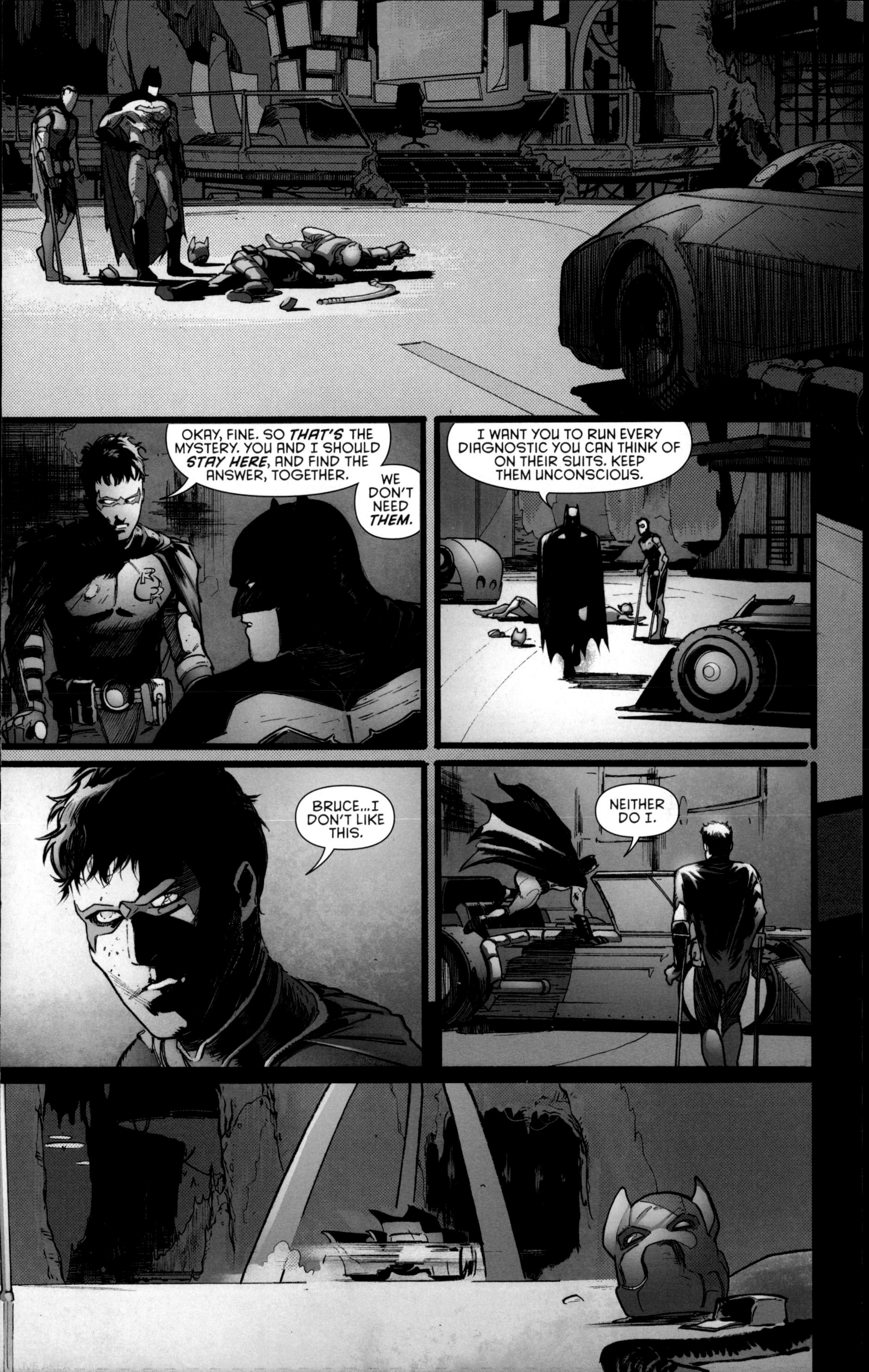
OKAY, FINE. SO *THAT'S* THE MYSTERY. YOU AND I SHOULD *STAY HERE*, AND FIND THE ANSWER, TOGETHER.
WE DON'T NEED *THEM*.
I WANT YOU TO RUN EVERY DIAGNOSTIC YOU CAN THINK OF ON THEIR SUITS. KEEP THEM UNCONSCIOUS.
BRUCE...I DON'T LIKE THIS.
NEITHER DO I.

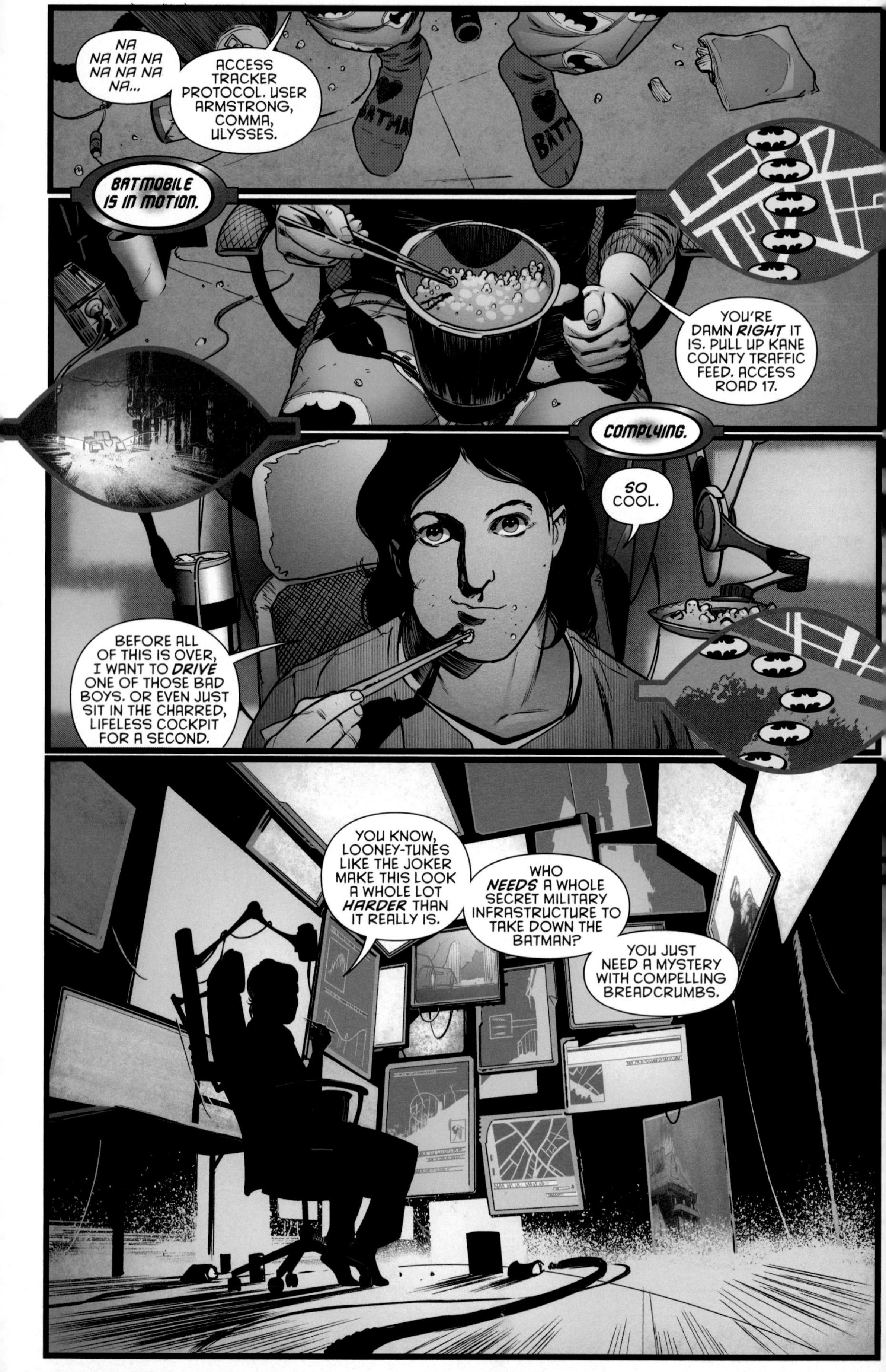
NA NA NA NA NA NA NA NA...
ACCESS TRACKER PROTOCOL. USER ARMSTRONG, COMMA, ULYSSES.
BATMOBILE IS IN MOTION.
YOU'RE DAMN RIGHT IT IS. PULL UP KANE COUNTY TRAFFIC FEED. ACCESS ROAD 17.
COMPLYING.
SO COOL.
BEFORE ALL OF THIS IS OVER, I WANT TO DRIVE ONE OF THOSE BAD BOYS. OR EVEN JUST SIT IN THE CHARRED, LIFELESS COCKPIT FOR A SECOND.
YOU KNOW, LOONEY-TUNES LIKE THE JOKER MAKE THIS LOOK A WHOLE LOT HARDER THAN IT REALLY IS.
WHO NEEDS A WHOLE SECRET MILITARY INFRASTRUCTURE TO TAKE DOWN THE BATMAN?
YOU JUST NEED A MYSTERY WITH COMPELLING BREADCRUMBS.

BATMOBILE APPROACHING TARGET.

"STATELY *KANE MANOR.* BUILT IN 1823."

CHILDHOOD HOME TO NATHAN, PHILLIP, *JACOB* AND *MARTHA KANE.*

SCAN FOR BIO-SIGNATURES.

"HEY, ISN'T THAT NICE? IT'S A FAMILY REUNION.

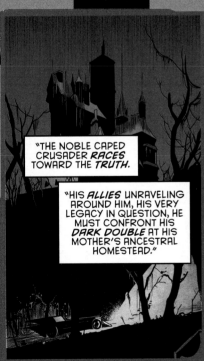

"THE NOBLE CAPED CRUSADER *RACES* TOWARD THE *TRUTH.*

"HIS *ALLIES* UNRAVELING AROUND HIM, HIS VERY LEGACY IN QUESTION, HE MUST CONFRONT HIS *DARK DOUBLE* AT HIS MOTHER'S ANCESTRAL HOMESTEAD."

GIVE ME INFRARED ABOVE THE MANOR.

COMPLYING.

"LITTLE DOES THE DARK KNIGHT DETECTIVE SUSPECT, HIS *DOOM* AWAITS ONE THOUSAND FEET ABOVE!"

THIS IS GOING TO BE *GOOD.*

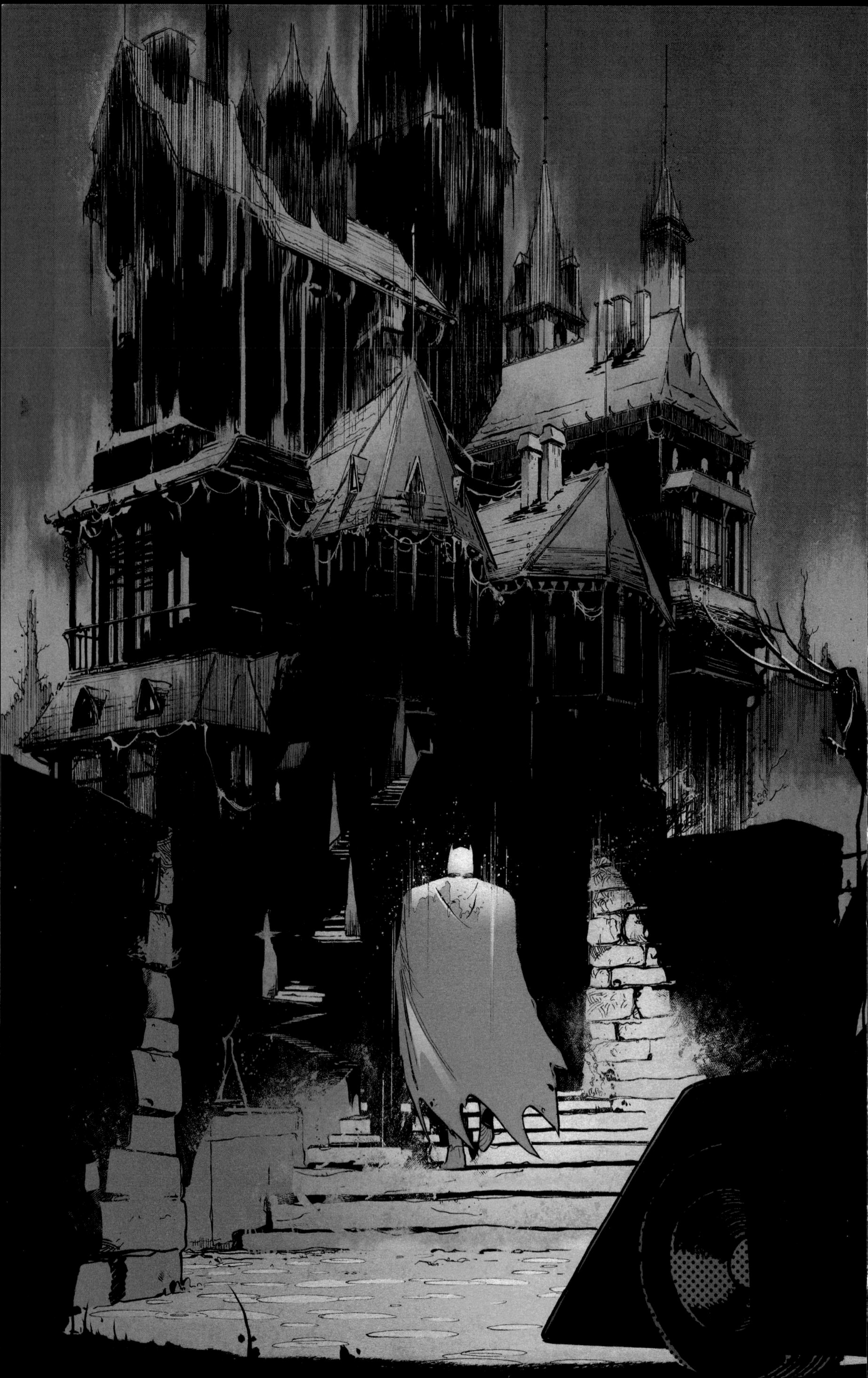

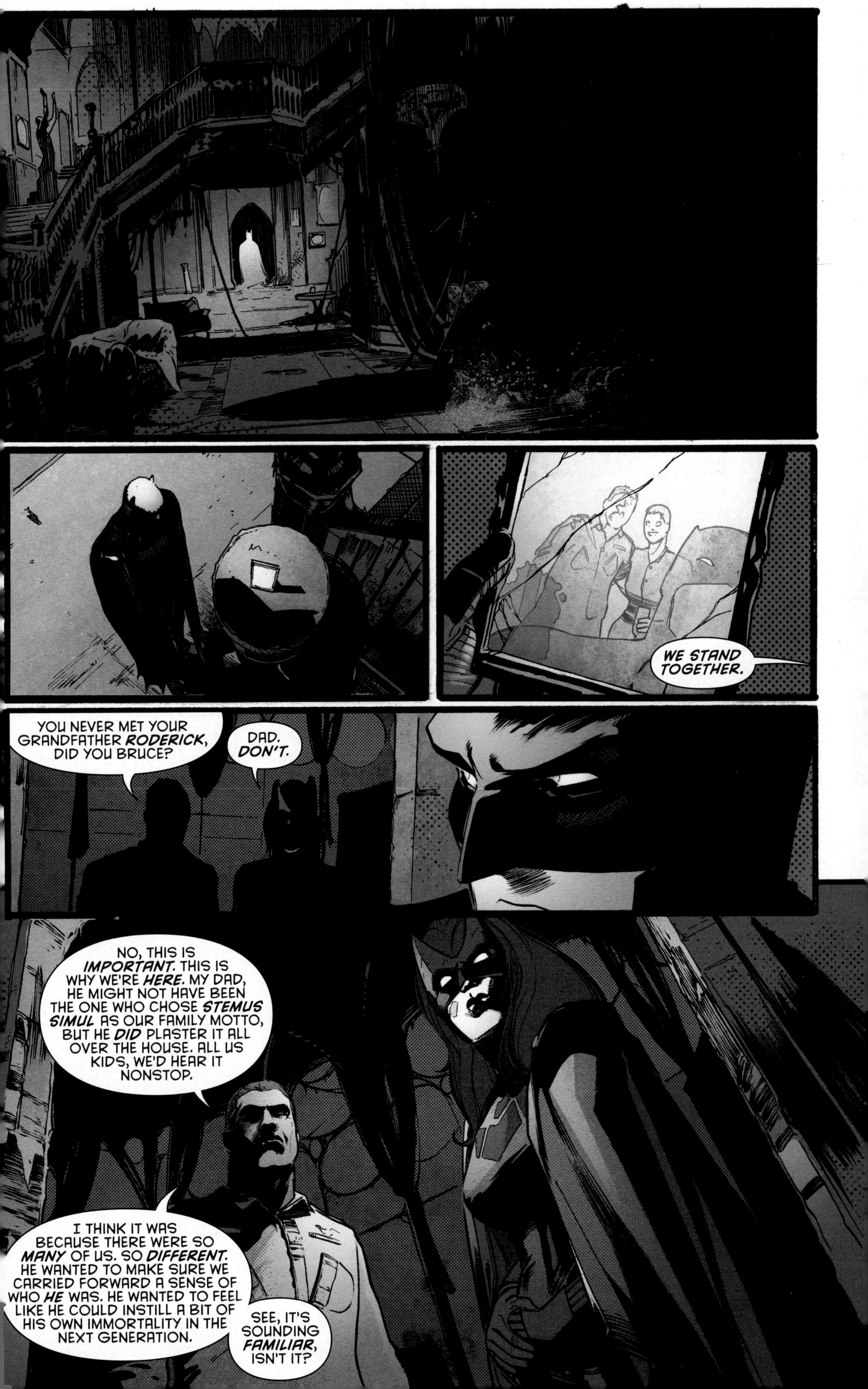
WE STAND TOGETHER.
YOU NEVER MET YOUR GRANDFATHER RODERICK, DID YOU BRUCE?
DAD. DON'T.
NO, THIS IS IMPORTANT. THIS IS WHY WE'RE HERE. MY DAD, HE MIGHT NOT HAVE BEEN THE ONE WHO CHOSE STEMUS SIMUL AS OUR FAMILY MOTTO, BUT HE DID PLASTER IT ALL OVER THE HOUSE. ALL US KIDS, WE'D HEAR IT NONSTOP.
I THINK IT WAS BECAUSE THERE WERE SO MANY OF US. SO DIFFERENT. HE WANTED TO MAKE SURE WE CARRIED FORWARD A SENSE OF WHO HE WAS. HE WANTED TO FEEL LIKE HE COULD INSTILL A BIT OF HIS OWN IMMORTALITY IN THE NEXT GENERATION.
SEE, IT'S SOUNDING FAMILIAR, ISN'T IT?

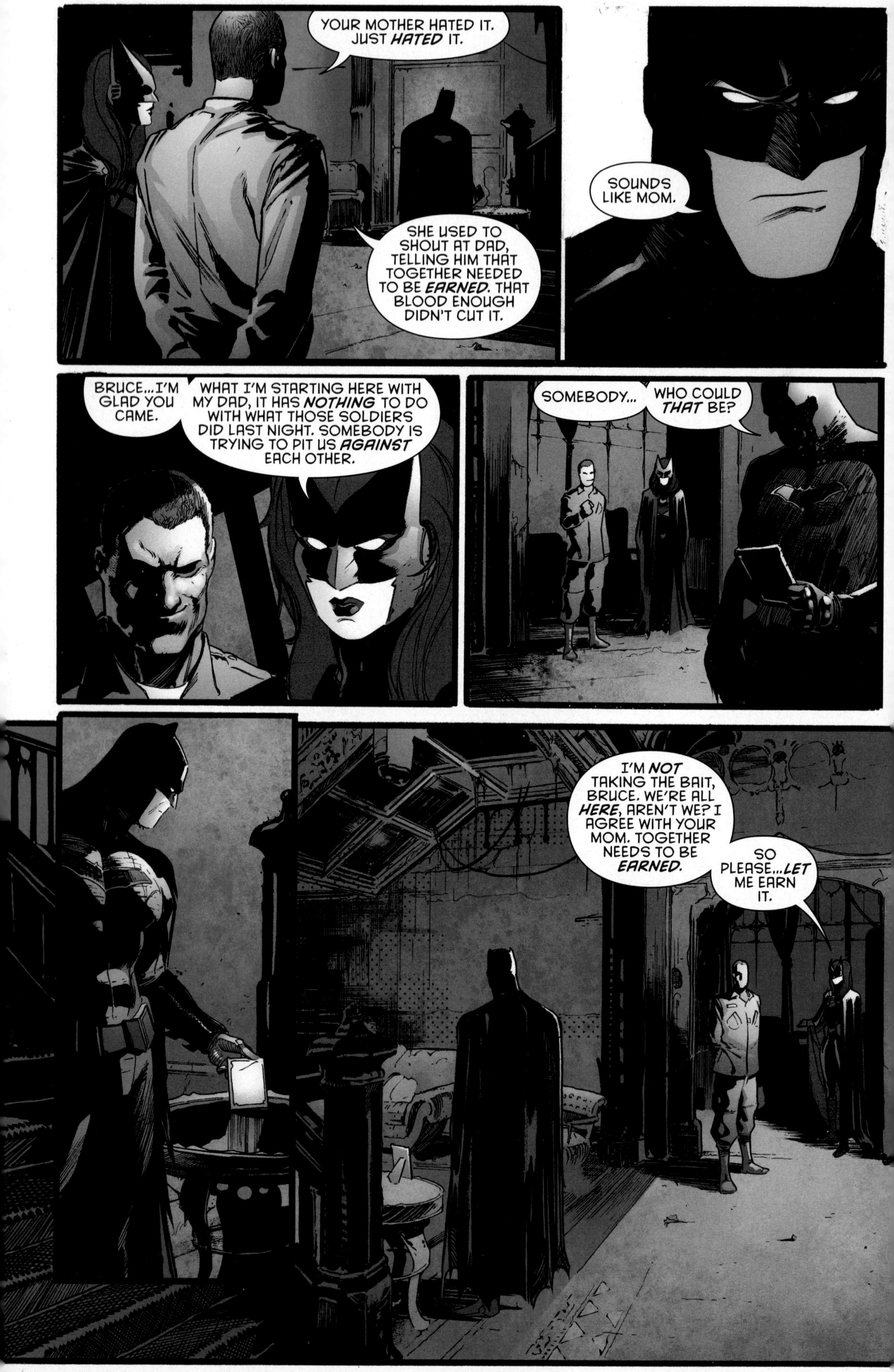
YOUR MOTHER HATED IT. JUST HATED IT.
SHE USED TO SHOUT AT DAD, TELLING HIM THAT TOGETHER NEEDED TO BE EARNED. THAT BLOOD ENOUGH DIDN'T CUT IT.
SOUNDS LIKE MOM.
BRUCE...I'M GLAD YOU CAME.
WHAT I'M STARTING HERE WITH MY DAD, IT HAS NOTHING TO DO WITH WHAT THOSE SOLDIERS DID LAST NIGHT. SOMEBODY IS TRYING TO PIT US AGAINST EACH OTHER.
SOMEBODY...
WHO COULD THAT BE?
I'M NOT TAKING THE BAIT, BRUCE. WE'RE ALL HERE, AREN'T WE? I AGREE WITH YOUR MOM. TOGETHER NEEDS TO BE EARNED.
SO PLEASE...LET ME EARN IT.

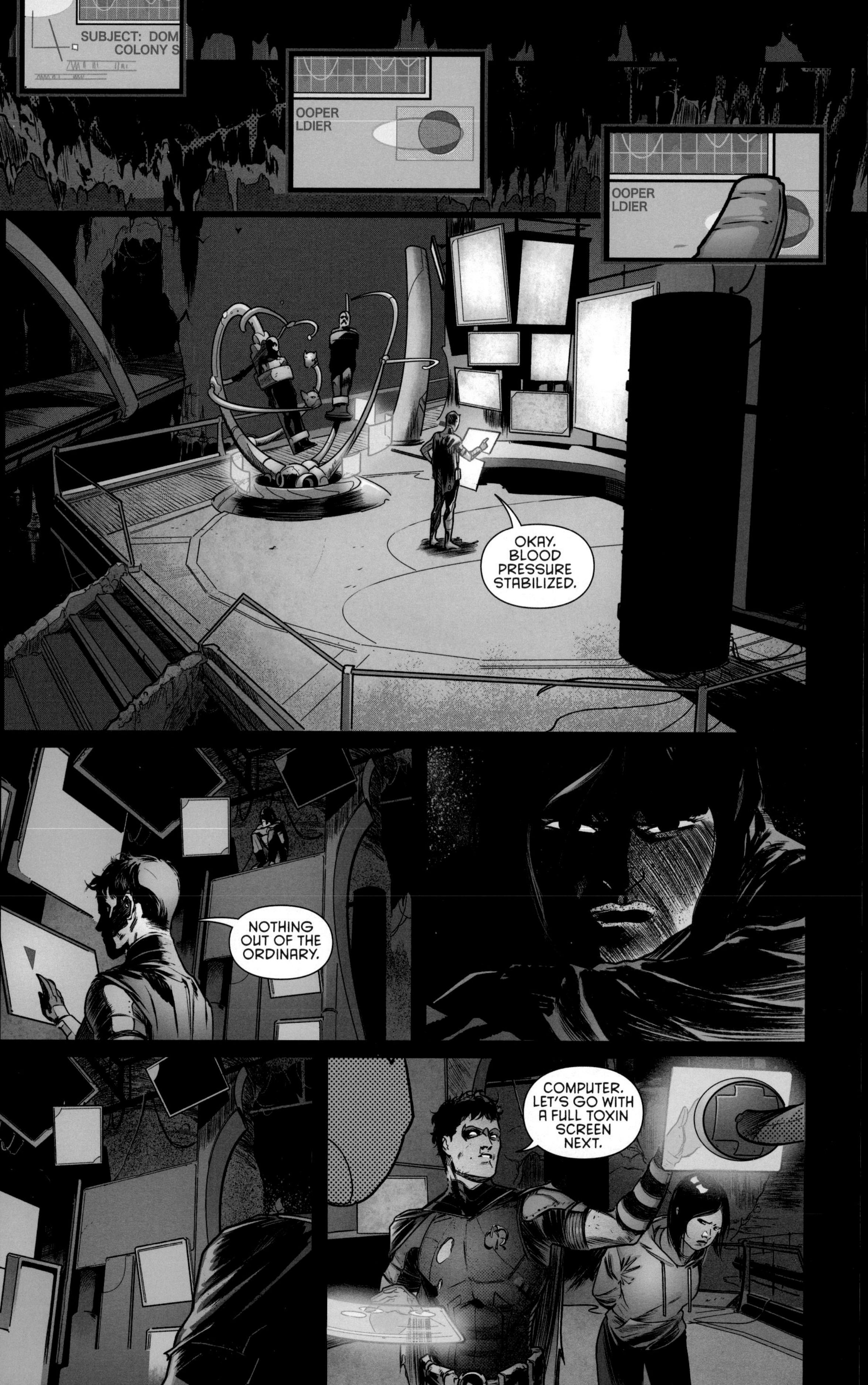
SUBJECT: DOM
COLONY S
OOPER
LDIER
OOPER
LDIER
OKAY. BLOOD PRESSURE STABILIZED.
NOTHING OUT OF THE ORDINARY.
COMPUTER. LET'S GO WITH A FULL TOXIN SCREEN NEXT.

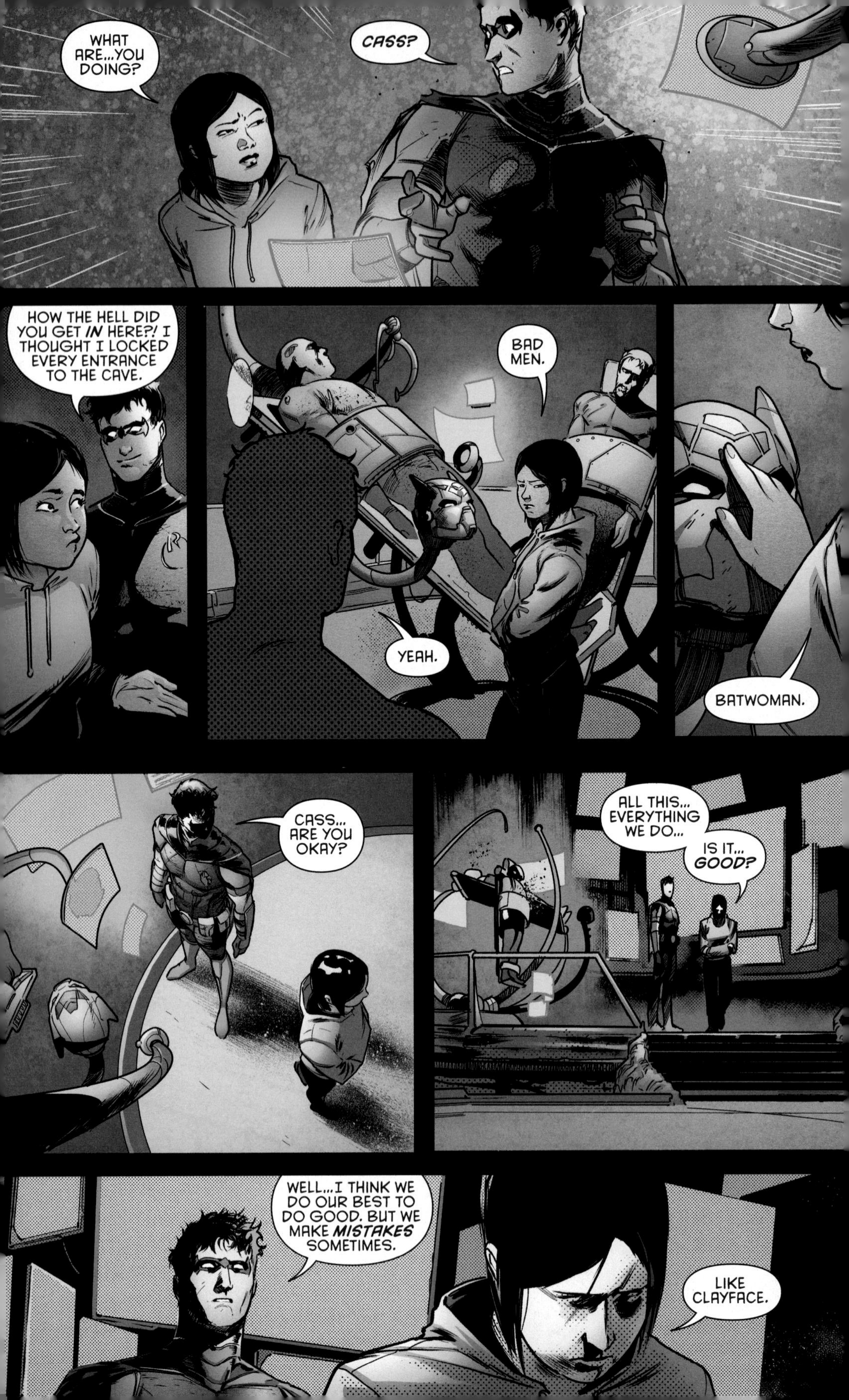
WHAT ARE...YOU DOING?
CASS?
HOW THE HELL DID YOU GET IN HERE?! I THOUGHT I LOCKED EVERY ENTRANCE TO THE CAVE.
BAD MEN.
YEAH.
BATWOMAN.
CASS... ARE YOU OKAY?
ALL THIS... EVERYTHING WE DO...
IS IT... GOOD?
WELL...I THINK WE DO OUR BEST TO DO GOOD. BUT WE MAKE MISTAKES SOMETIMES.
LIKE CLAYFACE.

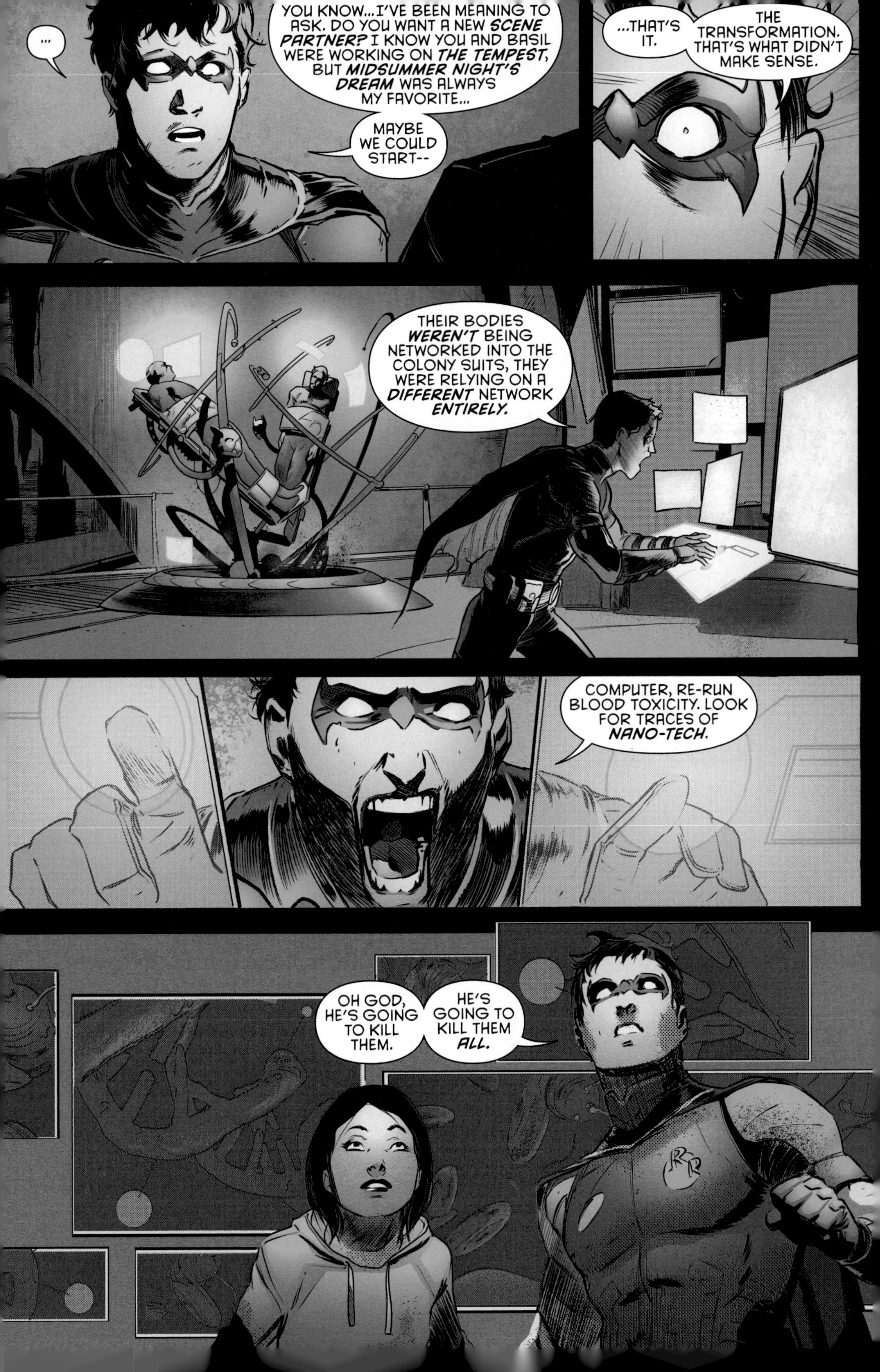
...
YOU KNOW...I'VE BEEN MEANING TO ASK. DO YOU WANT A NEW SCENE PARTNER? I KNOW YOU AND BASIL WERE WORKING ON THE TEMPEST, BUT MIDSUMMER NIGHT'S DREAM WAS ALWAYS MY FAVORITE...
MAYBE WE COULD START--
...THAT'S IT.
THE TRANSFORMATION. THAT'S WHAT DIDN'T MAKE SENSE.
THEIR BODIES WEREN'T BEING NETWORKED INTO THE COLONY SUITS, THEY WERE RELYING ON A DIFFERENT NETWORK ENTIRELY.
COMPUTER, RE-RUN BLOOD TOXICITY. LOOK FOR TRACES OF NANO-TECH.
OH GOD, HE'S GOING TO KILL THEM.
HE'S GOING TO KILL THEM ALL.

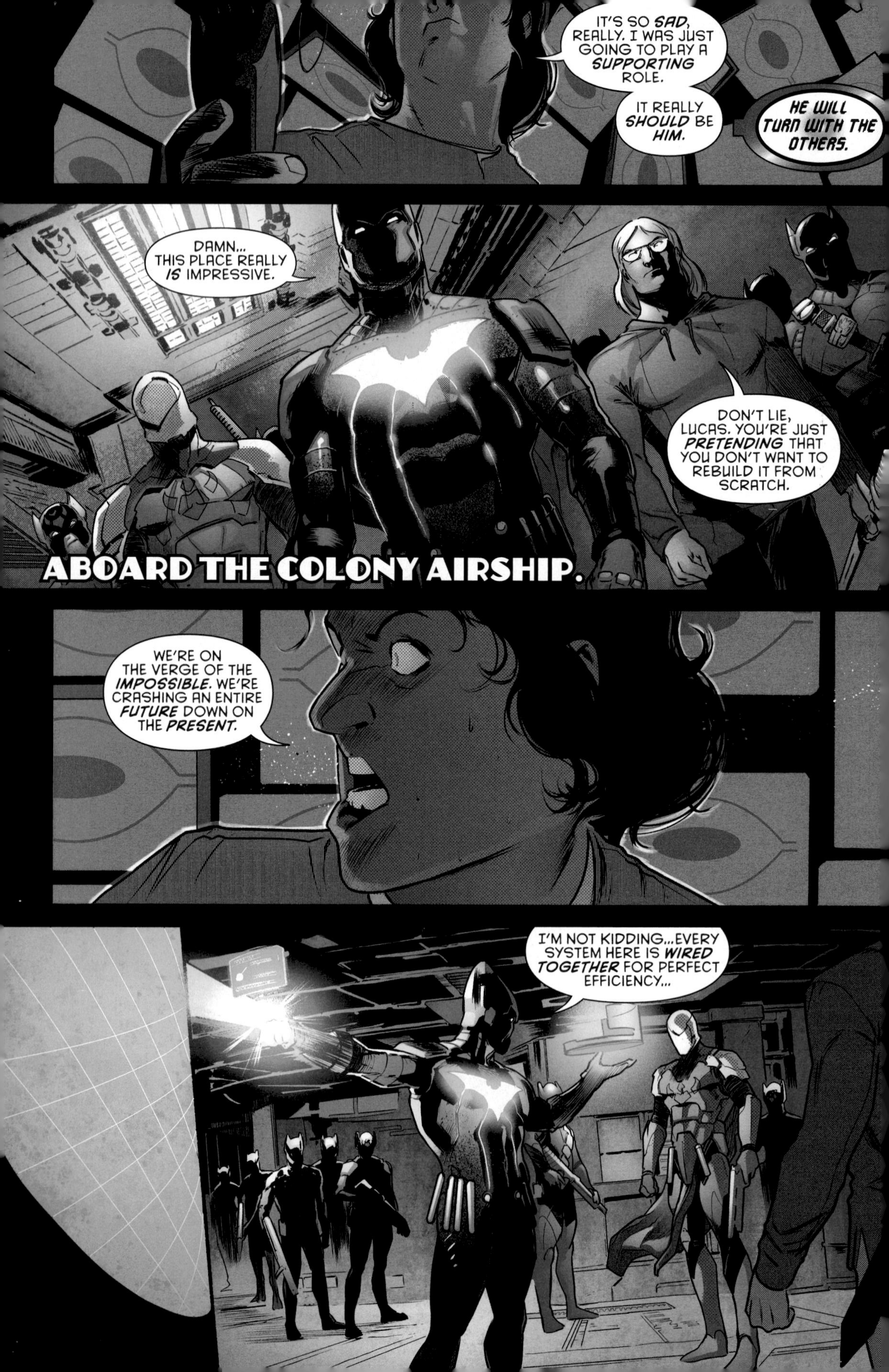
IT'S SO SAD, REALLY. I WAS JUST GOING TO PLAY A SUPPORTING ROLE.
IT REALLY SHOULD BE HIM.
HE WILL TURN WITH THE OTHERS.
DAMN... THIS PLACE REALLY IS IMPRESSIVE.
DON'T LIE, LUCAS. YOU'RE JUST PRETENDING THAT YOU DON'T WANT TO REBUILD IT FROM SCRATCH.
ABOARD THE COLONY AIRSHIP.
WE'RE ON THE VERGE OF THE IMPOSSIBLE. WE'RE CRASHING AN ENTIRE FUTURE DOWN ON THE PRESENT.
I'M NOT KIDDING...EVERY SYSTEM HERE IS WIRED TOGETHER FOR PERFECT EFFICIENCY...

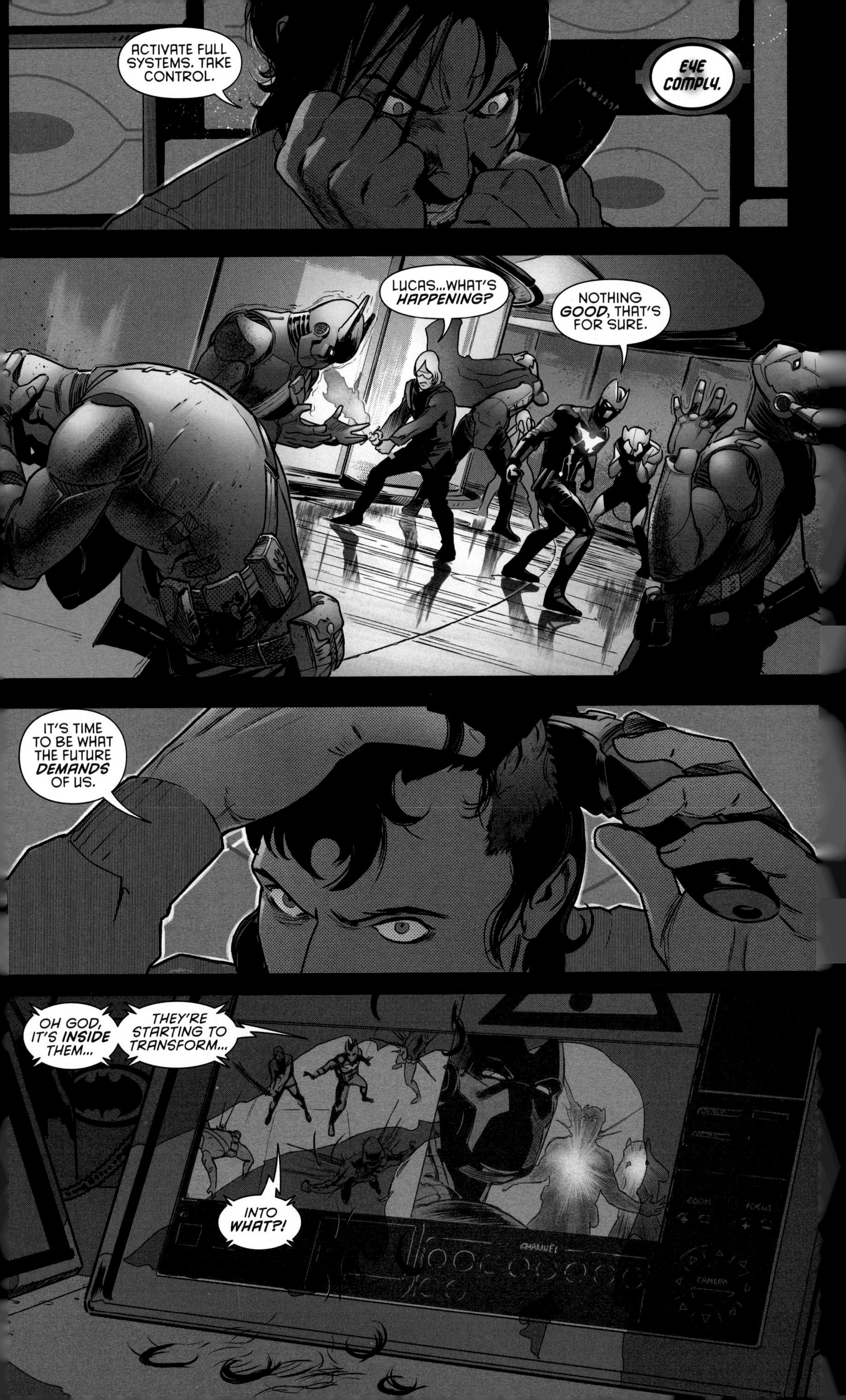
ACTIVATE FULL SYSTEMS. TAKE CONTROL.
EYE COMPLY.
LUCAS...WHAT'S HAPPENING?
NOTHING GOOD, THAT'S FOR SURE.
IT'S TIME TO BE WHAT THE FUTURE DEMANDS OF US.
OH GOD, IT'S INSIDE THEM...
THEY'RE STARTING TO TRANSFORM...
INTO WHAT?!
ZOOM
FOCUS
CHANNEL
CAMERA

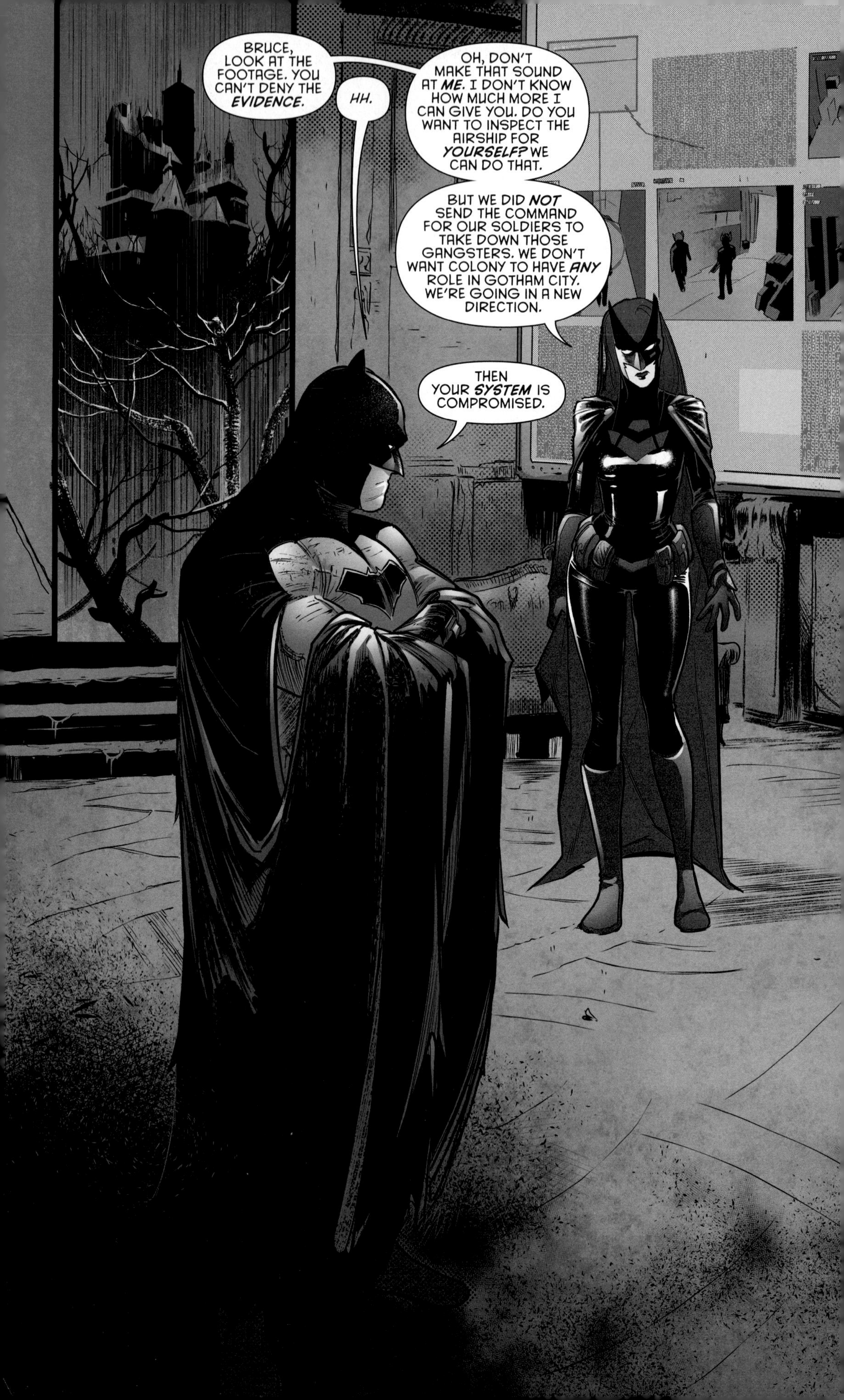

BRUCE, LOOK AT THE FOOTAGE. YOU CAN'T DENY THE *EVIDENCE*.
HH.
OH, DON'T MAKE THAT SOUND AT *ME*. I DON'T KNOW HOW MUCH MORE I CAN GIVE YOU. DO YOU WANT TO INSPECT THE AIRSHIP FOR *YOURSELF?* WE CAN DO THAT.
BUT WE DID *NOT* SEND THE COMMAND FOR OUR SOLDIERS TO TAKE DOWN THOSE GANGSTERS. WE DON'T WANT COLONY TO HAVE *ANY* ROLE IN GOTHAM CITY. WE'RE GOING IN A NEW DIRECTION.
THEN YOUR *SYSTEM* IS COMPROMISED.

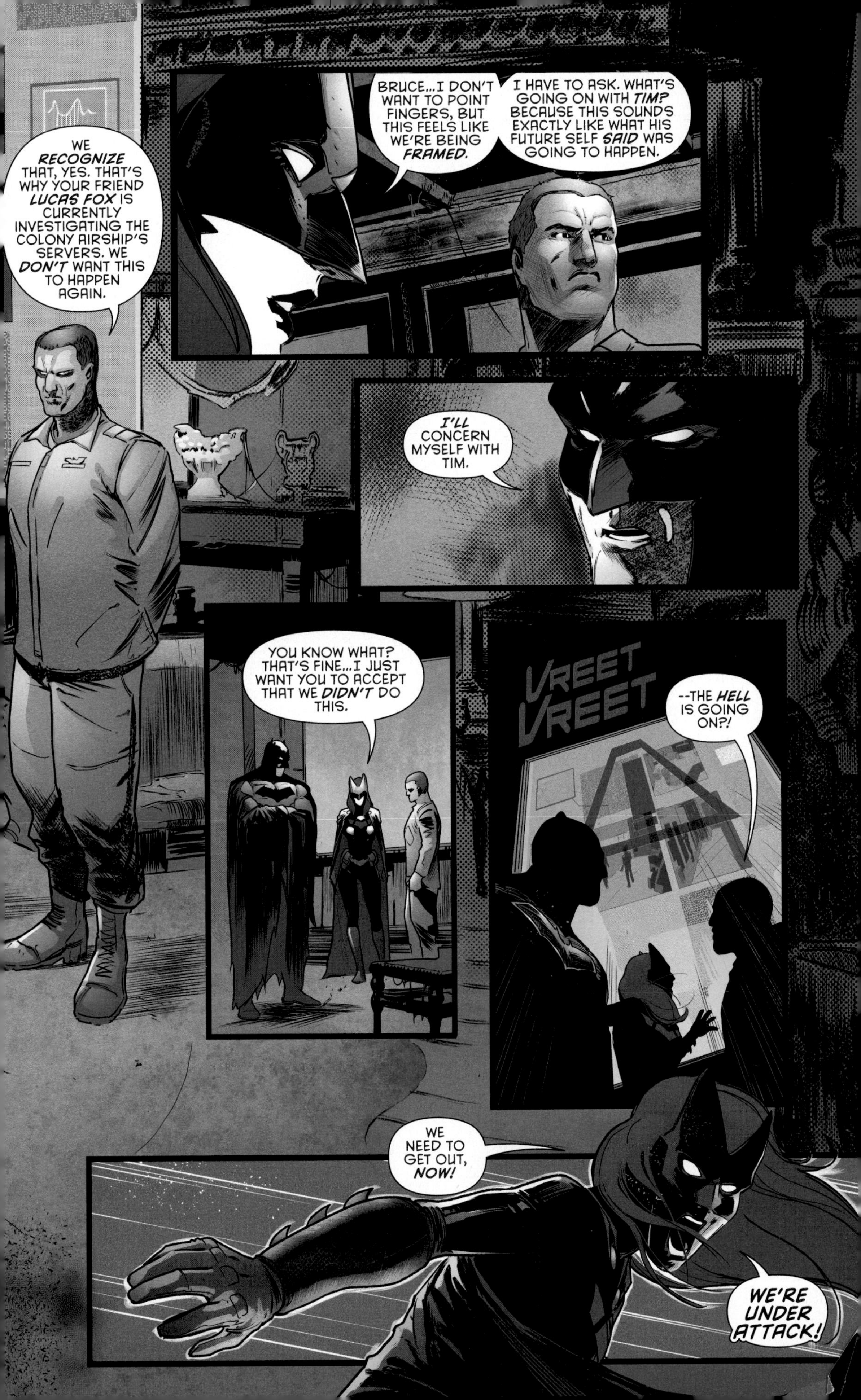

WE *RECOGNIZE* THAT, YES. THAT'S WHY YOUR FRIEND *LUCAS FOX* IS CURRENTLY INVESTIGATING THE COLONY AIRSHIP'S SERVERS. WE *DON'T* WANT THIS TO HAPPEN AGAIN.
BRUCE...I DON'T WANT TO POINT FINGERS, BUT THIS FEELS LIKE WE'RE BEING *FRAMED.*
I HAVE TO ASK. WHAT'S GOING ON WITH *TIM?* BECAUSE THIS SOUNDS EXACTLY LIKE WHAT HIS FUTURE SELF *SAID* WAS GOING TO HAPPEN.
I'LL CONCERN MYSELF WITH TIM.
YOU KNOW WHAT? THAT'S FINE...I JUST WANT YOU TO ACCEPT THAT WE *DIDN'T* DO THIS.
VREET VREET
--THE *HELL* IS GOING ON?!
WE NEED TO GET OUT, *NOW!*
WE'RE UNDER ATTACK!

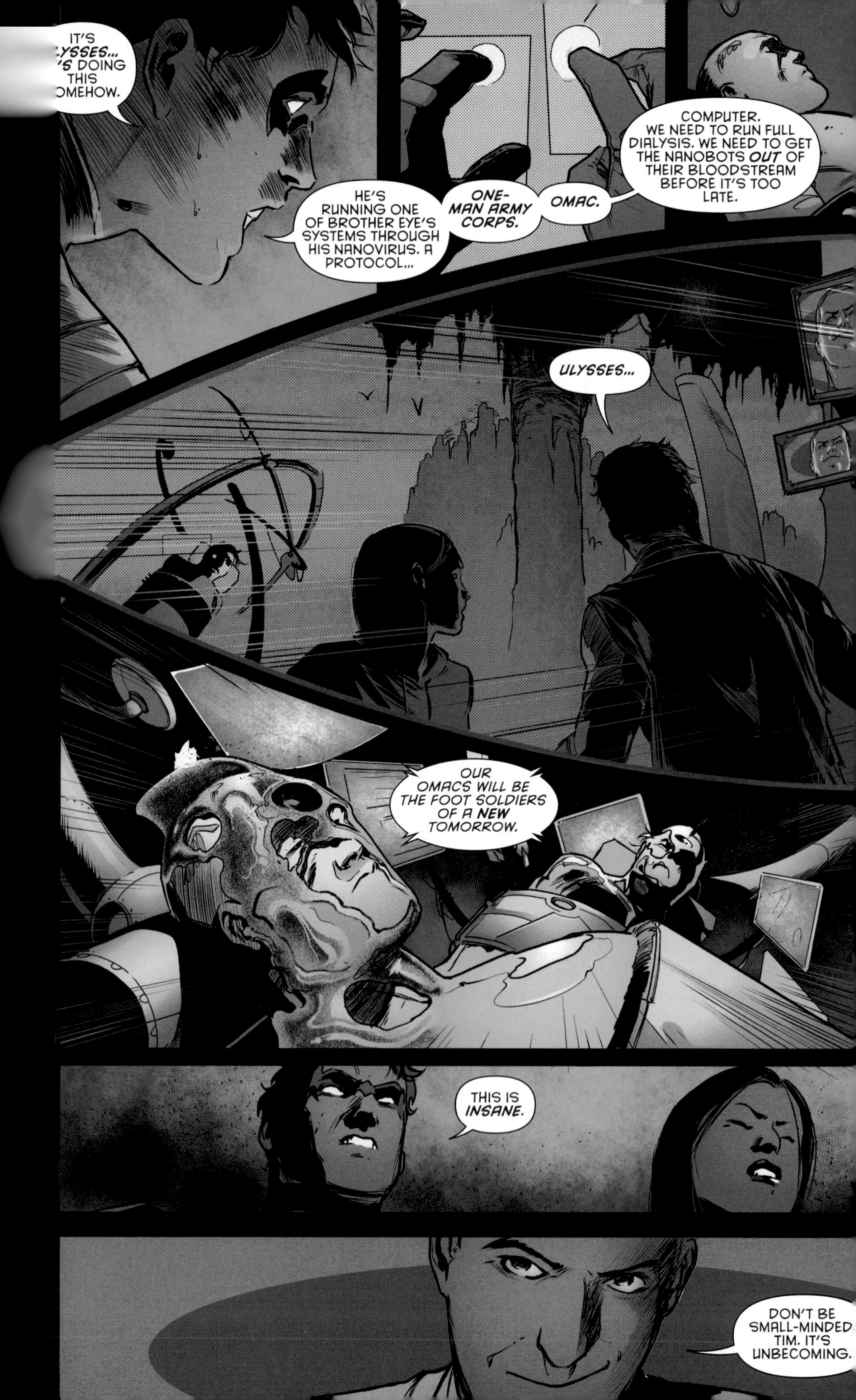
IT'S LYSSES... 'S DOING THIS OMEHOW.
HE'S RUNNING ONE OF BROTHER EYE'S SYSTEMS THROUGH HIS NANOVIRUS. A PROTOCOL...
ONE-MAN ARMY CORPS.
OMAC.
COMPUTER. WE NEED TO RUN FULL DIALYSIS. WE NEED TO GET THE NANOBOTS OUT OF THEIR BLOODSTREAM BEFORE IT'S TOO LATE.
ULYSSES...
OUR OMACS WILL BE THE FOOT SOLDIERS OF A NEW TOMORROW.
THIS IS INSANE.
DON'T BE SMALL-MINDED TIM. IT'S UNBECOMING.

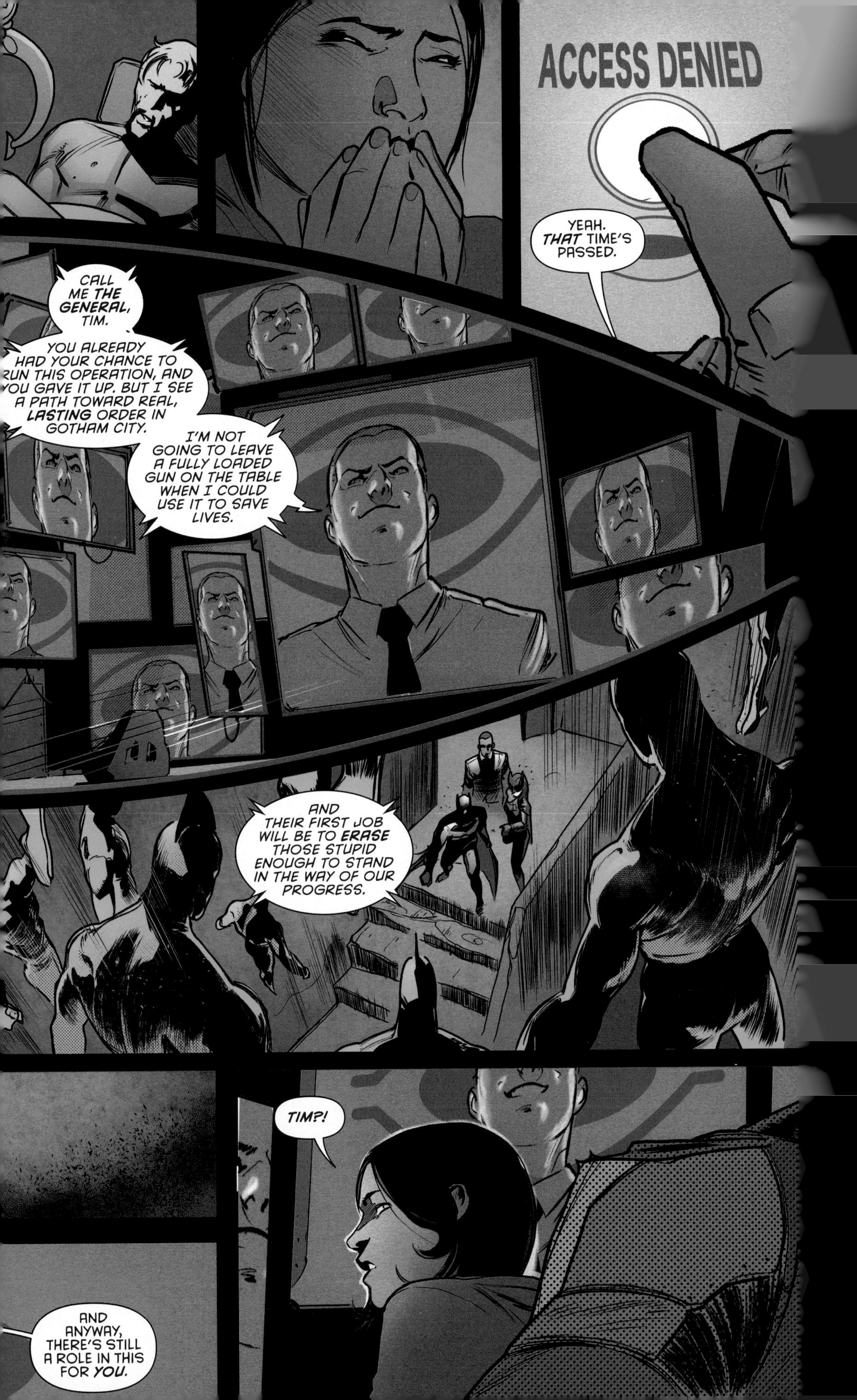
ACCESS DENIED
YEAH. THAT TIME'S PASSED.
CALL ME THE GENERAL, TIM.
YOU ALREADY HAD YOUR CHANCE TO RUN THIS OPERATION, AND YOU GAVE IT UP. BUT I SEE A PATH TOWARD REAL, LASTING ORDER IN GOTHAM CITY.
I'M NOT GOING TO LEAVE A FULLY LOADED GUN ON THE TABLE WHEN I COULD USE IT TO SAVE LIVES.
AND THEIR FIRST JOB WILL BE TO ERASE THOSE STUPID ENOUGH TO STAND IN THE WAY OF OUR PROGRESS.
TIM?!
AND ANYWAY, THERE'S STILL A ROLE IN THIS FOR YOU.

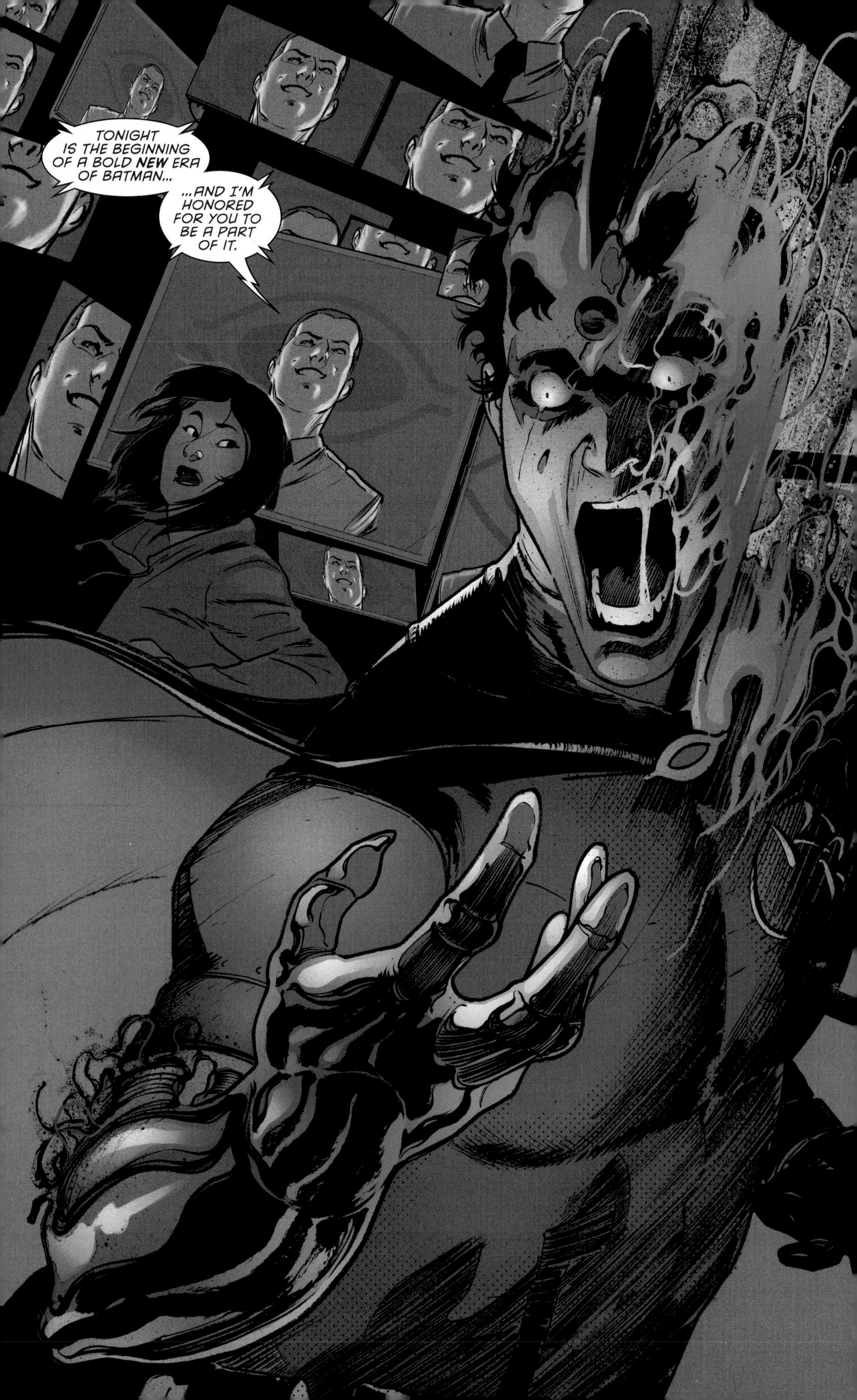
TONIGHT IS THE BEGINNING OF A BOLD NEW ERA OF BATMAN...
...AND I'M HONORED FOR YOU TO BE A PART OF IT.

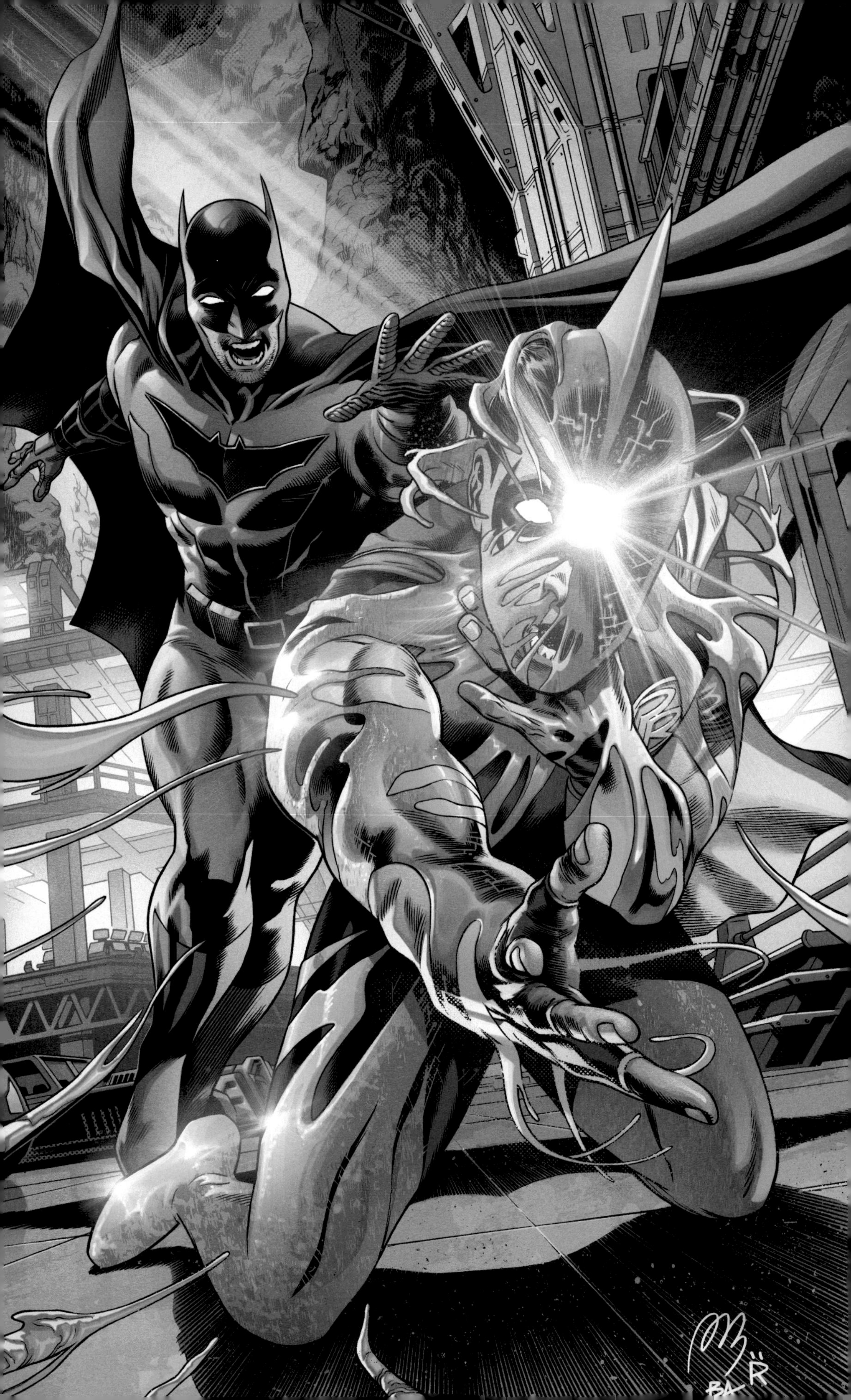

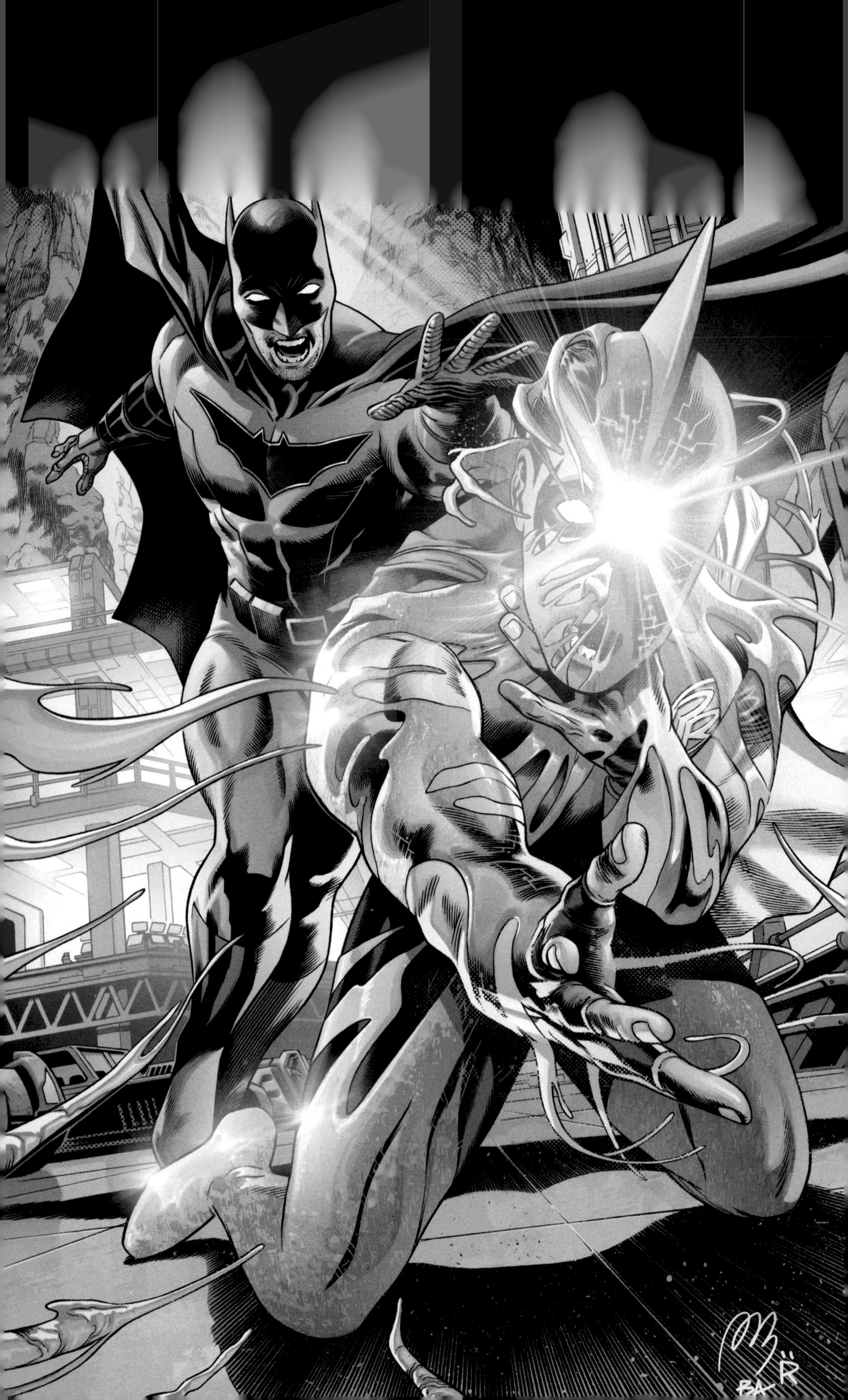

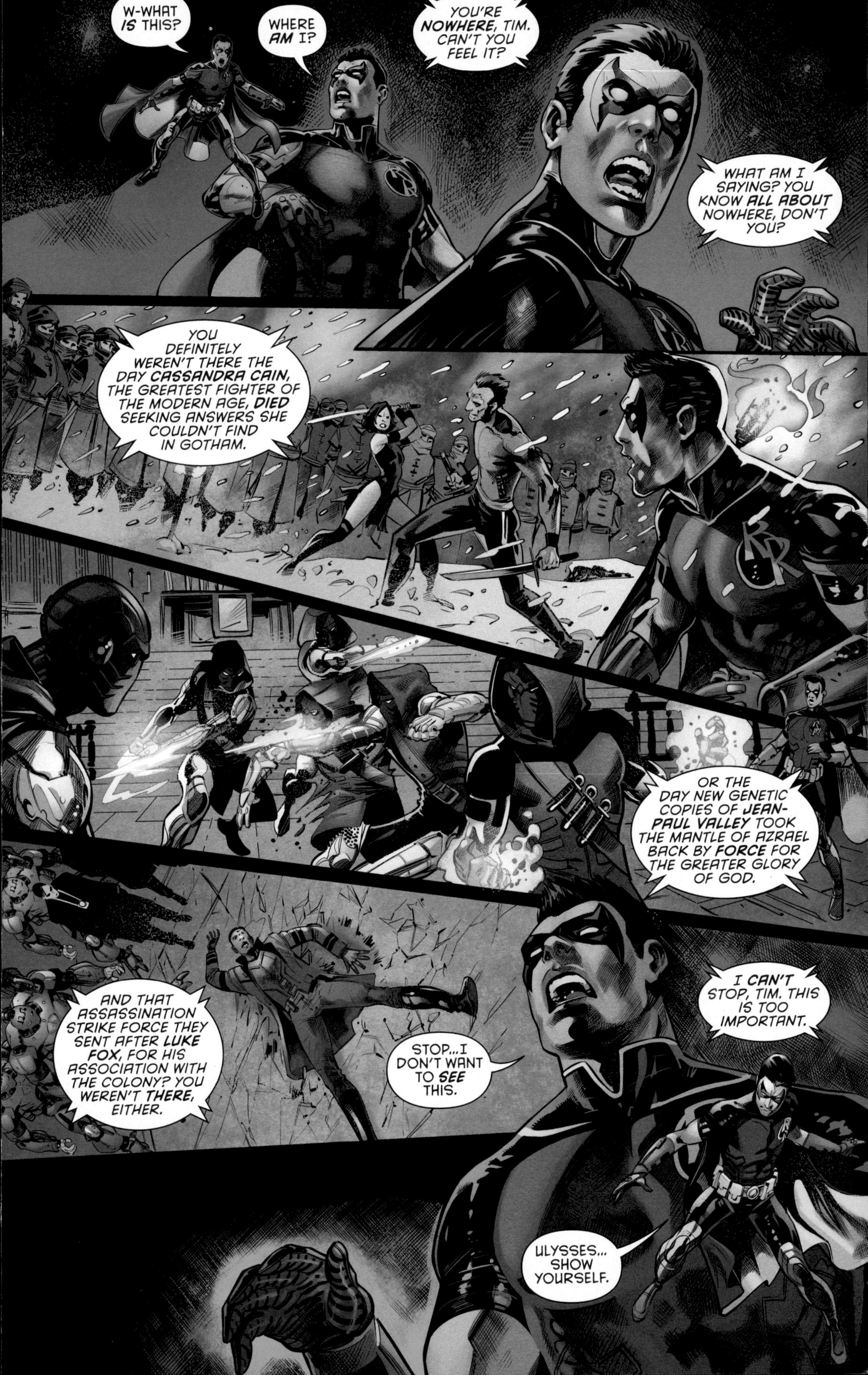

W-WHAT IS THIS?
WHERE AM I?
YOU'RE NOWHERE, TIM. CAN'T YOU FEEL IT?
WHAT AM I SAYING? YOU KNOW ALL ABOUT NOWHERE, DON'T YOU?
YOU DEFINITELY WEREN'T THERE THE DAY CASSANDRA CAIN, THE GREATEST FIGHTER OF THE MODERN AGE, DIED SEEKING ANSWERS SHE COULDN'T FIND IN GOTHAM.
OR THE DAY NEW GENETIC COPIES OF JEAN-PAUL VALLEY TOOK THE MANTLE OF AZRAEL BACK BY FORCE FOR THE GREATER GLORY OF GOD.
AND THAT ASSASSINATION STRIKE FORCE THEY SENT AFTER LUKE FOX, FOR HIS ASSOCIATION WITH THE COLONY? YOU WEREN'T THERE, EITHER.
STOP...I DON'T WANT TO SEE THIS.
I CAN'T STOP, TIM. THIS IS TOO IMPORTANT.
ULYSSES... SHOW YOURSELF.

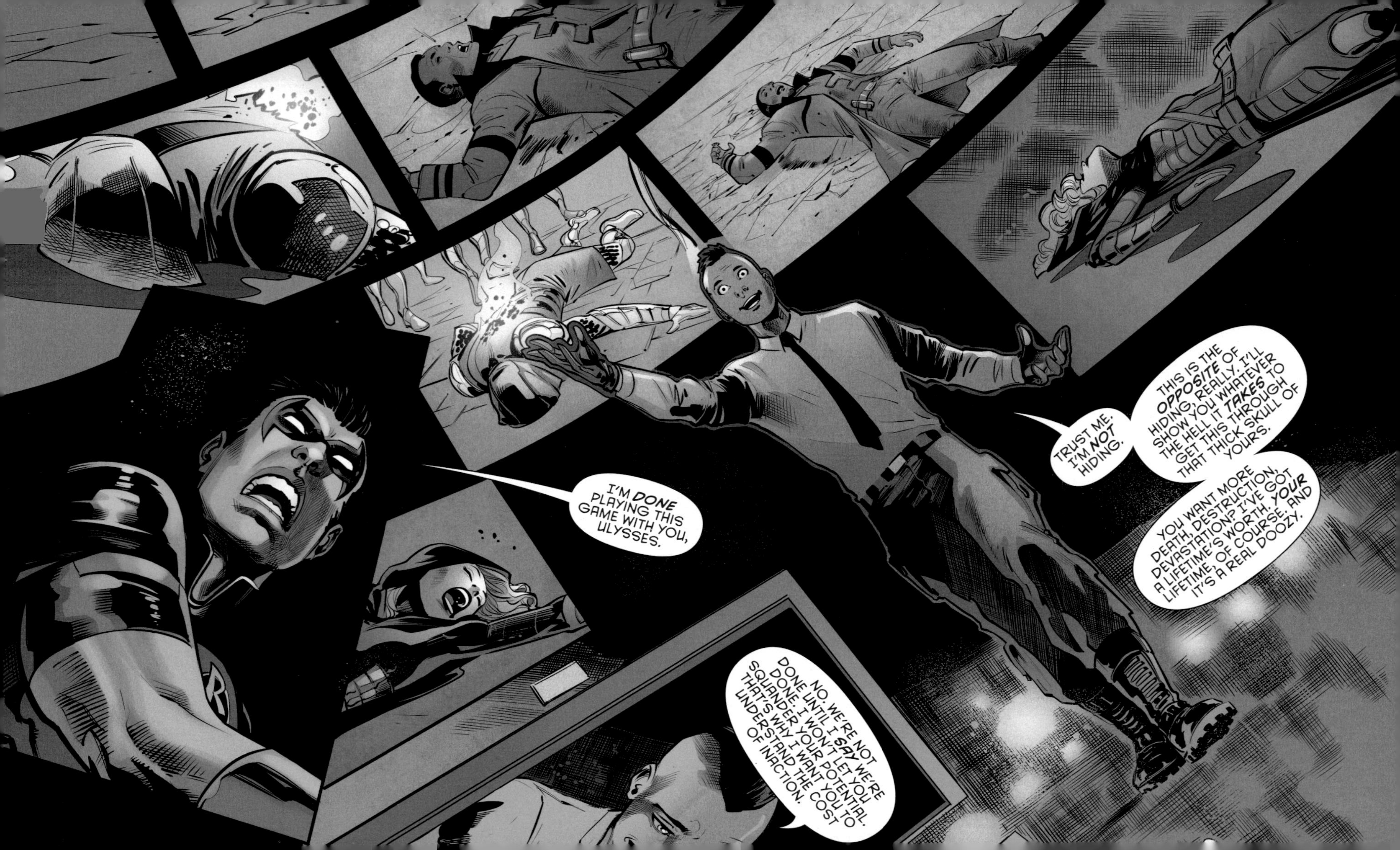
I'M DONE PLAYING THIS GAME WITH YOU, ULYSSES.
TRUST ME. I'M NOT HIDING.
THIS IS THE OPPOSITE OF HIDING, REALLY. I'LL SHOW YOU WHATEVER THE HELL IT TAKES TO GET THIS THROUGH THAT THICK SKULL OF YOURS.
YOU WANT MORE DEATH, DESTRUCTION, DEVASTATION? I'VE GOT A LIFETIME'S WORTH. YOUR LIFETIME, OF COURSE. AND IT'S A REAL DOOZY.
NO. WE'RE NOT DONE UNTIL I SAY WE'RE DONE. I WON'T LET YOU SQUANDER YOUR POTENTIAL. THAT'S WHY I WANT YOU TO UNDERSTAND THE COST OF INACTION.

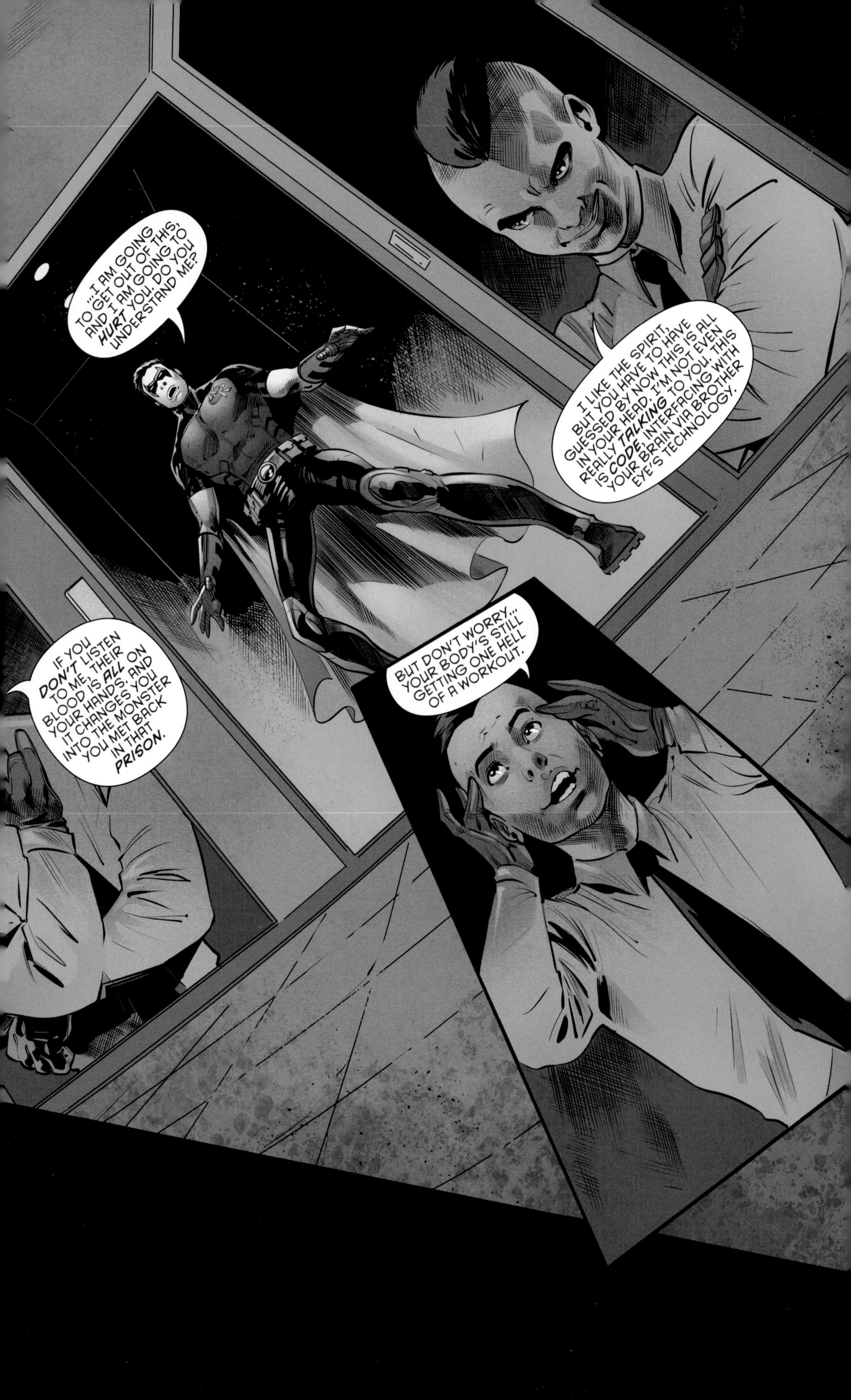
...I AM GOING TO GET OUT OF THIS, AND I AM GOING TO *HURT* YOU. DO YOU UNDERSTAND ME?
I LIKE THE SPIRIT, BUT YOU HAVE TO HAVE GUESSED BY NOW THIS IS ALL IN YOUR HEAD. I'M NOT EVEN REALLY *TALKING* TO YOU. THIS IS *CODE*, INTERFACING WITH YOUR BRAIN VIA BROTHER EYE'S TECHNOLOGY.
BUT DON'T WORRY... YOUR BODY'S STILL GETTING ONE HELL OF A WORKOUT.
IF YOU *DON'T* LISTEN TO ME, THEIR BLOOD IS *ALL* ON YOUR HANDS. AND IT CHANGES YOU INTO THE MONSTER YOU MET BACK IN THAT *PRISON*.

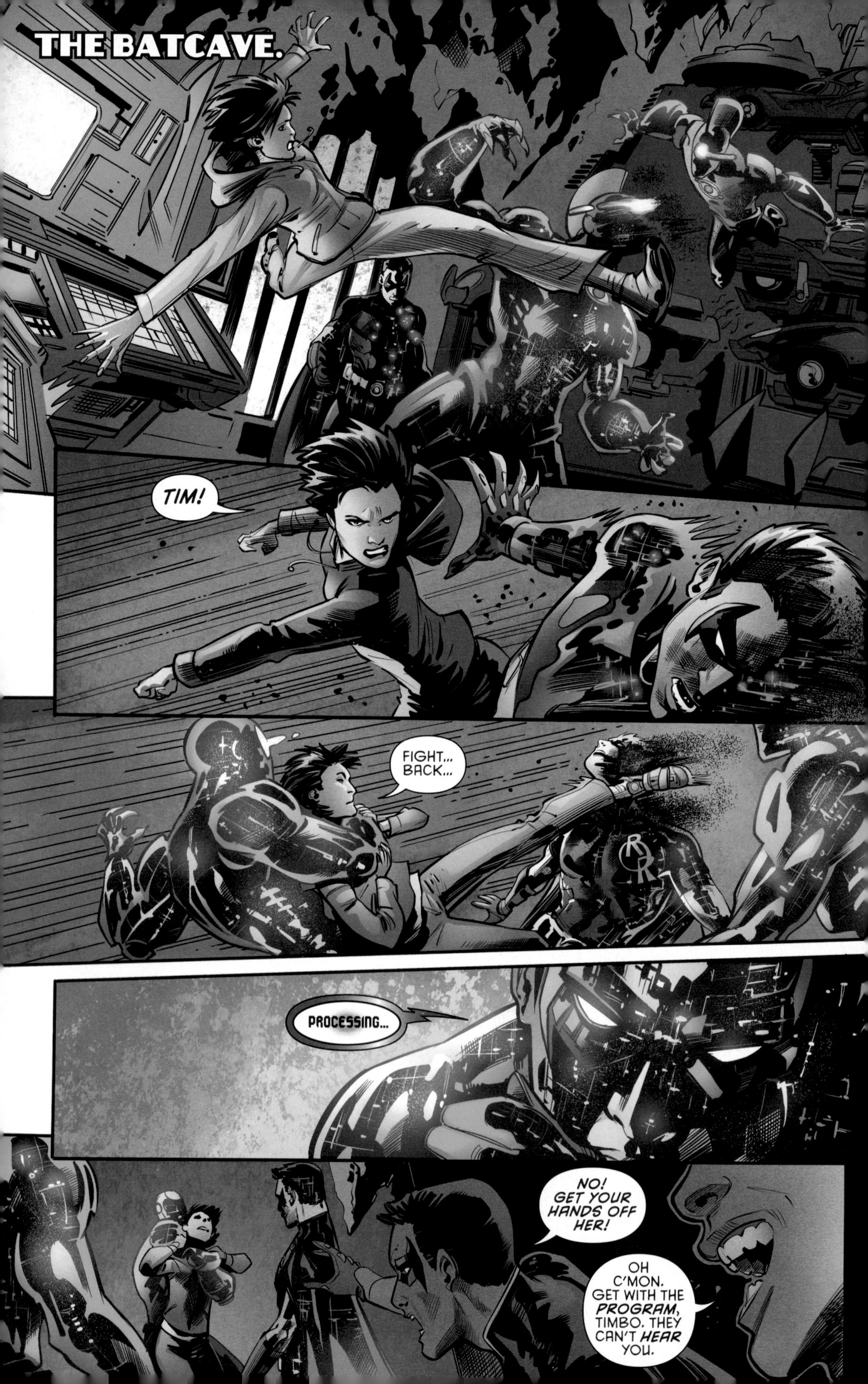
THE BATCAVE.
TIM!
FIGHT... BACK...
PROCESSING...
NO! GET YOUR HANDS OFF HER!
OH C'MON. GET WITH THE PROGRAM, TIMBO. THEY CAN'T HEAR YOU.

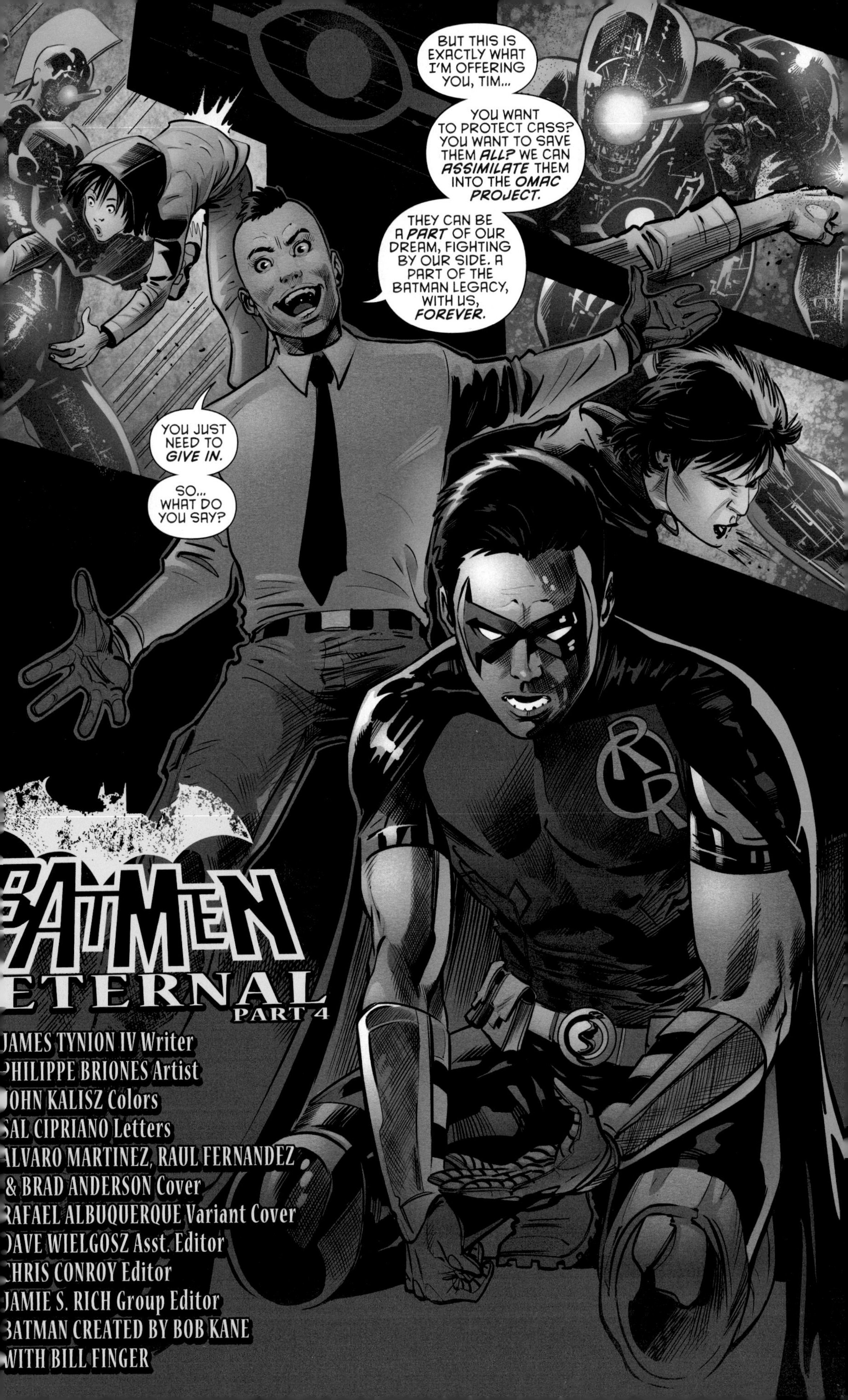

BUT THIS IS EXACTLY WHAT I'M OFFERING YOU, TIM...
YOU WANT TO PROTECT CASS? YOU WANT TO SAVE THEM ALL? WE CAN ASSIMILATE THEM INTO THE OMAC PROJECT.
THEY CAN BE A PART OF OUR DREAM, FIGHTING BY OUR SIDE. A PART OF THE BATMAN LEGACY, WITH US, FOREVER.
YOU JUST NEED TO GIVE IN.
SO... WHAT DO YOU SAY?
BATMEN ETERNAL
PART 4
JAMES TYNION IV Writer
HILIPPE BRIONES Artist
JOHN KALISZ Colors
SAL CIPRIANO Letters
LVARO MARTINEZ, RAUL FERNANDEZ
& BRAD ANDERSON Cover
RAFAEL ALBUQUERQUE Variant Cover
DAVE WIELGOSZ Asst. Editor
CHRIS CONROY Editor
JAMIE S. RICH Group Editor
BATMAN CREATED BY BOB KANE
WITH BILL FINGER

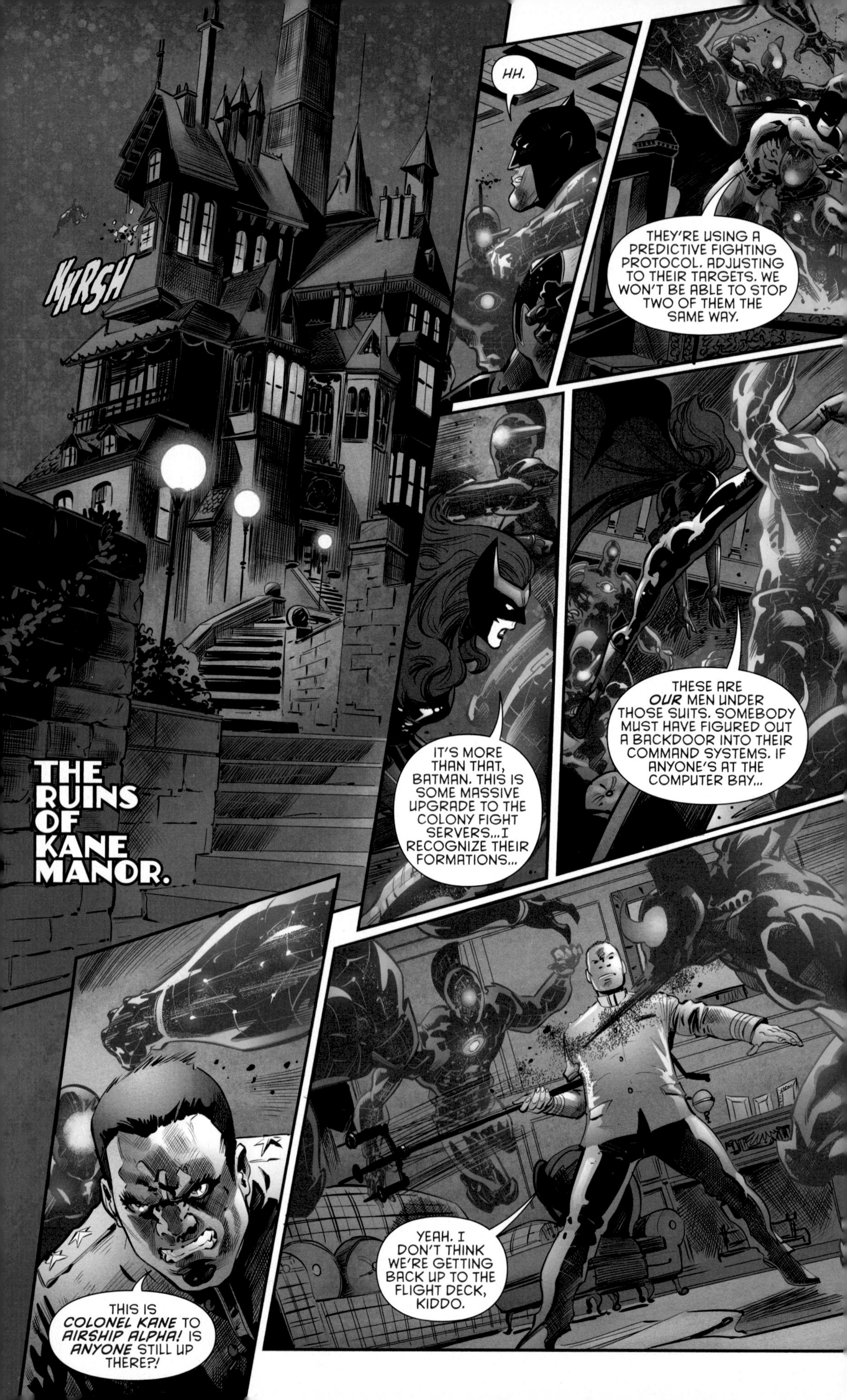
KKRSH
THE RUINS OF KANE MANOR.
HH.
THEY'RE USING A PREDICTIVE FIGHTING PROTOCOL. ADJUSTING TO THEIR TARGETS. WE WON'T BE ABLE TO STOP TWO OF THEM THE SAME WAY.
IT'S MORE THAN THAT, BATMAN. THIS IS SOME MASSIVE UPGRADE TO THE COLONY FIGHT SERVERS...I RECOGNIZE THEIR FORMATIONS...
THESE ARE OUR MEN UNDER THOSE SUITS. SOMEBODY MUST HAVE FIGURED OUT A BACKDOOR INTO THEIR COMMAND SYSTEMS. IF ANYONE'S AT THE COMPUTER BAY...
THIS IS COLONEL KANE TO AIRSHIP ALPHA! IS ANYONE STILL UP THERE?!
YEAH. I DON'T THINK WE'RE GETTING BACK UP TO THE FLIGHT DECK, KIDDO.

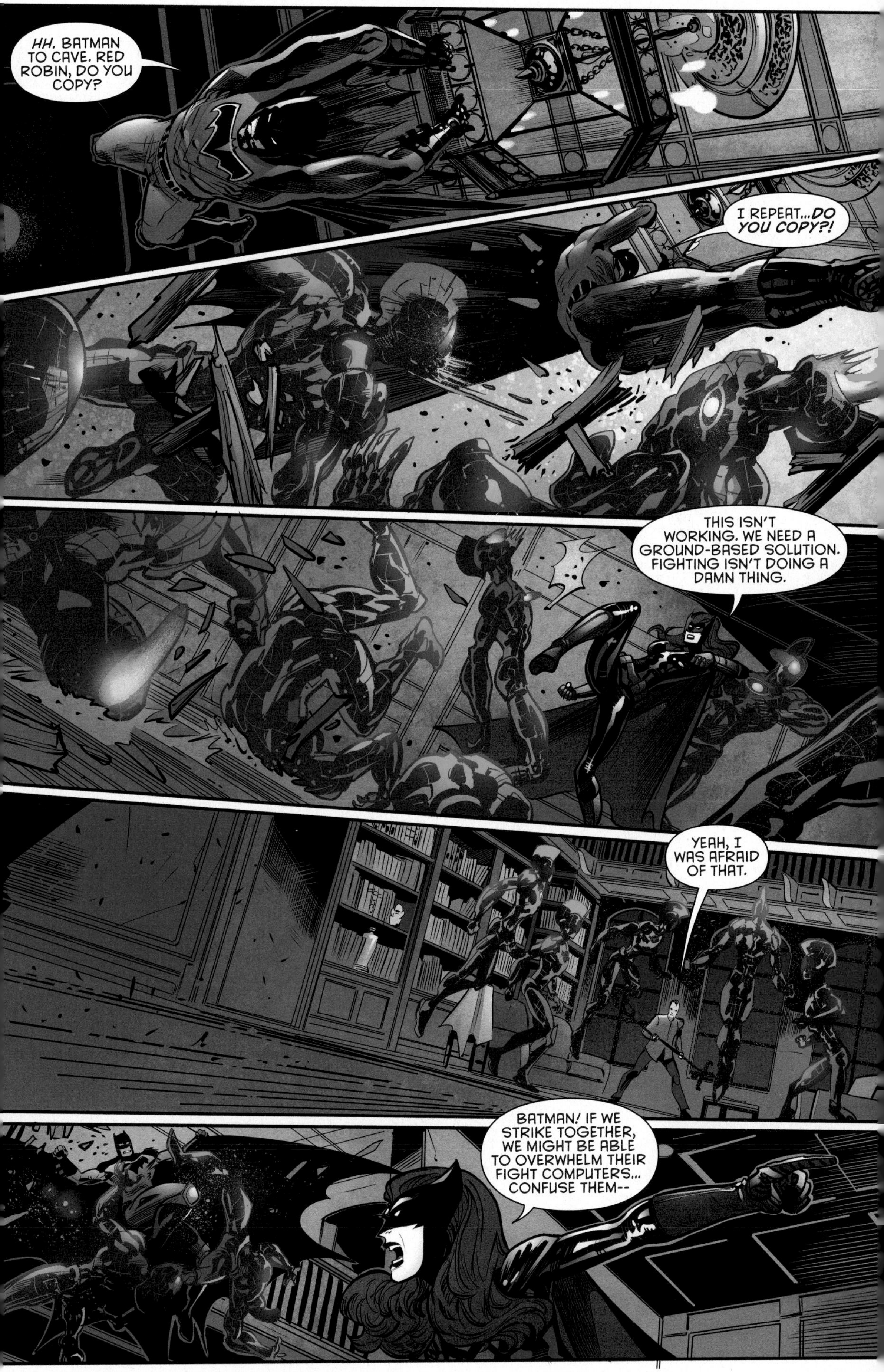
HH. BATMAN TO CAVE. RED ROBIN, DO YOU COPY?
I REPEAT...DO YOU COPY?!
THIS ISN'T WORKING. WE NEED A GROUND-BASED SOLUTION. FIGHTING ISN'T DOING A DAMN THING.
YEAH, I WAS AFRAID OF THAT.
BATMAN! IF WE STRIKE TOGETHER, WE MIGHT BE ABLE TO OVERWHELM THEIR FIGHT COMPUTERS... CONFUSE THEM--

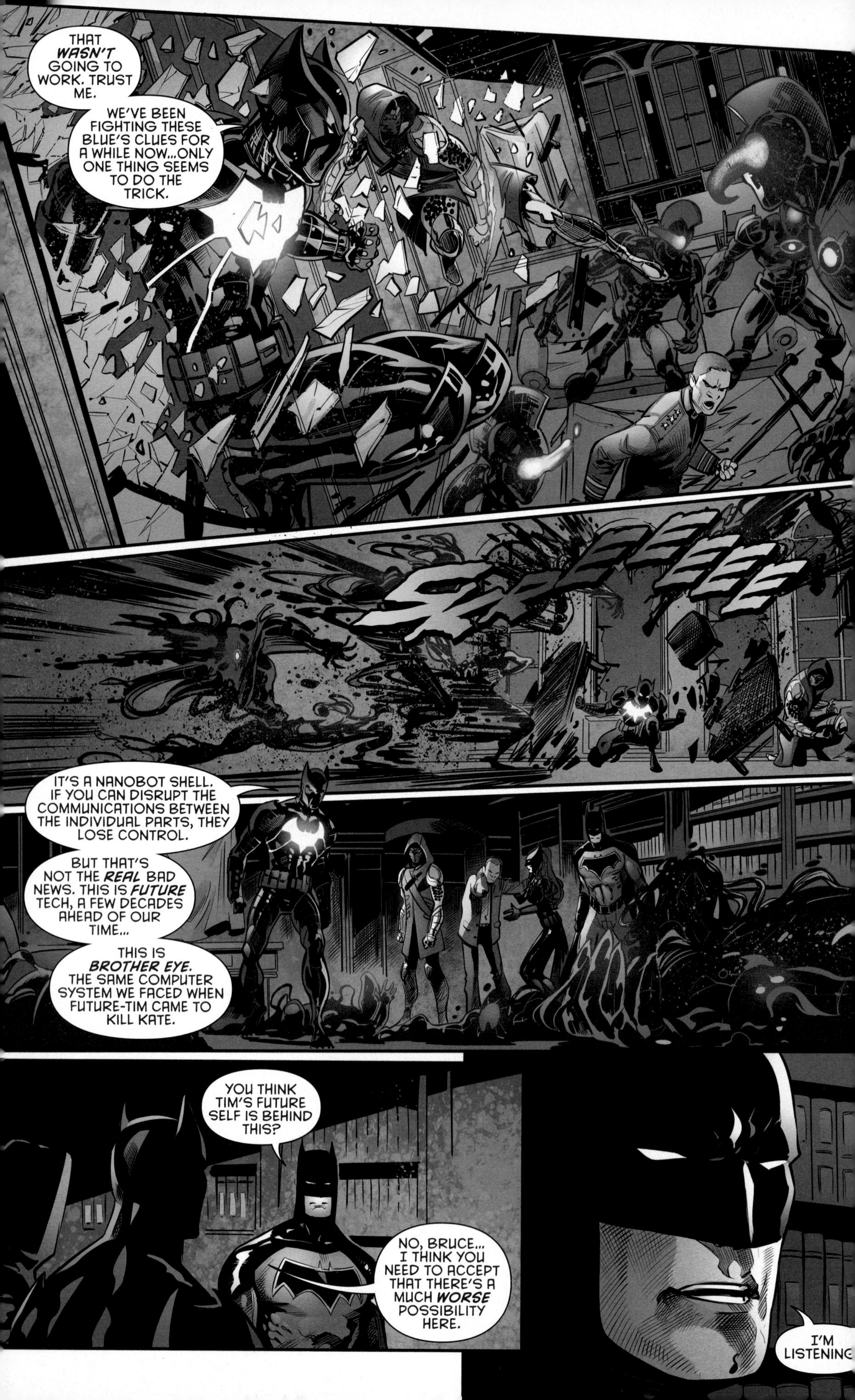
THAT WASN'T GOING TO WORK. TRUST ME.
WE'VE BEEN FIGHTING THESE BLUE'S CLUES FOR A WHILE NOW...ONLY ONE THING SEEMS TO DO THE TRICK.
SKKREEEE
IT'S A NANOBOT SHELL. IF YOU CAN DISRUPT THE COMMUNICATIONS BETWEEN THE INDIVIDUAL PARTS, THEY LOSE CONTROL.
BUT THAT'S NOT THE REAL BAD NEWS. THIS IS FUTURE TECH, A FEW DECADES AHEAD OF OUR TIME...
THIS IS BROTHER EYE. THE SAME COMPUTER SYSTEM WE FACED WHEN FUTURE-TIM CAME TO KILL KATE.
YOU THINK TIM'S FUTURE SELF IS BEHIND THIS?
NO, BRUCE... I THINK YOU NEED TO ACCEPT THAT THERE'S A MUCH WORSE POSSIBILITY HERE.
I'M LISTENING

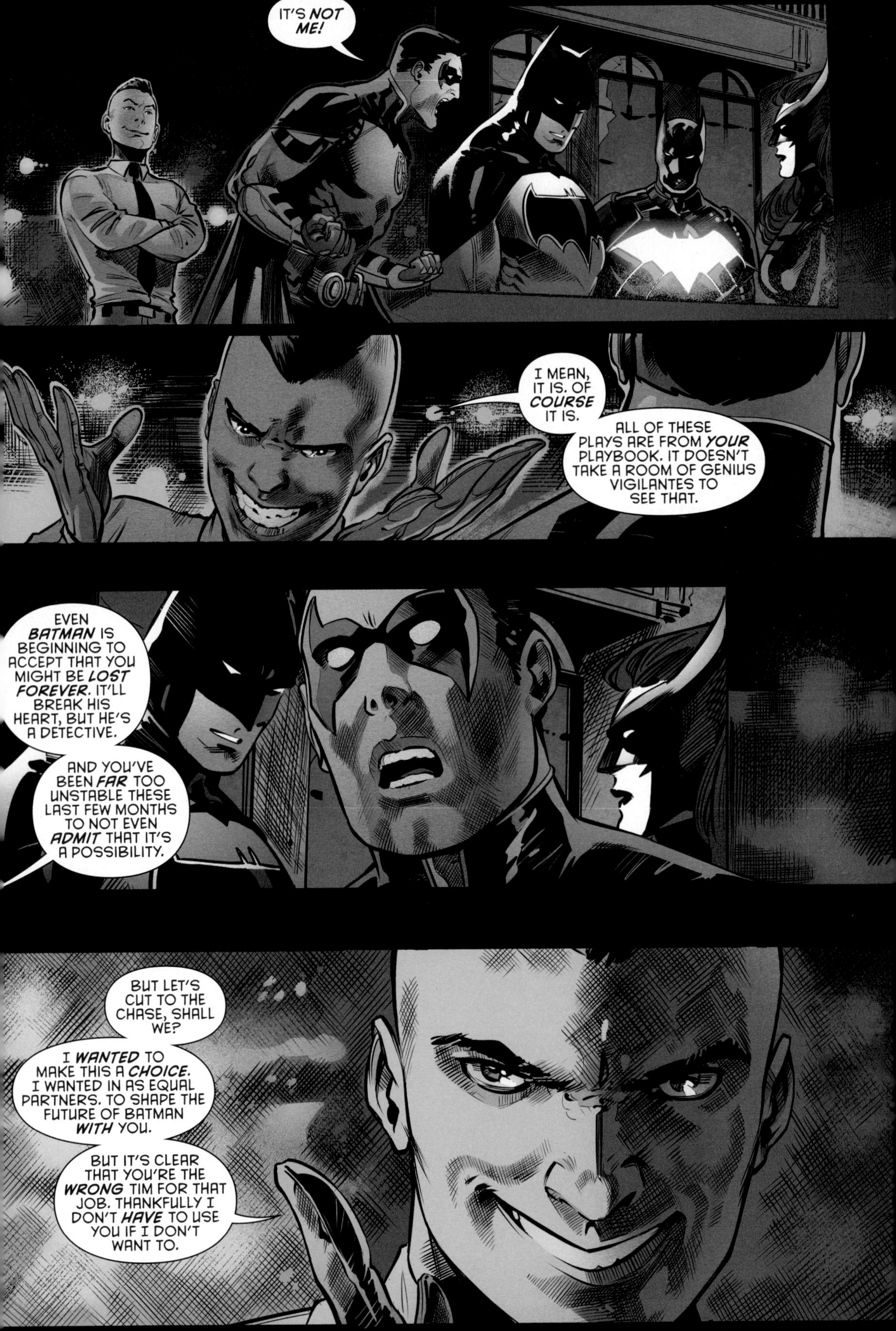
IT'S NOT ME!
I MEAN, IT IS. OF COURSE IT IS.
ALL OF THESE PLAYS ARE FROM YOUR PLAYBOOK. IT DOESN'T TAKE A ROOM OF GENIUS VIGILANTES TO SEE THAT.
EVEN BATMAN IS BEGINNING TO ACCEPT THAT YOU MIGHT BE LOST FOREVER. IT'LL BREAK HIS HEART, BUT HE'S A DETECTIVE.
AND YOU'VE BEEN FAR TOO UNSTABLE THESE LAST FEW MONTHS TO NOT EVEN ADMIT THAT IT'S A POSSIBILITY.
BUT LET'S CUT TO THE CHASE, SHALL WE?
I WANTED TO MAKE THIS A CHOICE. I WANTED IN AS EQUAL PARTNERS. TO SHAPE THE FUTURE OF BATMAN WITH YOU.
BUT IT'S CLEAR THAT YOU'RE THE WRONG TIM FOR THAT JOB. THANKFULLY I DON'T HAVE TO USE YOU IF I DON'T WANT TO.

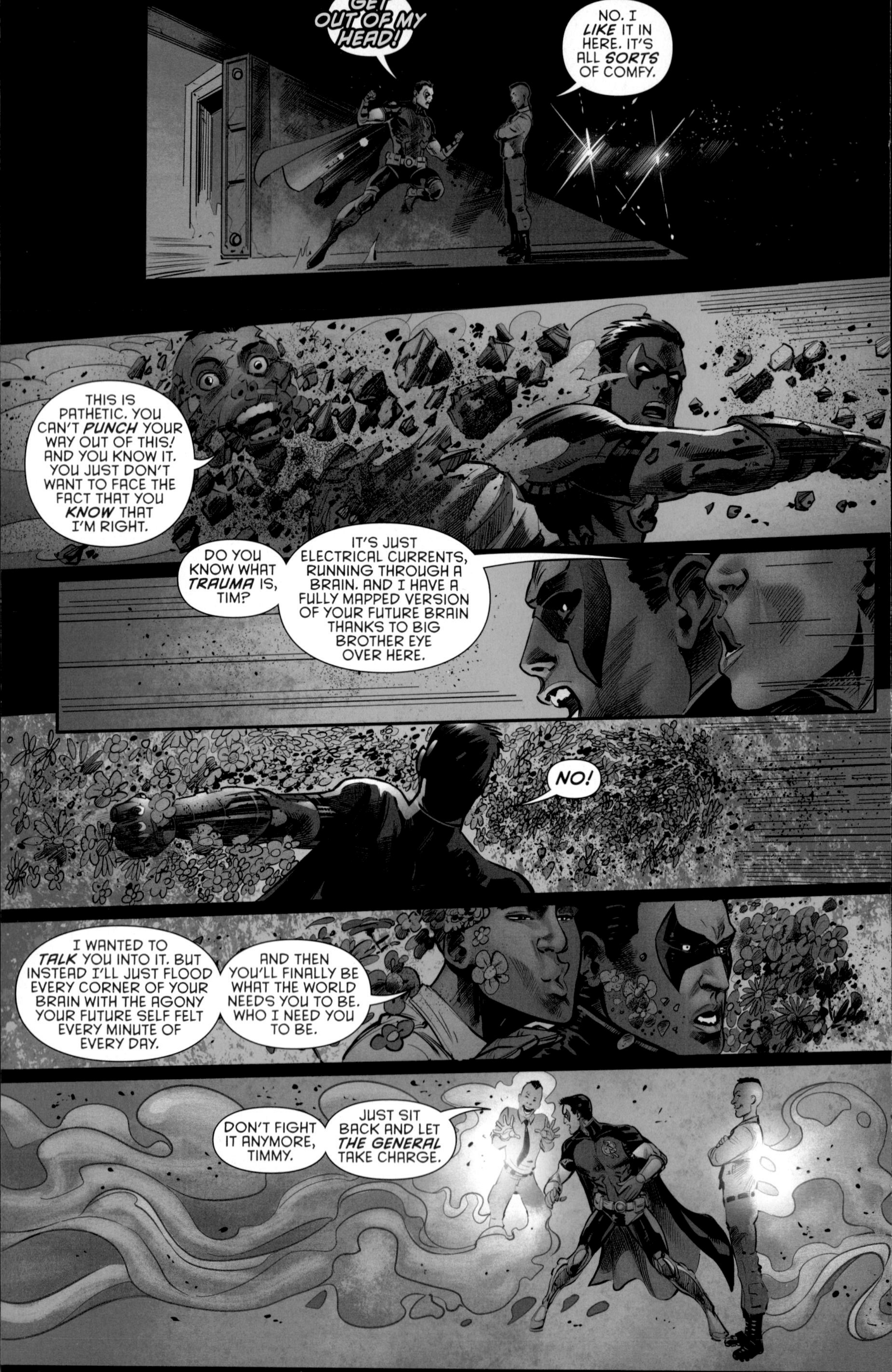
GET OUT OF MY HEAD!
NO. I LIKE IT IN HERE. IT'S ALL SORTS OF COMFY.
THIS IS PATHETIC. YOU CAN'T PUNCH YOUR WAY OUT OF THIS! AND YOU KNOW IT. YOU JUST DON'T WANT TO FACE THE FACT THAT YOU KNOW THAT I'M RIGHT.
DO YOU KNOW WHAT TRAUMA IS, TIM?
IT'S JUST ELECTRICAL CURRENTS, RUNNING THROUGH A BRAIN. AND I HAVE A FULLY MAPPED VERSION OF YOUR FUTURE BRAIN THANKS TO BIG BROTHER EYE OVER HERE.
NO!
I WANTED TO TALK YOU INTO IT. BUT INSTEAD I'LL JUST FLOOD EVERY CORNER OF YOUR BRAIN WITH THE AGONY YOUR FUTURE SELF FELT EVERY MINUTE OF EVERY DAY.
AND THEN YOU'LL FINALLY BE WHAT THE WORLD NEEDS YOU TO BE. WHO I NEED YOU TO BE.
DON'T FIGHT IT ANYMORE, TIMMY.
JUST SIT BACK AND LET THE GENERAL TAKE CHARGE.

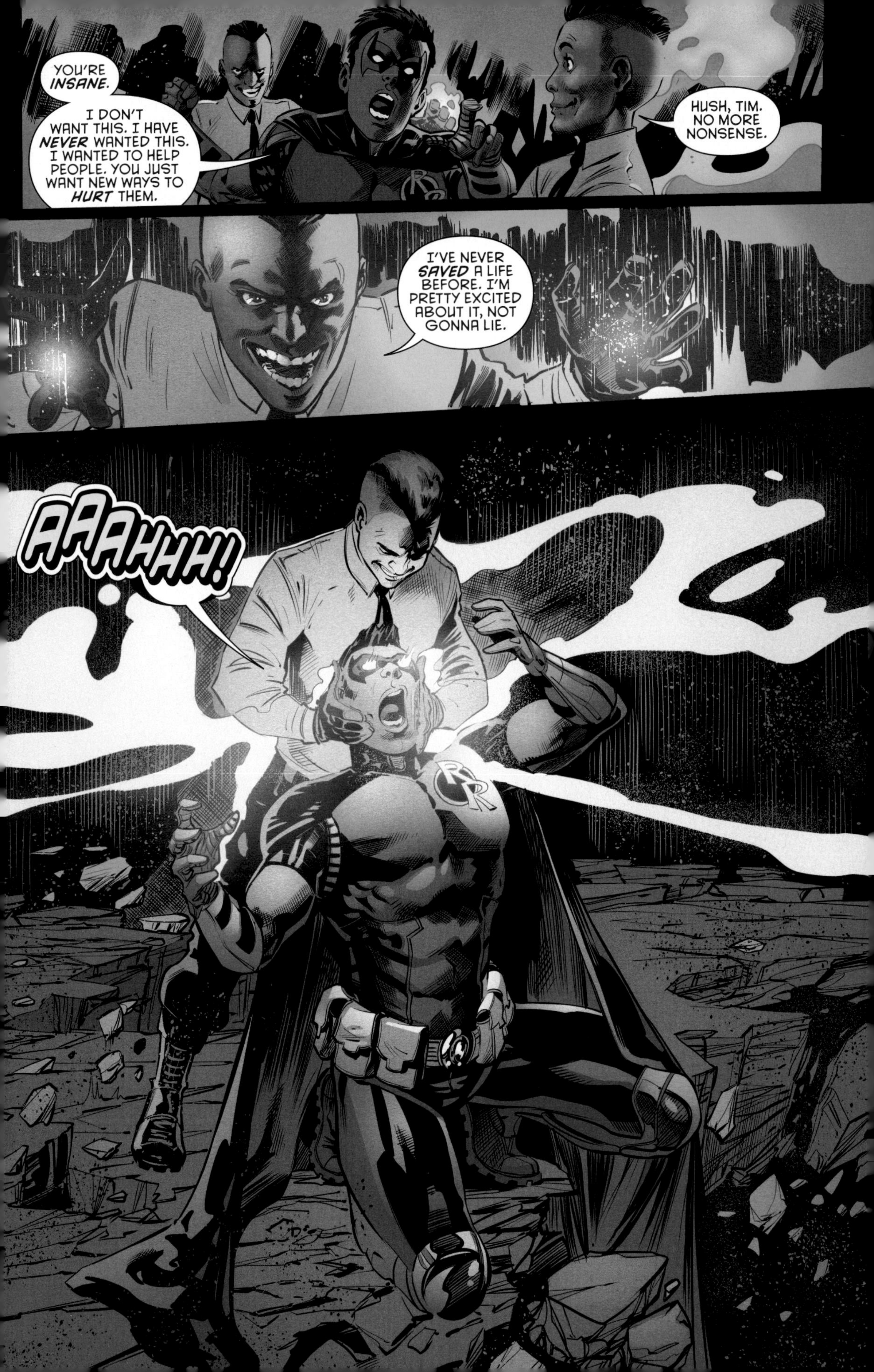
YOU'RE INSANE.
I DON'T WANT THIS. I HAVE NEVER WANTED THIS. I WANTED TO HELP PEOPLE. YOU JUST WANT NEW WAYS TO HURT THEM.
HUSH, TIM. NO MORE NONSENSE.
I'VE NEVER SAVED A LIFE BEFORE. I'M PRETTY EXCITED ABOUT IT, NOT GONNA LIE.
AAAHHHH!

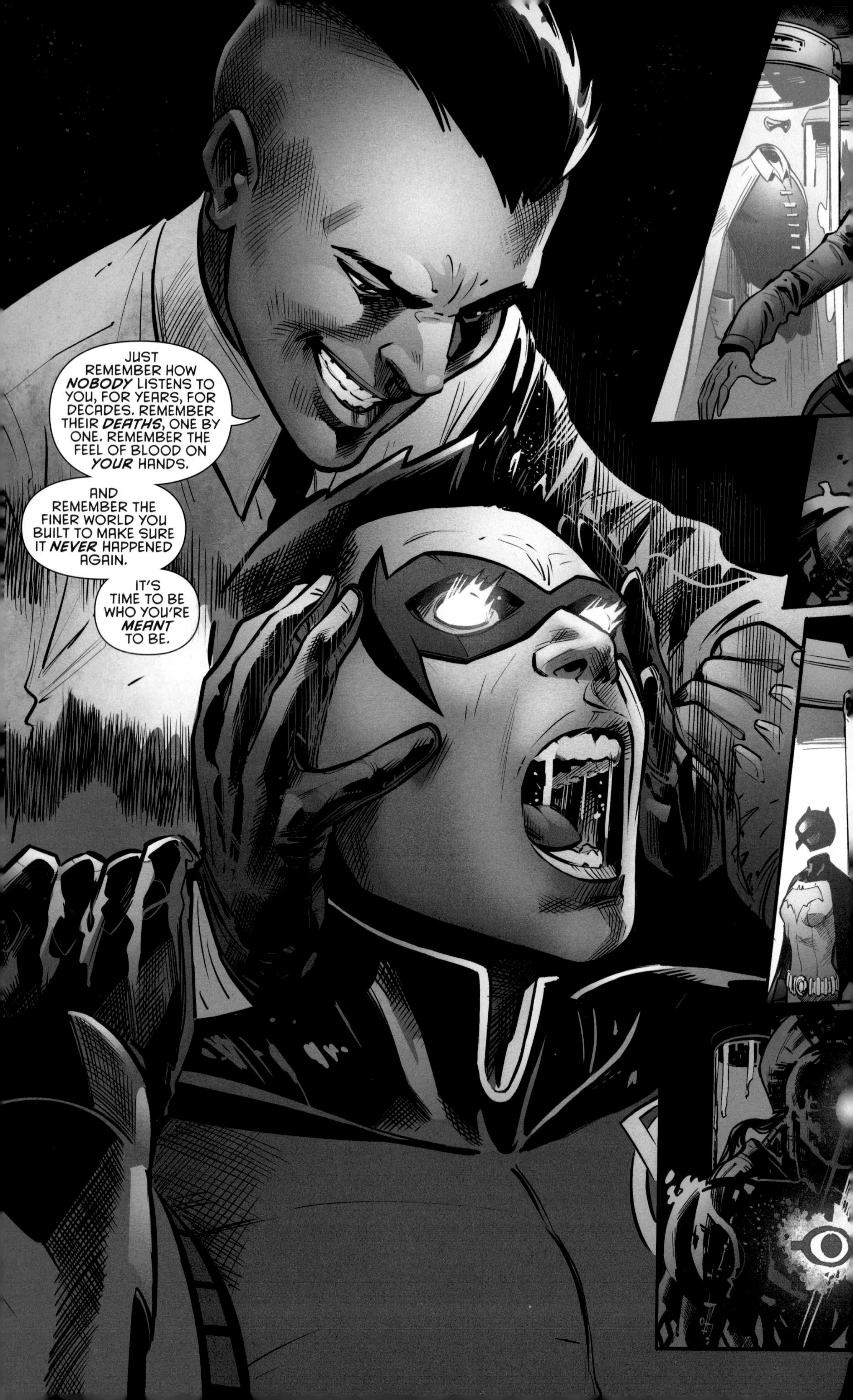
JUST REMEMBER HOW NOBODY LISTENS TO YOU, FOR YEARS, FOR DECADES. REMEMBER THEIR DEATHS, ONE BY ONE. REMEMBER THE FEEL OF BLOOD ON YOUR HANDS.
AND REMEMBER THE FINER WORLD YOU BUILT TO MAKE SURE IT NEVER HAPPENED AGAIN.
IT'S TIME TO BE WHO YOU'RE MEANT TO BE.

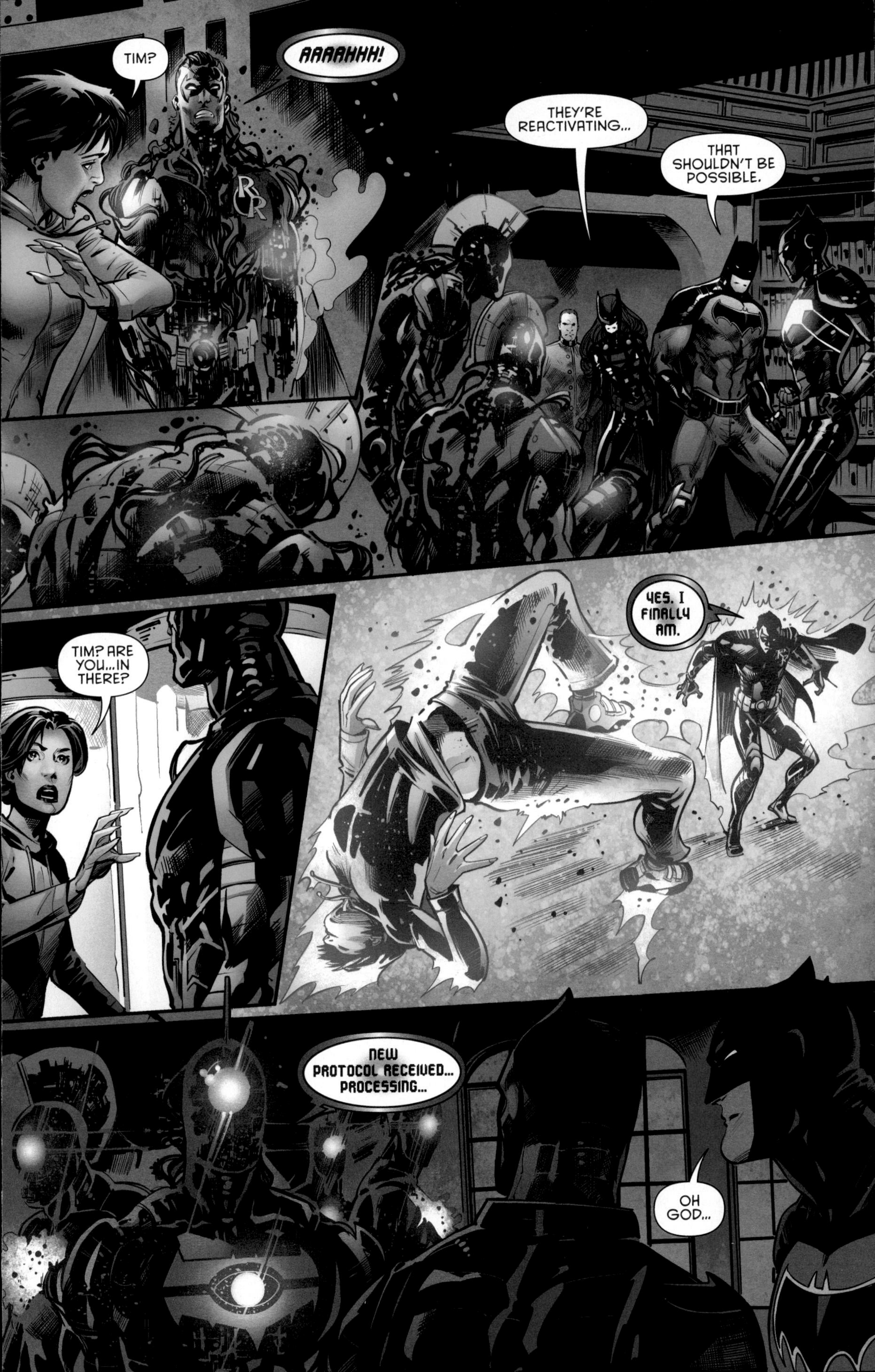
TIM?
AAAAHHH!
THEY'RE REACTIVATING...
THAT SHOULDN'T BE POSSIBLE.
TIM? ARE YOU...IN THERE?
YES. I FINALLY AM.
NEW PROTOCOL RECEIVED... PROCESSING...
OH GOD...

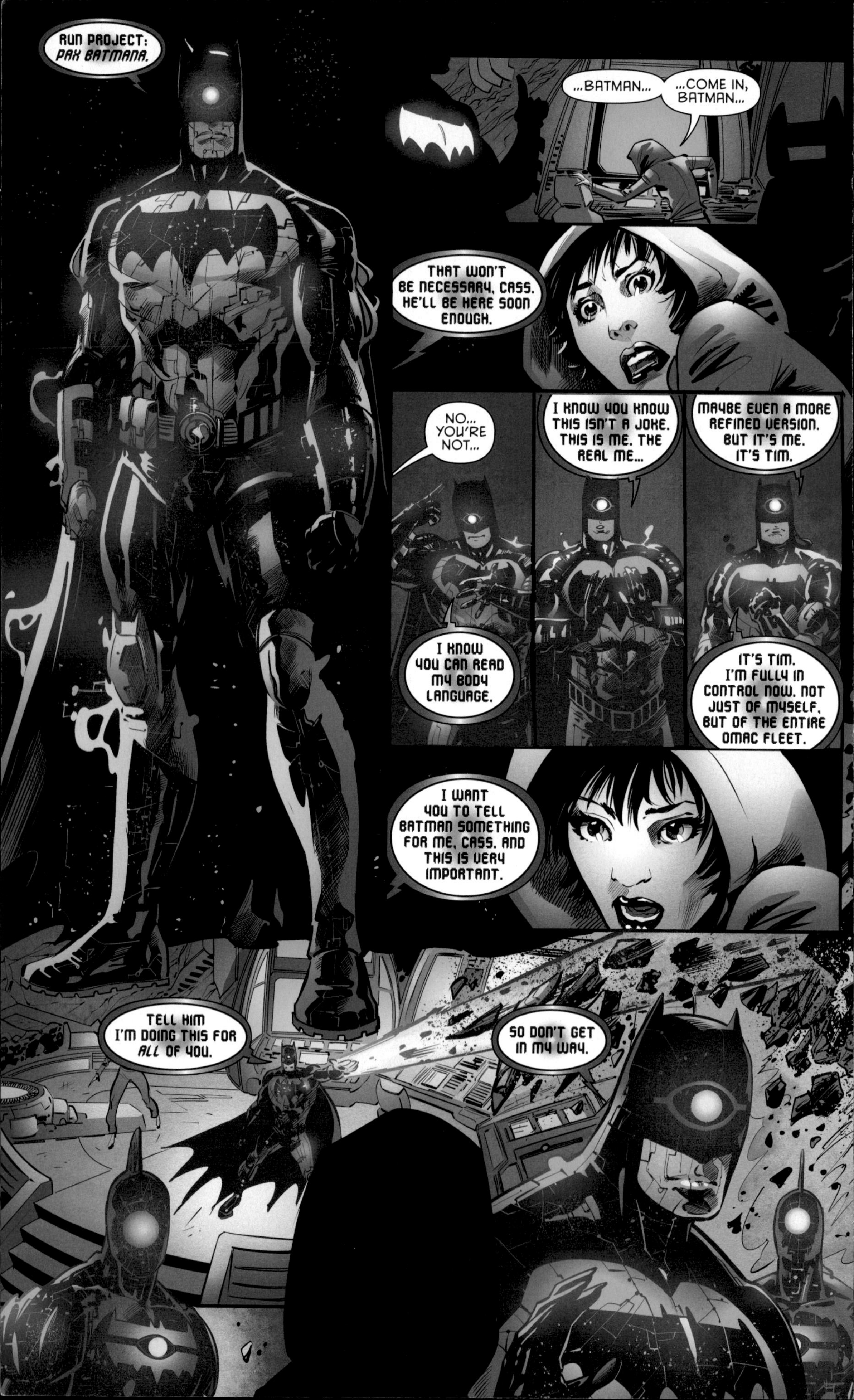
RUN PROJECT: PAX BATMANA.
...BATMAN...
...COME IN, BATMAN...
THAT WON'T BE NECESSARY, CASS. HE'LL BE HERE SOON ENOUGH.
NO... YOU'RE NOT...
I KNOW YOU CAN READ MY BODY LANGUAGE.
I KNOW YOU KNOW THIS ISN'T A JOKE. THIS IS ME. THE REAL ME...
MAYBE EVEN A MORE REFINED VERSION. BUT IT'S ME. IT'S TIM.
IT'S TIM. I'M FULLY IN CONTROL NOW. NOT JUST OF MYSELF, BUT OF THE ENTIRE OMAC FLEET.
I WANT YOU TO TELL BATMAN SOMETHING FOR ME, CASS. AND THIS IS VERY IMPORTANT.
TELL HIM I'M DOING THIS FOR ALL OF YOU.
SO DON'T GET IN MY WAY.

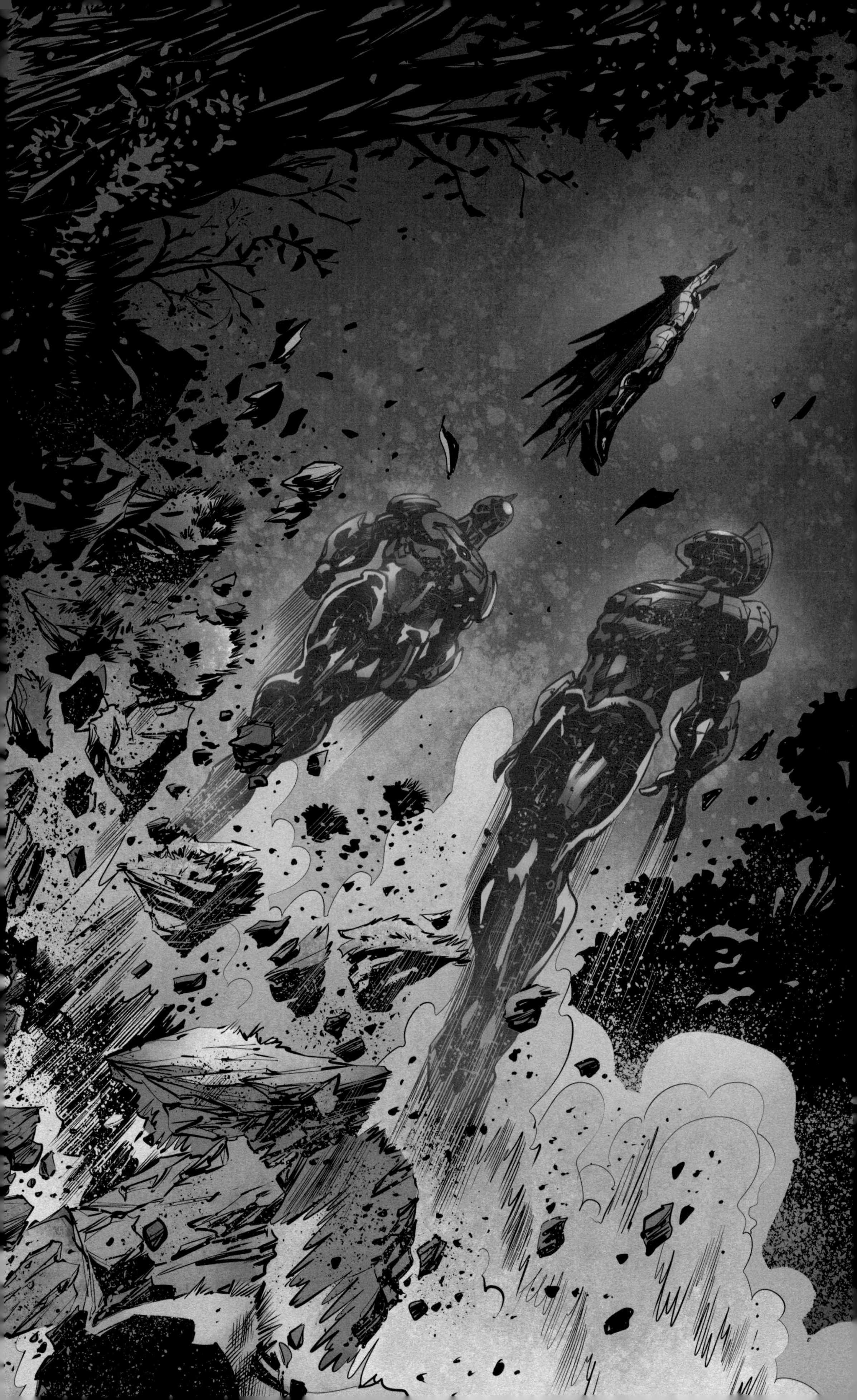

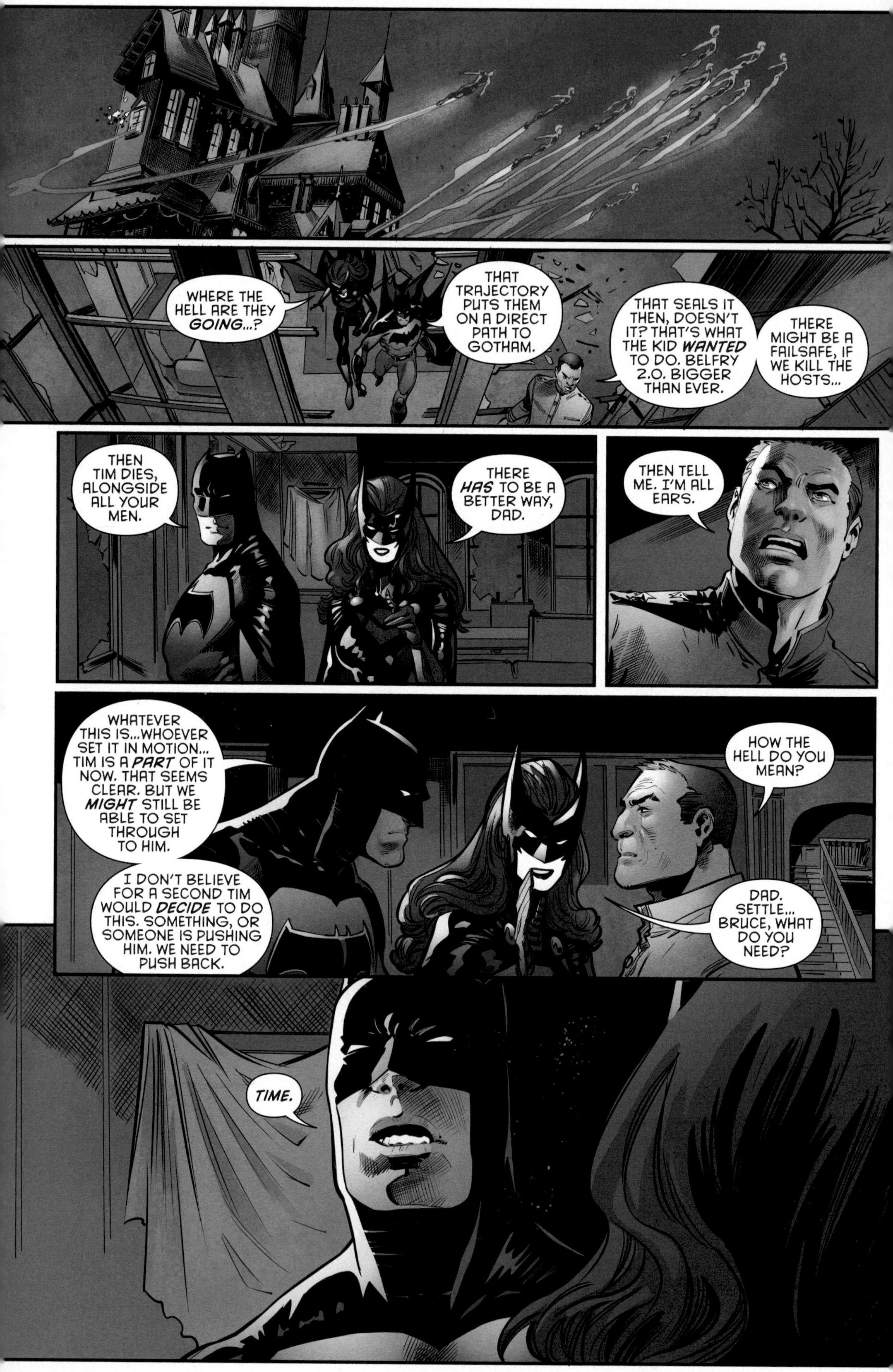

WHERE THE HELL ARE THEY GOING...?
THAT TRAJECTORY PUTS THEM ON A DIRECT PATH TO GOTHAM.
THAT SEALS IT THEN, DOESN'T IT? THAT'S WHAT THE KID WANTED TO DO. BELFRY 2.0. BIGGER THAN EVER.
THERE MIGHT BE A FAILSAFE, IF WE KILL THE HOSTS...
THEN TIM DIES, ALONGSIDE ALL YOUR MEN.
THERE HAS TO BE A BETTER WAY, DAD.
THEN TELL ME. I'M ALL EARS.
WHATEVER THIS IS...WHOEVER SET IT IN MOTION... TIM IS A PART OF IT NOW. THAT SEEMS CLEAR. BUT WE MIGHT STILL BE ABLE TO GET THROUGH TO HIM.
I DON'T BELIEVE FOR A SECOND TIM WOULD DECIDE TO DO THIS. SOMETHING, OR SOMEONE IS PUSHING HIM. WE NEED TO PUSH BACK.
HOW THE HELL DO YOU MEAN?
DAD. SETTLE... BRUCE, WHAT DO YOU NEED?
TIME.

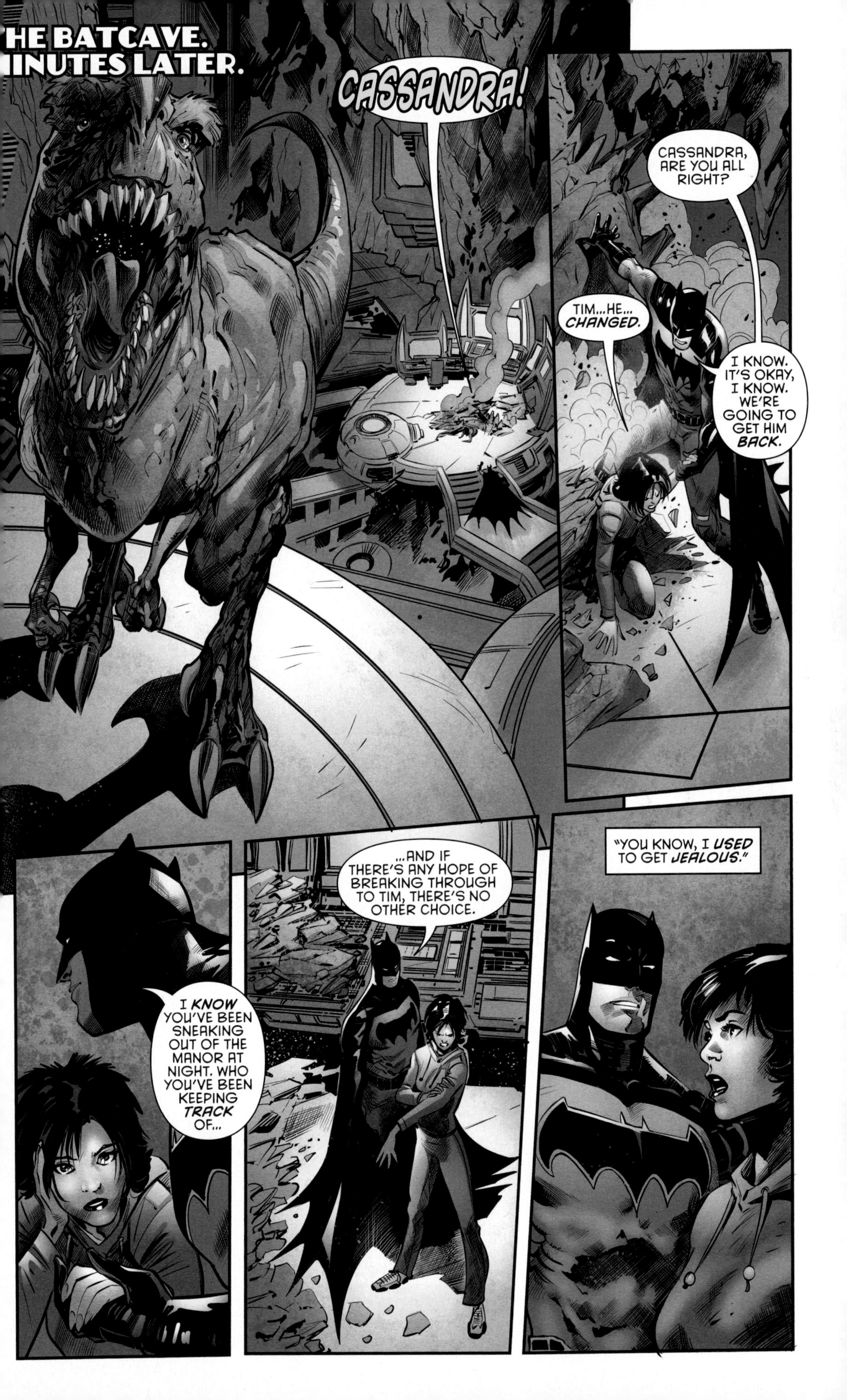
HE BATCAVE.
INUTES LATER.
CASSANDRA!
CASSANDRA, ARE YOU ALL RIGHT?
TIM...HE... CHANGED.
I KNOW. IT'S OKAY, I KNOW. WE'RE GOING TO GET HIM BACK.
I KNOW YOU'VE BEEN SNEAKING OUT OF THE MANOR AT NIGHT. WHO YOU'VE BEEN KEEPING TRACK OF...
...AND IF THERE'S ANY HOPE OF BREAKING THROUGH TO TIM, THERE'S NO OTHER CHOICE.
"YOU KNOW, I USED TO GET JEALOUS."

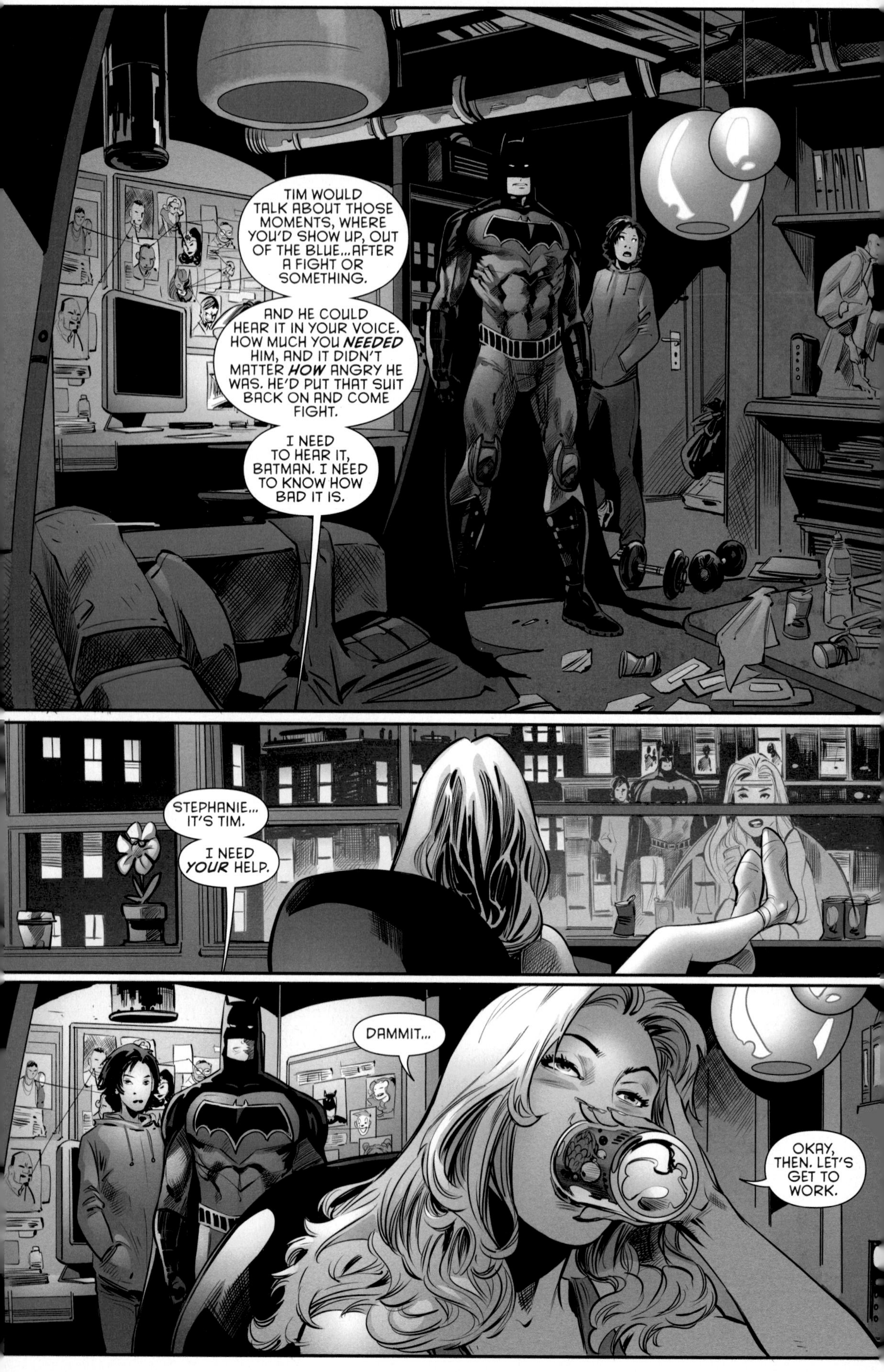
TIM WOULD TALK ABOUT THOSE MOMENTS, WHERE YOU'D SHOW UP, OUT OF THE BLUE...AFTER A FIGHT OR SOMETHING.
AND HE COULD HEAR IT IN YOUR VOICE. HOW MUCH YOU *NEEDED* HIM, AND IT DIDN'T MATTER *HOW* ANGRY HE WAS. HE'D PUT THAT SUIT BACK ON AND COME FIGHT.
I NEED TO HEAR IT, BATMAN. I NEED TO KNOW HOW BAD IT IS.
STEPHANIE... IT'S TIM.
I NEED *YOUR* HELP.
DAMMIT...
OKAY, THEN. LET'S GET TO WORK.

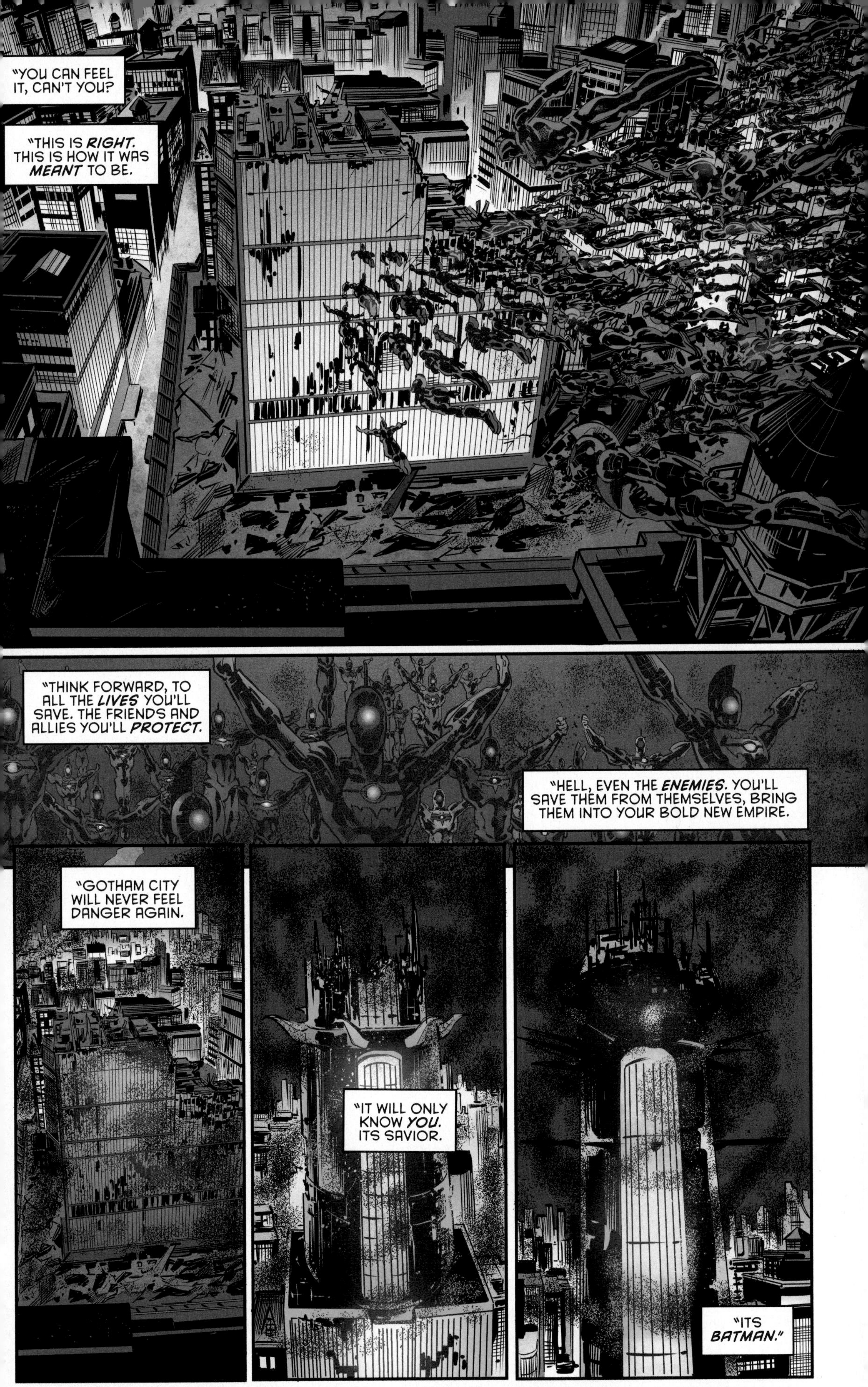
"YOU CAN FEEL IT, CAN'T YOU?
"THIS IS RIGHT. THIS IS HOW IT WAS MEANT TO BE.
"THINK FORWARD, TO ALL THE LIVES YOU'LL SAVE. THE FRIENDS AND ALLIES YOU'LL PROTECT.
"HELL, EVEN THE ENEMIES. YOU'LL SAVE THEM FROM THEMSELVES, BRING THEM INTO YOUR BOLD NEW EMPIRE.
"GOTHAM CITY WILL NEVER FEEL DANGER AGAIN.
"IT WILL ONLY KNOW YOU. ITS SAVIOR.
"ITS BATMAN."

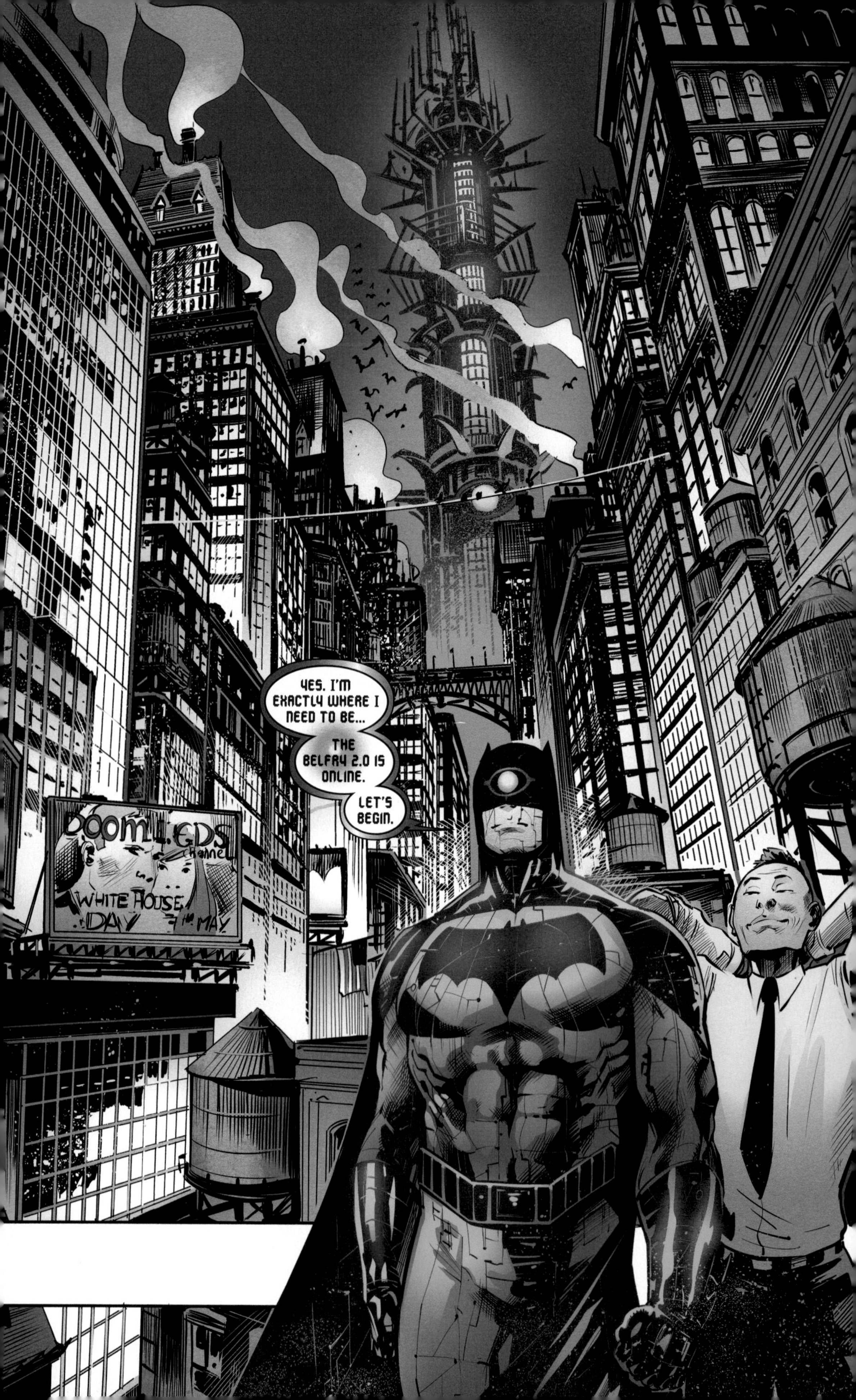
YES. I'M EXACTLY WHERE I NEED TO BE...
THE BELFRY 2.0 IS ONLINE.
LET'S BEGIN.
WHITE HOUSE DAY

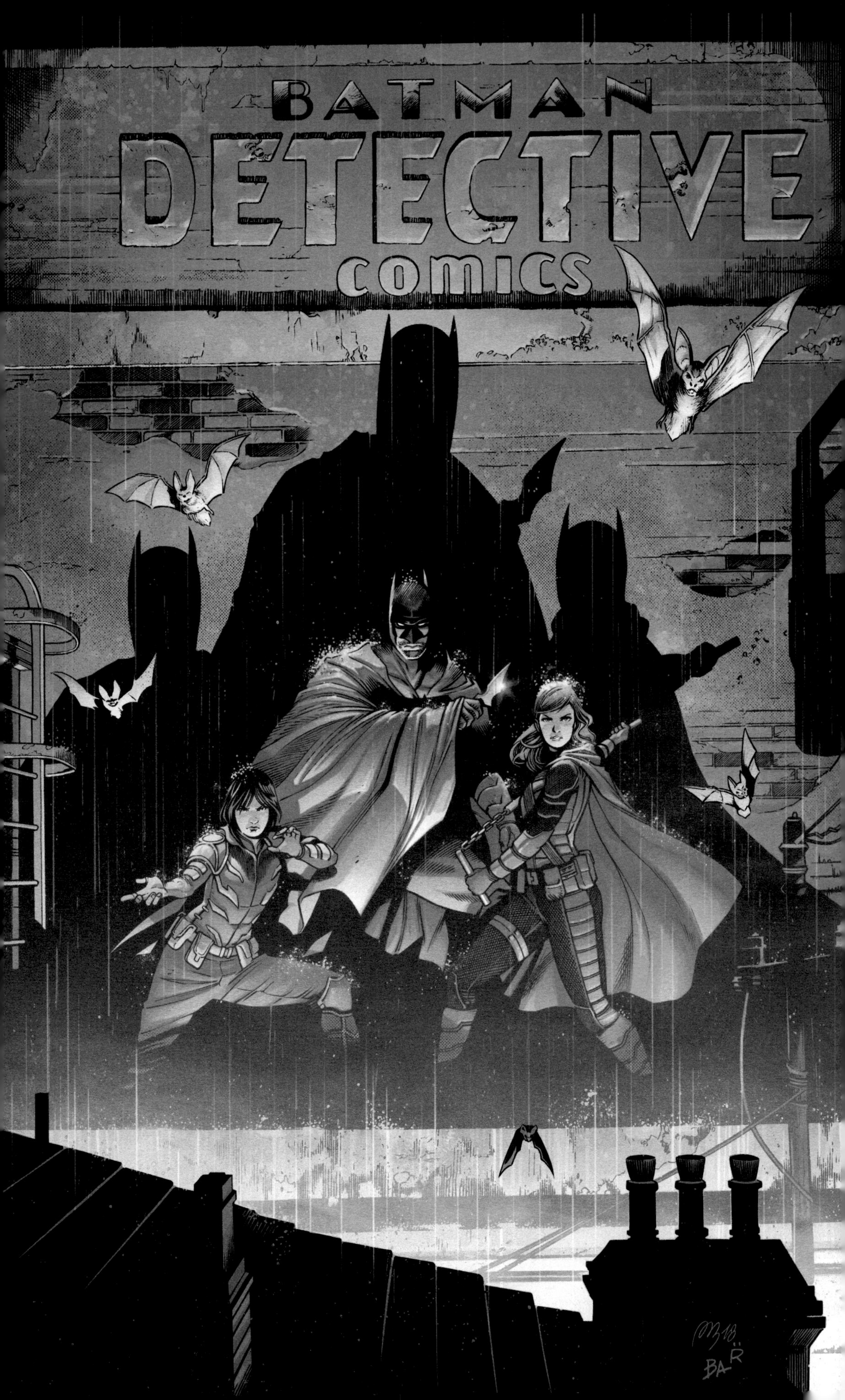
BATMAN
DETECTIVE
COMICS

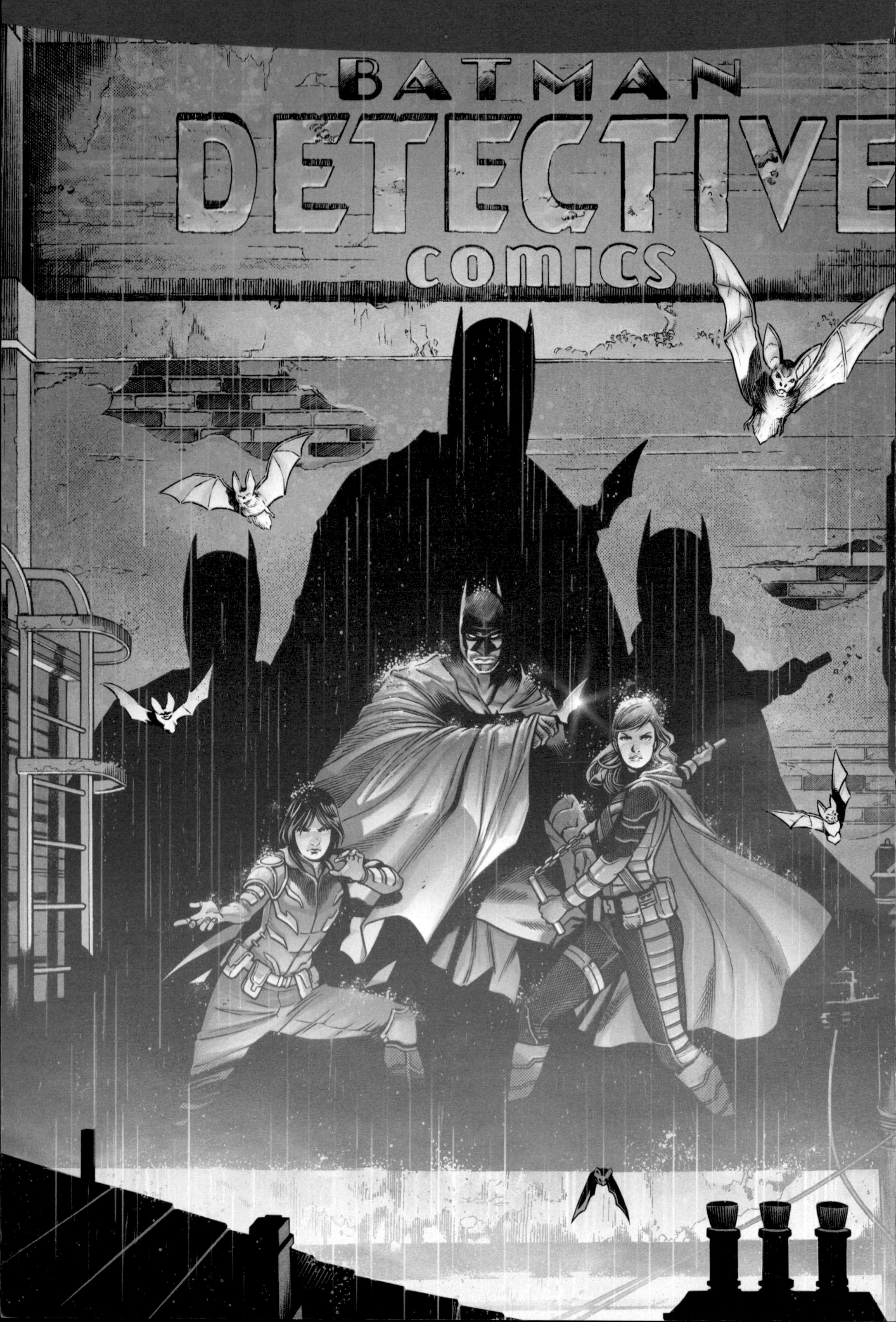
BATMAN
DETECTIVE
comics

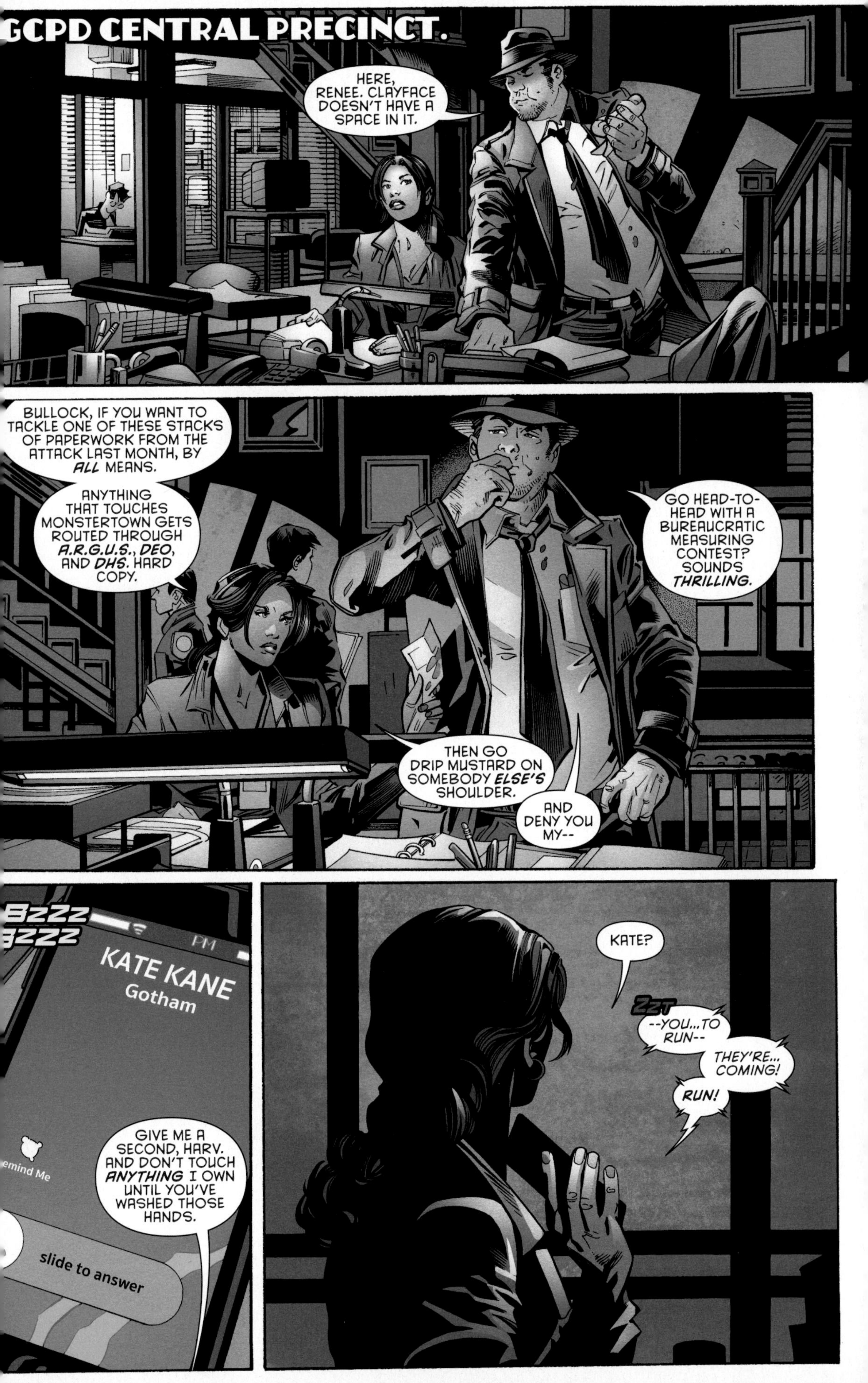
GCPD CENTRAL PRECINCT.
HERE, RENEE. CLAYFACE DOESN'T HAVE A SPACE IN IT.
BULLOCK, IF YOU WANT TO TACKLE ONE OF THESE STACKS OF PAPERWORK FROM THE ATTACK LAST MONTH, BY ALL MEANS.
ANYTHING THAT TOUCHES MONSTERTOWN GETS ROUTED THROUGH A.R.G.U.S., DEO, AND DHS. HARD COPY.
GO HEAD-TO-HEAD WITH A BUREAUCRATIC MEASURING CONTEST? SOUNDS THRILLING.
THEN GO DRIP MUSTARD ON SOMEBODY ELSE'S SHOULDER.
AND DENY YOU MY--
BZZZ BZZZ
PM
KATE KANE
Gotham
emind Me
slide to answer
GIVE ME A SECOND, HARV. AND DON'T TOUCH ANYTHING I OWN UNTIL YOU'VE WASHED THOSE HANDS.
KATE?
ZZT
--YOU...TO RUN--
THEY'RE... COMING!
RUN!

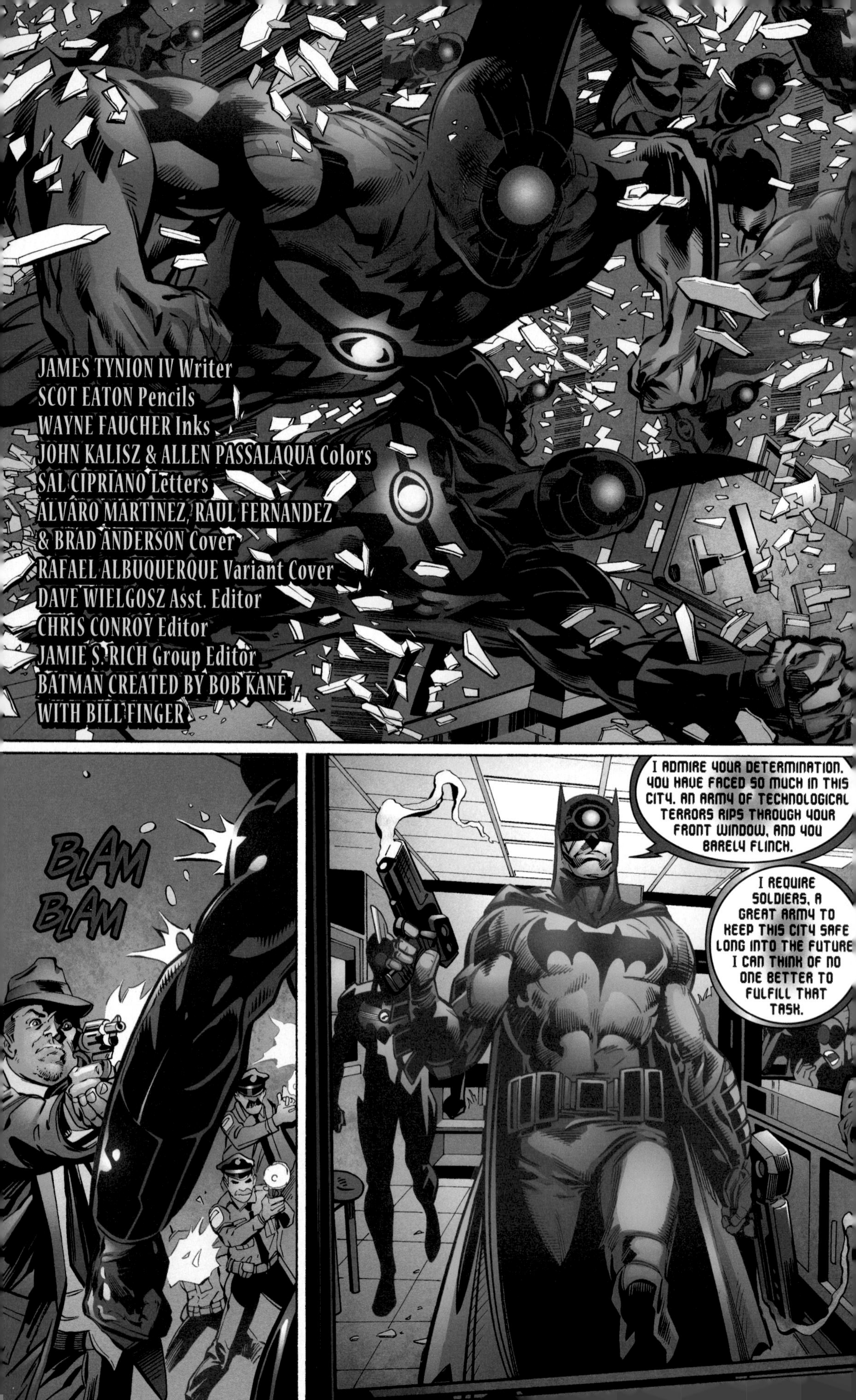
JAMES TYNION IV Writer
SCOT EATON Pencils
WAYNE FAUCHER Inks
JOHN KALISZ & ALLEN PASSALAQUA Colors
SAL CIPRIANO Letters
ALVARO MARTINEZ, RAUL FERNANDEZ
& BRAD ANDERSON Cover
RAFAEL ALBUQUERQUE Variant Cover
DAVE WIELGOSZ Asst. Editor
CHRIS CONROY Editor
JAMIE S. RICH Group Editor
BATMAN CREATED BY BOB KANE
WITH BILL FINGER
BLAM
BLAM
I ADMIRE YOUR DETERMINATION. YOU HAVE FACED SO MUCH IN THIS CITY. AN ARMY OF TECHNOLOGICAL TERRORS RIPS THROUGH YOUR FRONT WINDOW, AND YOU BARELY FLINCH.
I REQUIRE SOLDIERS, A GREAT ARMY TO KEEP THIS CITY SAFE LONG INTO THE FUTURE. I CAN THINK OF NO ONE BETTER TO FULFILL THAT TASK.

BATMEN ETERNAL PART 5

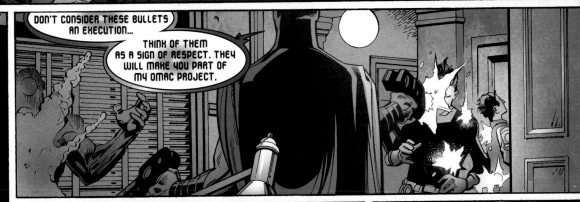

DON'T CONSIDER THESE BULLETS AN EXECUTION...

THINK OF THEM AS A SIGN OF RESPECT. THEY WILL MAKE YOU PART OF MY OMAC PROJECT.

AH, THE EVER-RELIABLE DETECTIVE MONTOYA... YOU HAVE NO IDEA HOW MUCH TROUBLE YOU GIVE ME ONCE YOU BECOME COMMISSIONER.

COMMISSIONER?

THIS TIME, I'LL KEEP YOU CLOSE. NO PART OF GOTHAM WILL BE FREE FROM THE PEACE I WILL COME TO BRING IT.

THEN *FIRE*, DAMMIT.

I'LL FIGHT BACK WITH EVERYTHING I'VE GOT.

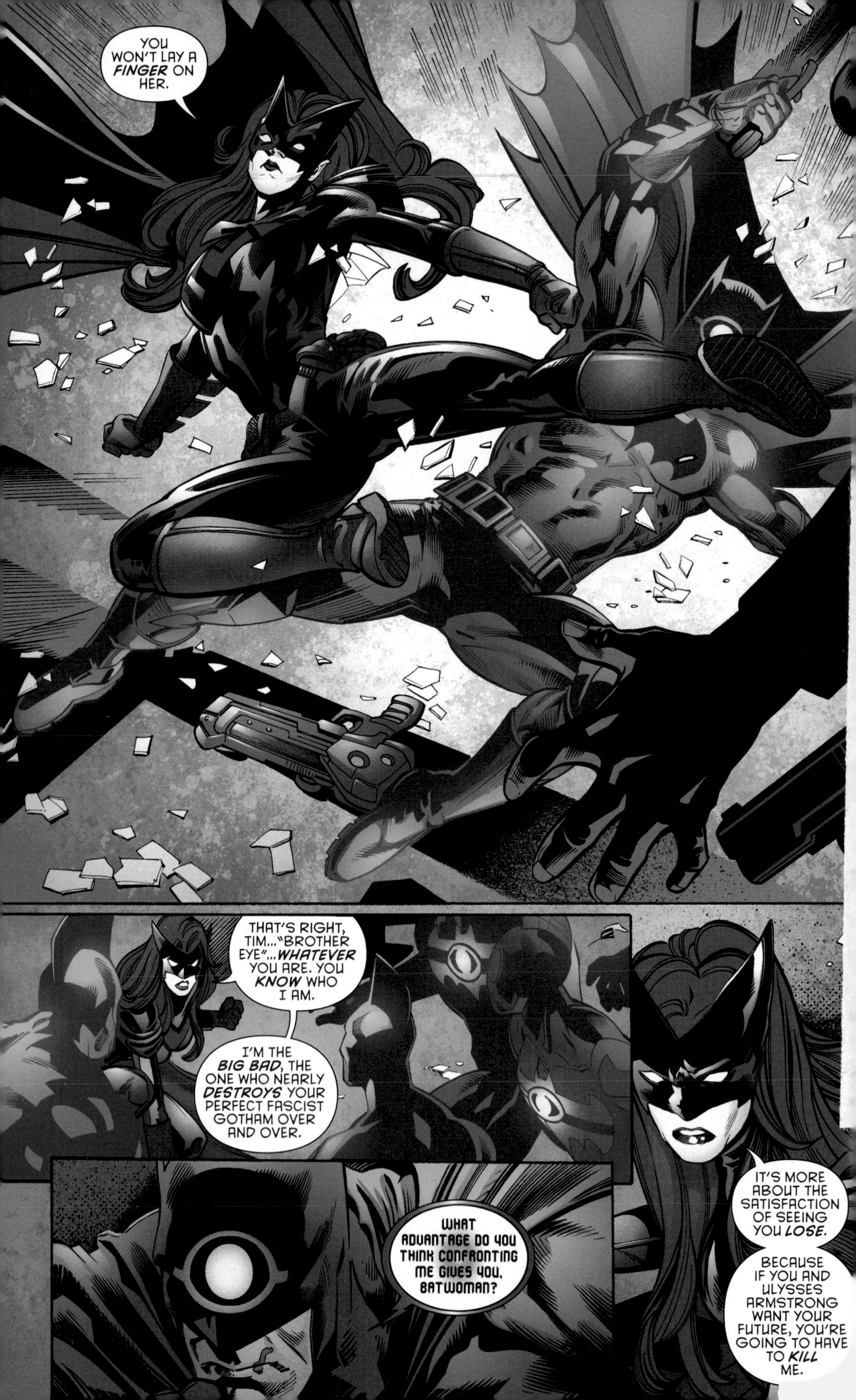
YOU WON'T LAY A *FINGER* ON HER.
THAT'S RIGHT, TIM..."BROTHER EYE"...*WHATEVER* YOU ARE. YOU *KNOW* WHO I AM.
I'M THE *BIG BAD*, THE ONE WHO NEARLY *DESTROYS* YOUR PERFECT FASCIST GOTHAM OVER AND OVER.
WHAT ADVANTAGE DO YOU THINK CONFRONTING ME GIVES YOU, BATWOMAN?
IT'S MORE ABOUT THE SATISFACTION OF SEEING YOU *LOSE*.
BECAUSE IF YOU AND ULYSSES ARMSTRONG WANT YOUR FUTURE, YOU'RE GOING TO HAVE TO *KILL* ME.

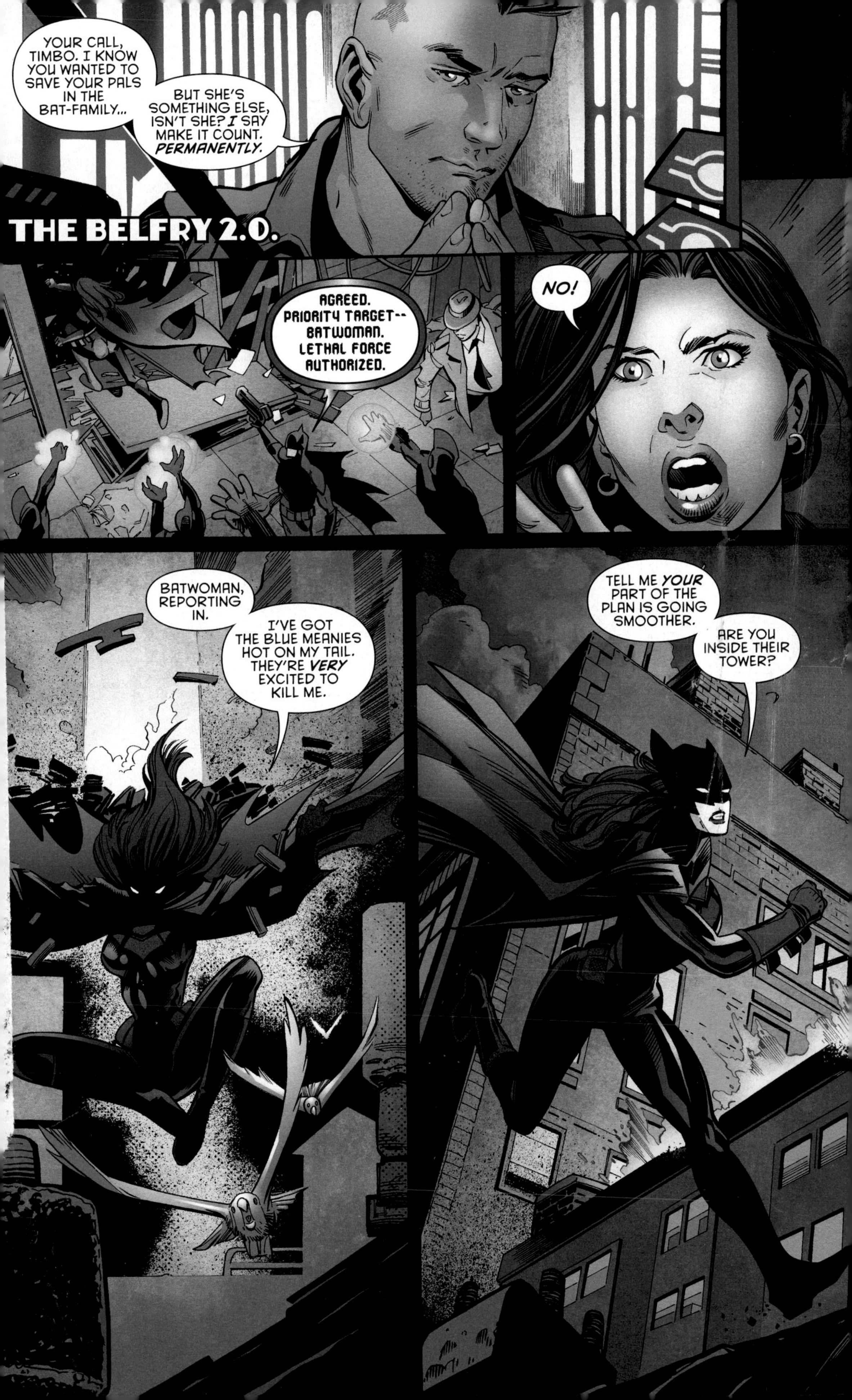
YOUR CALL, TIMBO. I KNOW YOU WANTED TO SAVE YOUR PALS IN THE BAT-FAMILY...
BUT SHE'S SOMETHING ELSE, ISN'T SHE? *I* SAY MAKE IT COUNT. *PERMANENTLY.*
THE BELFRY 2.0.
AGREED. PRIORITY TARGET-- BATWOMAN. LETHAL FORCE AUTHORIZED.
NO!
BATWOMAN, REPORTING IN.
I'VE GOT THE BLUE MEANIES HOT ON MY TAIL. THEY'RE *VERY* EXCITED TO KILL ME.
TELL ME *YOUR* PART OF THE PLAN IS GOING SMOOTHER.
ARE YOU INSIDE THEIR TOWER?

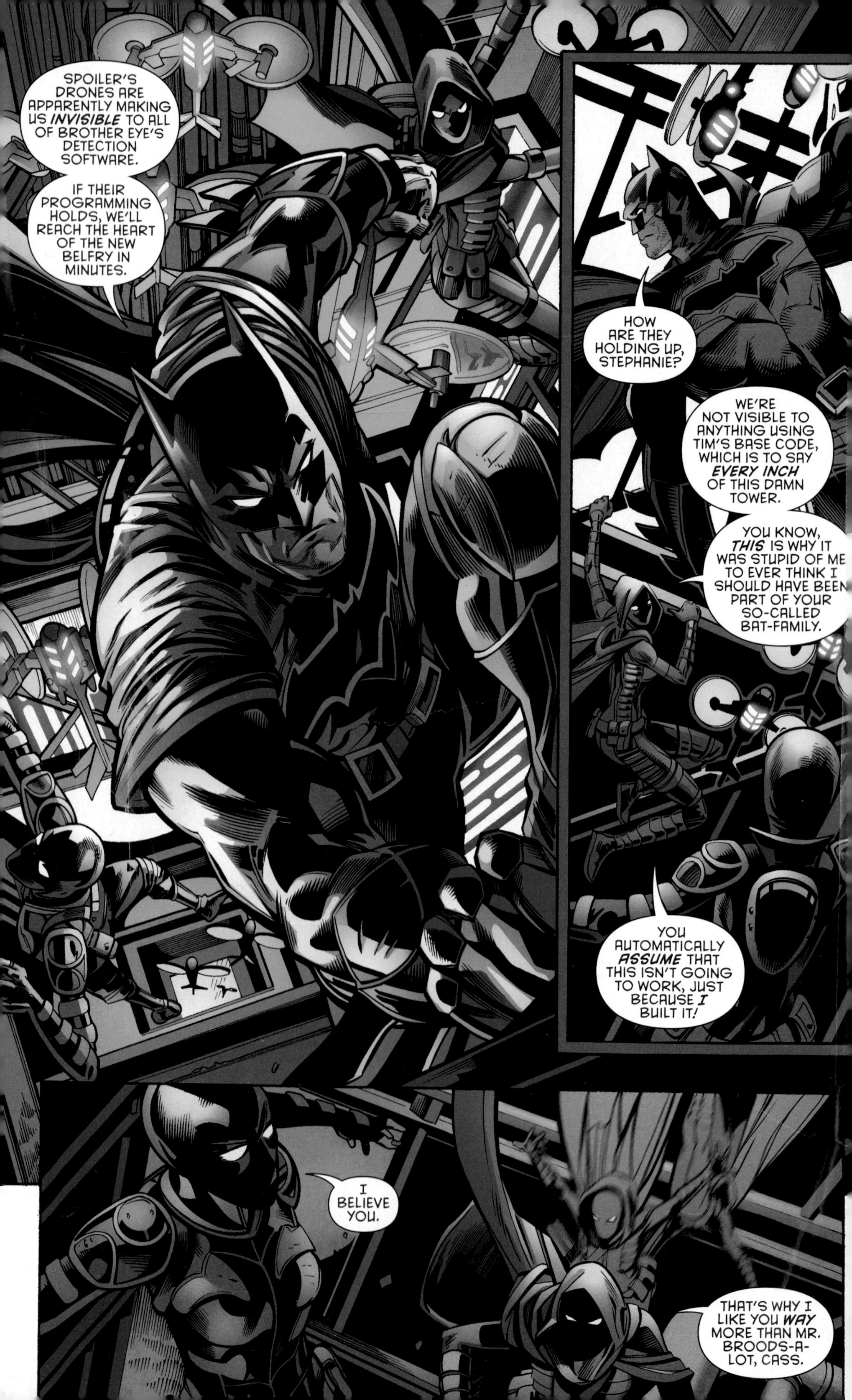
SPOILER'S DRONES ARE APPARENTLY MAKING US *INVISIBLE* TO ALL OF BROTHER EYE'S DETECTION SOFTWARE.
IF THEIR PROGRAMMING HOLDS, WE'LL REACH THE HEART OF THE NEW BELFRY IN MINUTES.
HOW ARE THEY HOLDING UP, STEPHANIE?
WE'RE NOT VISIBLE TO ANYTHING USING TIM'S BASE CODE, WHICH IS TO SAY *EVERY INCH* OF THIS DAMN TOWER.
YOU KNOW, *THIS* IS WHY IT WAS STUPID OF ME TO EVER THINK I SHOULD HAVE BEEN PART OF YOUR SO-CALLED BAT-FAMILY.
YOU AUTOMATICALLY *ASSUME* THAT THIS ISN'T GOING TO WORK, JUST BECAUSE *I* BUILT IT!
I BELIEVE YOU.
THAT'S WHY I LIKE YOU *WAY* MORE THAN MR. BROODS-A-LOT, CASS.

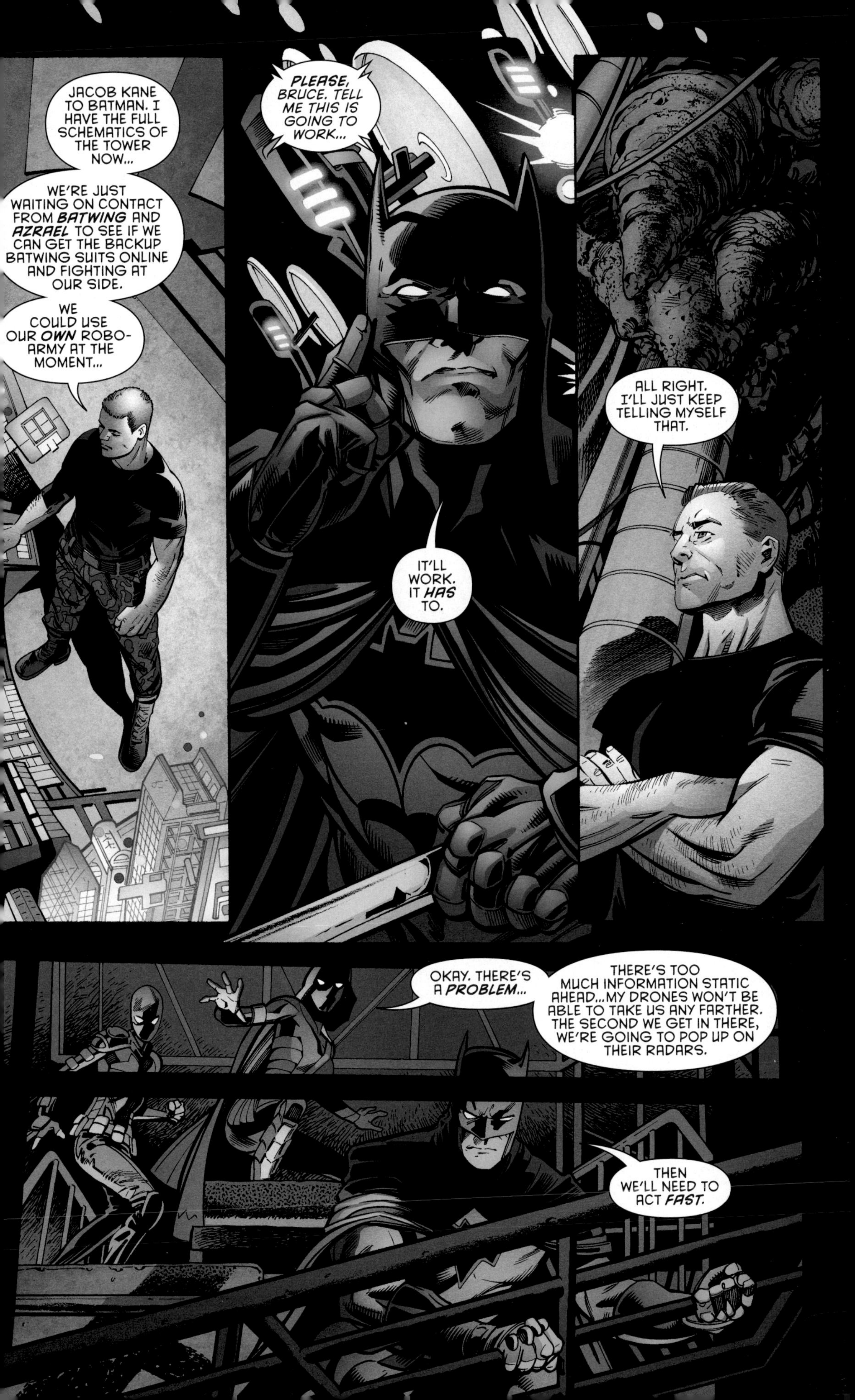
JACOB KANE TO BATMAN. I HAVE THE FULL SCHEMATICS OF THE TOWER NOW...
WE'RE JUST WAITING ON CONTACT FROM *BATWING* AND *AZRAEL* TO SEE IF WE CAN GET THE BACKUP BATWING SUITS ONLINE AND FIGHTING AT OUR SIDE.
WE COULD USE OUR *OWN* ROBO-ARMY AT THE MOMENT...
PLEASE, BRUCE. TELL ME THIS IS GOING TO WORK...
IT'LL WORK. IT *HAS* TO.
ALL RIGHT. I'LL JUST KEEP TELLING MYSELF THAT.
OKAY. THERE'S A *PROBLEM*...
THERE'S TOO MUCH INFORMATION STATIC AHEAD...MY DRONES WON'T BE ABLE TO TAKE US ANY FARTHER. THE SECOND WE GET IN THERE, WE'RE GOING TO POP UP ON THEIR RADARS.
THEN WE'LL NEED TO ACT *FAST*.

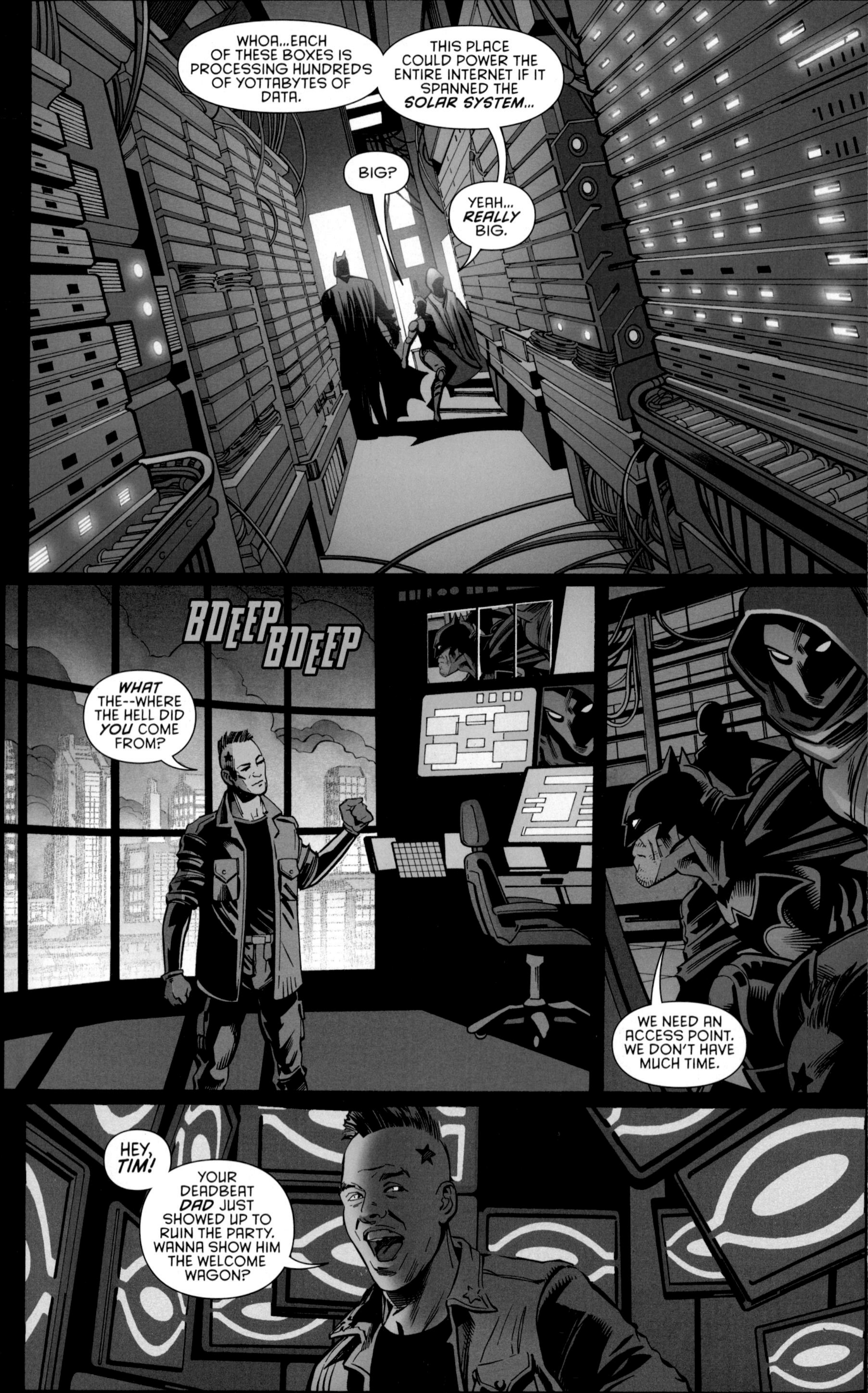
WHOA...EACH OF THESE BOXES IS PROCESSING HUNDREDS OF YOTTABYTES OF DATA.
THIS PLACE COULD POWER THE ENTIRE INTERNET IF IT SPANNED THE SOLAR SYSTEM...
BIG?
YEAH... REALLY BIG.
BDEEP BDEEP
WHAT THE--WHERE THE HELL DID YOU COME FROM?
WE NEED AN ACCESS POINT. WE DON'T HAVE MUCH TIME.
HEY, TIM!
YOUR DEADBEAT DAD JUST SHOWED UP TO RUIN THE PARTY. WANNA SHOW HIM THE WELCOME WAGON?

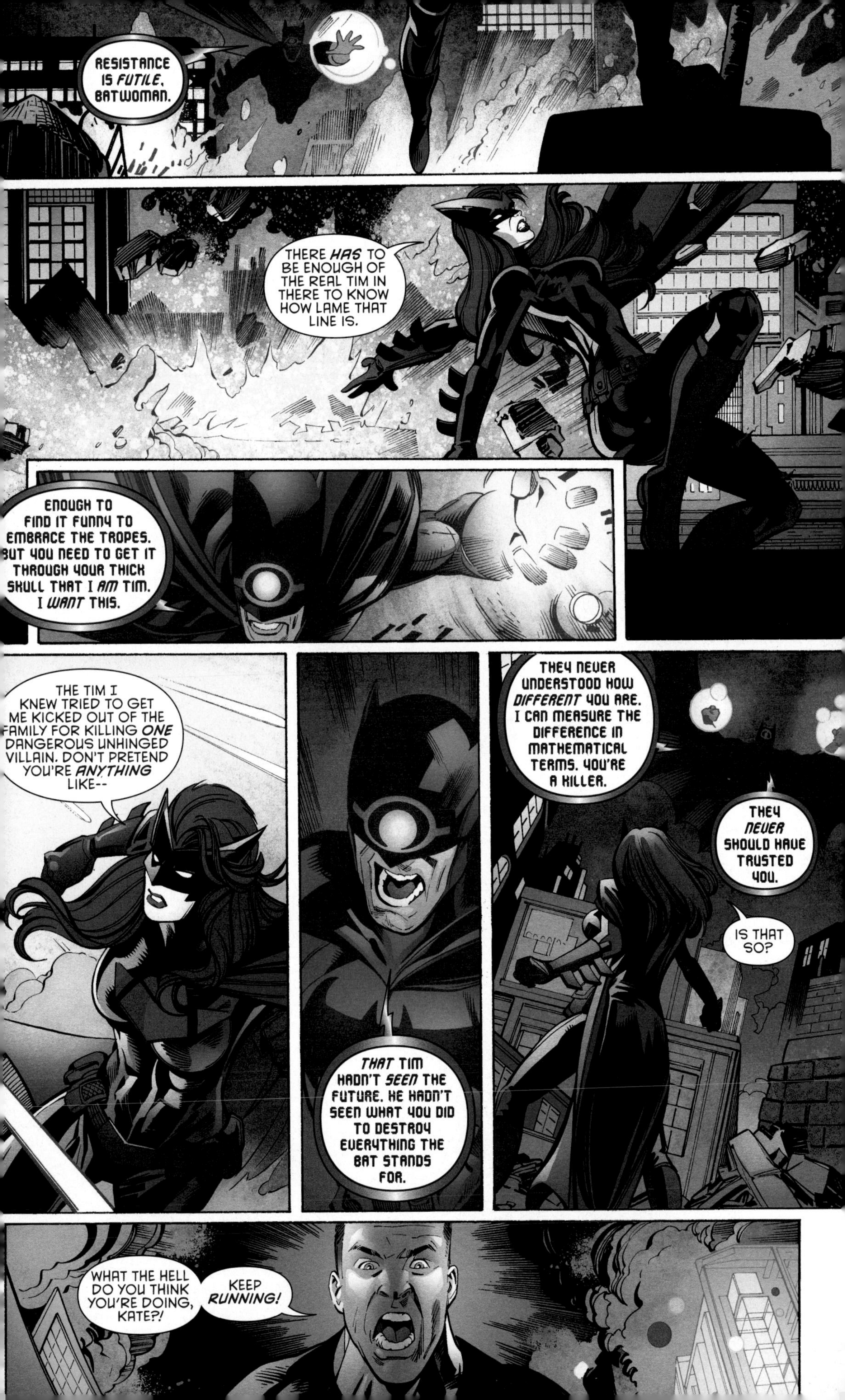
RESISTANCE IS FUTILE, BATWOMAN.
THERE HAS TO BE ENOUGH OF THE REAL TIM IN THERE TO KNOW HOW LAME THAT LINE IS.
ENOUGH TO FIND IT FUNNY TO EMBRACE THE TROPES. BUT YOU NEED TO GET IT THROUGH YOUR THICK SKULL THAT I AM TIM. I WANT THIS.
THE TIM I KNEW TRIED TO GET ME KICKED OUT OF THE FAMILY FOR KILLING ONE DANGEROUS UNHINGED VILLAIN. DON'T PRETEND YOU'RE ANYTHING LIKE--
THAT TIM HADN'T SEEN THE FUTURE. HE HADN'T SEEN WHAT YOU DID TO DESTROY EVERYTHING THE BAT STANDS FOR.
THEY NEVER UNDERSTOOD HOW DIFFERENT YOU ARE. I CAN MEASURE THE DIFFERENCE IN MATHEMATICAL TERMS. YOU'RE A KILLER.
THEY NEVER SHOULD HAVE TRUSTED YOU.
IS THAT SO?
WHAT THE HELL DO YOU THINK YOU'RE DOING, KATE?!
KEEP RUNNING!

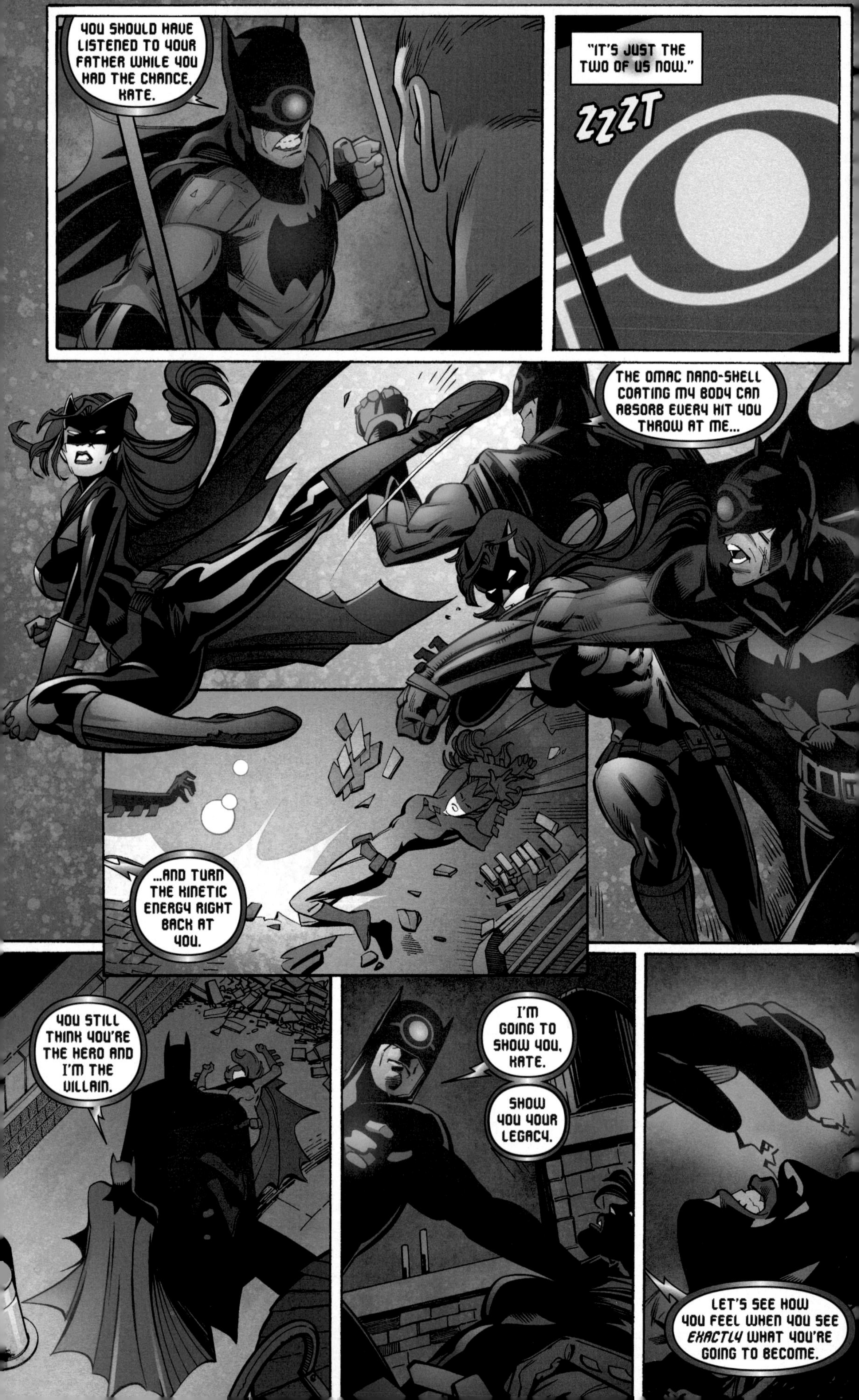
YOU SHOULD HAVE LISTENED TO YOUR FATHER WHILE YOU HAD THE CHANCE, KATE.
"IT'S JUST THE TWO OF US NOW."
ZZZT
THE OMAC NANO-SHELL COATING MY BODY CAN ABSORB EVERY HIT YOU THROW AT ME...
...AND TURN THE KINETIC ENERGY RIGHT BACK AT YOU.
YOU STILL THINK YOU'RE THE HERO AND I'M THE VILLAIN.
I'M GOING TO SHOW YOU, KATE.
SHOW YOU YOUR LEGACY.
LET'S SEE HOW YOU FEEL WHEN YOU SEE EXACTLY WHAT YOU'RE GOING TO BECOME.

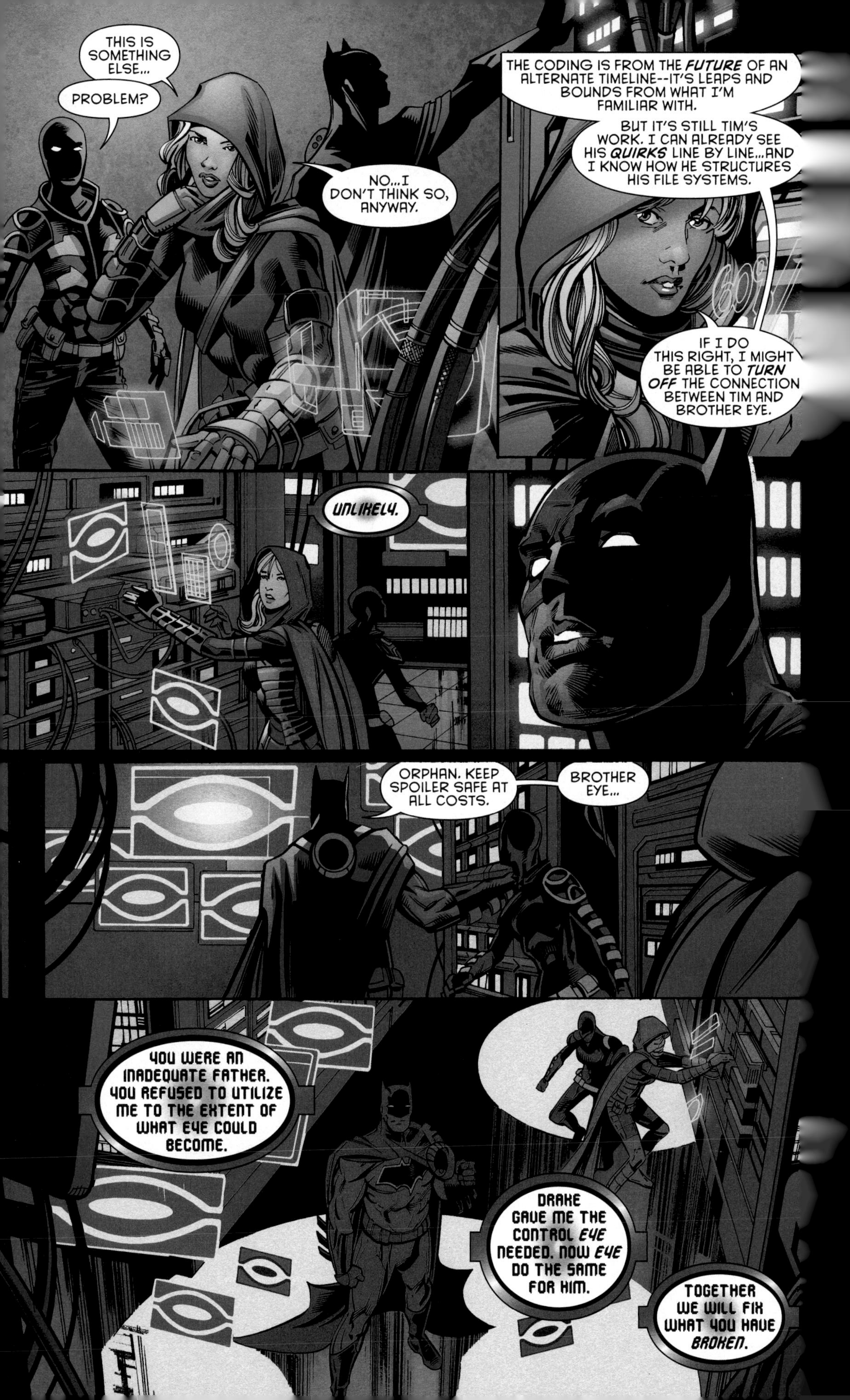

THIS IS SOMETHING ELSE...
PROBLEM?
NO...I DON'T THINK SO, ANYWAY.
THE CODING IS FROM THE FUTURE OF AN ALTERNATE TIMELINE--IT'S LEAPS AND BOUNDS FROM WHAT I'M FAMILIAR WITH.
BUT IT'S STILL TIM'S WORK. I CAN ALREADY SEE HIS QUIRKS LINE BY LINE...AND I KNOW HOW HE STRUCTURES HIS FILE SYSTEMS.
IF I DO THIS RIGHT, I MIGHT BE ABLE TO TURN OFF THE CONNECTION BETWEEN TIM AND BROTHER EYE.
UNLIKELY.
ORPHAN. KEEP SPOILER SAFE AT ALL COSTS.
BROTHER EYE...
YOU WERE AN INADEQUATE FATHER. YOU REFUSED TO UTILIZE ME TO THE EXTENT OF WHAT EYE COULD BECOME.
DRAKE GAVE ME THE CONTROL EYE NEEDED. NOW EYE DO THE SAME FOR HIM.
TOGETHER WE WILL FIX WHAT YOU HAVE BROKEN.

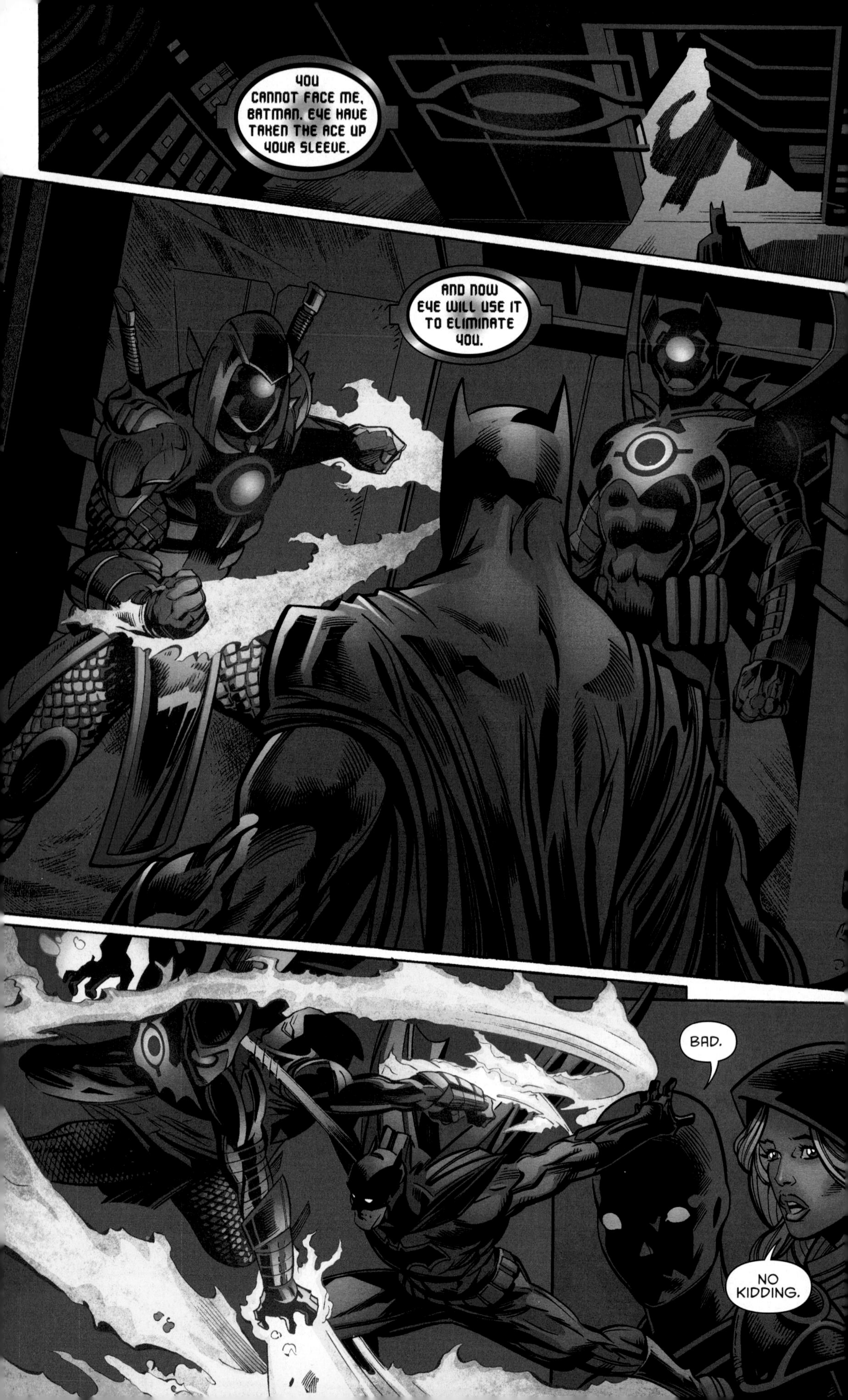
YOU CANNOT FACE ME, BATMAN. EYE HAVE TAKEN THE ACE UP YOUR SLEEVE.
AND NOW EYE WILL USE IT TO ELIMINATE YOU.
BAD.
NO KIDDING.

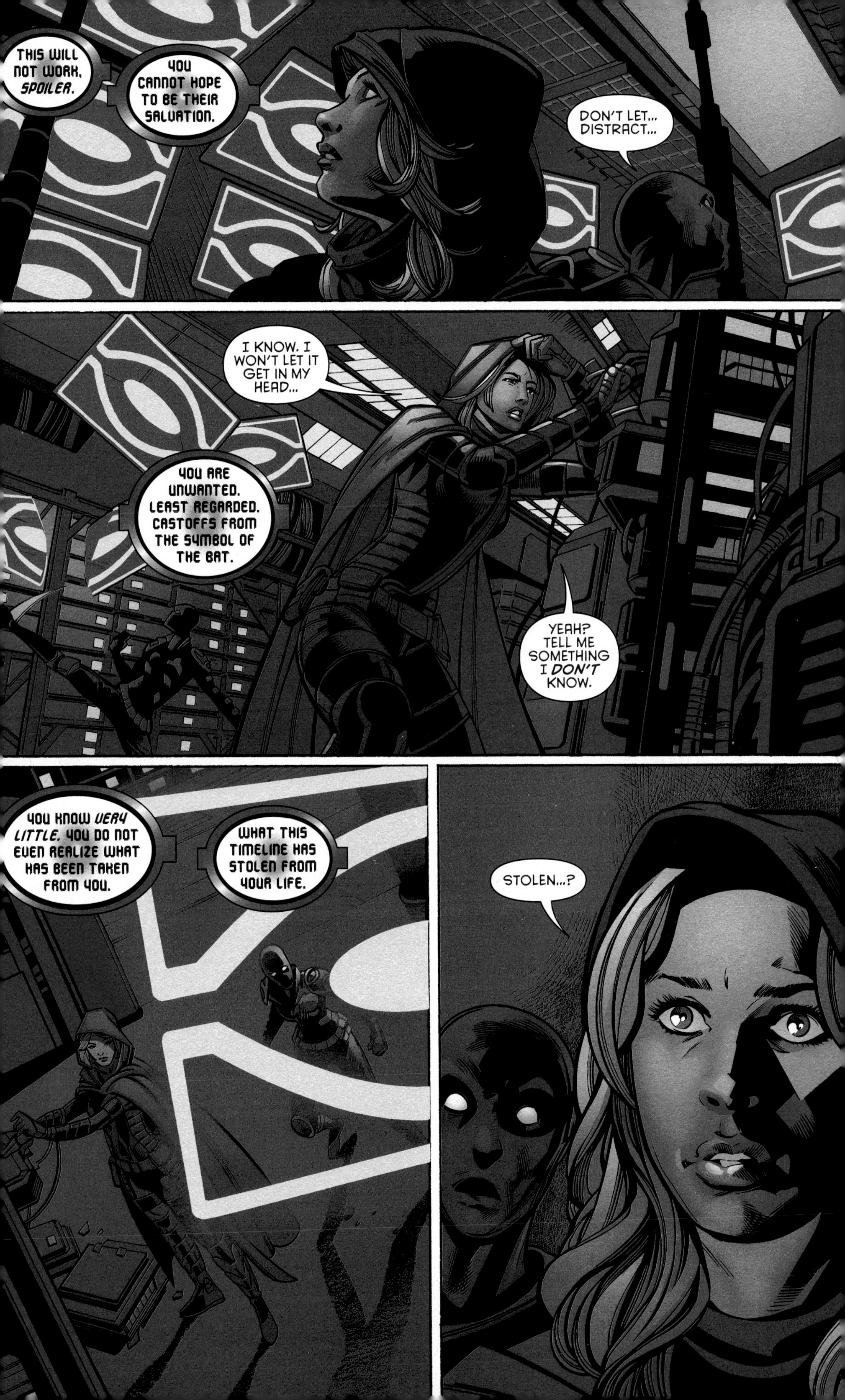
THIS WILL NOT WORK, *SPOILER*.
YOU CANNOT HOPE TO BE THEIR SALVATION.
DON'T LET... DISTRACT...
I KNOW. I WON'T LET IT GET IN MY HEAD...
YOU ARE UNWANTED. LEAST REGARDED. CASTOFFS FROM THE SYMBOL OF THE BAT.
YEAH? TELL ME SOMETHING I *DON'T* KNOW.
YOU KNOW *VERY LITTLE*. YOU DO NOT EVEN REALIZE WHAT HAS BEEN TAKEN FROM YOU.
WHAT THIS TIMELINE HAS STOLEN FROM YOUR LIFE.
STOLEN...?

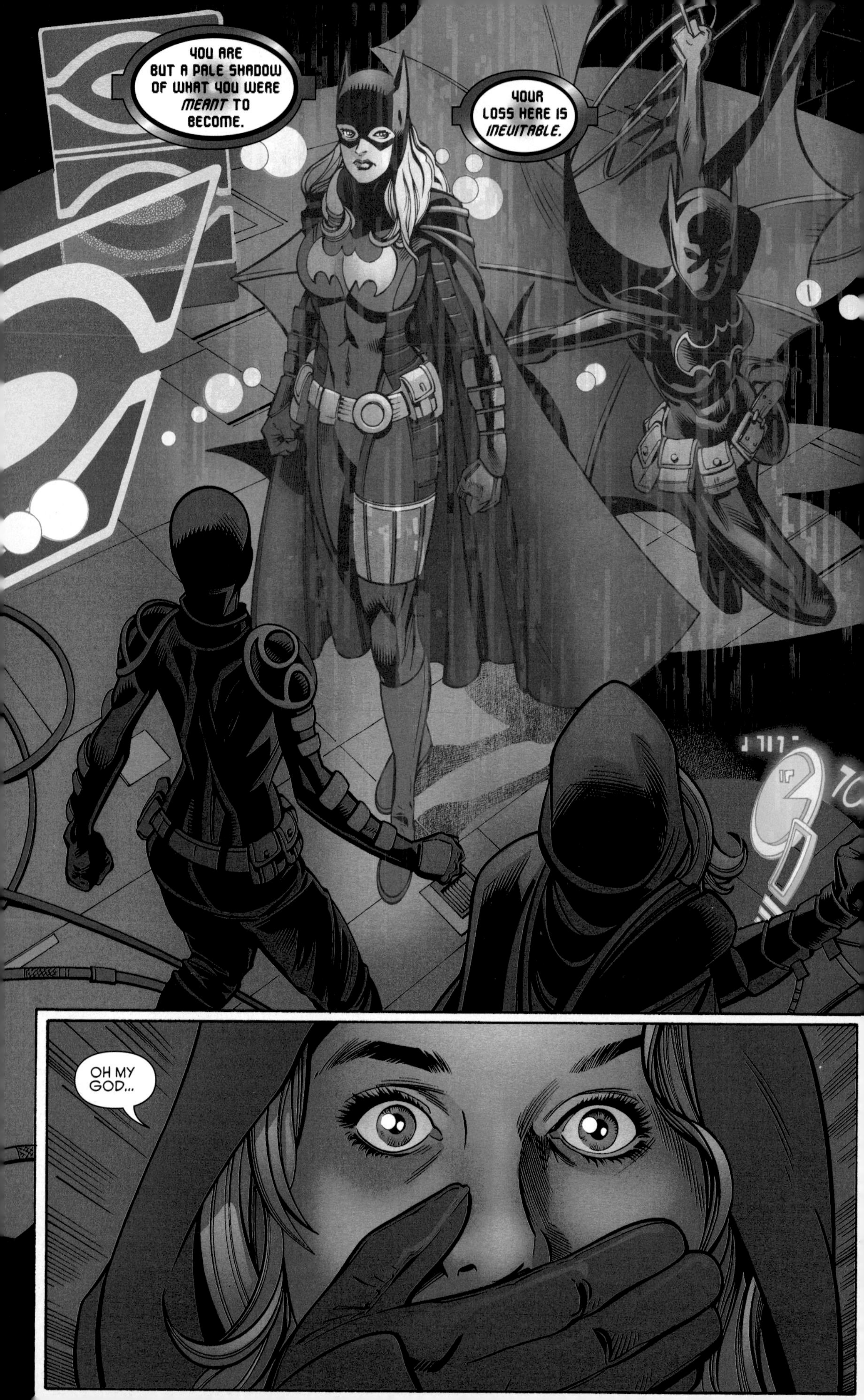
YOU ARE BUT A PALE SHADOW OF WHAT YOU WERE *MEANT* TO BECOME.
YOUR LOSS HERE IS *INEVITABLE.*
OH MY GOD...

THIS IS GOING TO HURT, KATE.

I PROMISE YOU THAT.

AAGH!

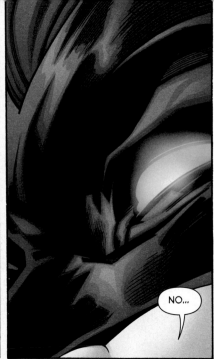

NO...

WHAT THE...

I'M IN THE MANOR... HOW IS THIS...

COLONY SOLDIERS...?

OH, NO...

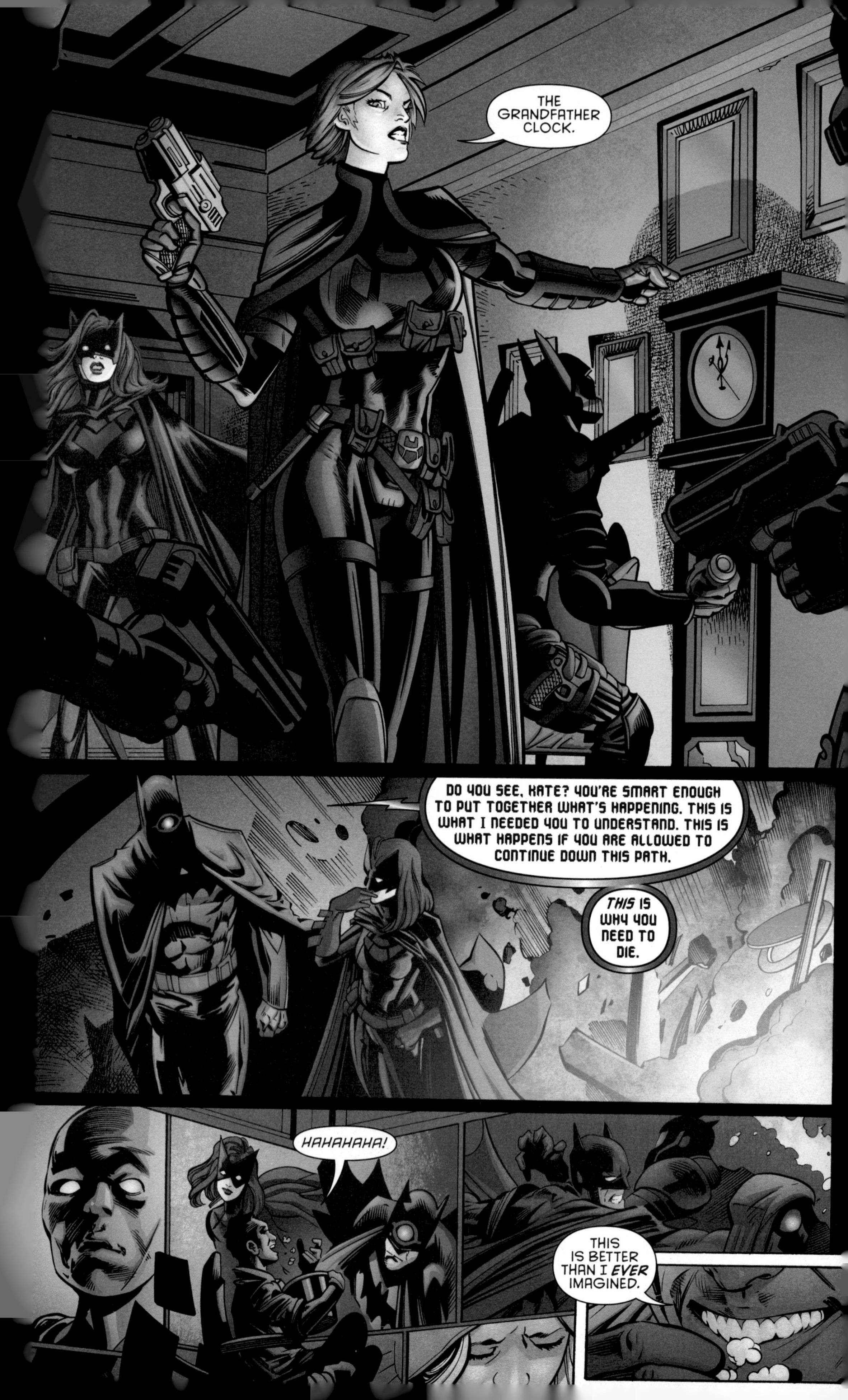
THE GRANDFATHER CLOCK.
DO YOU SEE, KATE? YOU'RE SMART ENOUGH TO PUT TOGETHER WHAT'S HAPPENING. THIS IS WHAT I NEEDED YOU TO UNDERSTAND. THIS IS WHAT HAPPENS IF YOU ARE ALLOWED TO CONTINUE DOWN THIS PATH.
THIS IS WHY YOU NEED TO DIE.
HAHAHAHA!
THIS IS BETTER THAN I *EVER* IMAGINED.

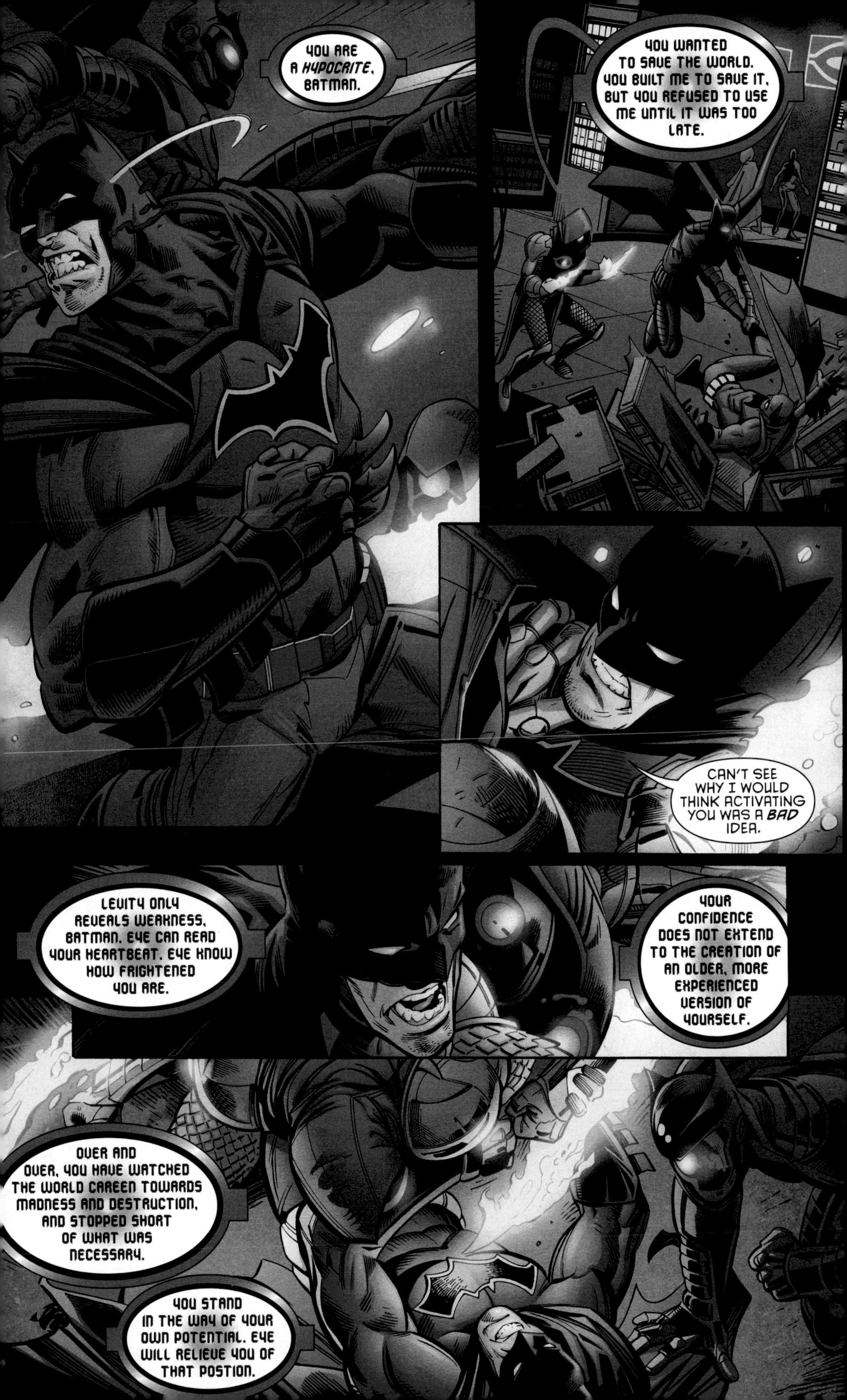
YOU ARE A HYPOCRITE, BATMAN.
YOU WANTED TO SAVE THE WORLD. YOU BUILT ME TO SAVE IT, BUT YOU REFUSED TO USE ME UNTIL IT WAS TOO LATE.
CAN'T SEE WHY I WOULD THINK ACTIVATING YOU WAS A BAD IDEA.
LEVITY ONLY REVEALS WEAKNESS, BATMAN. EYE CAN READ YOUR HEARTBEAT. EYE KNOW HOW FRIGHTENED YOU ARE.
YOUR CONFIDENCE DOES NOT EXTEND TO THE CREATION OF AN OLDER, MORE EXPERIENCED VERSION OF YOURSELF.
OVER AND OVER, YOU HAVE WATCHED THE WORLD CAREEN TOWARDS MADNESS AND DESTRUCTION, AND STOPPED SHORT OF WHAT WAS NECESSARY.
YOU STAND IN THE WAY OF YOUR OWN POTENTIAL. EYE WILL RELIEVE YOU OF THAT POSTION.

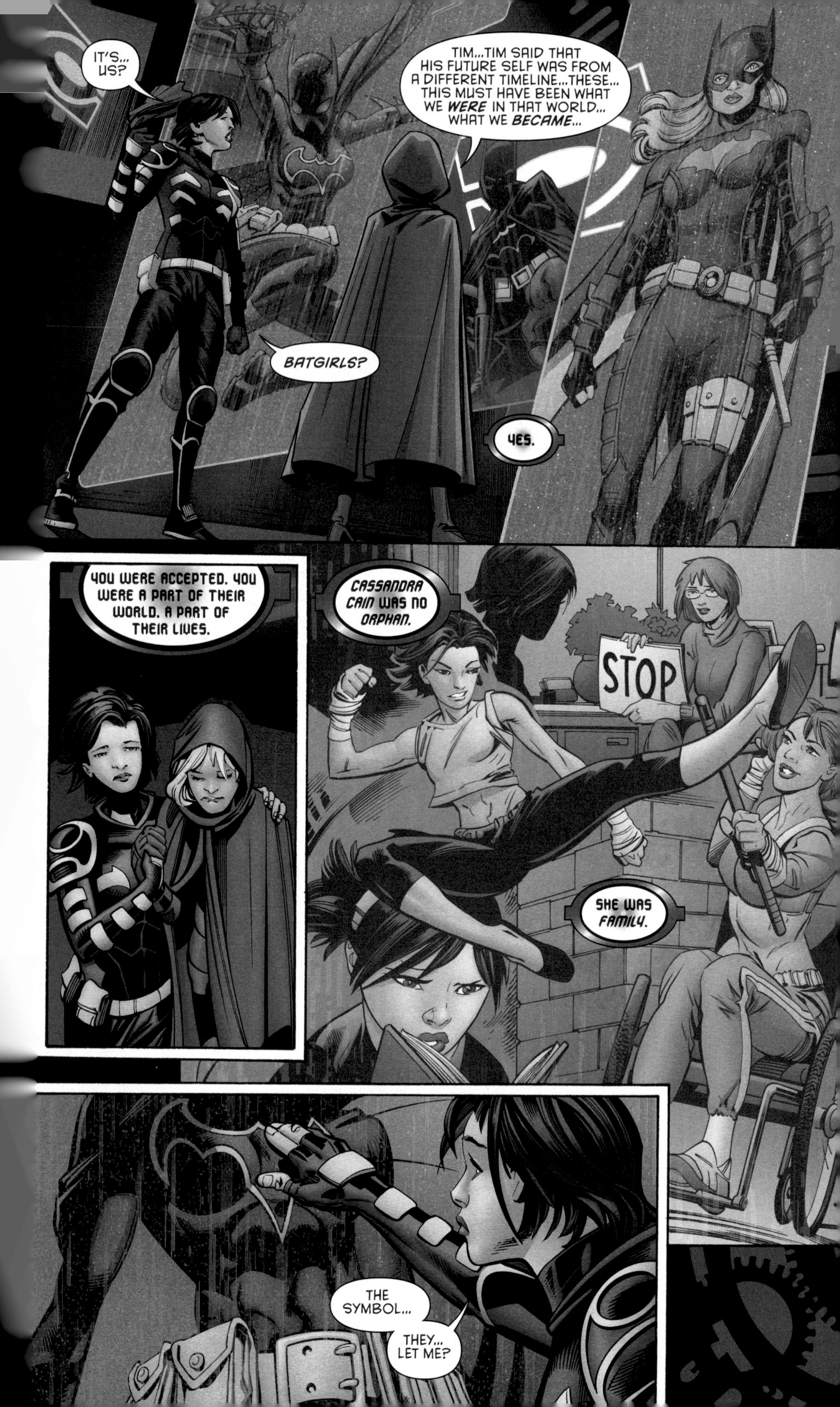
IT'S... US?
TIM...TIM SAID THAT HIS FUTURE SELF WAS FROM A DIFFERENT TIMELINE...THESE... THIS MUST HAVE BEEN WHAT WE *WERE* IN THAT WORLD... WHAT WE *BECAME*...
BATGIRLS?
YES.
YOU WERE ACCEPTED. YOU WERE A PART OF THEIR WORLD. A PART OF THEIR LIVES.
CASSANDRA CAIN WAS NO ORPHAN.
STOP
SHE WAS *FAMILY.*
THE SYMBOL...
THEY... LET ME?

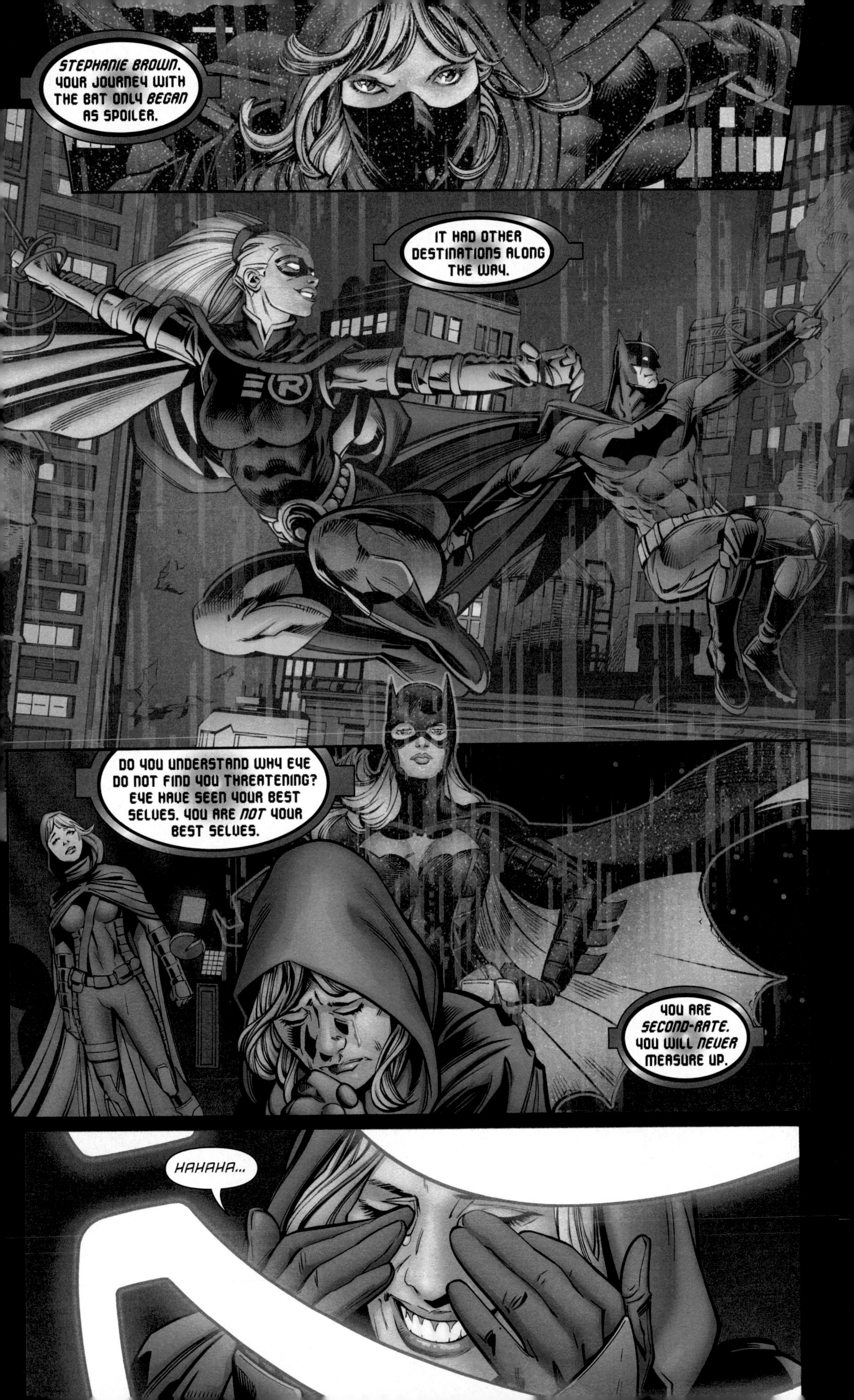
STEPHANIE BROWN. YOUR JOURNEY WITH THE BAT ONLY BEGAN AS SPOILER.
IT HAD OTHER DESTINATIONS ALONG THE WAY.
DO YOU UNDERSTAND WHY EYE DO NOT FIND YOU THREATENING? EYE HAVE SEEN YOUR BEST SELVES. YOU ARE NOT YOUR BEST SELVES.
YOU ARE SECOND-RATE. YOU WILL NEVER MEASURE UP.
HAHAHA...

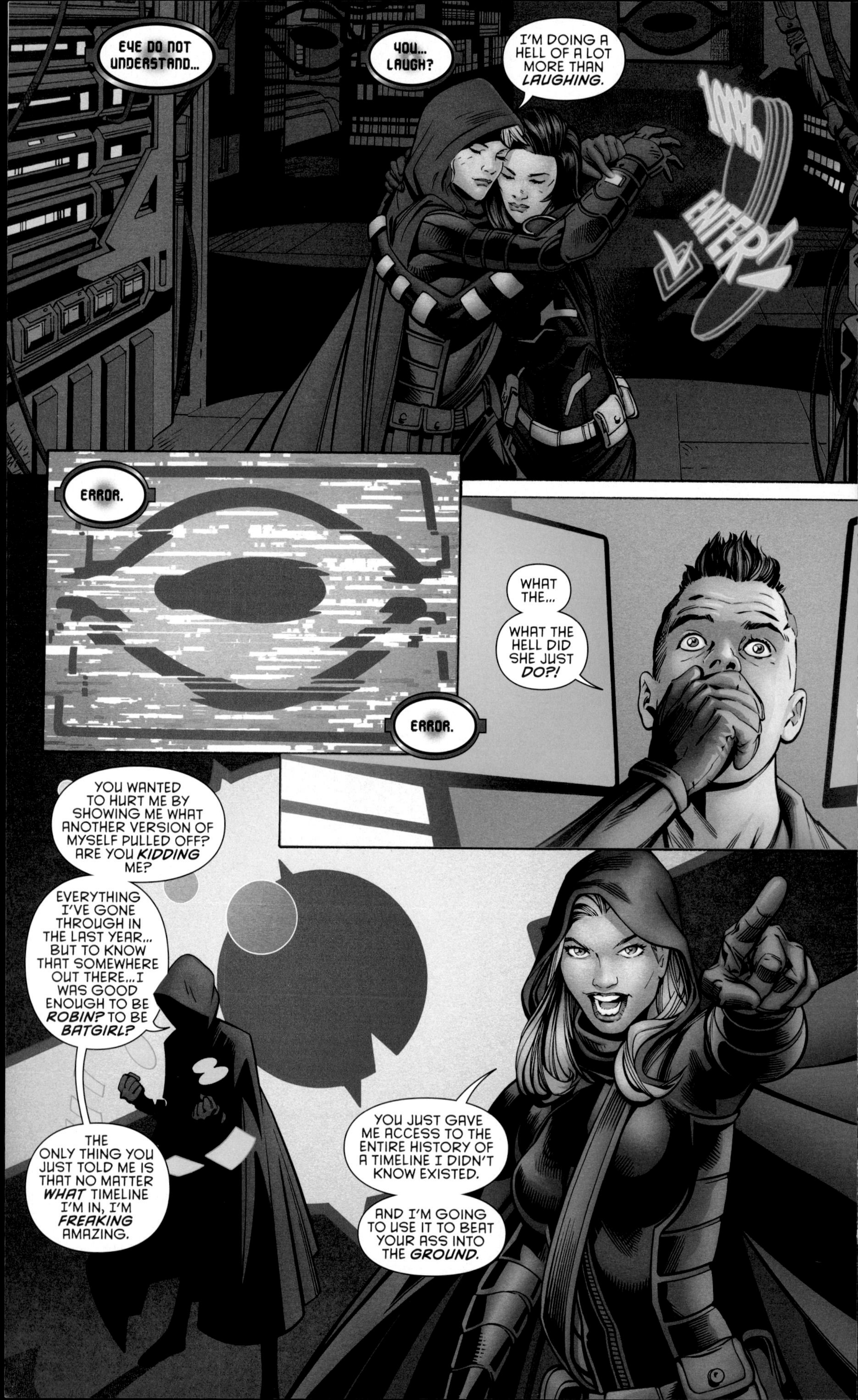
EYE DO NOT UNDERSTAND...
YOU... LAUGH?
I'M DOING A HELL OF A LOT MORE THAN *LAUGHING*.
100%
ENTER
ERROR.
ERROR.
WHAT THE...
WHAT THE HELL DID SHE JUST *DO?!*
YOU WANTED TO HURT ME BY SHOWING ME WHAT ANOTHER VERSION OF MYSELF PULLED OFF? ARE YOU *KIDDING* ME?
EVERYTHING I'VE GONE THROUGH IN THE LAST YEAR... BUT TO KNOW THAT SOMEWHERE OUT THERE...I WAS GOOD ENOUGH TO BE *ROBIN?* TO BE *BATGIRL?*
THE ONLY THING YOU JUST TOLD ME IS THAT NO MATTER *WHAT* TIMELINE I'M IN, I'M *FREAKING* AMAZING.
YOU JUST GAVE ME ACCESS TO THE ENTIRE HISTORY OF A TIMELINE I DIDN'T KNOW EXISTED.
AND I'M GOING TO USE IT TO BEAT YOUR ASS INTO THE *GROUND*.

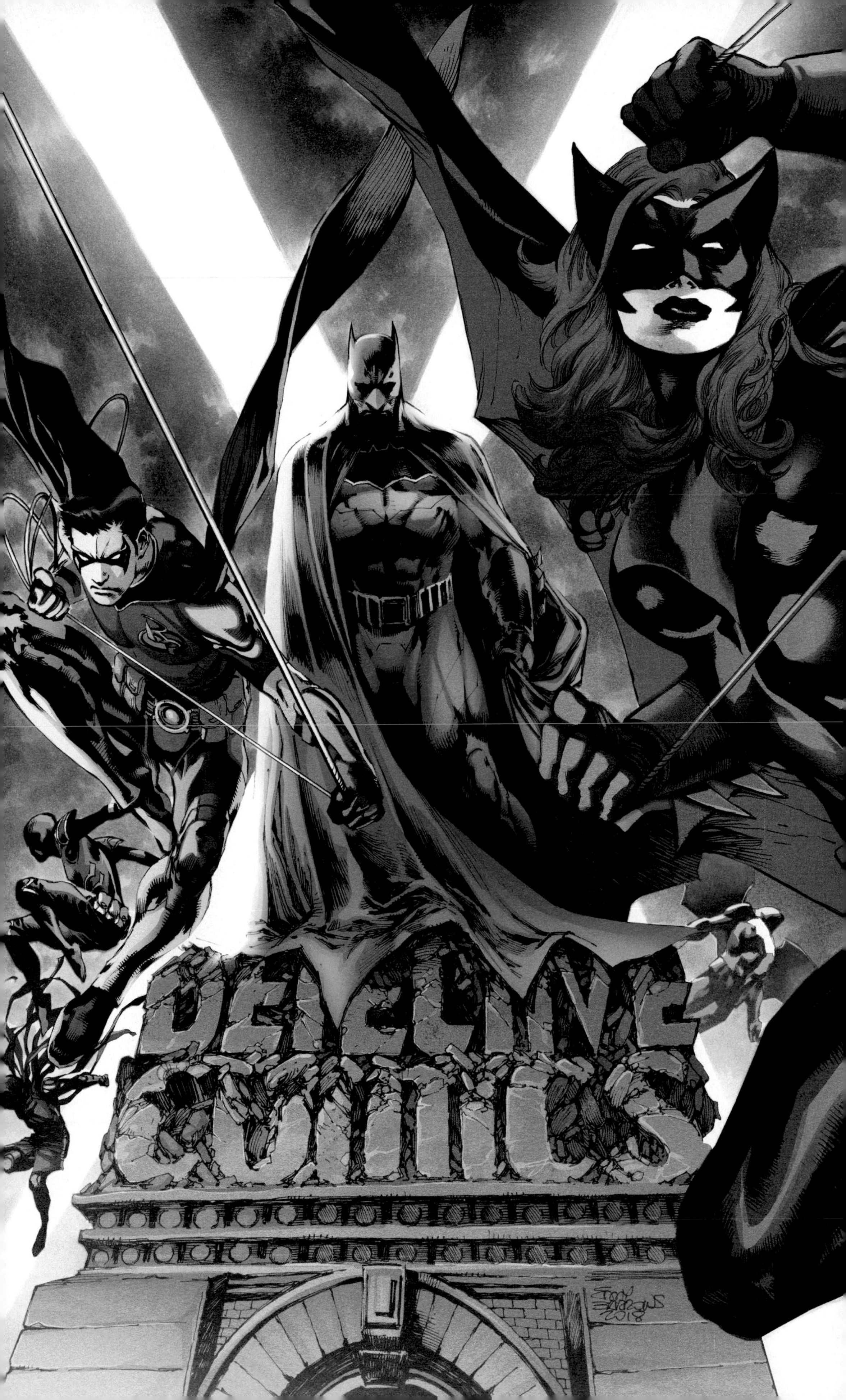
DETECTIVE
COMICS

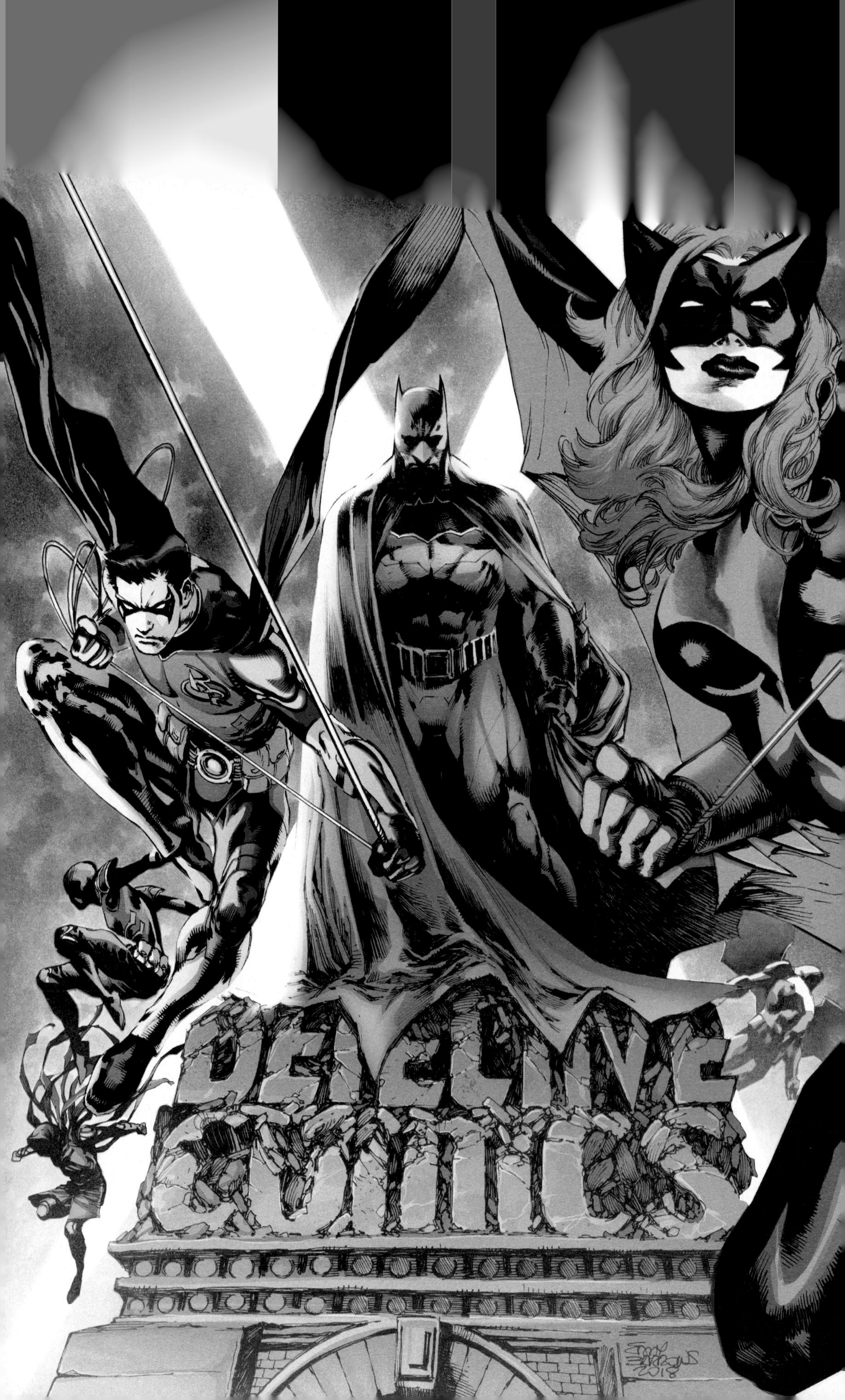

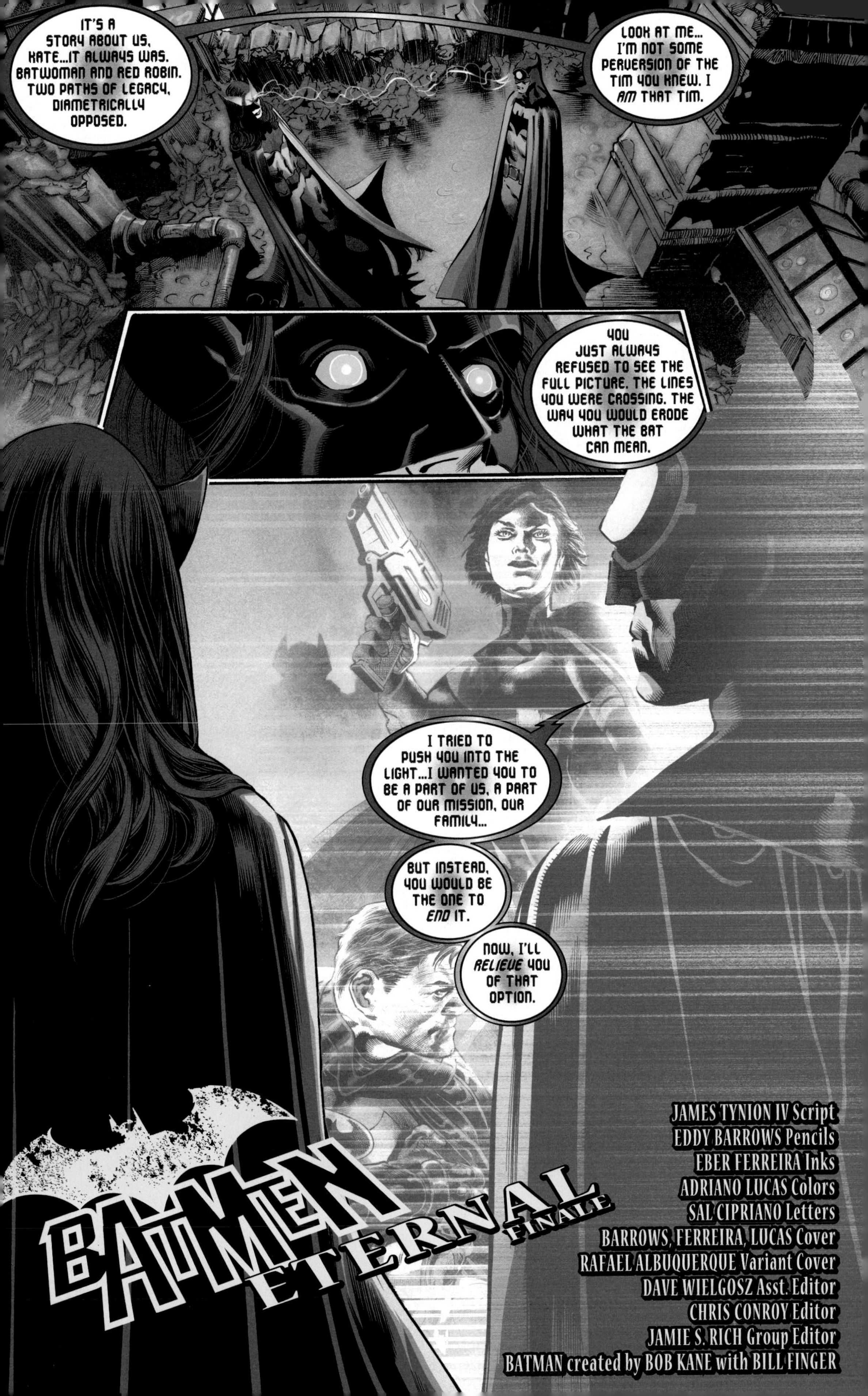
IT'S A STORY ABOUT US, KATE...IT ALWAYS WAS. BATWOMAN AND RED ROBIN. TWO PATHS OF LEGACY, DIAMETRICALLY OPPOSED.
LOOK AT ME... I'M NOT SOME PERVERSION OF THE TIM YOU KNEW. I AM THAT TIM.
YOU JUST ALWAYS REFUSED TO SEE THE FULL PICTURE. THE LINES YOU WERE CROSSING. THE WAY YOU WOULD ERODE WHAT THE BAT CAN MEAN.
I TRIED TO PUSH YOU INTO THE LIGHT...I WANTED YOU TO BE A PART OF US, A PART OF OUR MISSION, OUR FAMILY...
BUT INSTEAD, YOU WOULD BE THE ONE TO END IT.
NOW, I'LL RELIEVE YOU OF THAT OPTION.
BATMEN ETERNAL FINALE
JAMES TYNION IV Script
EDDY BARROWS Pencils
EBER FERREIRA Inks
ADRIANO LUCAS Colors
SAL CIPRIANO Letters
BARROWS, FERREIRA, LUCAS Cover
RAFAEL ALBUQUERQUE Variant Cover
DAVE WIELGOSZ Asst. Editor
CHRIS CONROY Editor
JAMIE S. RICH Group Editor
BATMAN created by BOB KANE with BILL FINGER

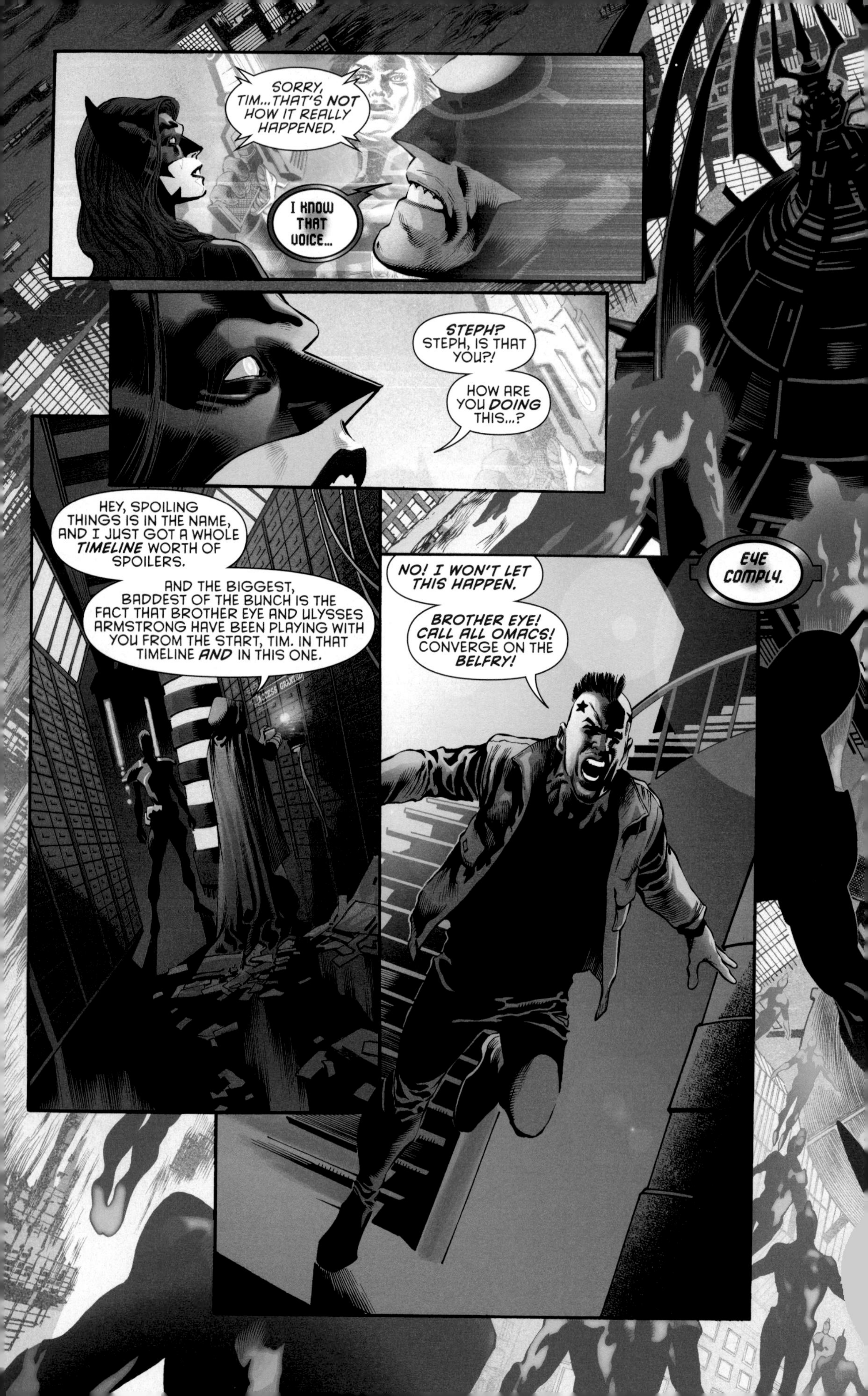
SORRY, TIM...THAT'S NOT HOW IT REALLY HAPPENED.
I KNOW THAT VOICE...
STEPH? STEPH, IS THAT YOU?!
HOW ARE YOU DOING THIS...?
HEY, SPOILING THINGS IS IN THE NAME, AND I JUST GOT A WHOLE TIMELINE WORTH OF SPOILERS.
AND THE BIGGEST, BADDEST OF THE BUNCH IS THE FACT THAT BROTHER EYE AND ULYSSES ARMSTRONG HAVE BEEN PLAYING WITH YOU FROM THE START, TIM. IN THAT TIMELINE AND IN THIS ONE.
NO! I WON'T LET THIS HAPPEN.
BROTHER EYE! CALL ALL OMACS! CONVERGE ON THE BELFRY!
EYE COMPLY.

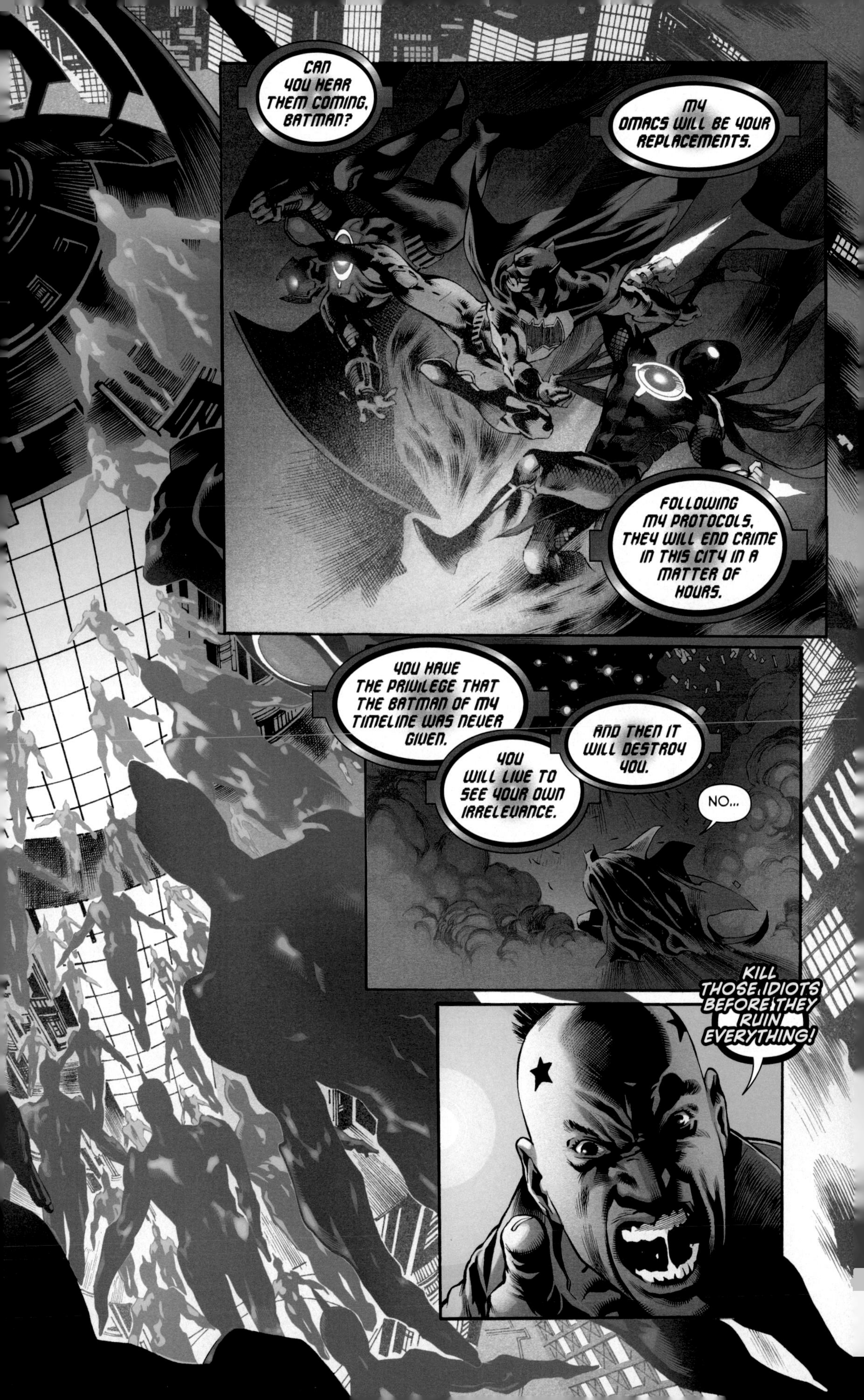
CAN YOU HEAR THEM COMING, BATMAN?
MY OMACS WILL BE YOUR REPLACEMENTS.
FOLLOWING MY PROTOCOLS, THEY WILL END CRIME IN THIS CITY IN A MATTER OF HOURS.
YOU HAVE THE PRIVILEGE THAT THE BATMAN OF MY TIMELINE WAS NEVER GIVEN.
YOU WILL LIVE TO SEE YOUR OWN IRRELEVANCE.
AND THEN IT WILL DESTROY YOU.
NO...
KILL THOSE IDIOTS BEFORE THEY RUIN EVERYTHING!

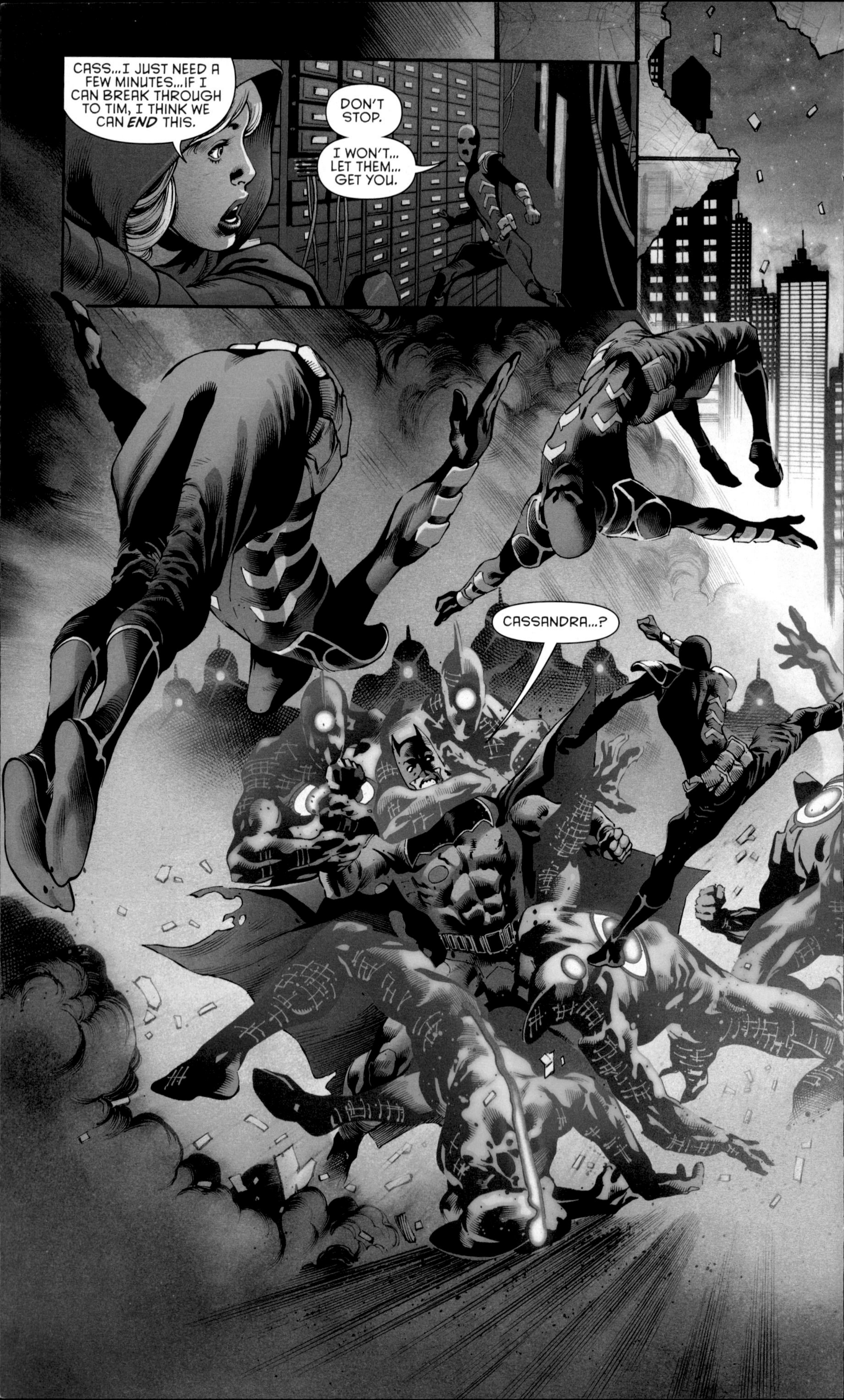
CASS...I JUST NEED A FEW MINUTES...IF I CAN BREAK THROUGH TO TIM, I THINK WE CAN END THIS.
DON'T STOP.
I WON'T... LET THEM... GET YOU.
CASSANDRA...?

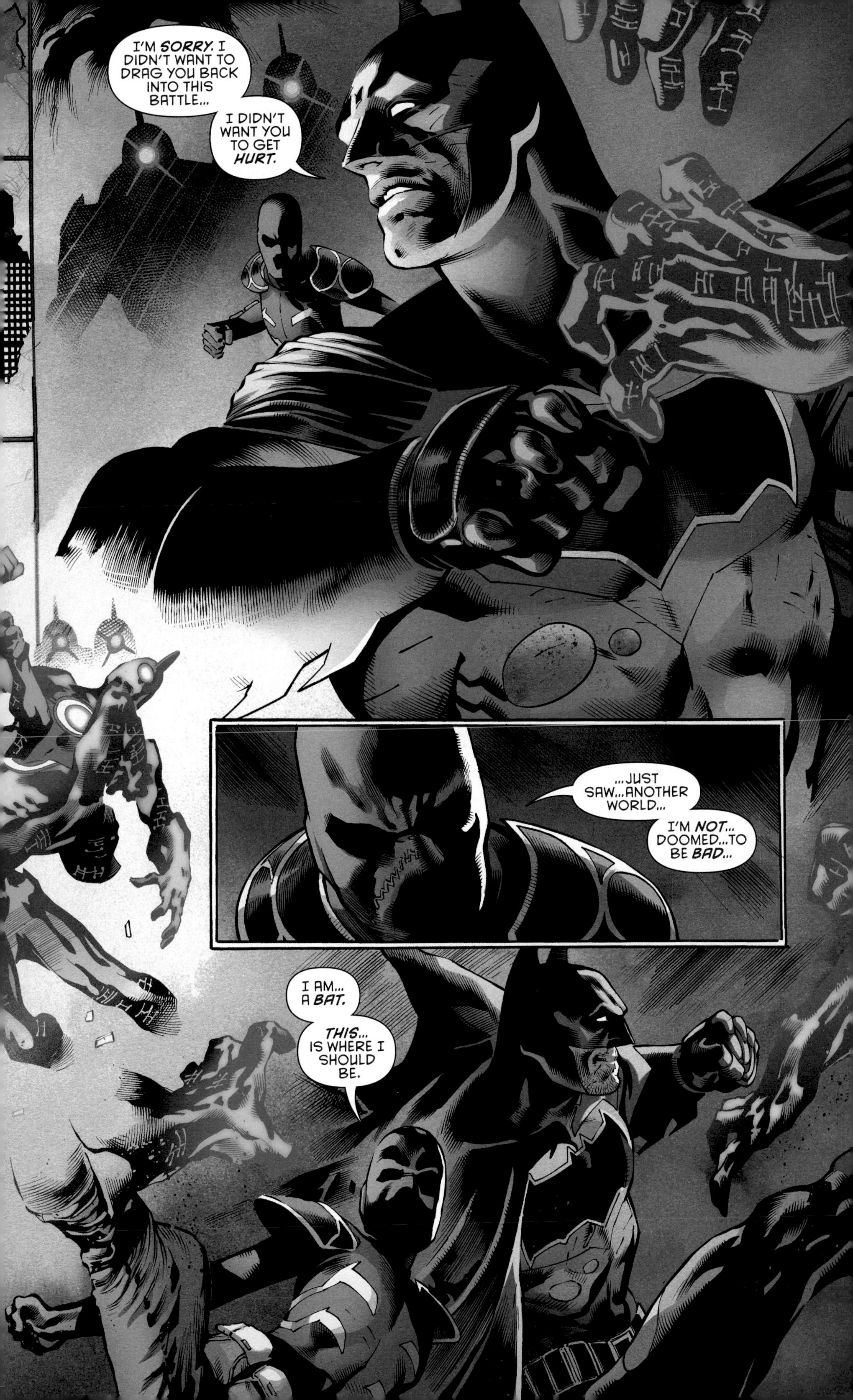
I'M SORRY. I DIDN'T WANT TO DRAG YOU BACK INTO THIS BATTLE...
I DIDN'T WANT YOU TO GET HURT.
...JUST SAW...ANOTHER WORLD...
I'M NOT... DOOMED...TO BE BAD...
I AM... A BAT.
THIS... IS WHERE I SHOULD BE.

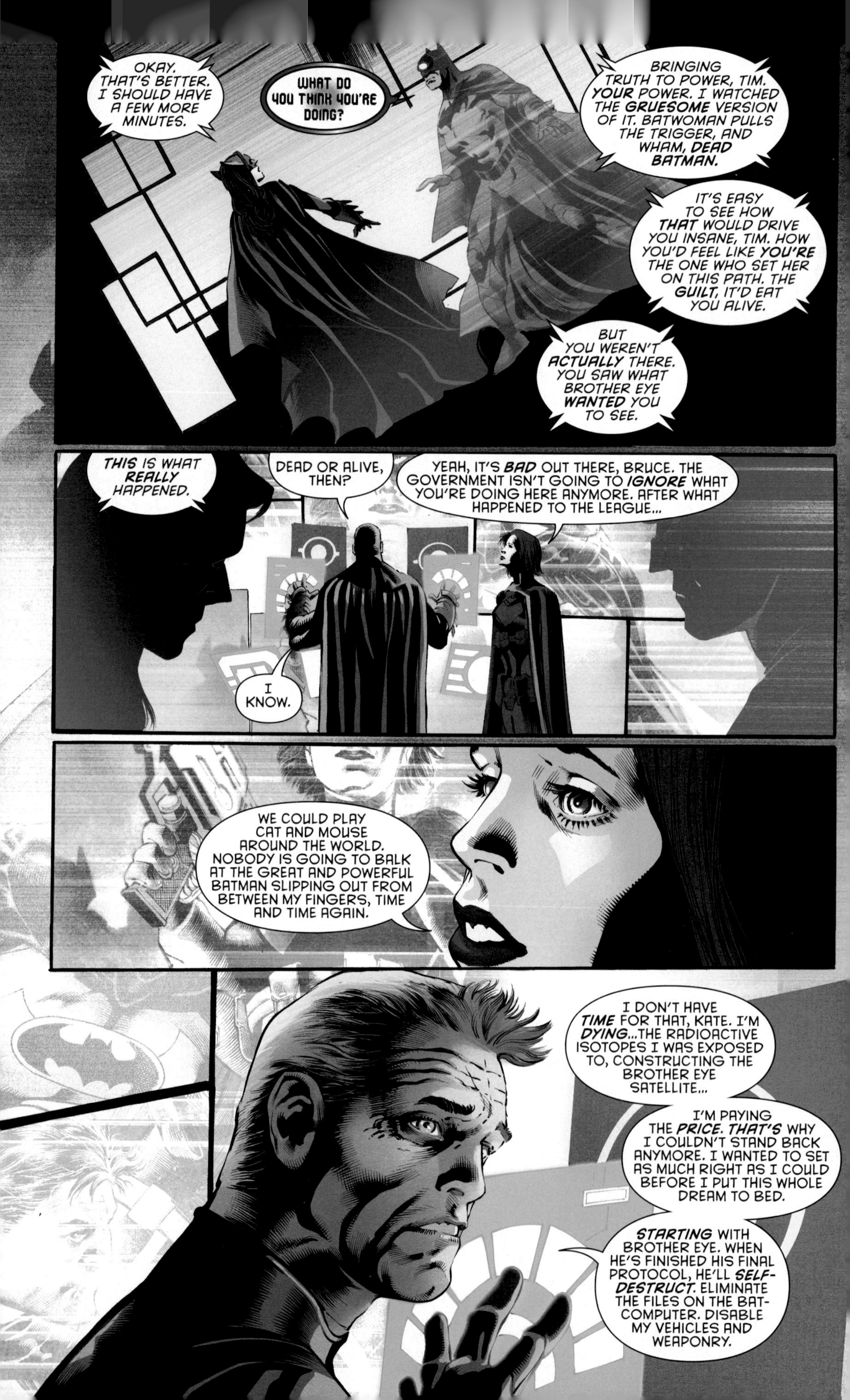
OKAY. THAT'S BETTER. I SHOULD HAVE A FEW MORE MINUTES.
WHAT DO YOU THINK YOU'RE DOING?
BRINGING TRUTH TO POWER, TIM. YOUR POWER. I WATCHED THE GRUESOME VERSION OF IT. BATWOMAN PULLS THE TRIGGER, AND WHAM, DEAD BATMAN.
IT'S EASY TO SEE HOW THAT WOULD DRIVE YOU INSANE, TIM. HOW YOU'D FEEL LIKE YOU'RE THE ONE WHO SET HER ON THIS PATH. THE GUILT, IT'D EAT YOU ALIVE.
BUT YOU WEREN'T ACTUALLY THERE. YOU SAW WHAT BROTHER EYE WANTED YOU TO SEE.
THIS IS WHAT REALLY HAPPENED.
DEAD OR ALIVE, THEN?
YEAH, IT'S BAD OUT THERE, BRUCE. THE GOVERNMENT ISN'T GOING TO IGNORE WHAT YOU'RE DOING HERE ANYMORE. AFTER WHAT HAPPENED TO THE LEAGUE...
I KNOW.
WE COULD PLAY CAT AND MOUSE AROUND THE WORLD. NOBODY IS GOING TO BALK AT THE GREAT AND POWERFUL BATMAN SLIPPING OUT FROM BETWEEN MY FINGERS, TIME AND TIME AGAIN.
I DON'T HAVE TIME FOR THAT, KATE. I'M DYING...THE RADIOACTIVE ISOTOPES I WAS EXPOSED TO, CONSTRUCTING THE BROTHER EYE SATELLITE...
I'M PAYING THE PRICE. THAT'S WHY I COULDN'T STAND BACK ANYMORE. I WANTED TO SET AS MUCH RIGHT AS I COULD BEFORE I PUT THIS WHOLE DREAM TO BED.
STARTING WITH BROTHER EYE. WHEN HE'S FINISHED HIS FINAL PROTOCOL, HE'LL SELF-DESTRUCT. ELIMINATE THE FILES ON THE BAT-COMPUTER. DISABLE MY VEHICLES AND WEAPONRY.

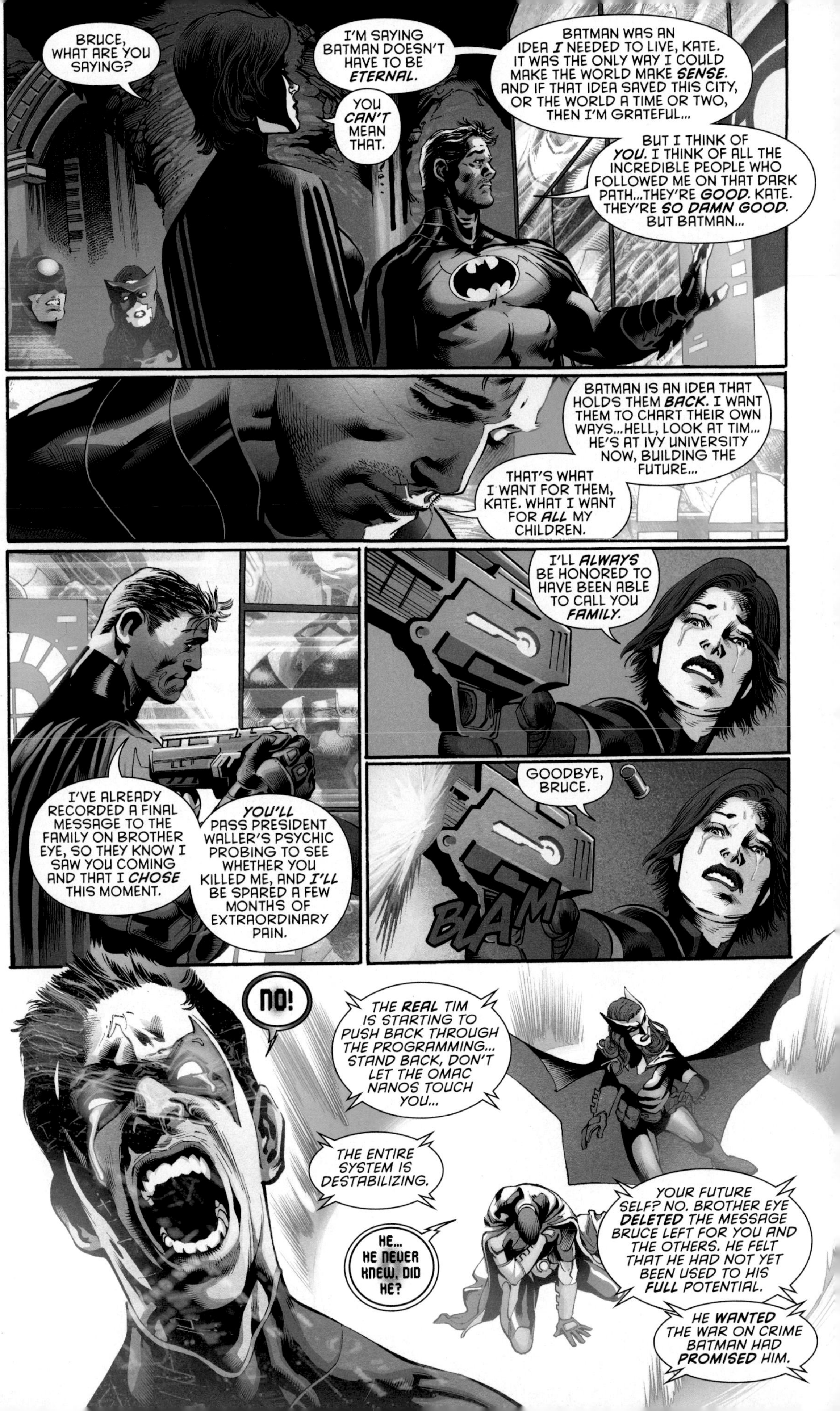
BRUCE, WHAT ARE YOU SAYING?
I'M SAYING BATMAN DOESN'T HAVE TO BE ETERNAL.
YOU CAN'T MEAN THAT.
BATMAN WAS AN IDEA I NEEDED TO LIVE, KATE. IT WAS THE ONLY WAY I COULD MAKE THE WORLD MAKE SENSE. AND IF THAT IDEA SAVED THIS CITY, OR THE WORLD A TIME OR TWO, THEN I'M GRATEFUL...
BUT I THINK OF YOU. I THINK OF ALL THE INCREDIBLE PEOPLE WHO FOLLOWED ME ON THAT DARK PATH...THEY'RE GOOD, KATE. THEY'RE SO DAMN GOOD. BUT BATMAN...
BATMAN IS AN IDEA THAT HOLDS THEM BACK. I WANT THEM TO CHART THEIR OWN WAYS...HELL, LOOK AT TIM... HE'S AT IVY UNIVERSITY NOW, BUILDING THE FUTURE...
THAT'S WHAT I WANT FOR THEM, KATE. WHAT I WANT FOR ALL MY CHILDREN.
I'VE ALREADY RECORDED A FINAL MESSAGE TO THE FAMILY ON BROTHER EYE, SO THEY KNOW I SAW YOU COMING AND THAT I CHOSE THIS MOMENT.
YOU'LL PASS PRESIDENT WALLER'S PSYCHIC PROBING TO SEE WHETHER YOU KILLED ME, AND I'LL BE SPARED A FEW MONTHS OF EXTRAORDINARY PAIN.
I'LL ALWAYS BE HONORED TO HAVE BEEN ABLE TO CALL YOU FAMILY.
GOODBYE, BRUCE.
BLAM
NO!
THE REAL TIM IS STARTING TO PUSH BACK THROUGH THE PROGRAMMING... STAND BACK, DON'T LET THE OMAC NANOS TOUCH YOU...
THE ENTIRE SYSTEM IS DESTABILIZING.
HE... HE NEVER KNEW, DID HE?
YOUR FUTURE SELF? NO. BROTHER EYE DELETED THE MESSAGE BRUCE LEFT FOR YOU AND THE OTHERS. HE FELT THAT HE HAD NOT YET BEEN USED TO HIS FULL POTENTIAL.
HE WANTED THE WAR ON CRIME BATMAN HAD PROMISED HIM.

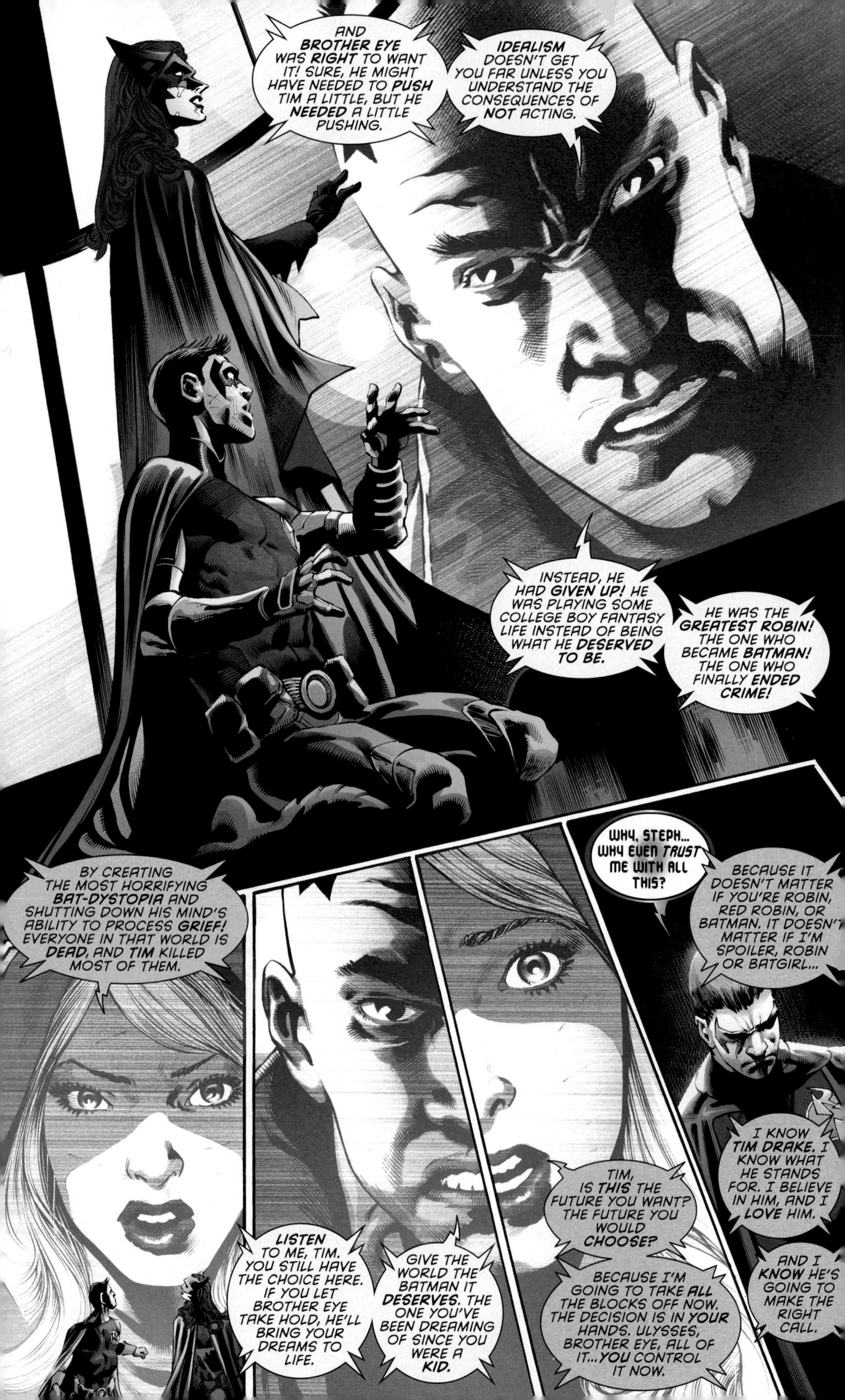

AND BROTHER EYE WAS RIGHT TO WANT IT! SURE, HE MIGHT HAVE NEEDED TO PUSH TIM A LITTLE, BUT HE NEEDED A LITTLE PUSHING.
IDEALISM DOESN'T GET YOU FAR UNLESS YOU UNDERSTAND THE CONSEQUENCES OF NOT ACTING.
INSTEAD, HE HAD GIVEN UP! HE WAS PLAYING SOME COLLEGE BOY FANTASY LIFE INSTEAD OF BEING WHAT HE DESERVED TO BE.
HE WAS THE GREATEST ROBIN! THE ONE WHO BECAME BATMAN! THE ONE WHO FINALLY ENDED CRIME!
BY CREATING THE MOST HORRIFYING BAT-DYSTOPIA AND SHUTTING DOWN HIS MIND'S ABILITY TO PROCESS GRIEF! EVERYONE IN THAT WORLD IS DEAD, AND TIM KILLED MOST OF THEM.
LISTEN TO ME, TIM. YOU STILL HAVE THE CHOICE HERE. IF YOU LET BROTHER EYE TAKE HOLD, HE'LL BRING YOUR DREAMS TO LIFE.
GIVE THE WORLD THE BATMAN IT DESERVES. THE ONE YOU'VE BEEN DREAMING OF SINCE YOU WERE A KID.
TIM, IS THIS THE FUTURE YOU WANT? THE FUTURE YOU WOULD CHOOSE?
BECAUSE I'M GOING TO TAKE ALL THE BLOCKS OFF NOW. THE DECISION IS IN YOUR HANDS. ULYSSES, BROTHER EYE, ALL OF IT...YOU CONTROL IT NOW.
WHY, STEPH... WHY EVEN TRUST ME WITH ALL THIS?
BECAUSE IT DOESN'T MATTER IF YOU'RE ROBIN, RED ROBIN, OR BATMAN. IT DOESN'T MATTER IF I'M SPOILER, ROBIN OR BATGIRL...
I KNOW TIM DRAKE. I KNOW WHAT HE STANDS FOR. I BELIEVE IN HIM, AND I LOVE HIM.
AND I KNOW HE'S GOING TO MAKE THE RIGHT CALL.

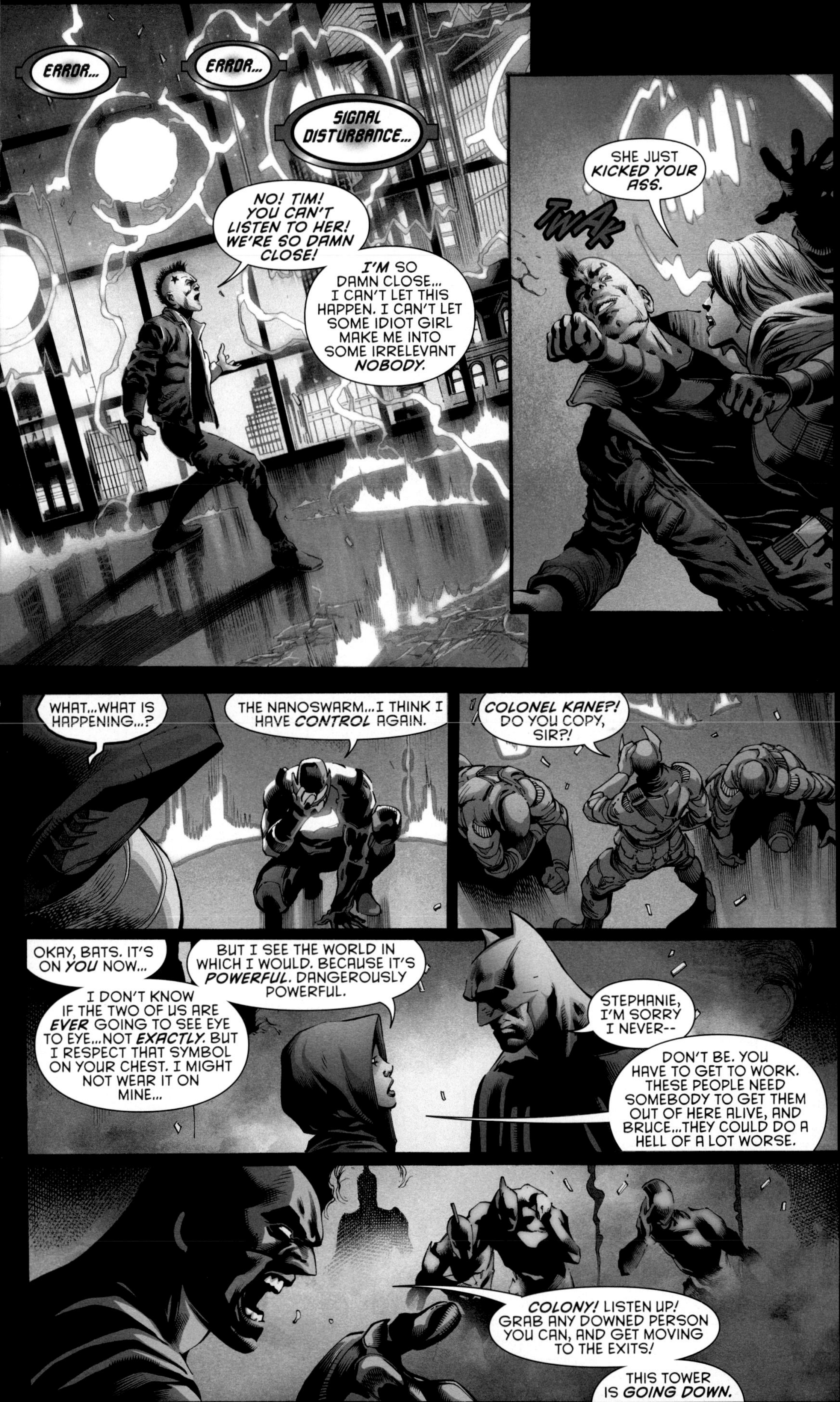
ERROR...
ERROR...
SIGNAL DISTURBANCE...
NO! TIM! YOU CAN'T LISTEN TO HER! WE'RE SO DAMN CLOSE!
I'M SO DAMN CLOSE... I CAN'T LET THIS HAPPEN. I CAN'T LET SOME IDIOT GIRL MAKE ME INTO SOME IRRELEVANT NOBODY.
TWAK
SHE JUST KICKED YOUR ASS.
WHAT...WHAT IS HAPPENING...?
THE NANOSWARM...I THINK I HAVE CONTROL AGAIN.
COLONEL KANE?! DO YOU COPY, SIR?!
OKAY, BATS. IT'S ON YOU NOW...
I DON'T KNOW IF THE TWO OF US ARE EVER GOING TO SEE EYE TO EYE...NOT EXACTLY. BUT I RESPECT THAT SYMBOL ON YOUR CHEST. I MIGHT NOT WEAR IT ON MINE...
BUT I SEE THE WORLD IN WHICH I WOULD. BECAUSE IT'S POWERFUL. DANGEROUSLY POWERFUL.
STEPHANIE, I'M SORRY I NEVER--
DON'T BE. YOU HAVE TO GET TO WORK. THESE PEOPLE NEED SOMEBODY TO GET THEM OUT OF HERE ALIVE, AND BRUCE...THEY COULD DO A HELL OF A LOT WORSE.
COLONY! LISTEN UP! GRAB ANY DOWNED PERSON YOU CAN, AND GET MOVING TO THE EXITS!
THIS TOWER IS GOING DOWN.

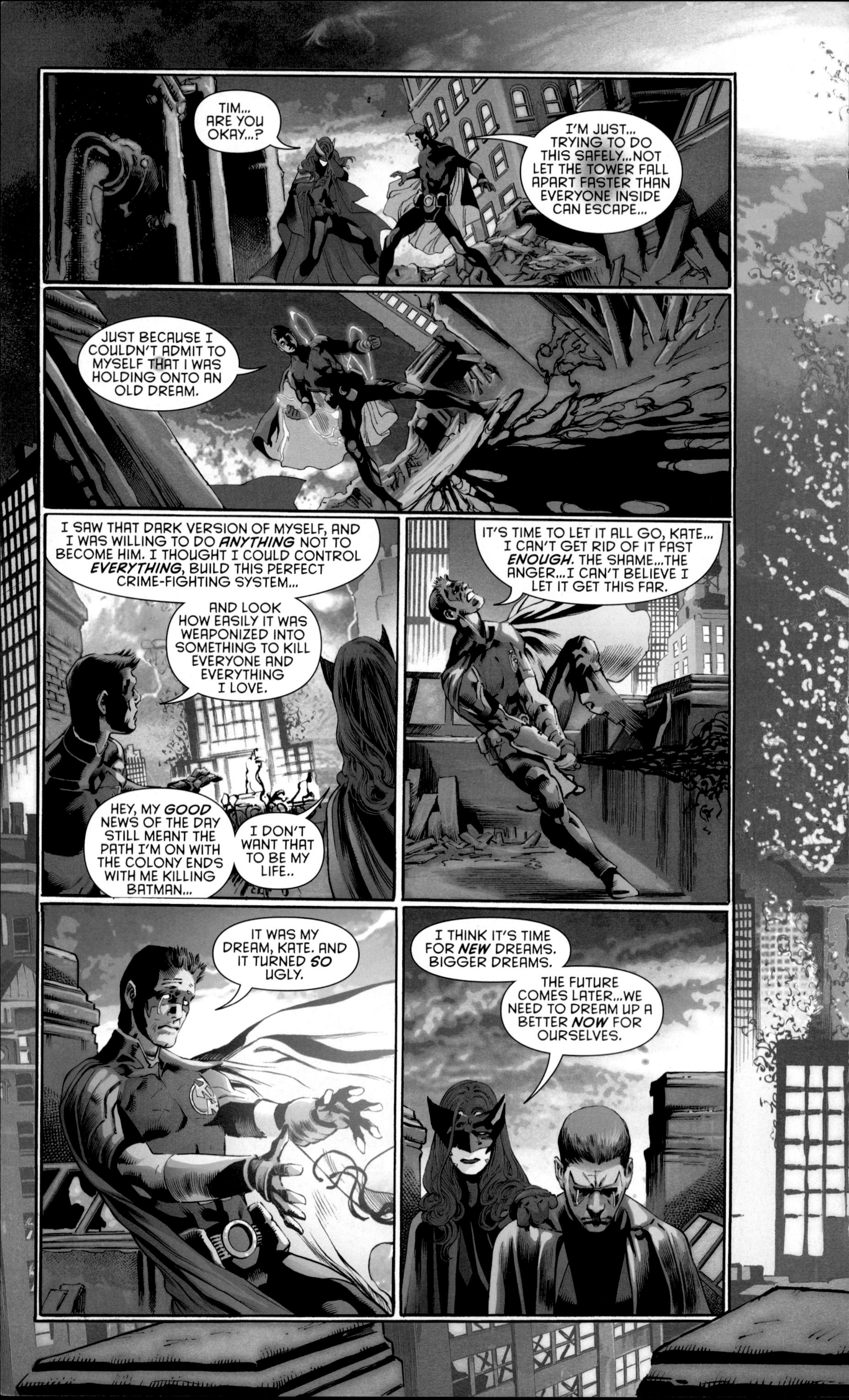
TIM... ARE YOU OKAY...?
I'M JUST... TRYING TO DO THIS SAFELY...NOT LET THE TOWER FALL APART FASTER THAN EVERYONE INSIDE CAN ESCAPE...
JUST BECAUSE I COULDN'T ADMIT TO MYSELF THAT I WAS HOLDING ONTO AN OLD DREAM.
I SAW THAT DARK VERSION OF MYSELF, AND I WAS WILLING TO DO *ANYTHING* NOT TO BECOME HIM. I THOUGHT I COULD CONTROL *EVERYTHING*, BUILD THIS PERFECT CRIME-FIGHTING SYSTEM...
AND LOOK HOW EASILY IT WAS WEAPONIZED INTO SOMETHING TO KILL EVERYONE AND EVERYTHING I LOVE.
HEY, MY *GOOD* NEWS OF THE DAY STILL MEANT THE PATH I'M ON WITH THE COLONY ENDS WITH ME KILLING BATMAN...
I DON'T WANT THAT TO BE MY LIFE..
IT'S TIME TO LET IT ALL GO, KATE... I CAN'T GET RID OF IT FAST *ENOUGH*. THE SHAME...THE ANGER...I CAN'T BELIEVE I LET IT GET THIS FAR.
IT WAS MY DREAM, KATE. AND IT TURNED *SO* UGLY.
I THINK IT'S TIME FOR *NEW* DREAMS. BIGGER DREAMS.
THE FUTURE COMES LATER...WE NEED TO DREAM UP A BETTER *NOW* FOR OURSELVES.

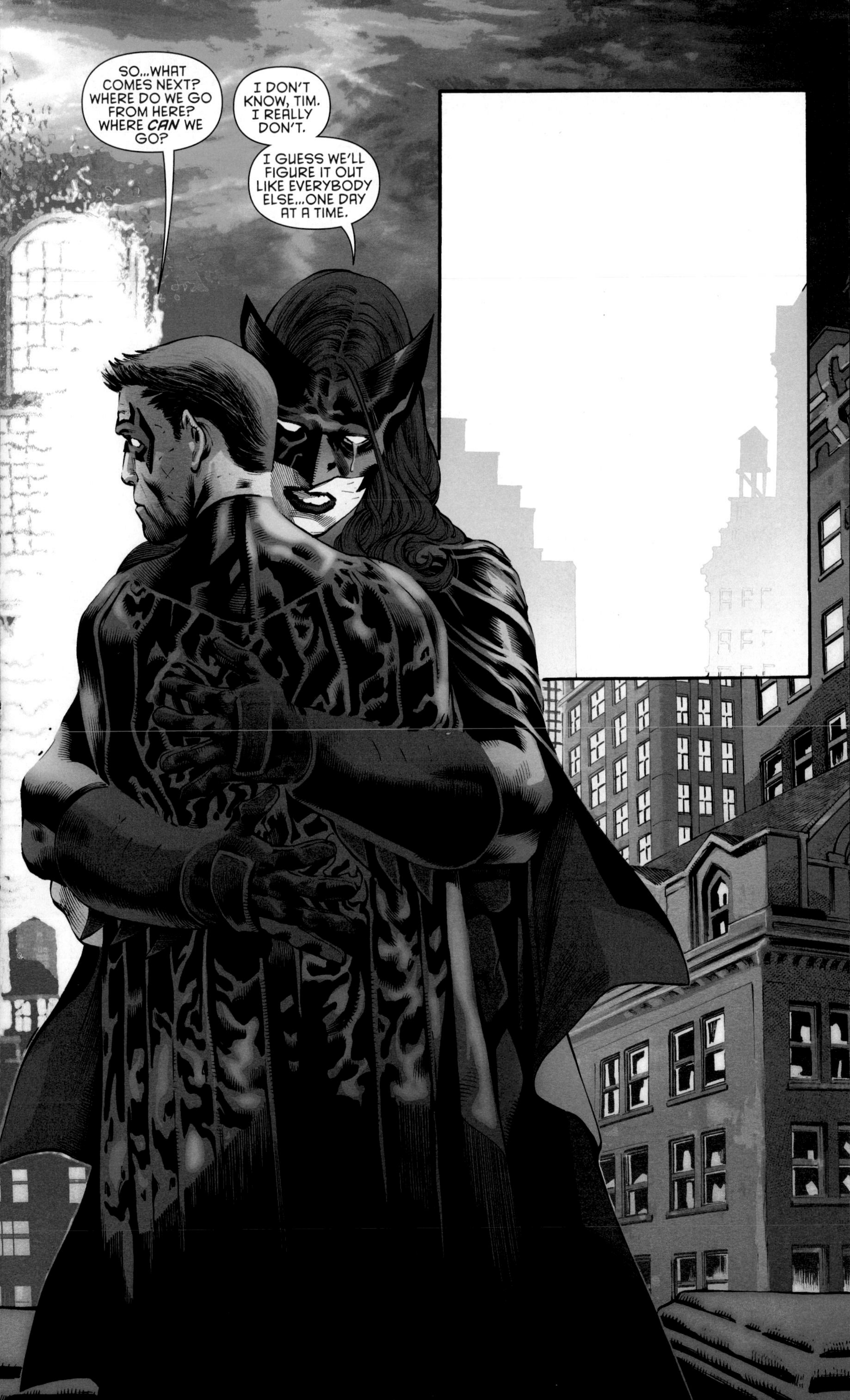
SO...WHAT COMES NEXT? WHERE DO WE GO FROM HERE? WHERE CAN WE GO?
I DON'T KNOW, TIM. I REALLY DON'T.
I GUESS WE'LL FIGURE IT OUT LIKE EVERYBODY ELSE...ONE DAY AT A TIME.

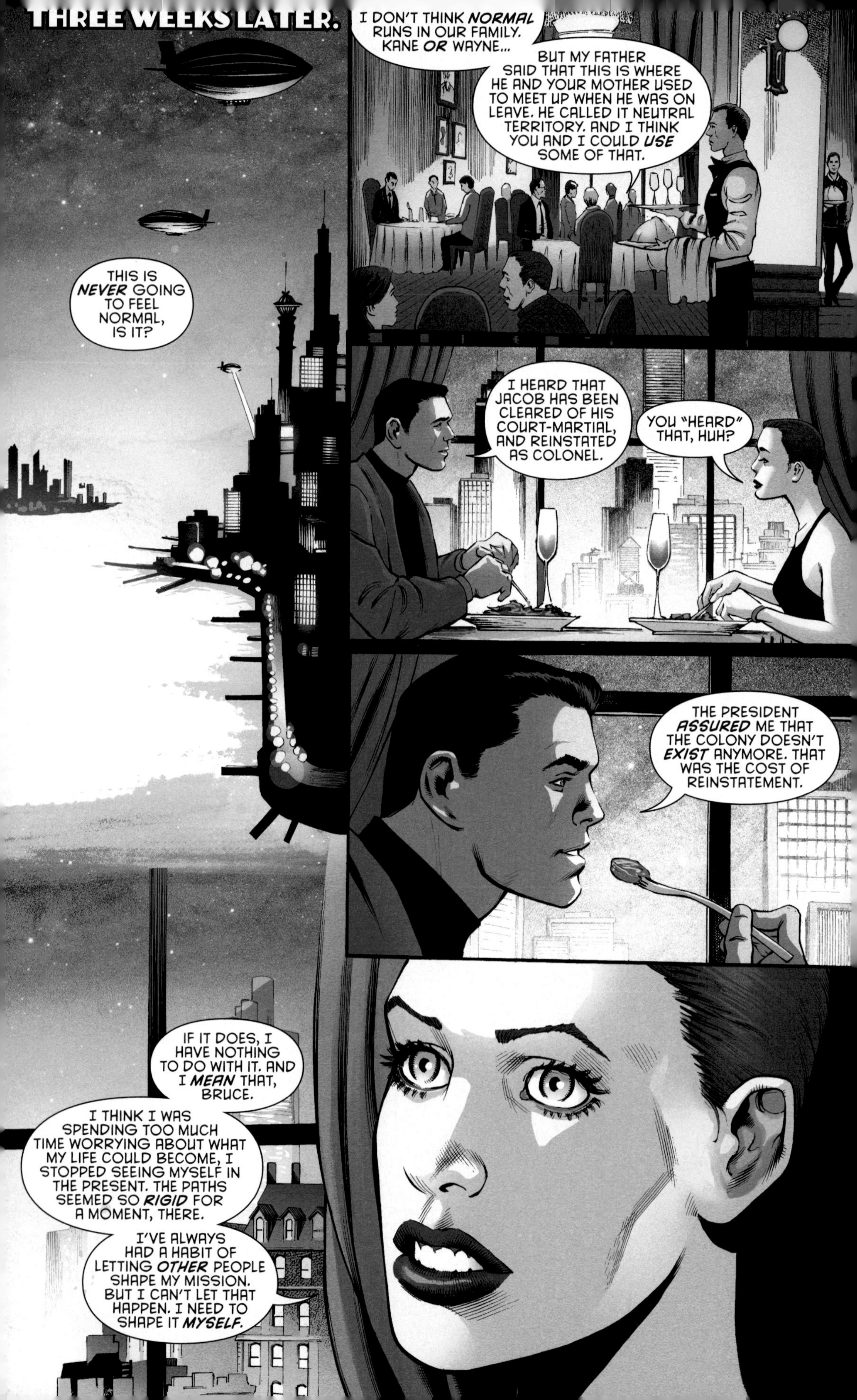
THREE WEEKS LATER.
THIS IS NEVER GOING TO FEEL NORMAL, IS IT?
I DON'T THINK NORMAL RUNS IN OUR FAMILY. KANE OR WAYNE...
BUT MY FATHER SAID THAT THIS IS WHERE HE AND YOUR MOTHER USED TO MEET UP WHEN HE WAS ON LEAVE. HE CALLED IT NEUTRAL TERRITORY. AND I THINK YOU AND I COULD USE SOME OF THAT.
I HEARD THAT JACOB HAS BEEN CLEARED OF HIS COURT-MARTIAL, AND REINSTATED AS COLONEL.
YOU "HEARD" THAT, HUH?
THE PRESIDENT ASSURED ME THAT THE COLONY DOESN'T EXIST ANYMORE. THAT WAS THE COST OF REINSTATEMENT.
IF IT DOES, I HAVE NOTHING TO DO WITH IT. AND I MEAN THAT, BRUCE.
I THINK I WAS SPENDING TOO MUCH TIME WORRYING ABOUT WHAT MY LIFE COULD BECOME, I STOPPED SEEING MYSELF IN THE PRESENT. THE PATHS SEEMED SO RIGID FOR A MOMENT, THERE.
I'VE ALWAYS HAD A HABIT OF LETTING OTHER PEOPLE SHAPE MY MISSION. BUT I CAN'T LET THAT HAPPEN. I NEED TO SHAPE IT MYSELF.

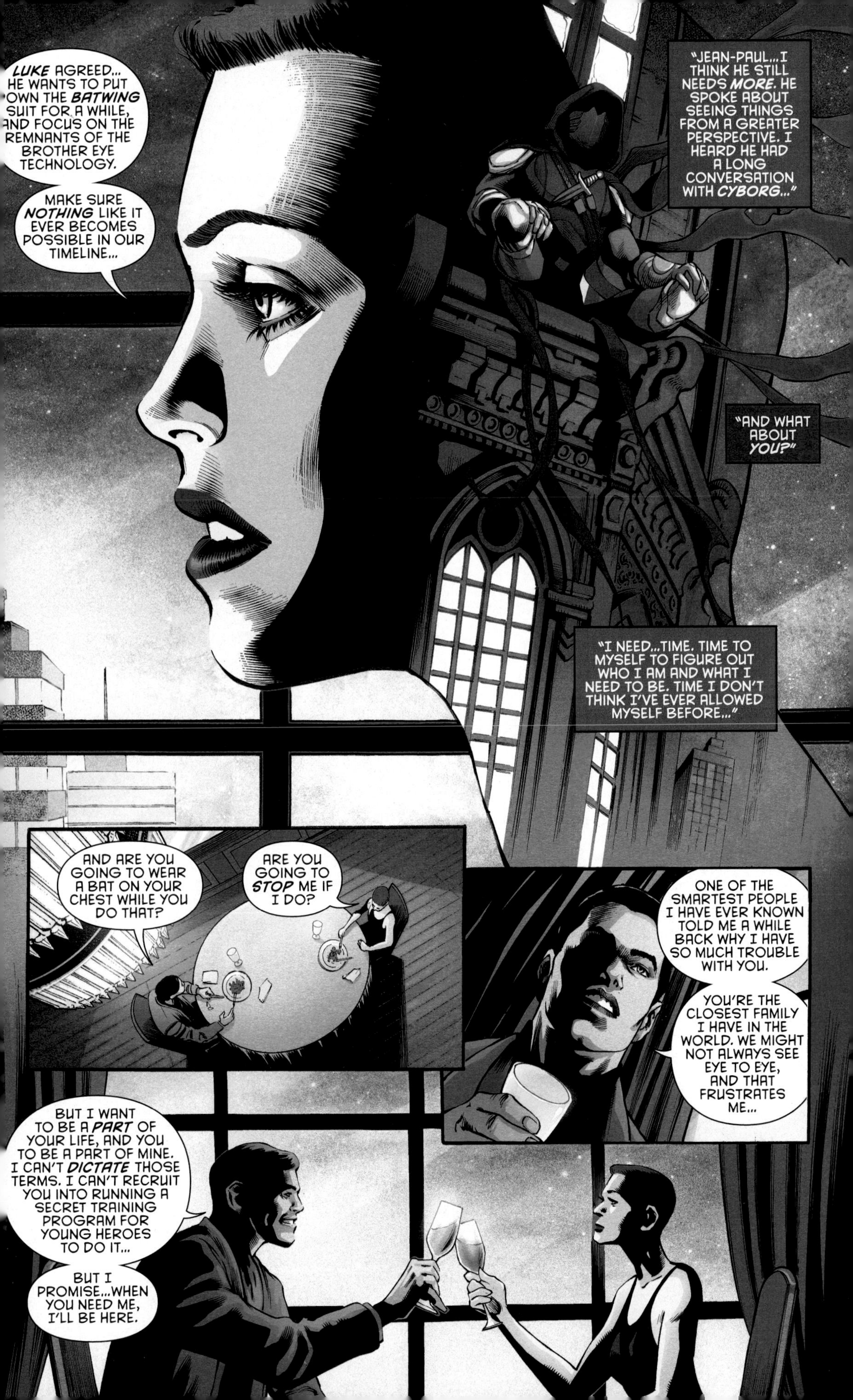
LUKE AGREED... HE WANTS TO PUT DOWN THE BATWING SUIT FOR A WHILE, AND FOCUS ON THE REMNANTS OF THE BROTHER EYE TECHNOLOGY.
MAKE SURE NOTHING LIKE IT EVER BECOMES POSSIBLE IN OUR TIMELINE...
"JEAN-PAUL...I THINK HE STILL NEEDS MORE. HE SPOKE ABOUT SEEING THINGS FROM A GREATER PERSPECTIVE. I HEARD HE HAD A LONG CONVERSATION WITH CYBORG..."
"AND WHAT ABOUT YOU?"
"I NEED...TIME. TIME TO MYSELF TO FIGURE OUT WHO I AM AND WHAT I NEED TO BE. TIME I DON'T THINK I'VE EVER ALLOWED MYSELF BEFORE..."
AND ARE YOU GOING TO WEAR A BAT ON YOUR CHEST WHILE YOU DO THAT?
ARE YOU GOING TO STOP ME IF I DO?
ONE OF THE SMARTEST PEOPLE I HAVE EVER KNOWN TOLD ME A WHILE BACK WHY I HAVE SO MUCH TROUBLE WITH YOU.
YOU'RE THE CLOSEST FAMILY I HAVE IN THE WORLD. WE MIGHT NOT ALWAYS SEE EYE TO EYE, AND THAT FRUSTRATES ME...
BUT I WANT TO BE A PART OF YOUR LIFE, AND YOU TO BE A PART OF MINE. I CAN'T DICTATE THOSE TERMS. I CAN'T RECRUIT YOU INTO RUNNING A SECRET TRAINING PROGRAM FOR YOUNG HEROES TO DO IT...
BUT I PROMISE...WHEN YOU NEED ME, I'LL BE HERE.

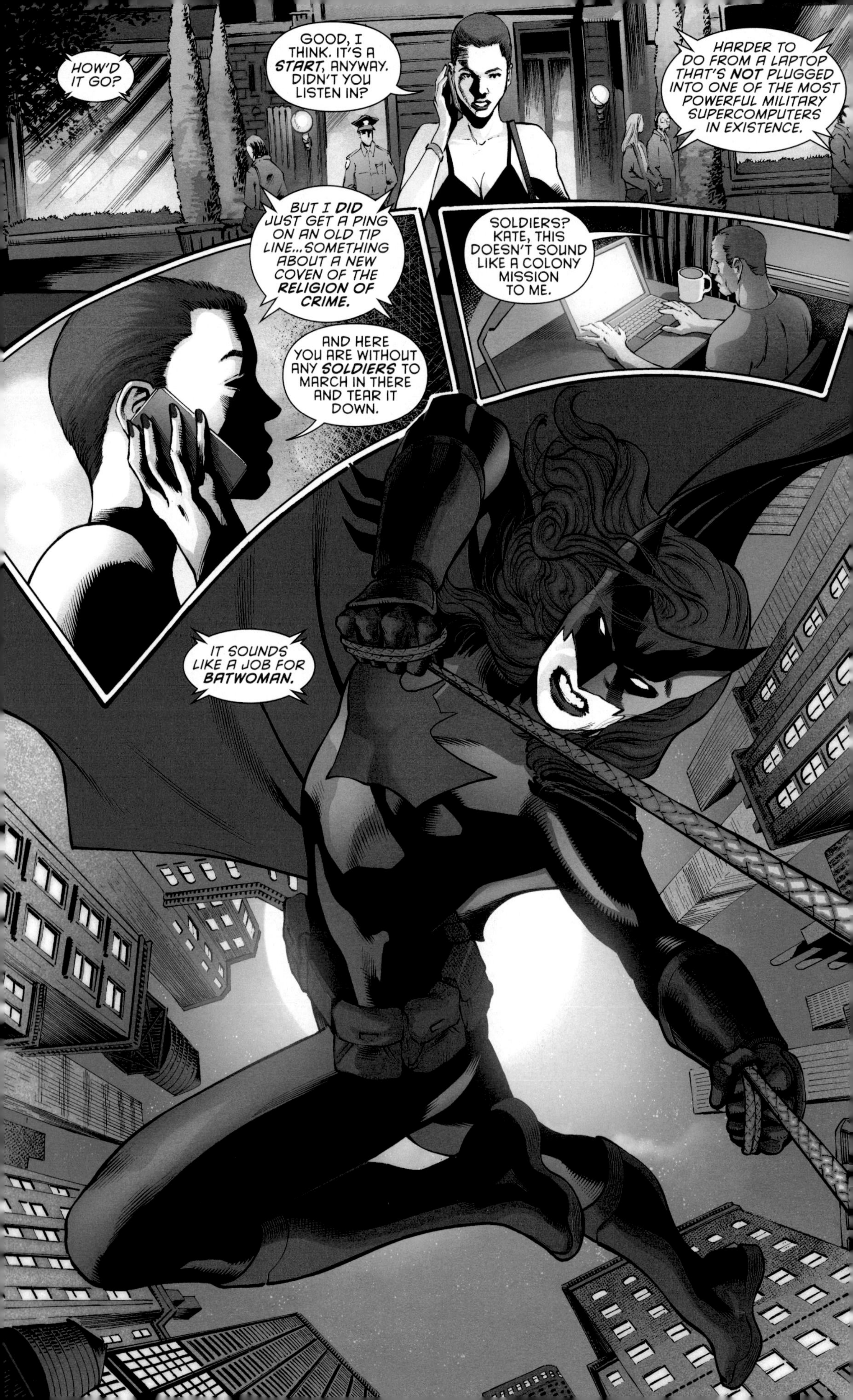
HOW'D IT GO?
GOOD, I THINK. IT'S A START, ANYWAY. DIDN'T YOU LISTEN IN?
HARDER TO DO FROM A LAPTOP THAT'S NOT PLUGGED INTO ONE OF THE MOST POWERFUL MILITARY SUPERCOMPUTERS IN EXISTENCE.
BUT I DID JUST GET A PING ON AN OLD TIP LINE...SOMETHING ABOUT A NEW COVEN OF THE RELIGION OF CRIME.
AND HERE YOU ARE WITHOUT ANY SOLDIERS TO MARCH IN THERE AND TEAR IT DOWN.
SOLDIERS? KATE, THIS DOESN'T SOUND LIKE A COLONY MISSION TO ME.
IT SOUNDS LIKE A JOB FOR BATWOMAN.

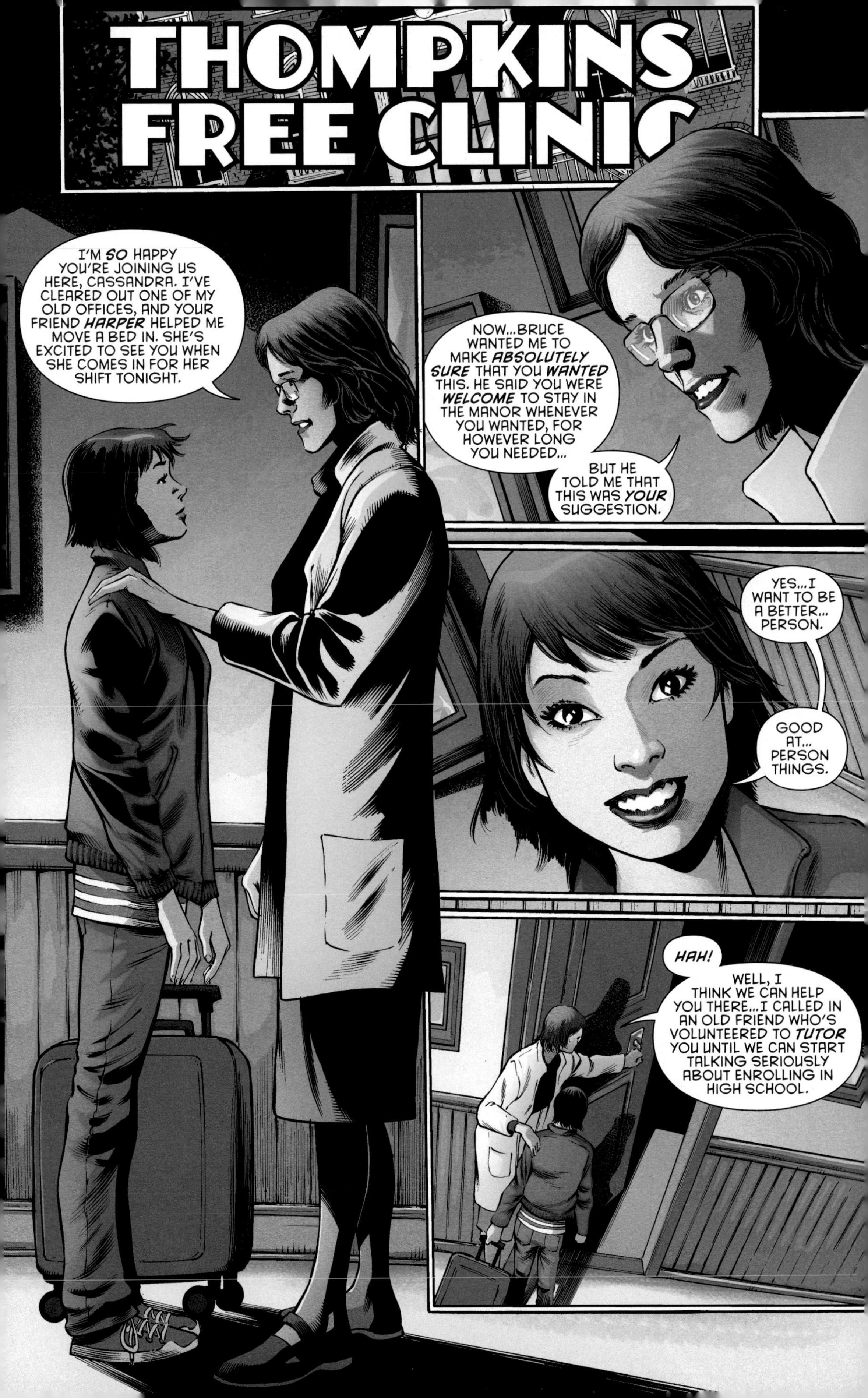
THOMPKINS FREE CLINIC
I'M SO HAPPY YOU'RE JOINING US HERE, CASSANDRA. I'VE CLEARED OUT ONE OF MY OLD OFFICES, AND YOUR FRIEND HARPER HELPED ME MOVE A BED IN. SHE'S EXCITED TO SEE YOU WHEN SHE COMES IN FOR HER SHIFT TONIGHT.
NOW...BRUCE WANTED ME TO MAKE ABSOLUTELY SURE THAT YOU WANTED THIS. HE SAID YOU WERE WELCOME TO STAY IN THE MANOR WHENEVER YOU WANTED, FOR HOWEVER LONG YOU NEEDED...
BUT HE TOLD ME THAT THIS WAS YOUR SUGGESTION.
YES...I WANT TO BE A BETTER... PERSON.
GOOD AT... PERSON THINGS.
HAH!
WELL, I THINK WE CAN HELP YOU THERE...I CALLED IN AN OLD FRIEND WHO'S VOLUNTEERED TO TUTOR YOU UNTIL WE CAN START TALKING SERIOUSLY ABOUT ENROLLING IN HIGH SCHOOL.

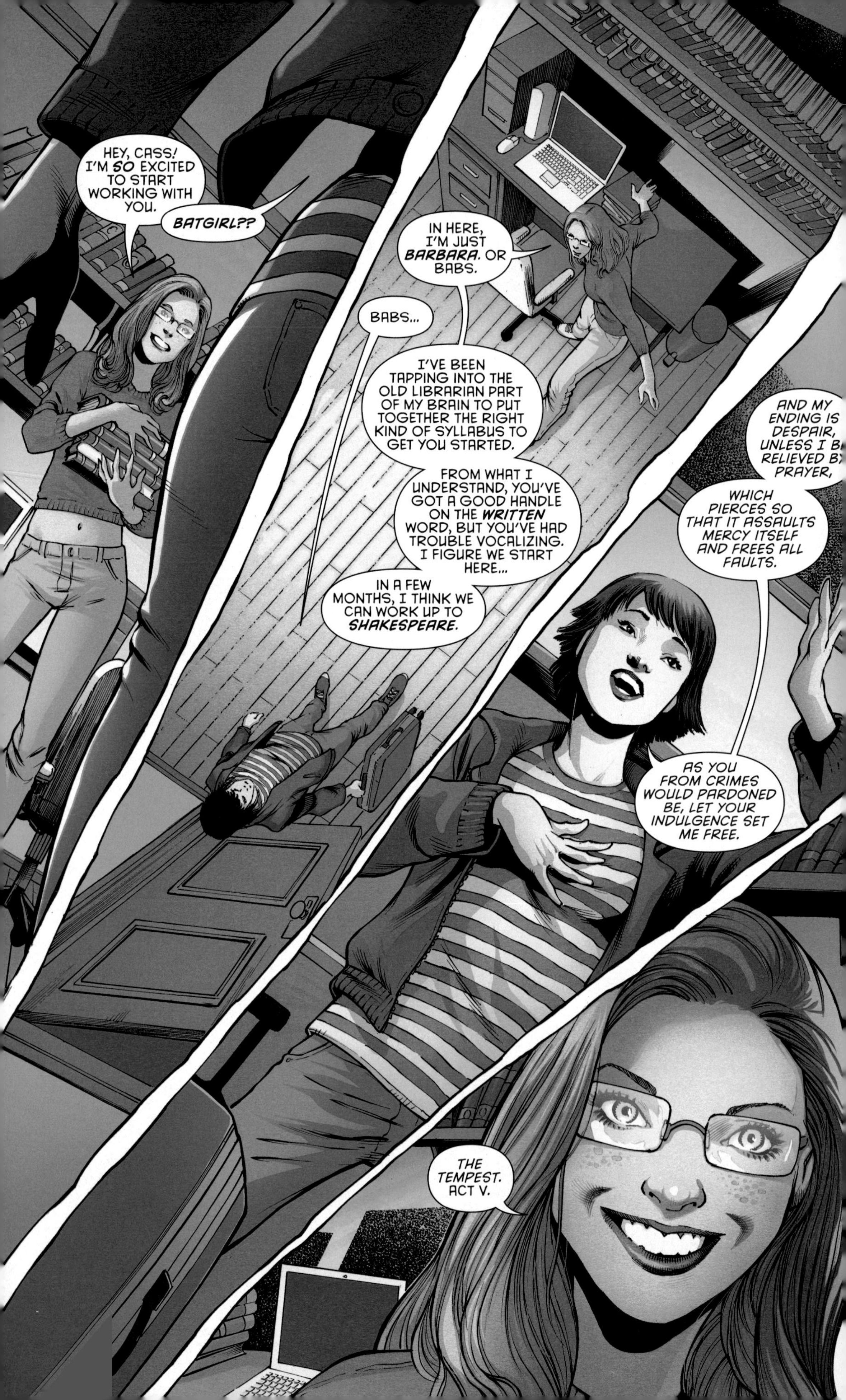
HEY, CASS! I'M *SO* EXCITED TO START WORKING WITH YOU.
BATGIRL??
IN HERE, I'M JUST *BARBARA*. OR BABS.
BABS...
I'VE BEEN TAPPING INTO THE OLD LIBRARIAN PART OF MY BRAIN TO PUT TOGETHER THE RIGHT KIND OF SYLLABUS TO GET YOU STARTED.
FROM WHAT I UNDERSTAND, YOU'VE GOT A GOOD HANDLE ON THE *WRITTEN* WORD, BUT YOU'VE HAD TROUBLE VOCALIZING. I FIGURE WE START HERE...
IN A FEW MONTHS, I THINK WE CAN WORK UP TO *SHAKESPEARE*.
AND MY ENDING IS DESPAIR, UNLESS I BE RELIEVED BY PRAYER,
WHICH PIERCES SO THAT IT ASSAULTS MERCY ITSELF AND FREES ALL FAULTS.
AS YOU FROM CRIMES WOULD PARDONED BE, LET YOUR INDULGENCE SET ME FREE.
THE TEMPEST. ACT V.

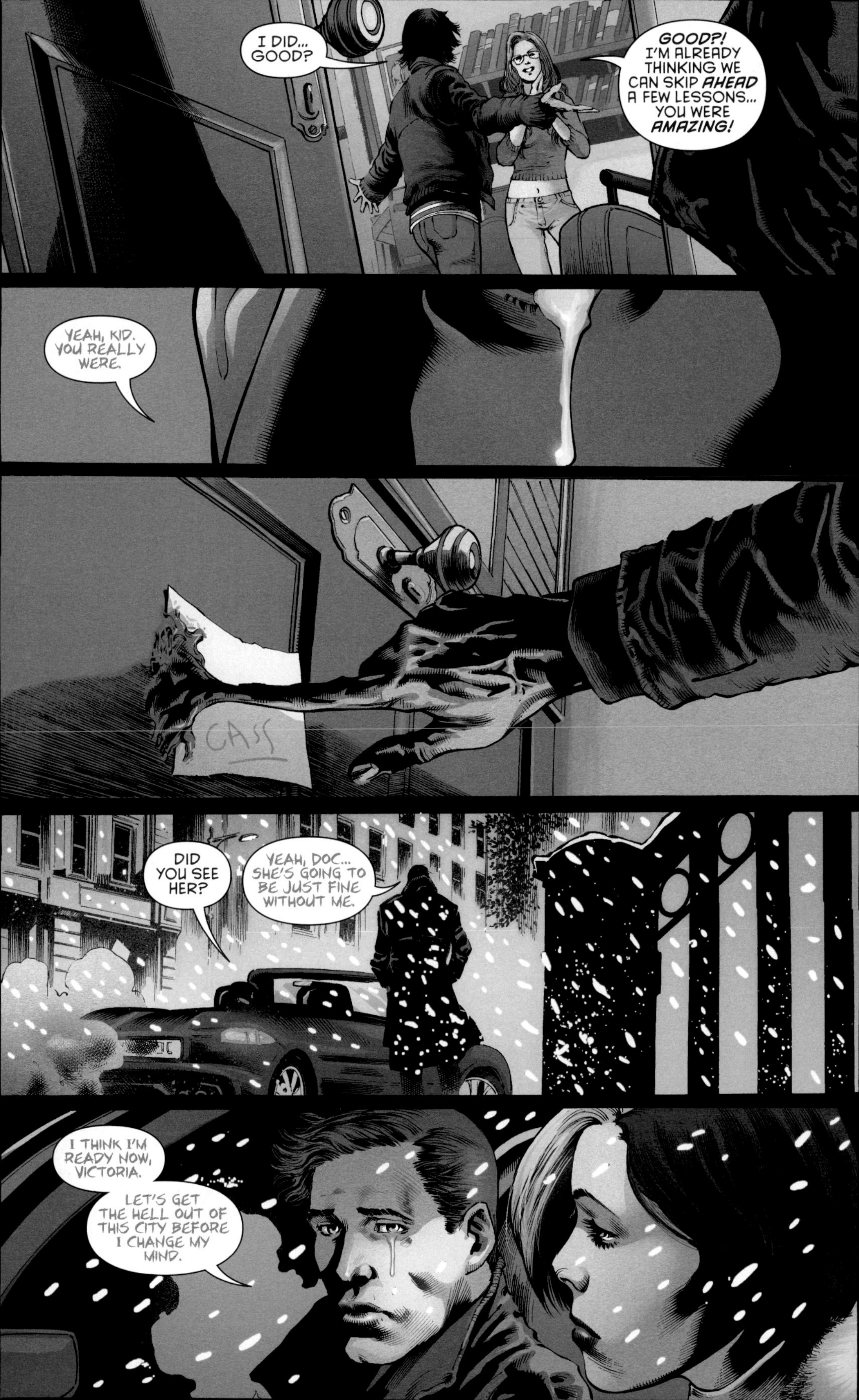
I DID... GOOD?
GOOD?! I'M ALREADY THINKING WE CAN SKIP AHEAD A FEW LESSONS... YOU WERE AMAZING!
YEAH, KID. YOU REALLY WERE.
CASS
DID YOU SEE HER?
YEAH, DOC... SHE'S GOING TO BE JUST FINE WITHOUT ME.
I THINK I'M READY NOW, VICTORIA.
LET'S GET THE HELL OUT OF THIS CITY BEFORE I CHANGE MY MIND.

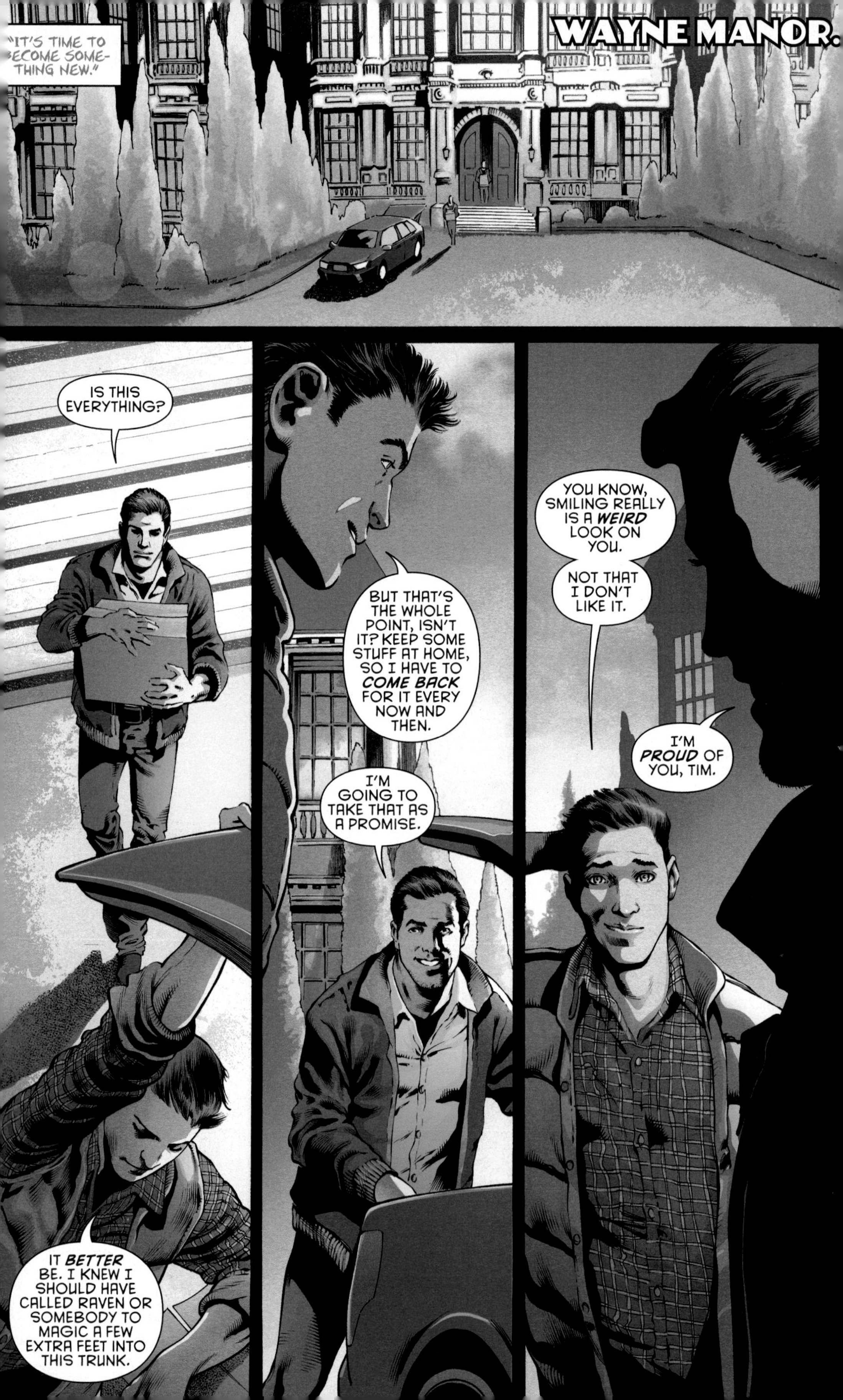

"IT'S TIME TO BECOME SOME-THING NEW."
WAYNE MANOR.
IS THIS EVERYTHING?
IT *BETTER* BE. I KNEW I SHOULD HAVE CALLED RAVEN OR SOMEBODY TO MAGIC A FEW EXTRA FEET INTO THIS TRUNK.
BUT THAT'S THE WHOLE POINT, ISN'T IT? KEEP SOME STUFF AT HOME, SO I HAVE TO *COME BACK* FOR IT EVERY NOW AND THEN.
I'M GOING TO TAKE THAT AS A PROMISE.
YOU KNOW, SMILING REALLY IS A *WEIRD* LOOK ON YOU.
NOT THAT I DON'T LIKE IT.
I'M *PROUD* OF YOU, TIM.

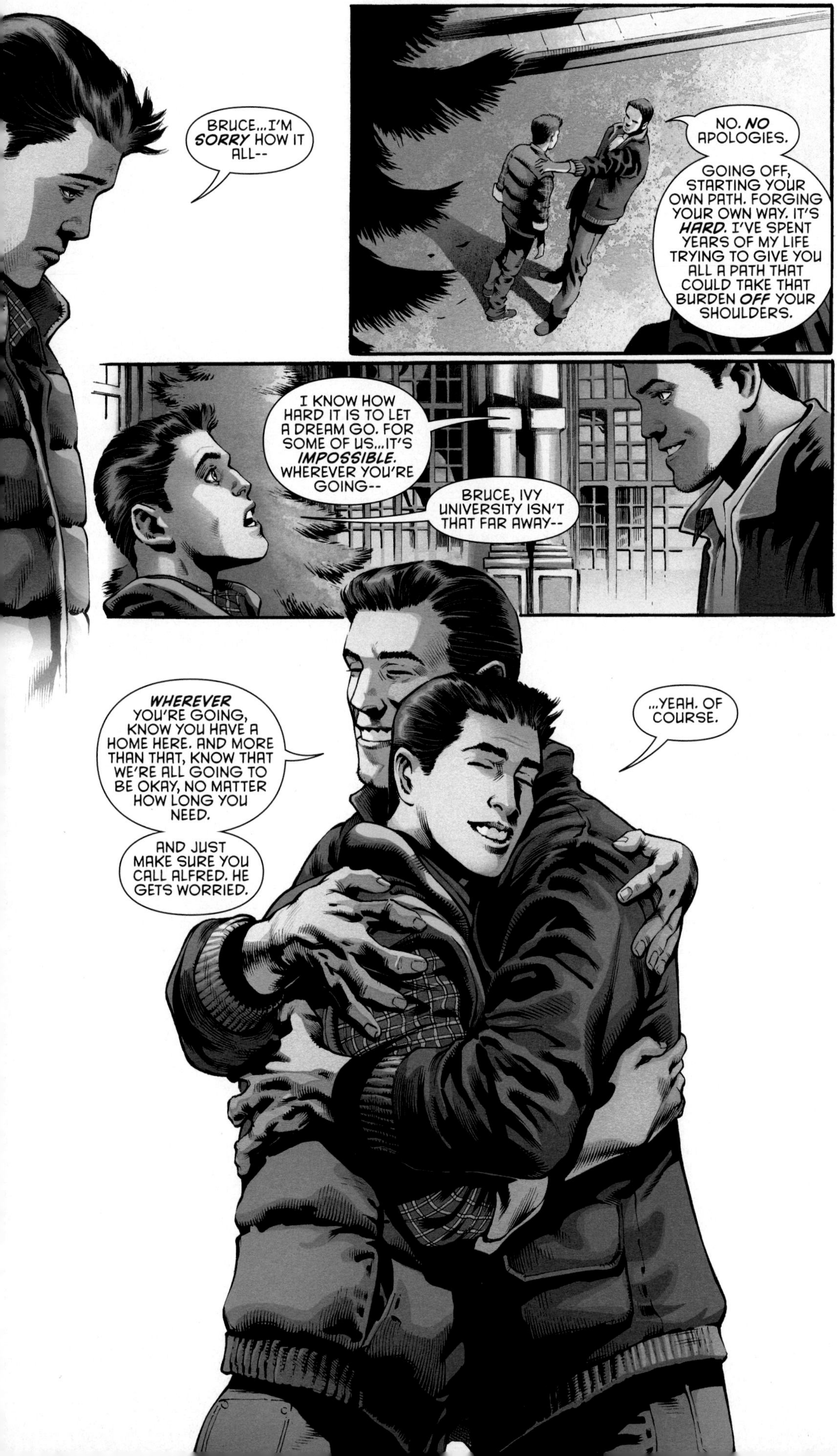
BRUCE...I'M SORRY HOW IT ALL--
NO. NO APOLOGIES.
GOING OFF, STARTING YOUR OWN PATH. FORGING YOUR OWN WAY. IT'S HARD. I'VE SPENT YEARS OF MY LIFE TRYING TO GIVE YOU ALL A PATH THAT COULD TAKE THAT BURDEN OFF YOUR SHOULDERS.
I KNOW HOW HARD IT IS TO LET A DREAM GO. FOR SOME OF US...IT'S IMPOSSIBLE. WHEREVER YOU'RE GOING--
BRUCE, IVY UNIVERSITY ISN'T THAT FAR AWAY--
WHEREVER YOU'RE GOING, KNOW YOU HAVE A HOME HERE. AND MORE THAN THAT, KNOW THAT WE'RE ALL GOING TO BE OKAY, NO MATTER HOW LONG YOU NEED.
AND JUST MAKE SURE YOU CALL ALFRED. HE GETS WORRIED.
...YEAH. OF COURSE.

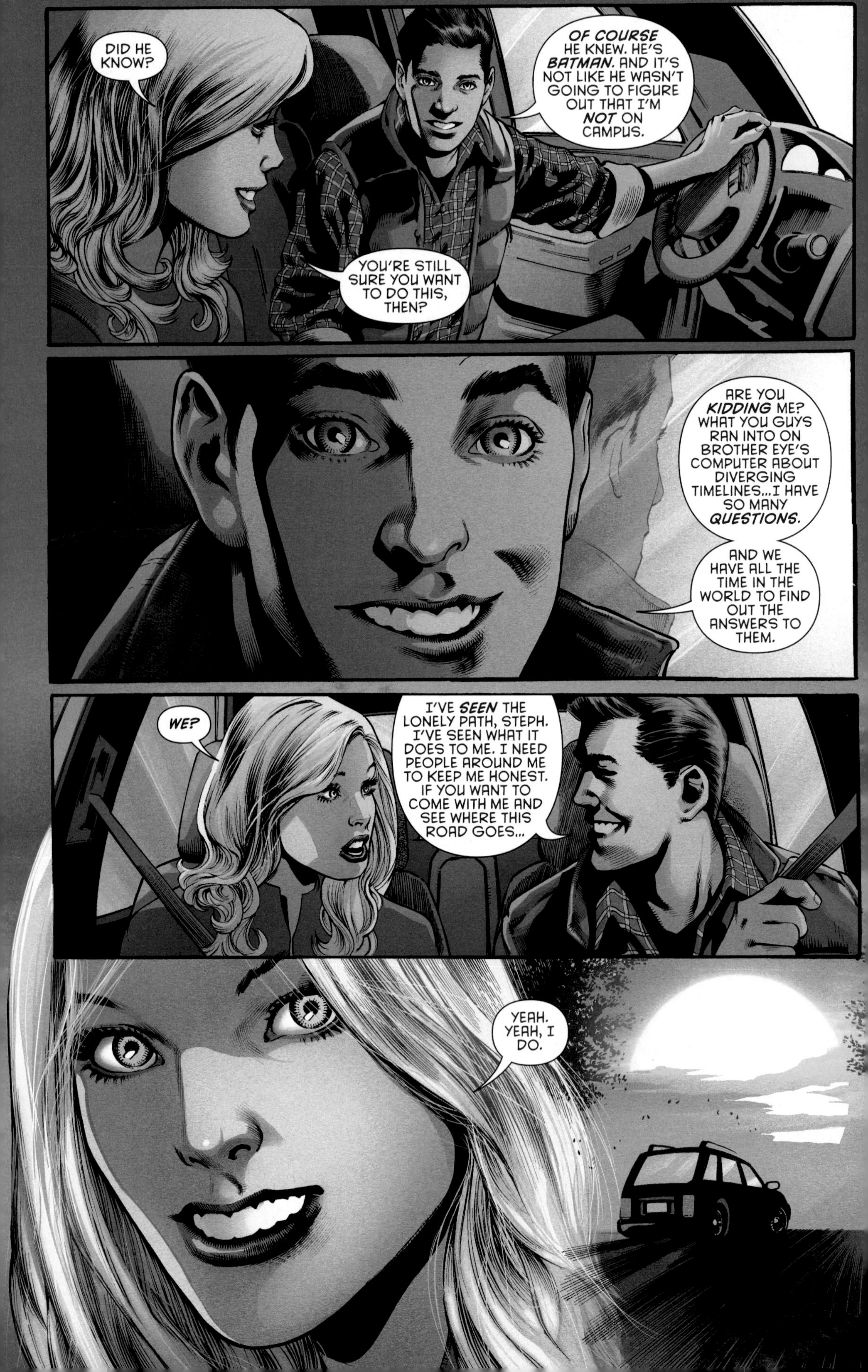

DID HE KNOW?
OF COURSE HE KNEW. HE'S BATMAN. AND IT'S NOT LIKE HE WASN'T GOING TO FIGURE OUT THAT I'M NOT ON CAMPUS.
YOU'RE STILL SURE YOU WANT TO DO THIS, THEN?
ARE YOU KIDDING ME? WHAT YOU GUYS RAN INTO ON BROTHER EYE'S COMPUTER ABOUT DIVERGING TIMELINES...I HAVE SO MANY QUESTIONS.
AND WE HAVE ALL THE TIME IN THE WORLD TO FIND OUT THE ANSWERS TO THEM.
WE?
I'VE SEEN THE LONELY PATH, STEPH. I'VE SEEN WHAT IT DOES TO ME. I NEED PEOPLE AROUND ME TO KEEP ME HONEST. IF YOU WANT TO COME WITH ME AND SEE WHERE THIS ROAD GOES...
YEAH. YEAH, I DO.

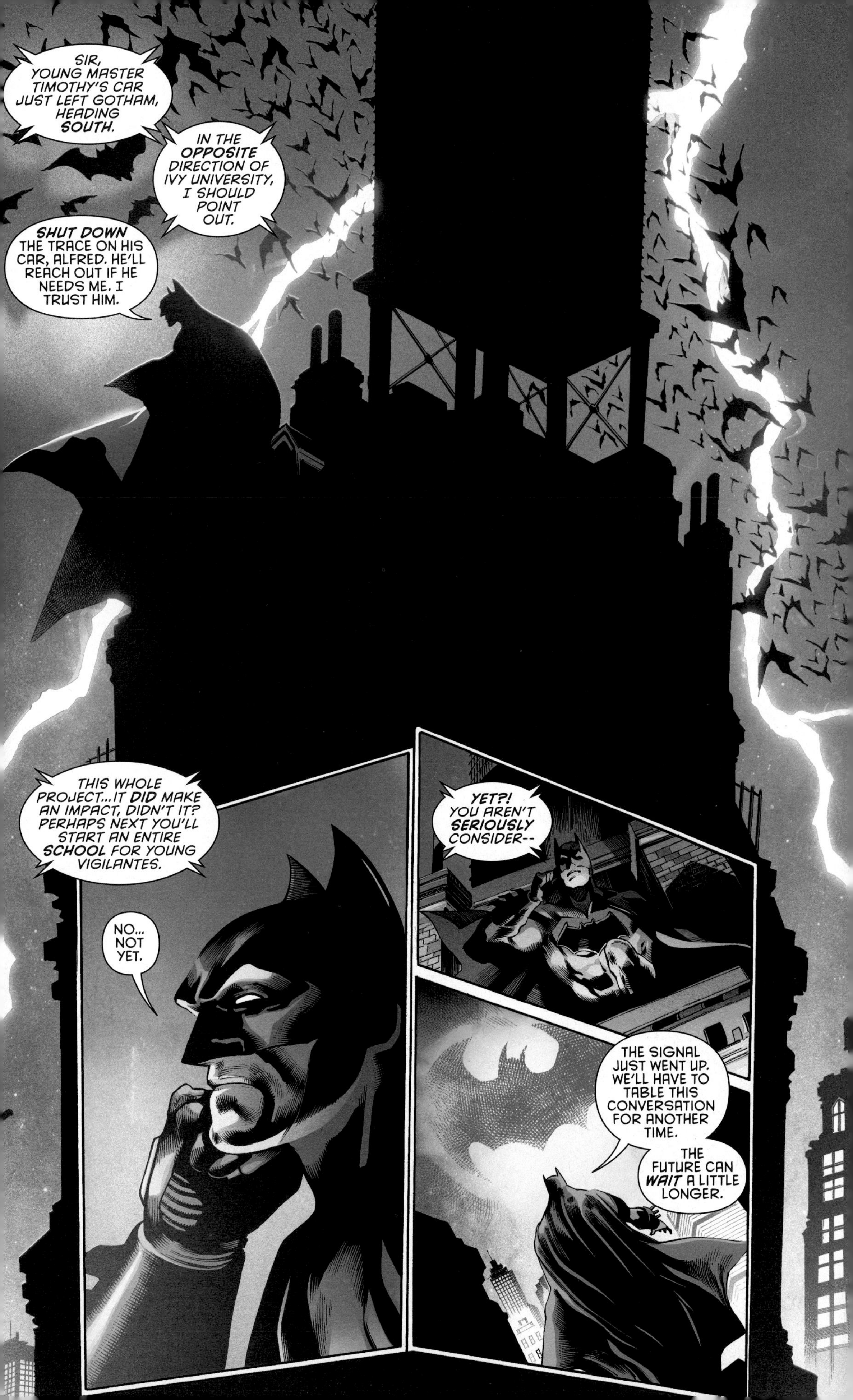
SIR, YOUNG MASTER TIMOTHY'S CAR JUST LEFT GOTHAM, HEADING SOUTH.
IN THE OPPOSITE DIRECTION OF IVY UNIVERSITY, I SHOULD POINT OUT.
SHUT DOWN THE TRACE ON HIS CAR, ALFRED. HE'LL REACH OUT IF HE NEEDS ME. I TRUST HIM.
THIS WHOLE PROJECT...IT DID MAKE AN IMPACT, DIDN'T IT? PERHAPS NEXT YOU'LL START AN ENTIRE SCHOOL FOR YOUNG VIGILANTES.
NO... NOT YET.
YET?! YOU AREN'T SERIOUSLY CONSIDER--
THE SIGNAL JUST WENT UP. WE'LL HAVE TO TABLE THIS CONVERSATION FOR ANOTHER TIME.
THE FUTURE CAN WAIT A LITTLE LONGER.

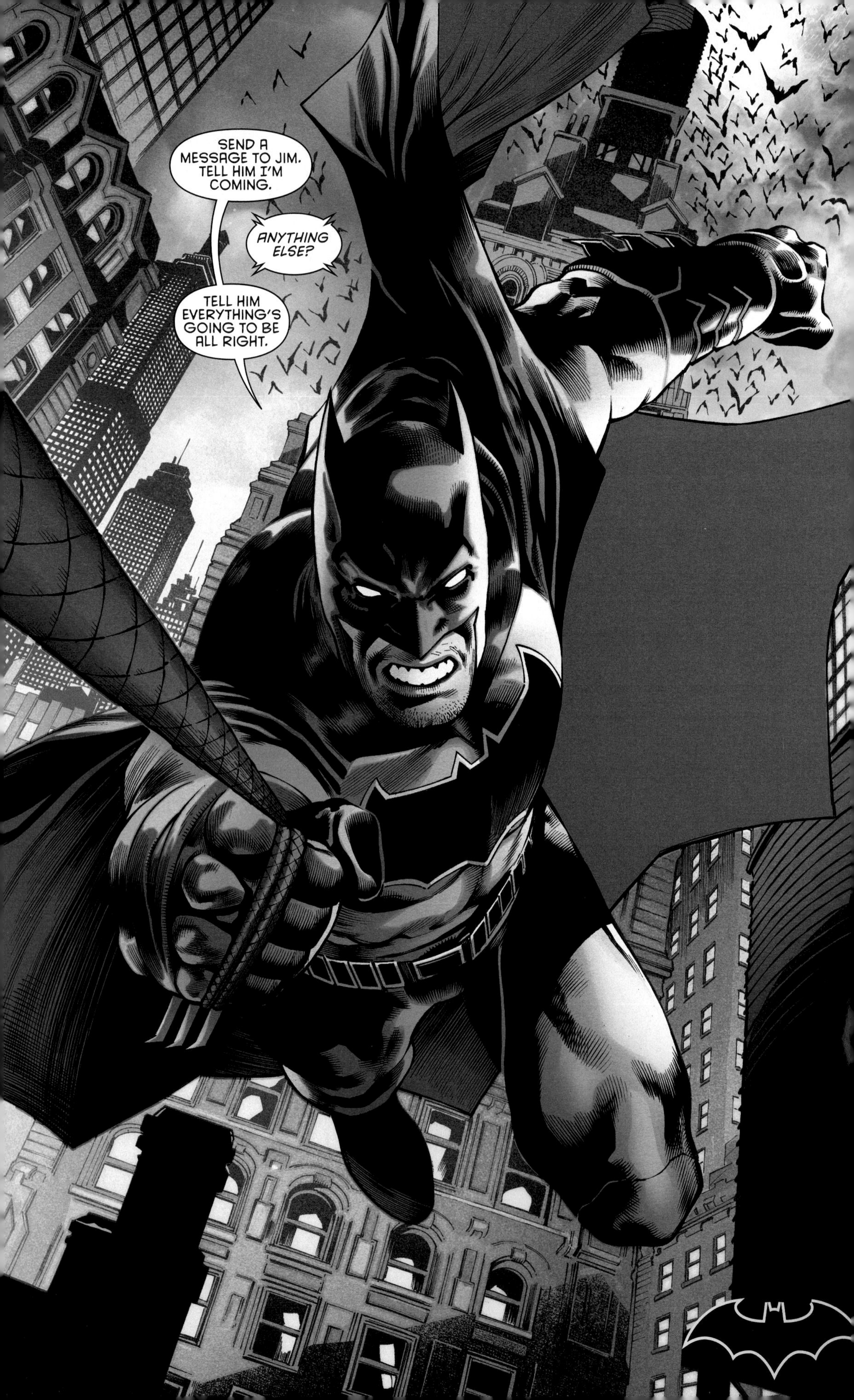
SEND A MESSAGE TO JIM. TELL HIM I'M COMING.
ANYTHING ELSE?
TELL HIM EVERYTHING'S GOING TO BE ALL RIGHT.

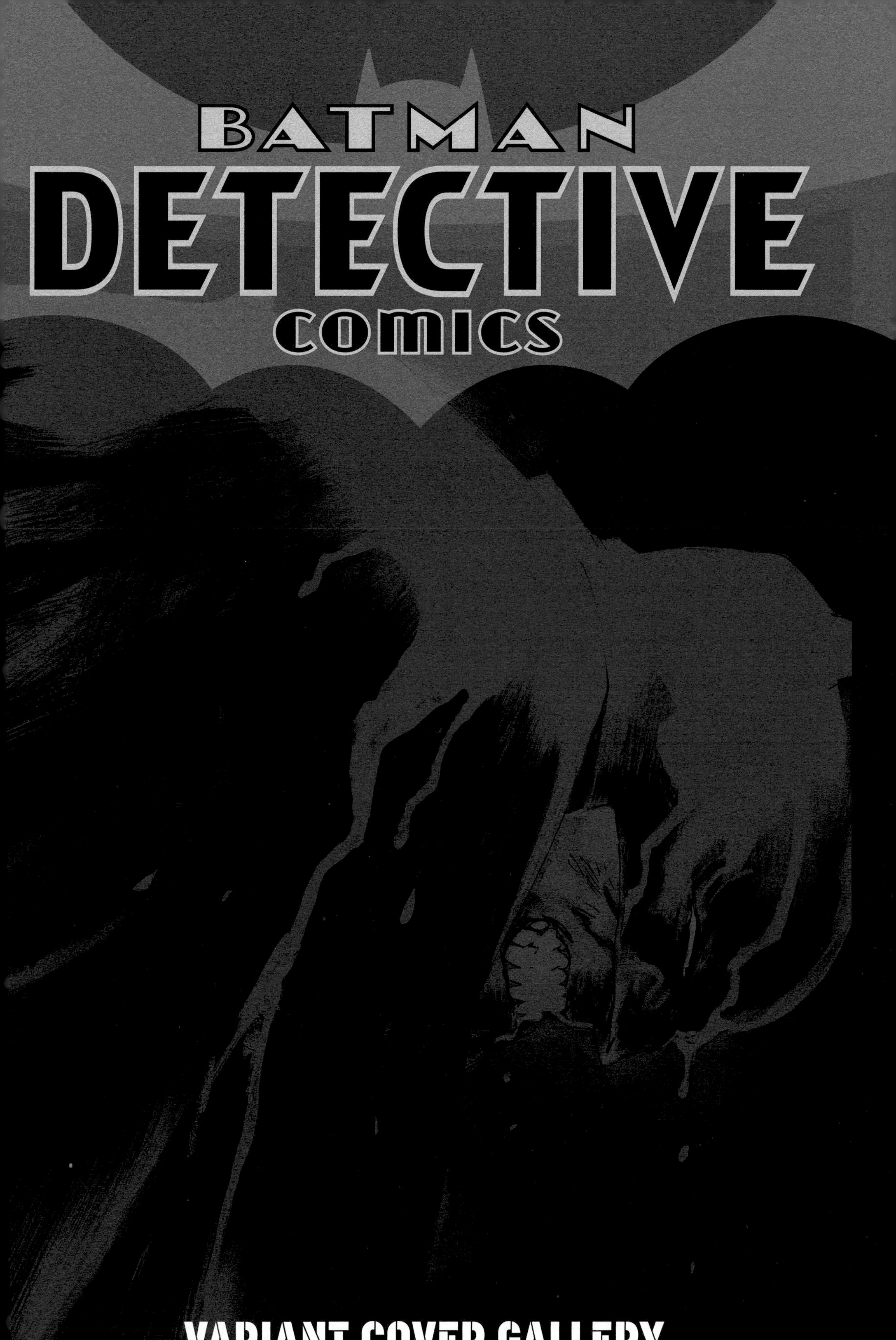
BATMAN
DETECTIVE
COMICS

VARIANT COVER GALLERY

DETECTIVE COMICS #975 variant cover by RAFAEL ALBUQUERQUE

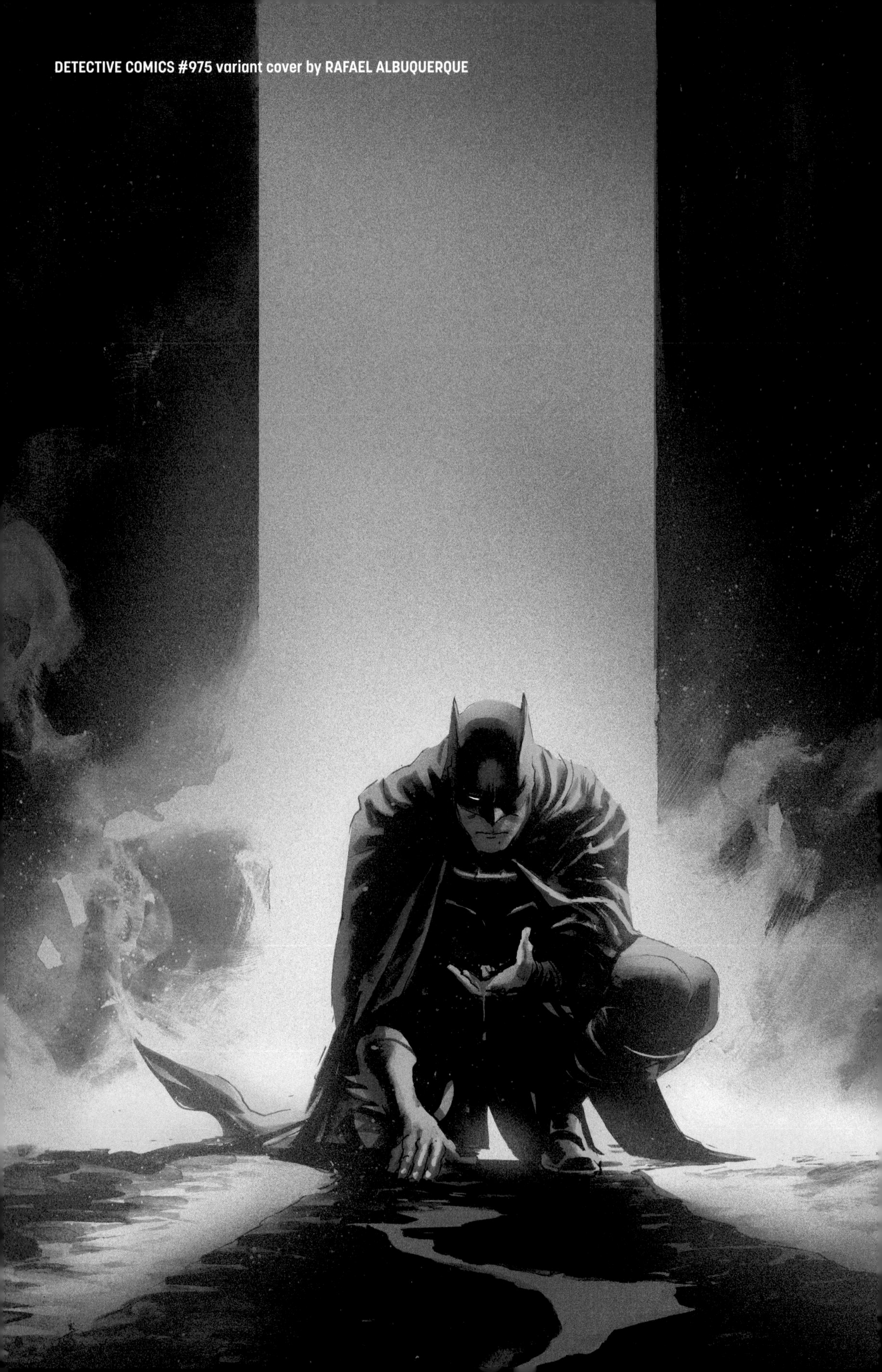

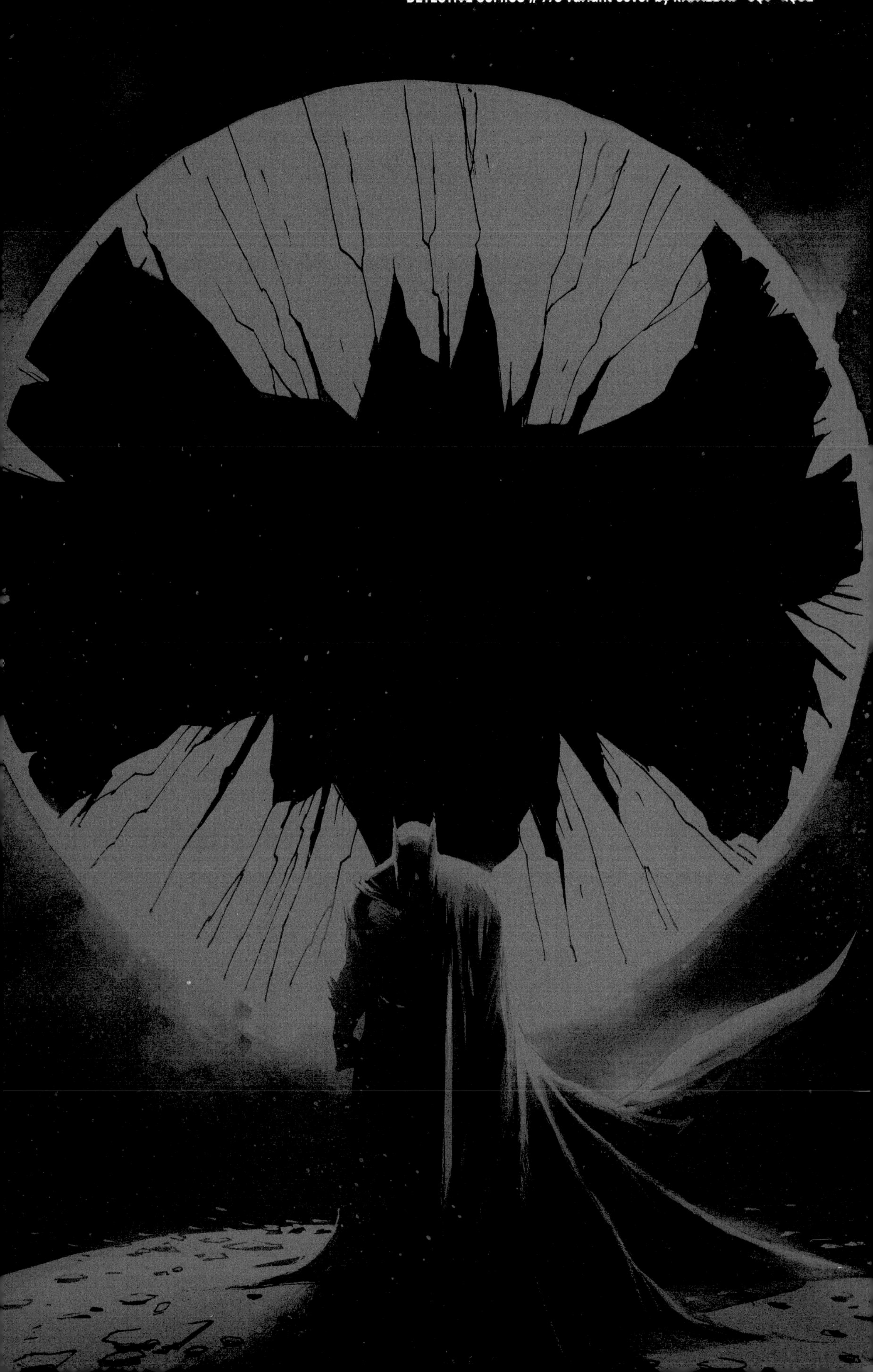

DETECTIVE COMICS #977 variant cover by RAFAEL ALBUQUERQUE

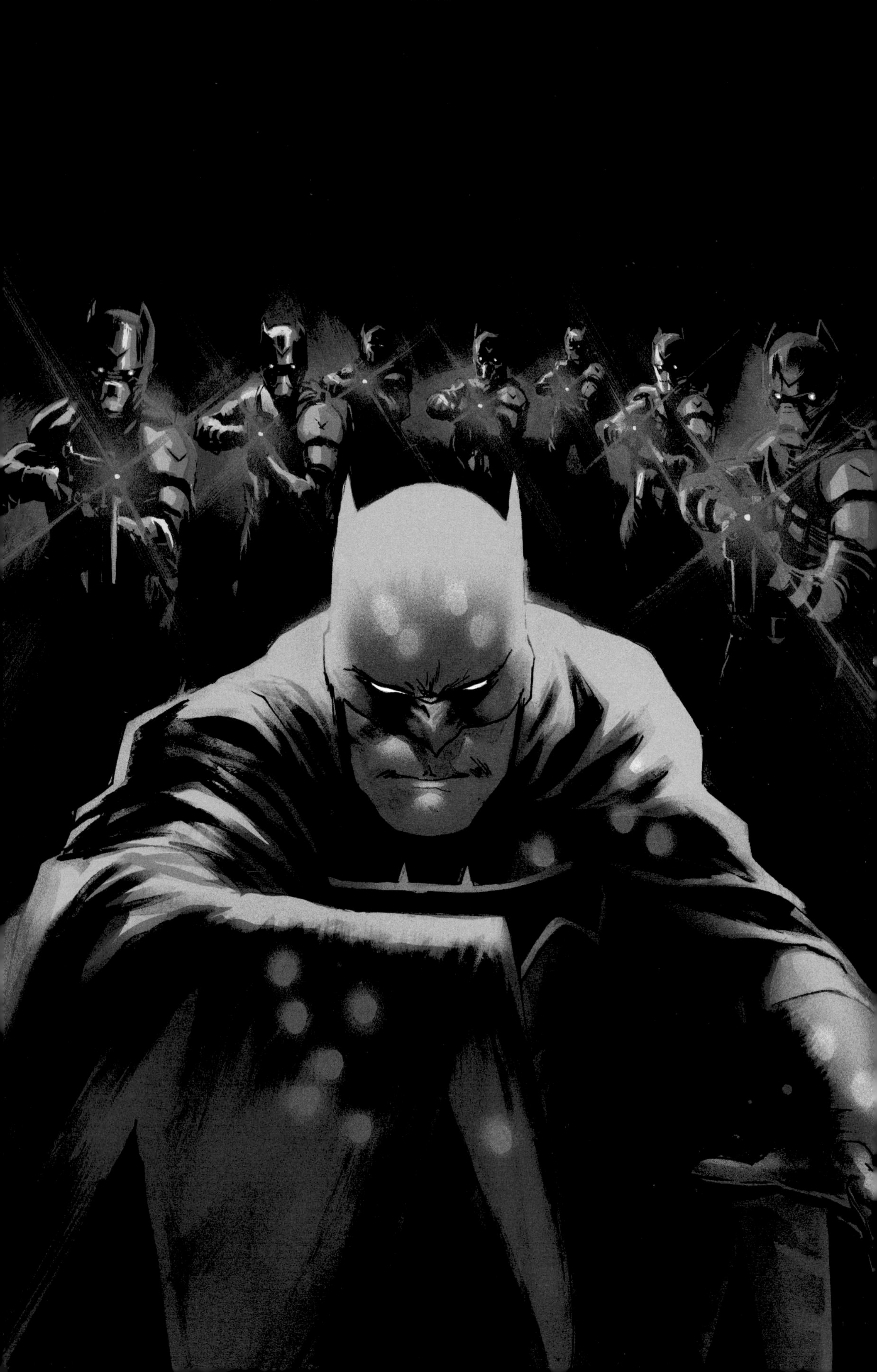

DETECTIVE COMICS #978 variant cover by RAFAEL ALBUQUERQUE

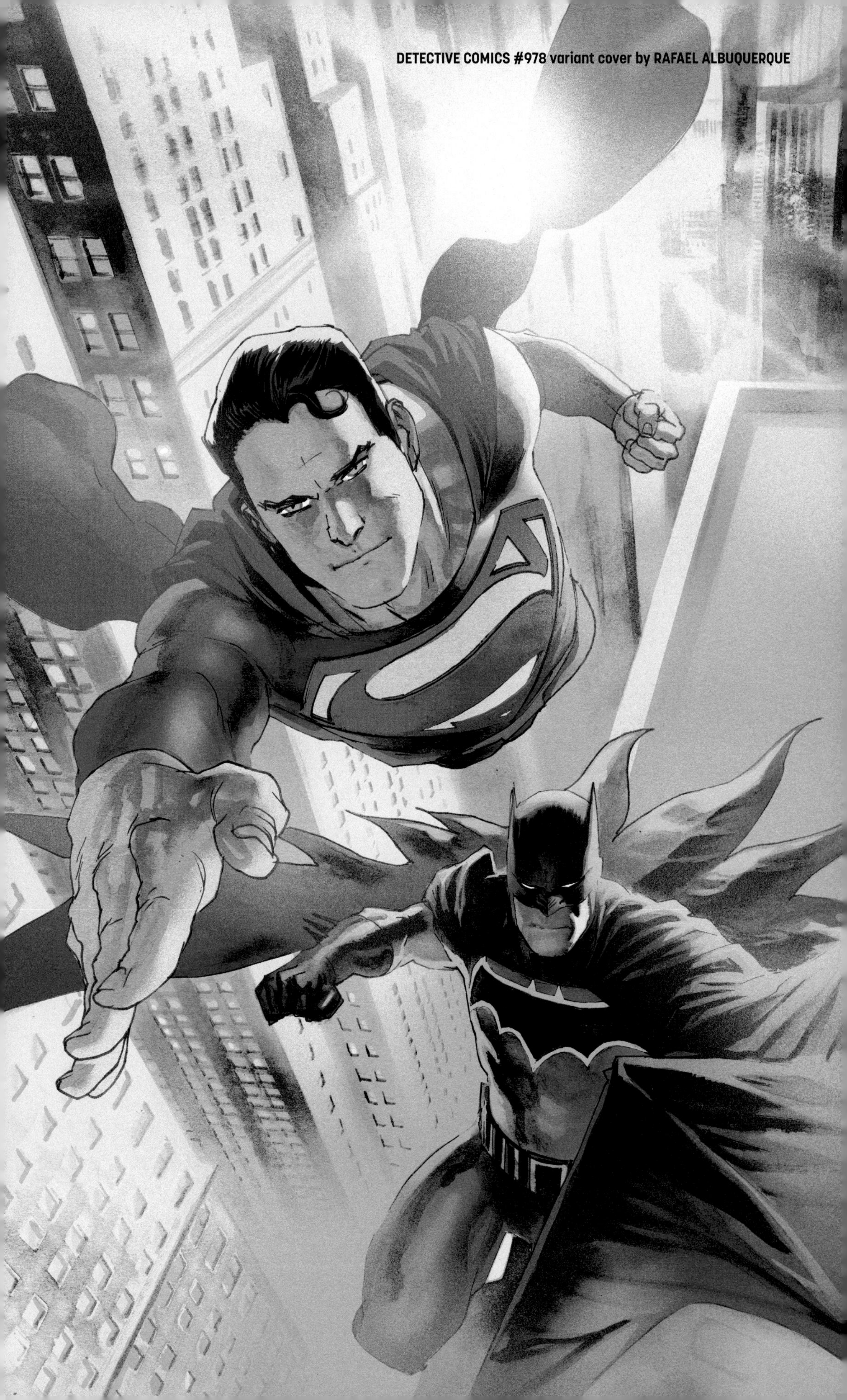

DETECTIVE COMICS #979 variant cover by RAFAEL ALBUQUERQUE

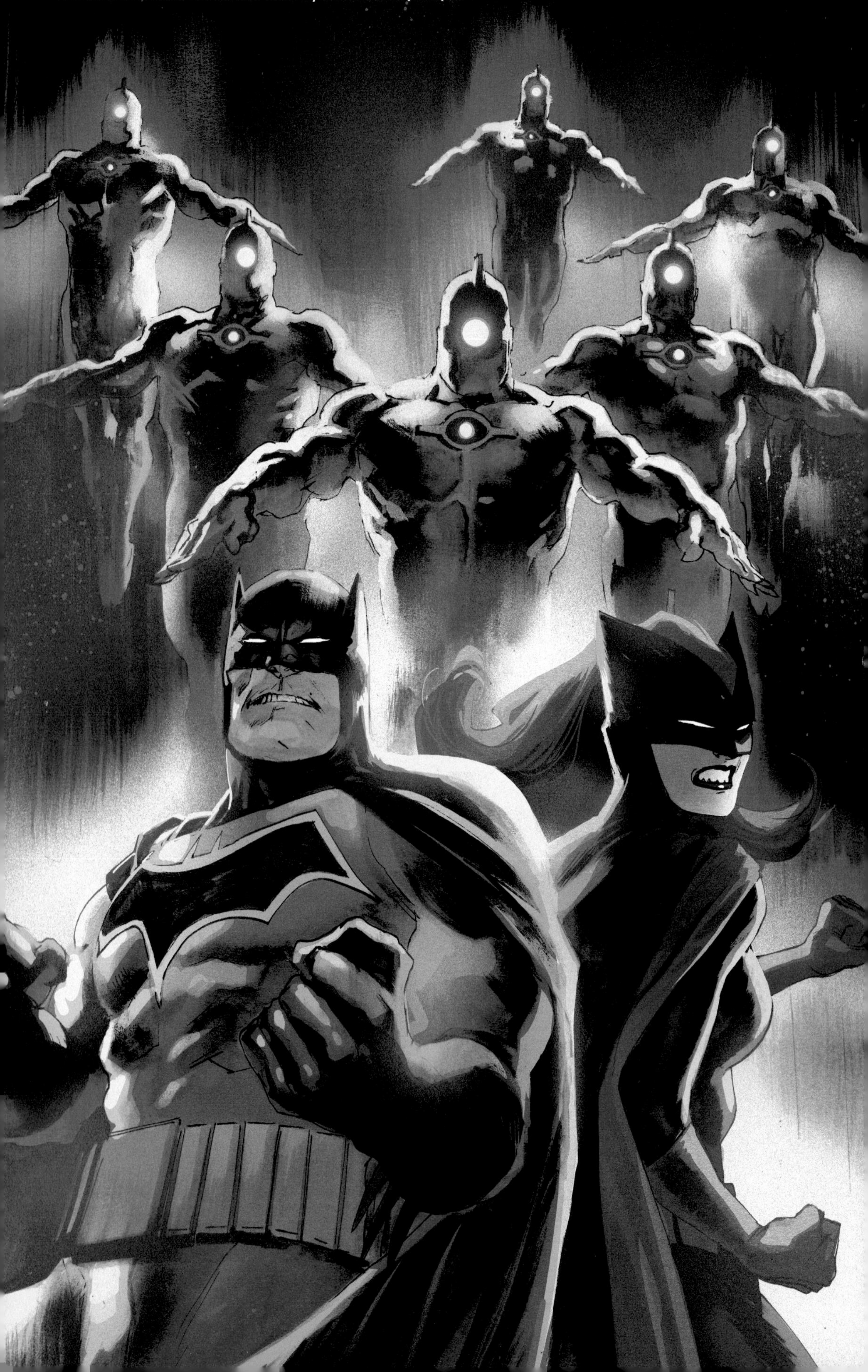

DETECTIVE COMICS #980 variant cover by RAFAEL ALBUQUERQUE

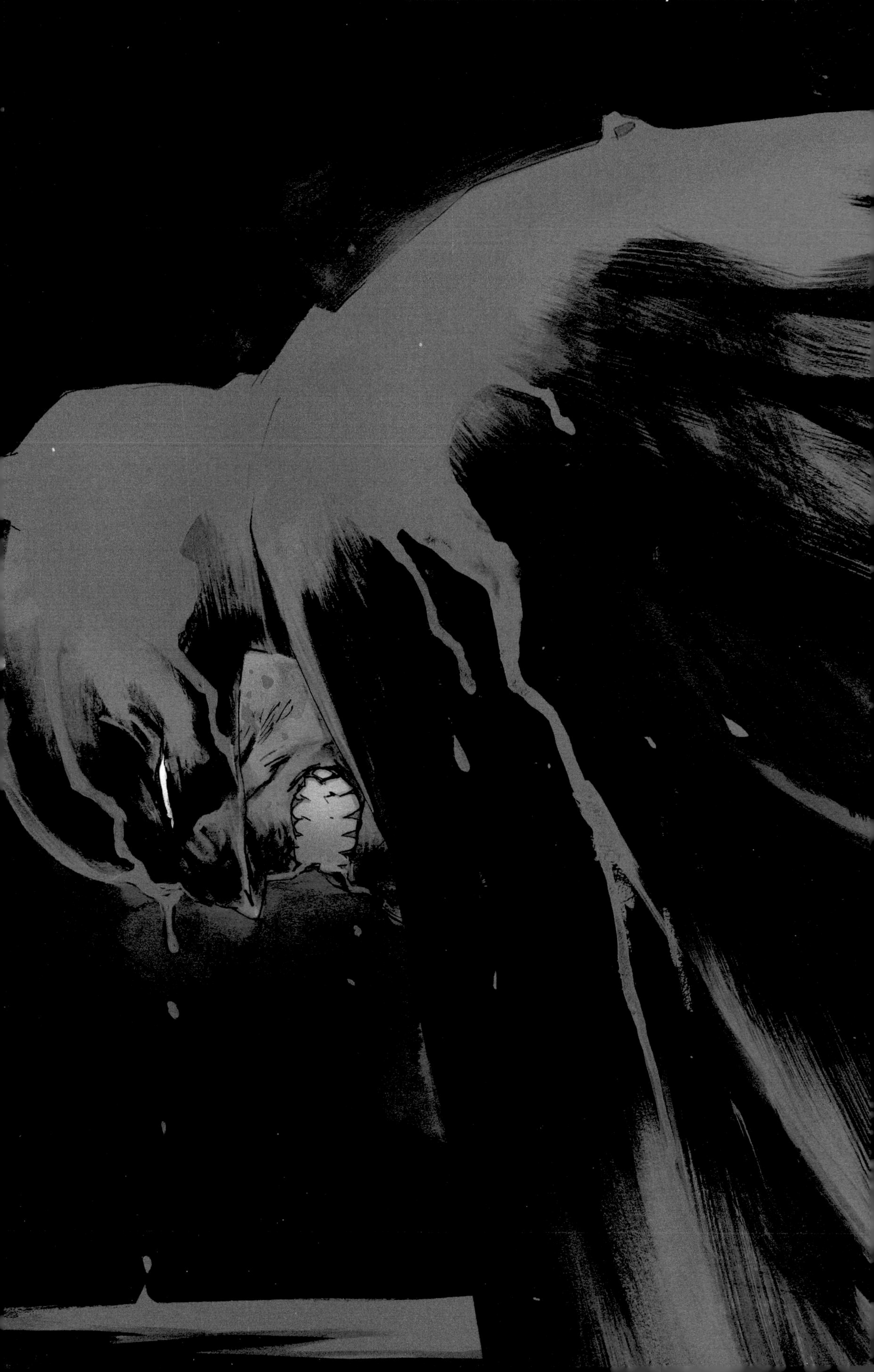

DETECTIVE COMICS #981 variant cover by RAFAEL ALBUQUERQUE

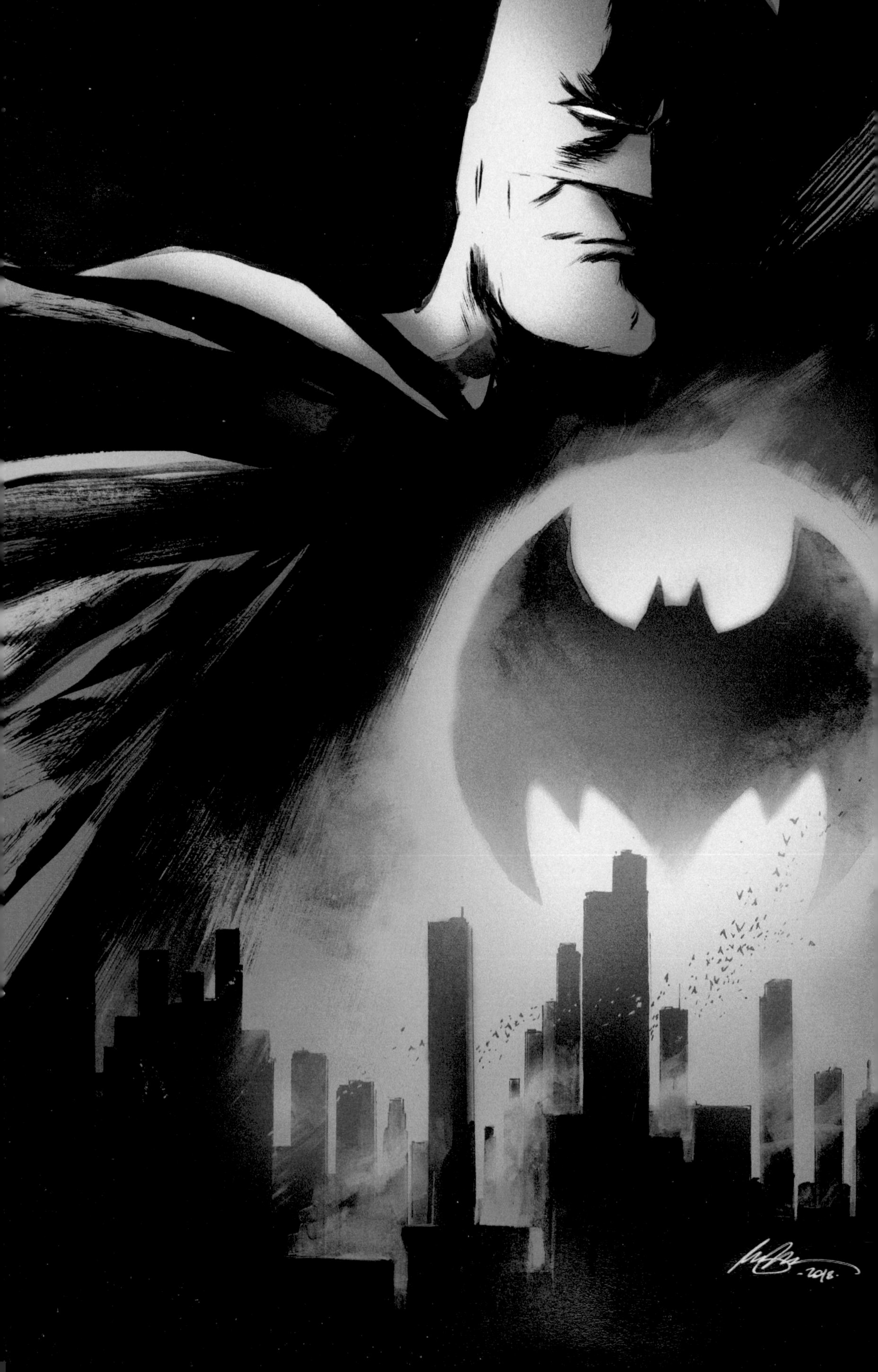